Habermas and the Public Sphere

edited by Craig Calhoun

The MIT Press, Cambridge, Massachusetts, and London, England

This book was set in Baskerville by DEKR Corporation and was printed and bound in the United States of America.

Library of Congress Cataloging-in-Publication Data

Habermas and the public sphere / edited by Craig Calhoun.
    p.   cm. — (Studies in contemporary German social thought)
  Includes bibliographical references and index.
  ISBN-13 978-0-262-03183-7 (hb), 978-0-262-53114-6 (pb)
  ISBN 0-262-03183-3 (hb), 0-262-53114-3 (pb)
  1. Sociology—Methodology—Congresses.   2. Habermas, Jürgen. Strukturwandel der Öffentlichkeit. English—Congresses.   3. Social structure—Congresses.
4. Middle classes—Congresses.   5. Political sociology—Congresses.   I. Calhoun, Craig J., 1952–   II. Series.
HM24.H322   1992
305—dc20   91-16736
                                                                          CIP

20 19 18 17 16 15 14 13 12

Habermas and the Public Sphere

Contents

II Historical Publics

III Public Communication

IV Conclusion and Response

Preface

Efforts to understand the history, foundations, and internal processes of public discourse are gaining importance in several disciplines. They inform democratic theory in political science, the self-reflection of literary and other cultural critics, the modernism/postmodernism debate in philosophy and cultural studies, new approaches in ethics and jurisprudence, and empirical studies in sociology, history, and communications. The debate has been influenced deeply by a variety of Jürgen Habermas's works. Surprisingly absent from the discussion, at least in English, has been one of Habermas's most important and directly relevant early works, *The Structural Transformation of the Public Sphere*.[1] Though this work has been among Habermas's most influential in German, and though it has been translated into several languages, it has only recently appeared in English, 27 years after publication of the German original.

The translation is propitiously timed. The book is certain to inform scholarship on problems of the relationship of state and civil society, the origins of and prospects for democracy, and the impact of the media. Perhaps even more important, the book's integrated treatment of these and other issues promises to enrich current work by drawing researchers from different disciplines into a common discourse. *Structural Transformation* will also surprise readers of Habermas's later work (including not only his fans but some who deride him as the new Parsons). This is by far the most historically concrete of Habermas's major works, building its theoretical argument largely out of synthetic empirical discussions of Britain, France, and Germany between the seventeenth and early twentieth centuries.

The present volume originated in a September 1989 conference on the occasion of the publication of the English translation of *The Structural Transformation of the Public Sphere*. Coming on the heels of China's prodemocracy movement and in the midst of the transformation of Central and Eastern Europe, the conference seemed more than a purely abstract, academic undertaking. In planning the conference, I tried to keep faith with the interdisciplinary nature of Habermas's undertaking. Participants came from backgrounds in history, the social sciences, literature, communications, and philosophy. One of the pleasures of the conference was in seeing how well the discourse sparked by Habermas's book could integrate themes from these various disciplines and from the many interdisciplinary concerns represented by participants: feminism, critical theory, cultural studies, democratic politics. The conference was also marked by a level of engagement and an absence of posturing that convinced many of us there that the public sphere was not altogether lost in the late twentieth century. Of course, this engagement also revealed some of the limits of that public sphere: at dinner one night the rational-critical discourse of twenty-some conferees rose to such a pitch that the proprietor of a local Polish restaurant felt compelled to bang on a glass and assert that the purpose of his establishment was peaceful dining, not loud conversation.

In organizing the conference and preparing this book for publication, I have incurred a number of debts. Tom McCarthy and Moishe Postone not only shaped my own reading of *Structural Transformation* but helped in the planning of the conference and offered useful comments on my introduction. Rekha Mirchandani and Ruth Slavin acted as able, supportive, and knowledgeable assistants throughout the planning and the conference; Ruth Slavin also prepared the index. Kevin Sargent came through with last-minute transportation and logistical assistance. The main financing for the conference came from the Provost's Office of the University of North Carolina as part of its support for the Program in Social Theory and Cross-

Cultural Studies. I am grateful also to my colleagues in that program, who provided an extremely stimulating community within which to prepare for and conduct the conference. The Center for Psychosocial Studies in Chicago contributed financially to the conference but also played an even more central role, since it was my reading of *Structural Transformation* in its seminar on social theory that occasioned the original idea for the conference.

At the conference, commentators played an especially important role, as papers were distributed rather than presented aloud; commentators had to take major responsibility for initiating discussion. Most also took the time to prepare careful, written comments that became the bases of their contributions to this book. Benjamin Lee, who had been an active participant, graciously stepped in to fill the place left when Fredric Jameson was at the last minute unable to complete his commentary. I am also grateful to Thomas Burger, who translated Habermas's essay revisiting the structural transformation of the public sphere for this volume; Leah Florence ably helped edit that translation.

Last but not least, I am grateful to Jürgen Habermas, who took time from a very busy schedule to participate in this conference. I only hope that he found it as valuable as the various participants all found his own contributions. His many comments from the floor and his open and constructive response at the conclusion were immensely clarifying and remarkable for their freedom from vanity and pretense.[2] Even for those of us who disagreed with him, he remains a model interlocutor of the public sphere.

Notes

1. Only a handful of earlier studies in English saw the significance of this work; the most prominent discussions are in P. Hohendahl, *The Institution of Criticism* (Ithaca, 1982); J. Cohen, "Why More Political Theory," *Telos* 40 (1979): 70–94; and D. Held, *An Introduction to Critical Theory* (London, 1982). *Structural Transformation* gets only very brief discussion in the main English language book on Habermas, T. McCarthy, *The Critical Theory of Jürgen Habermas* (Cambridge, Mass., 1978), and is not even mentioned in several others. More recently, *Structural Transformation* has been taken up in important ways in (particularly French) historical studies (see Baker's essay in this volume),

and from there it has spread to other historical discourse. Indeed, in the present book the philosophical writers still seem more inclined to treat Habermas's post-1970 theory of communicative action as his "real" work, with *Structural Transformation* viewed as preliminary, while others are more likely to find attractions in the earlier work and problems in the later (Hohendahl makes a related point in his remarks on Benhabib and McCarthy).

2. An edited selection of these concludes this book.

Habermas and the Public Sphere

1

Introduction: Habermas and the Public Sphere

Craig Calhoun

If we attend to the course of conversation in mixed companies consisting not merely of scholars and subtle reasoners but also of business people or women, we notice that besides storytelling and jesting they have another entertainment, namely, arguing.
Immanuel Kant[1]

Jürgen Habermas's important early book *The Structural Transformation of the Public Sphere* asks when and under what conditions the arguments of mixed companies could become authoritative bases for political action. The question, Habermas shows, is a crucial one for democratic theory. What are the social conditions, he asks, for a rational-critical debate about public issues conducted by private persons willing to let arguments and not statuses determine decisions? This is an inquiry at once into normative ideals and actual history. It focuses upon the bourgeois political life of the seventeenth through mid twentieth centuries, yet it aims to reach beyond the flawed realities of this history to recover something of continuing normative importance. This something is an institutional location for practical reason in public affairs and for the accompanying valid, if often deceptive, claims of formal democracy.

Habermas's social theory is often interpreted as moving over the years from a Hegelian-Marxist orientation to a sort of Kantian orientation. Though not without truth, this view underestimates the unity in his intellectual project. Kant occupies a central place in *Structural Transformation* as the theorist who offered the fullest articulation of the ideal of the bourgeois public sphere. In this public sphere, practical reason was institutionalized through norms of reasoned discourse in which arguments, not statuses or traditions, were to be decisive. Though Habermas rejects Kantian epistemology and its corollary ahistorical exaltation of philosophy as arbiter and foundation of all science and culture, in his recent work he nonetheless argues that something remains crucial from the Kantian view of modernity. Above all else, this is a notion of "procedural rationality and its ability to give credence to our views in the three areas of objective knowledge, moral-practical insight, and aesthetic judgment."[2] This procedural rationality is fundamentally a matter of basing judgment on reasons.

Habermas's task in *Structural Transformation* is to develop a critique of this category of bourgeois society showing both (1) its internal tensions and the factors that led to its transformation and partial degeneration and (2) the element of truth and emancipatory potential that it contained despite its ideological misrepresentation and contradictions. The key issues are implicit, if rather lightly expressed, in the quotation above from Kant. In a nutshell, a public sphere adequate to a democratic polity depends upon both quality of discourse and quantity of participation. Habermas develops the first requirement in elaborating how the classical bourgeois public sphere of the seventeenth and eighteenth centuries was constituted around rational critical argument, in which the merits of arguments and not the identities of arguers were crucial. The key point to draw from Kant, then, is the ubiquity of argument; this exercise of reason was the valuable kernel in the flawed ideology of the bourgeois public sphere. Kant betrayed a certain elitism in the way he noted that mere business people and even women might argue, but the emphasis can be put on the positive, since participation in argument is a means of education capable of overcoming the debilities that make some arguers inferior (and thus it is a very different matter from ascribed statuses that permanently exclude some people). On the other hand, reading Kant more negatively, we see that businesspeople and women were not "subtle reasoners," and we come across the dialectic leading to the decline of the public sphere.

The early bourgeois public spheres were composed of narrow segments of the European population, mainly educated, propertied men, and they conducted a discourse not only exclusive of others but prejudicial to the interests of those excluded. Yet the transformations of the public sphere that Habermas describes turn largely on its continual expansion to include more and more participants (as well as on the development of large scale social organizations as mediators of individual participation). He suggests that ultimately this inclusivity brought degeneration in the quality of discourse, but he contends that both the requirements of democracy and the nature of contemporary large-scale social organization mean that it is impossible to progress today by going back to an elitist public sphere.

Among the writers represented in this book, as among others responding to *Structural Transformation*, there are those who stress the issue of rational, critical debate and the questions of from whence it came, whether it was ever reality as much as ideal, and why it declined, if indeed it did. There are also those who stress the issue of participation, focusing on the exclusionary character of the early public sphere and the gains won by those who fought to enter it and transform it. Several, including Benhabib, Fraser, Eley, and Ryan, focus on the issue of gender, an exclusion that Habermas noted but one that is only problematically grasped by the Marxism that shaped his own early analysis and that of some of his most prominent early critics.[3] The gendered character of the early public sphere is also less clearly linked to the theme of transformation by "massification" than is exclusion on class grounds; inclusion of small numbers of elite, literate women would not have transformed the bourgeois public sphere into a mass. Schudson focuses on the extent of participation as an essential dimension of publicness, a key criterion for evaluating a public sphere. At the same time he raises questions about whether earlier constitutions of the public sphere really produced more rational-critical debate than those of recent years. Indeed, to some contemporary theorists, the very emphasis on rational-critical debate implies an incapacity to deal fairly with "identity politics" and concerns for difference. It is with this in mind that Warner, for example, focuses on publicity in general, rather than on its intersection with rational-critical debate. Garnham and Warner, somewhat relatedly, focus on Habermas's fairly wholesale incorporation of the Frankfurt School's critique of mass culture, and they raise questions about whether his understanding of modern mass media is adequate. In all these cases, and they are just a small sampling, one of the challenges of reading and responding to *Structural Transformation* is to keep fully in mind Habermas's two-sided constitution of the category of public sphere as simultaneously about the quality or form of rational-critical discourse and the quantity of, or openness to, popular participation. This informs not just his definition but his whole approach, inasmuch as he attempts to recover the enduringly valuable ideal of the bourgeois public sphere from its historically contradictory and partial realization.

In this introductory essay I propose mainly to offer a snyopsis of *The Structural Transformation of the Public Sphere* for the benefit of readers not familiar with that work. I will briefly situate *Structural Transformation* in the larger trajectory of Habermas's intellectual project and will add a few critical comments and elaborations of my own. Since the papers in this book speak for themselves and are the subject of detailed commentaries printed here, I will introduce them only very briefly.

1

The Structural Transformation of the Public Sphere was born in controversy and is likely to continue to spark controversy. It originated as Habermas's *Habilitationschrift* (thesis for the postdoctoral qualification required of German professors) and was intended for submission to Max Horkheimer (and Theodor Adorno) at Frankfurt. Horkheimer and Adorno, however, apparently thought it at once insufficiently critical of the illusions and dangerous tendencies of an Enlightenment conception of democratic public life, especially in mass society, and too radical in its politically focused call for an attempt to go beyond liberal constitutional protections in pursuit of truer democracy. Habermas successfully submitted it to Wolfgang Abendroth at Marburg.[4] Influential in the early years of the student movement, *Structural Transformation* soon drew criticism from that direction as well when young leftists attacked it for focusing on the bourgeois public sphere to the exclusion of the proletarian one, for an inadequate grasp of everyday life (including mass media) in advanced capitalism, and for exaggerating the emancipatory potential in the idealized bourgeois public sphere.[5] Habermas himself was apparently unhappy with the work, or at least conscious of the large amount of empirical research done on themes relevant to it during the 1960s, for one of the reasons for the delayed translation was that he had intended for years to rework this text. He never did, but readers may be surprised how many of Habermas's later themes are prefigured (and often given their most sociological formulation and historically specific treatment) in this work. It also enters into an interesting and important dialogue with other key work of the mid twentieth century, notably that of Hannah Arendt.[6] And the book remains extraordinarily suggestive, still the most significant modern work on its subject.

That subject is the historically specific phenomenon of the bourgeois public sphere created out of the relations between capitalism and the state in the seventeenth and eighteenth centuries. Habermas sets out to establish what the category of public meant in bourgeois society and how its meaning and material operation were transformed in the centuries after its constitution. The motivation for this lies largely in an attempt to revive the progressive potential in "formal" democracy and law and thus to counterbalance their neglect in the Marxist tradition.[7] More specifically, it is part of Habermas's lifelong effort to reground the Frankfurt School project of critical theory in order to get out of the pessimistic cul de sac in which Horkheimer and Adorno found themselves in the postwar era. In a nutshell, the attempt to ground a vision of societal transformation and human emancipation on the proletariat had foundered. The experience of fascism and the rise of the cultural industry and "engineered consent" seemed to indicate that there was no historical subject on which critics might pin their hopes for transcending capitalism. Habermas turned away from the search for such a subject and developed an account of intersubjective communicative processes and their emancipatory potential in place of any philosophy (or politics) of the subject. At the same time Habermas sought to incorporate into his theory a full appreciation of the implications of changes that had occurred in both capitalism and state structures through the period of Western modernity. The rise of the large corporation, the problematization of consumption (as a response to successful increases in productive capacity), the development of the social-welfare state and mass democracy all altered both the conditions that framed the view of classical Marxism and the conditions of bourgeois society itself. In this respect, *Structural Transformation* also parallels much of the older Frankfurt School's analysis of the transition from liberal to "organized" capitalism.

The importance of the public sphere lies in its potential as a mode of societal integration. Public discourse (and what Habermas later and more generally calls communicative action) is a possible mode of coordination of human life, as are state power and market economies. But money and power are non-discursive modes of coordination, as Habermas's later theory stresses; they offer no intrinsic openings to the identification of reason and will, and they suffer from tendencies toward domination and reification. State and economy are thus both crucial topics for and rivals of the democratic public sphere.

Structural Transformation approaches these concerns first by trying to develop a historically specific understanding of the modern category of publicness. The bourgeois public sphere is "a category that is typical of an epoch. It cannot be abstracted from the unique developmental history of that 'civil society' (*bürgerliche Gesellschaft*) originating in the European High Middle Ages; nor can it be transferred, ideal typically generalized, to any number of historical situations that represent formally similar constellations" (p. xvii).[8] The Enlightenment category thus is different from its classical Greek ancestor, just as it is different from its transformed contemporary descendant. Greek thought made a strong division between public and private affairs. But in the private realm of the *oikos*, the Greek head of a household confronted only necessity. Freedom was to be found in public, though of course the public realm of autonomous citizens rested on the private autonomy of each as master of a household (most of whose members were ex-

cluded from the public). The bourgeois public sphere that
Habermas explores shares some features with this picture, but
it reverses a key element. It is defined as the public of *private*
individuals who join in debate of issues bearing on state authority. Unlike the Greek conception, individuals are here
understood to be formed primarily in the private realm, including the family. Moreover, the private realm is understood
as one of freedom that has to be defended against the domination of the state.[9]

The seventeenth- and eighteenth-century notion developed
alongside the rise and transformation of the modern state, as
well as on the basis of capitalist economic activity. The modern
state constituted the public as a specific realm again (as had
the Greek polis). In the middle ages, publicness had been more
of a "status attribute" (p. 7). It was a characteristic of the ruler,
borne even by his person. In a world of kings who could say
"L'etat, c'est moi," the public of a country did not exist apart
from a king and his court. This was the heyday of "representative publicity," and lordship was represented "not for but
'before' the people" (p. 8). Gradually, however, court society
developed into the new sort of sociability of eighteenth-century
salons. Aristocrats played leading roles in the early bourgeois
public sphere. Habermas does not mean to suggest that what
made the public sphere bourgeois was simply the class composition of its members.[10] Rather, it was *society* that was bourgeois, and bourgeois society produced a certain form of public
sphere.[11] The new sociability, together with the rational-critical
discourse that grew in the salons (and coffee houses and other
places), depended on the rise of national and territorial power
states on the basis of the early capitalist commercial economy.
This process led to an idea of society separate from the ruler
(or the state) and of a private realm separate from the public.

This notion of civil society is basic to Habermas's account of
the public sphere, and his account in turn offers a great deal
of richness to current discussions of civil society that come close
to equating it with the private market.[12] Civil society, in the
seventeenth and eighteenth centuries, developed as "the genuine domain of private autonomy [that] stood opposed to the
state" (p. 12). Capitalist market economies formed the basis of

this civil society, but it included a good deal more than that. It included institutions of sociability and discourse only loosely related to the economy. Transformations of the economy none-theless produced transformations in all of civil society.

In an account that partially prefigures Benedict Anderson's analysis of "print capitalism," Habermas shows the intimate involvement of print media in the early extensions of market economies beyond local arenas.[13] Long-distance trade, for ex-ample, meant a traffic in news almost as immediately as a traffic in commodities. Merchants needed information about prices and demand, but the newsletters that supplied those needs very quickly began to carry other sorts of information as well. The same processes helped to engender both a more wide-spread literacy and an approach to the printed word as a source of currently significant "public" information. These develop-ments became revolutionary in the era of mercantilism, when town economies were extended into national territories and the modern state grew up to administer these territories. The development of the state bureaucracies as agents of permanent administration, buttressed by standing armies, created a new sphere of public authority. "Now continuous state activity cor-responded to the continuity of contact among those trafficking in commodities and news (stock market, press)" (p. 18). Public authority thus was consolidated into a palpable object distinct from the representative publicity of the ruler and the older estates as well as from the common people, who were excluded from it. "'Public' in this narrower sense was synonymous with 'state-related'" (p. 18). But the public sphere was not cotermi-nous with the state apparatus, for it included all those who might join in a discussion of the issues raised by the adminis-tration of the state. The participants in this discussion included agents of the state and private citizens.

The public sphere, like civil society in general, could only be conceptualized in this full sense once the state was constituted as an *impersonal* locus of authority. Unlike the ancient notion of the public, therefore, the modern notion depended on the possibility of counterposing state and society. Here Habermas joins with Arendt in stressing how a private sphere of society could take on a public relevance. "Civil society came into existence as the corollary of a depersonalized state authority" (p. 19). It became possible to recognize society in the relationships and organizations created for sustaining life and to bring these into public relevance by bringing them forward as interests for a public discussion and/or the action of the state.[14] In this way a certain educated elite came to think of itself as constituting the public and thereby transformed the abstract notion of the *publicum* as counterpart to public authority into a much more concrete set of practices. The members of this elite public began to see themselves through this category not just as the object of state actions but as the opponent of public authority.

Because, on the one hand, the society now confronting the state clearly separated a private domain from public authority and because, on the other hand, it turned the reproduction of life into something transcending the confines of private domestic authority and becoming a subject of public interest, that zone of continuous administrative contact became "critical" also in the sense that it provoked the critical judgment of a public making use of its reason. (P. 24)

The last phrase of the quote is crucial. The bourgeois public sphere institutionalized, according to Habermas, not just a set of interests and an opposition between state and society but a practice of rational-critical discourse on political matters. Thus, for example, critical reasoning entered the press in the early eighteenth century, supplementing the news with learned articles and quickly creating a new genre of periodical. The very idea of the public was based on the notion of a general interest sufficiently basic that discourse about it need not be distorted by particular interests (at least in principle) and could be a matter of rational approach to an objective order, that is to say, of truth.

The bourgeois public sphere may be conceived above all as the sphere of private people come together as a public; they soon claimed the public sphere regulated from above against the public authorities themselves, to engage them in a debate over the general rules governing relations in the basically privatized but publicly relevant sphere of commodity exchange and social labor. The medium of this political confrontation was peculiar and without historical precedent: people's public use of their reason. (P. 27)

2

With the general category of public sphere established, we can now look at several of Habermas's more specific arguments about its transformations. After its introductory section, *Structural Transformation* is organized as a repeated series of themes: social structure, political functions, and ideology are analyzed first for the constitution of the classical sphere and then for its degenerative transformation.[15] Though the book has perhaps been more often read for its account of the degeneration of the public sphere, the earlier argument about its constitution is both more original and more interesting. Throughout, one sees precursors of themes familiar to readers of Habermas's later work.

Two processes helped to institutionalize the public sphere as it developed out of court society and urban corporations in the early modern era. First, the family was reconstituted as an intimate sphere that grounded both the evaluative affirmation of ordinary life and of economic activity alluded to above and the participation of its patriarchal head in the public sphere. Second, the public sphere was initially constituted in the world of letters, which paved the way for that oriented to politics. The two processes were intertwined. For example, early novels helped to circulate a vision of intimate sentimentality, communicating to the members of the literary public sphere just how they should understand the heart of private life.

The intimate sphere figures importantly in Habermas's account: "The public's understanding of the public use of reason was guided specifically by such private experiences as grew out of the audience-oriented subjectivity of the conjugal family's intimate domain. Historically, the latter was the source of privateness in the modern sense of a saturated and free interiority" (p. 28). In the new conjugal family, "private" meant not merely the burden of necessity, as in classical Greece, and not only the property-owning privacy of economic control either. Rather, the family was understood as at least partially differentiated from material reproduction. Just as state and society were split, so economy and family (the intimate sphere) were distinguished within the private realm. The subjectivity the family nurtured was "audience-oriented" because it was played out in dramas staged for the other members of the family (mirroring the ideal types offered by the sentimental literature of the period).

In this way the reconceived family helped lead to a reconceptualization of humanity itself.[16] It emphasized, first off, the autonomy of its head. This rested on the private ownership of property, but the notion of the intimate family excluded that from its core, thus providing a key element of the false consciousness of the bourgeois. The family was believed to be independent of the market, "whereas in truth it was profoundly caught up in the requirements of the market. The ambivalence of the family as an agent of society yet simultaneously as the anticipated emancipation from society manifested itself in the situation of the family members: on the one hand, they were held together by patriarchal authority; on the other, they were bound to one another by human closeness. As a privatized individual, the bourgeois was two things in one: owner of goods and persons and one human being among others, i.e., *bourgeois* and *homme*" (p. 55). The family was idealized as the purely human realm of "intimate relationships between human beings who, under the aegis of the family, were nothing more than human" (p. 48). At the same time, the intimacy of the family promised a liberation from the constraints of what existed, from necessity, because it was a realm of pure interiority following its own laws and not any external purpose. "In this specific notion of humanity a conception of what existed was promulgated within the bourgeois world which promised redemption from the constraint of what existed without escaping into a transcendental realm. This conception's transcendence of what was immanent was the element of truth that raised bourgeois ideology above ideology itself, most fundamentally in that area where the experience of 'humanity' originated" (p. 48). The family thus provided a crucial basis for the immanent critique of the bourgeois public sphere itself, for it taught that there was something essential to humanness that economic or other status could not take away.[17]

Literature of the period, especially sentimental early novels like Richardson's *Pamela,* relied on and reinforced this same sense of humanness. This was a matter not just of their content but of the author-reader relationship developed by the genre: "The relations between author, work, and public changed. They became intimate mutual relationships between privatized individuals who were psychologically interested in what was 'human,' in self-knowledge, and in empathy" (p. 50). At the same time, the literary public sphere helped to develop the distinctively modern idea of culture as an autonomous realm: "Inasmuch as culture became a commodity and thus finally evolved into 'culture' in the specific sense (as something that pretends to exist merely for its own sake), it was claimed as the ready topic of a discussion through which an audience-oriented subjectivity communicated with itself" (p. 29).

Beyond this subjectivity, the greatest contributions of the literary public sphere to the political sphere lay in the development of institutional bases. These ranged from meeting places to journals to webs of social relationships. Thus early British businessmen met in coffee houses to discuss matters of trade, including the "news," which was coming into ever-wider circulation. London had 3,000 coffee houses by the first decade of the eighteenth century, each with a core of regulars. The conversation of these little circles branched out into affairs of state administration and politics. Journals of opinion were created, which linked the thousands of smaller circles in London and throughout the country. These were often based at particular coffee houses and replicated in their contents the style of convivial exchange. In France, salons, pubic institutions located in private homes, played a crucial role, bridging a literary public sphere dominated by aristocrats with the emergent bourgeois political public sphere.[18] In Germany, table societies drew together especially academics but also other sorts of people. The public outside these institutions was very small.

In all these instances, several features were crucial. The first and perhaps most basic was "a kind of social intercourse that, far from presupposing the equality of status, disregarded status altogether" (p. 36). Of course, this was not fully realized, but the idea had an importance of its own.[19] This "mutual willingness to accept the given roles and simultaneously to suspend their reality was based on the justifiable trust that within the public—presupposing its shared class interest—friend-or-foe relations were in fact impossible" (p. 131). The notion of common interest in truth or right policy thus undergirded the "bracketing" of status differences. This was in turn linked to a second crucial feature, the notion that rational argument was the sole arbiter of any issue.[20] However often the norm was breached, the idea that the best rational argument and not the identity of the speaker was supposed to carry the day was institutionalized as an available claim. Third, "discussion within such a public presupposed the problematization of areas that until then had not been questioned" (p. 36). All sorts of topics over which church and state authorities had hitherto exercised a virtual monopoly of interpretation were opened to discussion, inasmuch as the public defined its discourse as focusing on all matters of common concern. Fourth, the emerging public established itself as inclusive in principle. Anyone with access to cultural products—books, plays, journals—had at least a potential claim on the attention of the culture-debating public. "However exclusive the public might be in any given instance, it could never close itself off entirely and become consolidated as a clique; for it always understood and found itself immersed within a more inclusive public of all private people, persons who—insofar as they were propertied and educated—as readers, listeners, and spectators could avail themselves via the market of the objects that were subject to discussion" (p. 37).

This literary public sphere produced the practice of literary criticism (see also Hohendahl 1982). The division between critics and "mere readers" was not initially sharp, for "when reviewers of the caliber of Schiller and Schlegel did not regard themselves as too good for voluminous incidental activity of this sort, the lay judgment of the private people with an interest in literature had been institutionalized" (p. 167). It thus institutionalized a form of rational-critical discourse about objects of common concern that could be carried over directly into political discussion: "The process in which the state-governed public sphere was appropriated by the public of private people making use of their reason and was established as a sphere of criticism of public authority was one of functionally converting the public sphere in the world of letters already equipped with institutions of the public and with forums for discussion" (p. 51). A central topic for the transformational discourse was the question of absolute sovereignty versus the rule of general, abstract, depersonalized laws. The new public sphere of civil society made its initial political mark through commitment to the latter, and assertion of "itself (i.e., public opinion) as the only legitimate source of this law" (p. 54).

3

This argument is most famously that between Hobbes and those, such as Locke and Montesquieu, who would limit or qualify absolute sovereignty. Its primary locus was Britain, and indeed, Britain serves Habermas as the model case of the development of the public sphere. It was there, for example, that the elimination of the institution of censorship first marked a new stage in the development of public discourse. The free provision of information was, alongside education, crucial to putting the public in a position to arrive at a considered, rather than merely a common, opinion. It was in Britain too, after the Glorious Revolution, that national-level political opposition shifted away from resort to violence, so that "through the critical debate of the public, it took the form of a permanent controversy between the governing party and the opposition" (p. 64).

In France a public that critically debated political issues arose only near the middle of the eighteenth century. Even then it lacked the capacity to institutionalize its critical impulses until the Revolution. There was nothing like the British Parliament, with its attendant political press, nor was the state amenable to any notion of a "loyal opposition." Only in the years just before the Revolution did the philosophes turn their critical attention from art, literature, and religion to politics. The founding of clubs and journals focused on economic policy toward English inspiration in the 1770s. The physiocrats were central, and they were the first to combine activity in this public discourse and membership in the government—a sign that public opinion was becoming effective. The occasion for this, as for the summoning of the Estates General, was the government's growing financial crisis. Revolution followed quickly, and from the beginning it was a matter of bourgeois public discourse as much as mob action. The clubs played a central role, and almost overnight an extraordinary range of publications sprang up. The Constitution of 1791 declared that "the free communication of ideas and opinions is one of the most precious rights of man" (p. 70).

Germany lagged behind France. There "the public's rational-critical debate of political matters took place predominantly in the private gatherings of the bourgeoisie" (p. 72). The nobility remained completely dependent on the courts and thus failed to develop strong enough lines of communication with bourgeois intellectuals to participate in creating a strong civil society separate from the state. Nonetheless, journals with political content proliferated and were debated in reading societies, even if the political efficacy of this public remained limited.

In all three settings some degree of institutional basis for a public sphere was established. Habermas stresses the economic foundations: "The social precondition for this 'developed' bourgeois public sphere was a market that, tending to be liberalized, made affairs in the sphere of social reproduction as much as possible a matter of private people left to themselves and so finally completed the privatization of civil society" (p. 74). This institutionalization of a new and stronger sense of privacy as free control of productive property was a crucial contribution of capitalism to the public sphere. It was reflected on the Continent in the codification of civil law, where basic private freedoms were guaranteed. At the same time a fundamental parity among persons was established, corresponding to that among owners of commodities in the market and among educated individuals in the public sphere. Though not all people were full legal subjects, all such legal subjects were joined in a more or less undifferentiated category of persons.[21] The extension of these notions into the doctrines of laissez-faire and even free trade among nations brought the development of "civil society as the private sphere emancipated from public authority" to its fullest extent, though it lasted only for "one blissful moment in the long history of capitalist development" (p. 79).

Conceptually, from the physiocrats through classical economists, it was crucial that the laws of the market were seen as a natural order. Hence, civil society could be understood as neutral regarding power and domination, and its discourse only a matter of discovering the right policies for allowing its full development: "The constitutional state predicated on civil rights pretended, on the basis of an effective public sphere, to be an organization of public power ensuring the latter's subordination to the needs of a private sphere itself taken to be neutralized as regards power and domination. Thus the constitutional norms implied a model of civil society that by no means corresponded to its reality" (p. 84). This contradiction would in time become transformative. In this period of its classical flowering, however, the public still understood itself as using its critical debate not to achieve compromises or to exercise power, but rather to discover laws immanent to its form of society. "The 'domination' of the public, according to its own idea, was an order in which domination itself was dissolved. . . . Public debate was supposed to transform *voluntas* into a *ratio* that in the public competition of private arguments came into being as the consensus about what was practically necessary in the interest of all" (pp. 82–83). Here we see reflected not only economic conditions but also the idea of formless or pure humanity developed out of the bourgeois family's conjugal sphere.

The public sphere in this era remained rooted in the world of letters even as it assumed political functions. It took that older, elite public as constitutive of the whole relevant citizenry. Education and property ownership were its two criteria for admission. Restrictions of the franchise did not have to be viewed as restrictions of the public sphere but could be interpreted rather as "mere legal ratification of a status attained economically in the private sphere" (p. 85). These qualifications defined a "man," that is, the fully capable and autonomous person competent to enter into the rational-critical discourse about the general interest. "For the private person, there was no break between *homme* and *citoyen*, as long as the *homme* was simultaneously an owner of private property who as *citoyen* was to protect the stability of the property order as a private one"

(p. 87). So central was this phenomenon that Habermas (echoing stresses of the young Marx) sees in it the origin of ideology itself, in the strong sense that grounds immanent critique as well as describes false consciousness:

If ideologies are not only manifestations of the socially necessary consciousness in its essential falsity, if there is an aspect to them that can lay a claim to truth inasmuch as it transcends the status quo in utopian fashion, even if only for purposes of justification, then ideology exists at all only from this period on. Its origin would be the identification of "property owner" with "human being as such" in the role accruing to private people as members of the public in the political public sphere of the bourgeois constitutional state. (P. 88)

4

In chapter 4 Habermas turns to ideology, especially in the realm of the most "advanced" ideas and greatest thinkers of the time. Here the movement is essentially from Hobbes through Locke, the physiocrats, and Rousseau to Kant and then on to Hegel, Marx, Mill, and Tocqueville. What is being developed and then critiqued is a conception of public opinion as a reasoned form of access to truth. This replaces the notions of public opinion as the "mere opinion" (or arbitrary views) of isolated individuals taken in the aggregate, the reputation that emerges in the mirror of dispersed opinions, and the opinion of the "common" sort of people. Rather, public opinion comes to refer more positively to the views held by those who join in rational-critical debate on an issue.

Despite his unpublic doctrine of absolute sovereignty, Hobbes did bring new respect to opinion by identifying it with conscience (and consciousness). His very devaluation of religious conviction meant a corresponding upward revaluation of other opinion. But it was Locke who fully freed opinion from the taint of pure prejudice. Reason and criticism constructed an educated opinion that was fundamentally different from the "mere" opinion that had been seen as so vulgar. The physiocrats moved still further along this path of separating critique from opinion, at least for the enlightened public.

Rousseau, of course, was more complicated. "The physiocrats spoke out in favor of an absolutism complemented by a public sphere that was a place of critical activity; Rousseau wanted democracy without public debate" (p. 99). The general will was nonetheless a sort of public opinion, a consensus of hearts rather than arguments. However polarized in substance, both sides followed Guizot's injunction "to seek after truth, and to tell it to power" (quoted on p. 101). Since truth was the object of critical reflection and the general will alike, these could be interpreted as in a sense apolitical. The task was to rationalize politics in the name of morality as well as truth, not simply to engage in it.

In this pursuit, Kant become the paradigmatic voice, following Rousseau on the idea of the will of the whole people but the philosophes and the British Enlightenment thinkers on the centrality of critical reason. His was the most fully developed philosophy of the bourgeois public sphere. By themselves, Kant reasoned in "What Is Enlightenment?" individuals would have a hard time working their way out of tutelage, the inability to make use of understanding without external direction. Enlightenment became more possible in free public discourse. "In regard to enlightenment, therefore, thinking for oneself seemed to coincide with thinking aloud and the use of reason with its public use" (p. 104). Communication and criticism were central.[22] Thus even Kantian notions of universality, cosmopolitanism, and science were constituted in the communication of rational beings. When Kant called on Enlightenment thinkers to address the "world," or to be men of the world, the public sphere was essential to its definition; the very unity and dignity of the human species was revealed, in part, by its capacity to join in public discourse: "'World' here pointed to humanity as a species, but in that guise in which its unity presented itself in appearance: the world of a critically debating reading public that at the time was just evolving within the broader bourgeois strata" (p. 106). Engagement in the public sphere was the means by which the conflicting private wills of rational people could be brought into harmony. This could happen because society, particularly the private economy, necessarily gave rise to the conditions for turning politics into morality. *Bourgeois* could be conflated with *homme* because the private economy was a natural order, so constructed that justice was immanent in free commerce.[23]

If Kant offered the fullest philosophy of bourgeois publicness, Hegel offered the first critique, denouncing the public of civil society as ideology. Public opinion had the form of common sense; it was dispersed among people in the form of prejudices, not true knowledge; it took the fortuitous for the permanent. "Hegel took the teeth out of the idea of the public sphere of civil society; for anarchic and antagonistic civil society did not constitute the public sphere, emancipated from domination and insulated from the interference of power, in which autonomous private people related to one another" (p. 122). This did not provide the basis for transforming political authority into rational authority, force or interest into reason. Civil society could not dispense with domination but on the contrary required it because of a tendency toward disintegration.

It was only a short step to Marx's denunciation of public opinion as a mask for bourgeois class interests. "The public sphere with which Marx saw himself confronted contradicted its own principle of universal accessibility—the public could no longer claim to be identical with the nation, civil society with all of society" (p. 124). Similarly, of course, property owners could not be seen as equivalent to human beings in general. Indeed, the very division of state and society entailed an alienating division of the person into public and private. The private realm did not offer true respite from public tensions, for the family and the intimate sphere in general were marked by the necessity of labor, patriarchal property ownership, and domination. In Marx's vision, the state would be absorbed into society, and rational planning would enable the development of "an intimate sphere set free from economic functions" (p. 129). In this vision, interaction would be emancipated from the demands of social labor, and private relationships would be freed from the need for any legal regulations. Behind the Marxist view, however, was still the idea of a natural order— Marx disagreed not with the general idea but only with the claim that bourgeois civil society constituted the natural order that could give rise to harmonious human relationships.

Liberals like Mill and Tocqueville were willing, Habermas suggests, to take the step of discarding the notion of an underlying natural order adequate to ground a philosophy of history in which politics would become morality. Accepting the disharmony of much of capitalist civil society, the liberalism they developed sought protections and ameliorations, relative not perfect freedom. The political public sphere, in their account, did not rest on any natural basis, though some form of the bourgeois public sphere did need to be defended through common sense, prudence, and realism.[24] The key issue that they confronted was how to maintain the virtues of public life while its size increased and its composition changed. This democratization of the public sphere was an inevitable result of the tension between its original class limitations and its principled openness. "Electoral reform was the topic of the nineteenth century: no longer the principle of publicity as such, as had been true in the eighteenth century, but of the enlargement of the public" (p. 133). As the public was enlarged, however, public opinion itself came to seem a threat, particularly when it seemed to involve a compulsion toward conformity more than critical discourse. Thus it was that both Mill and Tocqueville worried, for example, about protecting minorities from persecution by majorities. This was actually a matter, in part, of protecting the possibility of free, critical thought from public opinion itself. Here we clearly see an initial theoretical response to the structural transformation of the public sphere.[25]

Mill and Tocqueville thus accepted an individualism without a comparable notion of the whole and resigned themselves to a more imperfect world.

This resignation before the inability to resolve rationally the competition of interests in the public sphere was disguised as perspectivist epistemology: because the particular interests were no longer measured against the general, the opinions into which they were ideologically transposed possessed an irreducible kernel of faith. . . . The unity of reason and of public opinion lacked the objective guarantee

of a concordance of interests existing in society, the rational de-
monstrability of a universal interest as such. (P. 135)

The "principle" of the public sphere, critical public discourse,
seemed to lose in strength in proportion as it extended as a
sphere, partly because its very foundations in the private realm
were undermined.

5

The undermining of the foundations of the public sphere came
about, Habermas suggests, through a "refeudalization" of society. "The model of the bourgeois public sphere presupposed
strict separation of the public from the private realm in such
a way that the public sphere, made up of private people gathered together as a public and articulating the needs of society
with the state, was itself considered part of the private realm"
(pp. 175–176). Structural transformation came about, however,
as private organizations began increasingly to assume public
power on the one hand, while the state penetrated the private
realm on the other. State and society, once distinct, became
interlocked. The public sphere was necessarily transformed as
the distinction between public and private realms blurred, the
equation between the intimate sphere and private life broke
down with a polarization of family and economic society, rational-critical debate gave way to the consumption of culture.

The blurring of relations between private and public involved centrally the loss of the notion that private life (family,
economy) created autonomous, relatively equal persons who in
public discourse might address the general or public interest.
First, the inequalities always present in civil society ceased to
be "bracketed" and became instead the basis of discussion and
action. This happened both because these inequalities grew
greater (as in the case of giant corporations) and because the
inclusion of more people in the public sphere made it impossible to escape addressing the class divisions of civil society
(because, for example, some of these people were excluded
from the franchise or lacked the private ownership of the
means of production that were the basis of the putative auton-

omy of *bourgeois* and *homme*). Second and relatedly, the notion of an objective general interest was replaced, even ideally, with one of a fairly negotiated compromise among interests.[26] The functioning of the public sphere thus shifted from rational-critical debate to negotiation. "The process of the politically relevant exercise and equilibration of power now takes place directly between the private bureaucracies, special-interest associations, parties, and public administration. The public as such is included only sporadically in this circuit of power, and even then it is brought in only to contribute its acclamation" (p. 176). This second process marked the beginning of the movement toward the welfare state as interest groups in civil society used the public sphere to demand "social rights"—the services or protection of the state. Attempts were made, in other words, to transfer to a political level those conflicts, e.g., between workers and employers, that were not resolvable in the private sphere alone. "The more society became transparent as a mere nexus of coercive constraints, the more urgent became the need for a strong state" (p. 144). But "the occupation of the political public sphere by the unpropertied masses led to an interlocking of state and society which [contrary to Marx's expectations] removed from the new public sphere its former basis without supplying a new one" (p. 177).

Civil society was changed also by the establishment of a world of work as a sphere of its own right between the public and private realms. Large organizations, both public and private, played the central role in separating work from the purely private sphere of the household or the paternalisticly managed workplace. The private sphere in turn was reduced to the family. An "externalization of what is declared to be the inner life" occurred. "To the extent that private people withdrew from their socially controlled roles as property owners into the purely 'personal' ones of their noncommittal use of leisure time, they came directly under the influence of semi-public authorities, without the protection of an institutionally respected domestic domain" (p. 159).[27]

At the same time, and largely as a consequence of these trends, the public sphere was turned into a sham semblance of its former self. The key tendency was to replace the shared, critical activity of public discourse by a more passive culture consumption on the one hand and an apolitical sociability on the other.[28] Habermas's account here is typical of the critique of mass culture in which members of the Frankfurt School had already played a prominent role. He also borrows descriptions of suburban social life from William H. Whyte's *Organization Man* to illustrate the pursuit of "groupness" as an end in itself. Thus participants in social gatherings lost the sense of the pleasures and virtues of argument that Kant and the members of the eighteenth-century public sphere had made central to public life: "In the course of our century, the bourgeois forms of sociability have found substitutes that have one tendency in common despite their regional and national diversity: abstinence from literary and political debate. On the new model the convivial discussion among individuals gave way to more or less noncommittal group activities" (p. 163). This did not mean that there was not a sharing of culture, only that it was a joint consumption rather than a more active participation in mutual critique (and production). "Individual satisfaction of needs might be achieved in a public fashion, namely, in the company of many others; but a public sphere itself did not emerge from such a situation. . . . Rational-critical debate had a tendency to be replaced by consumption, and the web of public communication unraveled into acts of individuated reception, however uniform in mode" (p. 161). Where works of literature, for example, had previously been appropriated not just through individual reading but through group discussion and the critical discourse of literary publications, the modern media and the modern style of appropriation "removed the ground for a communication about what has been appropriated" (p. 163).[29] Thus, "the world fashioned by the mass media is a public sphere in appearance only" (p. 171).

What happened was that in the expansion of access, the form of participation was fatally altered. Innovations that opened economic access to the public sphere and the realm of "high" culture, e.g., cheaper editions of books (not to mention higher incomes of readers), are worthy of praise. But alongside these there has been a psychological facilitation of access by lowering the threshold capacity required for appreciation or participation. "Serious involvement with culture produces facility, while the consumption of mass culture leaves no lasting trace; it affords a kind of experience which is not cumulative but regressive" (p. 166). The distinction between "serious involvement" and "consumption of mass culture" is perhaps overdrawn, if familiar; that between economically opening access and psychologically facilitating it is clearer. It is surprising, however, that Habermas does not consider the various ways in which access was opened that do not fall into either category—the extension of public education and mass literacy, for example, or the increase in working-class leisure time.[30] In any case, what he is charting is simultaneously the depoliticization of the public sphere and its impoverishment by removal of critical discourse. "In relation to the expansion of the news-reading public, therefore, the press that submitted political issues to critical discussion in the long run lost its influence. Instead, the culture-consuming public whose inheritance derived from the public sphere in the world of letters more than from that in the political realm attained a remarkable dominance" (p. 169).

The eighteenth-century public sphere had been constituted in the discourse of private persons but was based on a distinction between the private activities that formed them for public life and provided its motivations and that public life itself. By contrast, "the sphere generated by the mass media has taken on the traits of a secondary realm of intimacy" (p. 172). We experience radio, film, and television communication with an immediacy far greater than that characteristic of the printed word.[31] One of the effects of this on public discourse is that "bracketing" personal attributes and concentrating on the rational-critical argument becomes more difficult. This feeds into a more general "sentimentality toward persons and corresponding cynicism toward institutions," which curtails "subjective capacity for rational criticism of public authority, even where it might objectively still be possible" (p. 172). A personalized politics revives representative publicity by making candidates into media stars.[32] At the same time the new public-relations industry finds it easy to engineer consent among the consumers of mass culture. Even states must address citizens as consumers when they, like private corporations or political candidates, seek to cultivate an "uncommitted friendly disposition" (p. 195). This of course involves an element of false consciousness in which the degenerate mass public sphere understands itself on the model of its more effective predecssor: "The awakened readiness of the consumers involves the false consciousness that as critically reflecting private people they contribute responsibly to public opinion" (p. 194). Even legislatures are affected, as they become arenas for staged displays aimed at persuading the masses rather than forums for critical debate among their members. The mass-consumption mentality substitutes a pursuit of acclamation for the development of rational-critical consensus.[33]

The weakening of the public is not just a matter of new (lower class) entrants being mere consumers or substandard participants. On the contrary, Habermas asserts (with some empirical evidence), the consumption of mass culture increases with wealth, status, and urbanization. The most that can be said is that the consumption levels are highest for those whose wealth has outstripped their education. And the result is that the public sphere as a whole is transformed, not just diluted around the edges.

This transformation involves a literal disintegration. With the loss of a notion of general interest and the rise of a consumption orientation, the members of the public sphere lose their common ground. The consumption orientation of mass culture produces a proliferation of products designed to please various tastes. Not only are these not subjected, according to Habermas, to much critical discussion; none of them reaches the whole of the public. "Of Richardson's *Pamela* it could be said that it was read by the entire public, that is, by 'everyone' who could read at all" (p. 174). Nothing attains such general currency today.[34] This break involves not only segmentation of audiences but transformation of the once intimate relationship between cultural producers and consumers. It is, Habermas argues, precisely with this break that intellectuals begin to form a distinct stratum of those who produce culture and its critical commentaries. Once they are so distinguished, they have to explain to themselves their isolation from the public of the

educated bourgeoisie. The ideology of the free-floating intelligentsia responds to precisely this predicament. At the same
time, however, even the elite of producers and critics under-
goes a specialization that undercuts its public function. "The
sounding board of an educated stratum tutored in the public
use of reason has been shattered; the public is split apart into
minorities of specialists [e.g., lawyers, academics] who put their
reason to use nonpublicly and the great mass of consumers
whose receptiveness is public but uncritical" (p. 175).

6

By means of these transformations, the public sphere has become more an arena for advertising than a setting for rational-
critical debate. Legislators stage displays for constituents. Special-interest organizations use publicity work to increase the
prestige of their own positions, without making the topics to
which those positions refer subjects of genuine public debate.
The media are used to create occasions for consumers to identify with the public positions or personas of others. All this
amounts to the return of a version of representative publicity,
to which the public responds by acclamation, or the withhold-
ing of acclamation, rather than critical discourse. In this respect, the latter sections of *Structural Transformation* directly
foreshadow Habermas's arguments in *Legitimation Crisis* (1975).
The public sphere becomes a setting for states and corporate
actors to develop legitimacy not by responding appropriately
to an independent and critical public but by seeking to instill
in social actors motivations that conform to the needs of the
overall system dominated by those states and corporate actors.
The only difference is that in the earlier book Habermas implies that organized capitalism has a more successful legitimation regime.

Even political parties reflect the transformation of the public
sphere. From the nineteenth century these ceased to be groups
of voters so much as bureaucratic organizations aimed at motivating voters and attracting their psychological identification
and acclamation by voting. Modern parties "in the proper
sense" are thus "organized supralocally and with a bureaucratic

apparatus and aimed at the ideological integration and the political mobilization of the broad voting masses." Their attention is focused on attracting the votes of those not yet committed (and in some cases motivating those whose opinions, but not actual participation, they can count on). Such parties attempt to move people to offer their acclamation without providing political education or remedies for the "political immaturity" of voters (p. 203).[35] Plebiscites replace public discourse. When parties were constituted as groups of voters, they were simultaneously groups of participants in the rational-critical public sphere. Legislators were given free mandates, the argument went, because they, *like their constituents*, were autonomous parties to the public sphere with parity of standing in its rational-critical debate; they could not be bound to a position in advance of the discourse. But with the consumption orientation of mass culture and the interpenetration of state and society through organized interest groups and corporations, legislators become agents (or principals) of parties. Instead of joining with their constituents in rational-critical debate, they attempt to garner the support not just of independent constituents (as anachronistic liberal theory has it) but also of special-interest groups. They do this not through rational-critical debate but through offering to represent those interests in bargaining. "Direct mutual contact between the members of the public was lost in the degree that the parties, having become integral parts of a system of special-interest associations under public law, had to transmit and represent at any given time the interests of several such organizations that grew out of the private sphere into the public sphere" (p. 204).

As parties dominate politics and as state and society are generally intertwined, the material conditions for the old sort of public sphere disappear. The new version of representative publicity responds to a "democratic" broadening of the constituency of the public, but at the cost of its internally democratic functioning. No attempt to go back to the old bourgeois public sphere can be progressive, for social change has made its contradictory foundations manifest. "Any attempt at restoring the liberal public sphere through the reduction of its plebiscitarily expanded form will only serve to weaken even more the residual functions genuinely remaining within it" (p. 208). The struggle instead must be to find a form of democratic public discourse that can salvage critical reason in an age of large-scale institutions and fuzzy boundaries between state and society. The answer, Habermas suggests, lies in what in the 1960s came sometimes to be called "the long march through the institutions." That is, parties, parastatal agencies, and bureaucracies of all sorts must themselves be internally democratized and subjected to critical publicity. In the case of the media, for example, some mechanism for insuring more democratic access and selection is needed as a response to the concentration of ownership and increasing scale of media organizations. There may be no alternative to a politics based on negotiation of interests among organized groups.[36] But the trend for these organizations to become less open to rational-critical discourse can be reversed. "To be able to satisfy these functions in the sense of democratic opinion and consensus formation their inner structure must first be organized in accord with the principle of publicity and must institutionally permit an intra-party or intra-association democracy—to allow for unhampered communication and public rational-critical debate" (p. 209).

The struggle to transform institutions and reclaim the public sphere, to make good on the kernel of truth in the ideology of the bourgeois public sphere, is a struggle to make publicity a source of reasoned, progressive consensus formation rather than an occasion for the manipulation of popular opinion. Only thereby can the public realm become an authority for politics rather than merely its playing field: " 'Public opinion' takes on a different meaning depending on whether it is brought into play as a critical authority in connection with the normative mandate that the exercise of political and social power be subject to publicity or as the object to be molded in connection with a staged display of, and manipulative propagation of, publicity in the service of persons and institutions, consumer goods, and programs" (p. 236). The often touted democratic potential of plebiscites and public-opinion research is minimal, because neither in itself offers an occasion for discursive will formation.[37] "Publicity was, according to its very idea, a principle of democracy not because anyone could in principle announce, with equal opportunity, his personal inclinations, wishes, and convictions—opinions; it could only be realized in the measure that these personal opinions could evolve through the rational-critical debate of a public into public opinion" (p. 219). Public-opinion research is more akin to the simultaneously developed field of group psychology than to democratic practice; it is an auxiliary science to public administration rather than a basis or substitute for true public discourse.

The ideal of the public sphere calls for social integration to be based on rational-critical discourse. Integration, in other words, is to be based on communication rather than domination. "Communication" in this context means not merely sharing what people already think or know but also a process of potential transformation in which reason is advanced by debate itself. This goal cannot be realized by a denial of the implications of large-scale social organization, by imagining a public sphere occupied only by autonomous private individuals, with no large organizations and with no cleavages of interest inhibiting the identification of the general good, as liberal theory suggests. "Institutionalized in the mass democracy of the social-welfare state, . . . the idea of publicity . . . is today realizable only as a rationalization . . . of the exercise of societal and political power under the mutual control of rival organizations themselves committed to publicity as regards both their internal structure and their interaction with one another and with the state" (p. 210). The rationalization is limited, just as it was in the bourgeois public sphere of critical debate among private people, but it is rationalization nonetheless.

7

The second half of *Structural Transformation* is less satisfying than the first. If the early chapters succeed in recovering a valuable critical ideal from the classical bourgeois public sphere, Habermas ultimately cannot find a way to ground his hopes for its realization very effectively in his account of the social institutions of advanced or organized capitalism. While his idea of intraorganizational publicity and democracy is important, in the absence of a unifying general interest, it can only improve representation in compromise, not achieve the identification of the political with the moral through the agency of rational-critical debate. At the center of this impass is Habermas's inability to find in advanced capitalist societies an institutional basis for an effective political public sphere corresponding in character and function to that of early capitalism and state formation but corresponding in scale and participation to the realities of later capitalism and states.

Habermas responds to this problem in three ways.[38] First, especially in *Legitimation Crisis,* he addresses the consequences of extensive state intervention into the economy. This, as I noted above, is shown in *Structural Transformation* to undermine the bases in civil society for the development of a public sphere as a part of the private realm. Habermas's next move is to argue that this state intervention effectively prevents a focus on the contradictions of capital as such and thus orients political action away from the bases of potential fundamental transformation and toward the state itself. Welfare state democracy demands that states legitimate themselves by demonstrating that their policies serve the overall interests of their constituents. This is a result not only of state intervention as such (which is functionally required to maintain stable socioeconomic function) but also of the transformation of the public sphere into an arena in which a wide range of social interests vie for state action. Because those interests conflict, states are left to face a crisis in which they are unable simultaneously to produce adequate motivation for work and loyalty to the existing regime.[39]

Second, Habermas takes up the division between system and lifeworld. He argues that advanced capitalist society cannot be conceptualized as a social totality, because it is split into separate realms integrated on different bases. The lifeworld is the realm of personal relationships and (at its best) communicative action. But to it is counterposed a system ordered on the basis of nonlinguistic steering media (money and power), integrating society impersonally through functional or cybernetic feedback. This split cannot be overcome, Habermas argues, because there is no immanent logic of capitalism to produce its dialectical transcendence and because large-scale modern society would be impossible without such systemic integration (and dreams of doing away with such large-scale societal integration are not only romantic but dangerous because reduction in scale can come about only in catastrophic ways).[40] Nonetheless, the lifeworld is the locus for basic human values and is undergoing rationalization processes of its own; it needs to be defended against the continual encroachment of systemic media.

Third, Habermas shifted his attention from the institutional construction of a public sphere as the basis for democratic will formation to the validity claims universally implicit in all speech.[41] In the latter he finds the basis for a progressive rationalization of communication and the capacity for noninstrumental organization of interpersonal relationships. Habermas thus turns away from historically specific grounding for democracy (though the public sphere remains the institutional locus for democratic political practice) toward reliance on a transhistorical capacity of human communication.[42] Communicative action thus provides an alternative to money and power as a basis for societal integration. On the one hand, Habermas idealizes the directly interpersonal relations of the lifeworld as counterpoint to systemic integration with its dehumanization and reification. On the other hand, especially in more recent work, he explores the capacity of specific institutionalized discourses like law to develop communicative action as a means of societal rationalization and integration.[43] More generally, "a radical-democratic change in the process of legitimation aims at a new balance between the forces of societal integration so that the social-integrative power of solidarity—the 'communicative force of production'—can prevail over the powers of the other two control resources, i.e., money and administrative power, and therewith successfully assert the practically oriented demands of the lifeworld."[44]

Habermas thus continues to seek a way to recover the normative ideal of formal democracy from early bourgeois political theory and practice and to develop a basis for discerning the social directions by which it might progress.[45] More specifically, he continues to see the development of welfare state capitalism as producing impasses (rather than crises born of a dialectic, which will resolve them) but destroying earlier bases for addressing them through utopian collective action.[46] However, where *Structural Transformation* located the basis for the application of practical reason to politics in the historically specific social institutions of the public sphere, the theory of communicative action locates them in transhistorical, evolving communicative capacities or capacities of reason conceived intersubjectively as in its essence a matter of communication. The public sphere remains an ideal, but it becomes a contingent product of the evolution of communicative action, rather than its basis.

What happened in *Structural Transformation* to make these moves seem necessary? More precisely, did Habermas have to abandon the more historically specific and social-institutional strategy of *Structural Transformation* to locate bases for the simultaneous rationalization and democratization of politics? I think the answer lies in the last chapters of the book. In a sense, Habermas himself seems to have been persuaded more by his account of the degeneration of the public sphere than by his suggestions of its revitalization through intraorganizational reforms and the application of norms of publicity to interorganizational relations. He seems to have seen no bases for progress in social institutions as such, either those of capitalism and civil society or those of the state, and so turned elsewhere to look for them. The crucial question was what might underpin the development and recognition of a truly general interest.[47] No longer believing in the capacity of either the public sphere as such or of socialist transformation of civil society to meet this need, Habermas sought a less historical, more transcendental basis for democracy. This is what he found in an evolutionary account of human communicative capacity that stressed the potentials implicit in all speech. This gave him the basis for revitalizing Kantian ideals, and more generally democratic ideals, in a world still torn asunder and subjected to domination by capitalism and bureaucratic power.

8

Habermas's work has changed more in strategy than in overall goal. The reasons for this may not be simply "theoretical progress," however, but some more specific internal weaknesses of *Structural Transformation*. In the remainder of this introduction I can only suggest a few of these (while drawing on and introducing the chapters that follow); I cannot remedy any. Most tend to be problems of underdevelopment or omission of significant issues. Mentioning them thus points directly to possibilities for extending and improving on the analysis in *Structural Transformation*. This is important, for though it is far less theoretically developed, the historical specificity and grasp of concrete social-institutional foundations give *Structural Transformation* some advantages over Habermas's later theory.[48]

A central weakness is that *Structural Transformation* does not treat the "classical" bourgeois public sphere and the postransformation public sphere of "organized" or "late" capitalism symmetrically. Habermas tends to judge the eighteenth century by Locke and Kant, the nineteenth century by Marx and Mill, and the twentieth century by the typical suburban television viewer. Thus Habermas's account of the twentieth century does not include the sort of intellectual history, the attempt to take leading thinkers seriously and recover the truth from their ideologically distorted writings, that is characteristic of his approach to seventeenth, eighteenth, and nineteenth centuries. Conversely, his treatment of the earlier period doesn't look at "penny dreadfuls," lurid crime and scandal sheets, and other less than altogether rational-critical branches of the press or at the demagoguery of traveling orators, and glances only in passing at the relationship of crowds to political discourse.[49] The result is perhaps an overestimation of the degeneration of the public sphere. The revitalization of a critical political public during the 1960s (and its refusal to quite go away since then) lends further credence to this view. Moreover, the public consequences of mass media are not necessarily as uniformly negative as *Structural Transformation* suggests, and there may be more room than Habermas realized for alternative democratic media strategies.[50]

Another important issue is Habermas's treatment of culture and identity. Eley (chapter 12), for example, points to the remarkable absence of nationalism from Habermas's discussion of the public sphere (though the history of nationalism does not necessarily challenge the account Habermas offers). This may be due partly to the general lack of attention to the nineteenth-century public sphere, which Eley sets out specifically to remedy. It seems, however, also to be part of a thinness of attention to matters of culture and the construction of identity.[51] Indeed, this is reflected methodologically, as it were, in Habermas's inattention to cultural variation in his empirical accounts; as Baker notes (chapter 8), he tends to typify epochs with little regard to national or other cultural specificity.[52]

This bears also on the question of "degeneration" of the public sphere. Even if we grant that the problem-solving functions of the public sphere are being performed less well than in the past, this does not mean that public discourse has ceased to be at least as vibrant a source of understanding, including self-understanding. In the terms Habermas has adopted, we might say that the public sphere plays a crucial "world-disclosing" role alongside of, or possibly independently of, its problem-solving one. And this world-disclosing role is not limited to nonpolitical culture. Phenomena like nationalism, feminism, and gay, ethnic, or youth consciousness often involve crucial redefinitions of the issues and identities involved in political struggles. As Warner suggests (chapter 15), one of the key changes in the public sphere since its "classical" heyday has been an increasing prominence of what may be called identity politics (though it should not be thought that this theme was ever absent). Warner's and Eley's chapters point especially to this theme, but it is also implicit in the whole rethinking of the boundary between public and private broached by feminist discourse and in this volume especially by Fraser and Ryan (chapters 5 and 11). Indeed, feminist thought has probably done more than any other intellectual discourse to point up the difficulties inherent in assuming the public/private dichotomy to exist as neatly as Habermas assumes. The difficulties also go deeper, because Habermas sees maintaining the division as an important task. This is not just a description of bourgeois thought, for it reemerges in a new form in his discussion of the defense of lifeworld boundaries against systemic intrusion.

When Habermas treats identities and interests as settled within the private world and then brought fully formed into the public sphere, he impoverishes his own theory. In the first place, his own discussion of the literary public sphere showed in a preliminary way how fiction serves to facilitate a discussion about selfhood and subjectivity and to reinforce a vesting of primary identity in a newly constructed intimate sphere. The central theme of the ideological conflation of *bourgeois* and *homme* is a construction of identity on which the bourgeois public sphere may depend but that also takes place in public discourse. As Nancy Fraser suggests, public deliberation need not be understood as simply *about* an already established common good; it may be even more basically an occasion for the clarification (and I would add, constitution) of interests. The very dichotomous understandings of public/private and system/lifeworld are thus among the reasons why Habermas reaches an impasse in his search of a general interest; his theoretical scheme requires him to look for that interest in advance of public life, and his assumptions lead him to locate it along with "true humanity" in the lifeworld or private realm. The feminist critique thus shows not just that Habermas failed to pay enough attention to the gendered nature of the public sphere, nor even that he sees the solution to this problem only in gender neutrality rather than in thematizing the issue of gender. It also points up that the public/private dichotomy itself imposes a neutralizing logic on differential identity by establishing qualification for publicness as a matter of abstraction from private identity (see chapter 15 and less directly chapter 3). Difference may be "bracketed" or tolerated; it is hard on Habermas's account to see the need for it to be positively thematized.

Habermas's neglect of religion, noted by Zaret (chapter 9), is closely related. Habermas implicitly follows the philosophes in imagining that religion and science must stand in a sort of hydraulic relationship to one another. For all their criticism of the Enlightenment, Adorno and Horkheimer (at least until his old age) also shared this view that religion must decline as enlightenment progresses. That secularization is part and parcel of modernity and, closely linked to the rise of rational-critical discourse, goes unquestioned. This view contributes to Habermas's blind spot on the role of religion both as a central thematic topic in the early public sphere and as one of its enduring institutional bases.[53] This is true not only of England, where religious debate was perhaps as important as literary discourse in paving the way for the political public sphere. It was also true in France, where the anticlerical obsessions of many leading Enlightenment thinkers were ancestors of the very antireligious assumptions Habermas inherits.

Science may also have played an important role, as Zaret suggests, particularly by providing a model of "disinterested" discourse, or rather, discourse shaped by a general interest in knowledge that at least in ideology held the particular interests of participants in check and rendered their private identities irrelevant. This was like a highly restricted version of the literary public sphere, but as Habermas's own later work suggests, the extension of the idea of science to social science was a key moment in the creation of the liberal public sphere.[54] On the other hand, the ideology of science was one source of views that saw rightness in public policy as distinctly ascertainable from public discourse and potentially superordinate over it. In the name of science one thus could (and can) still treat public opinion as mere opinion. Thus, as Baker notes, the physiocrats and Condorcet in particular saw public discourse as vital, but not primary. For them, unlike many republicans, it was but one of the means that might serve the end of rational social progress. It is not only in the late twentieth-century era of organized capitalism that a specialized nonpublic science has been deployed in the service of administrative rationality and in competition with the public sphere.

Related to these issues of culture and identity is Habermas's neglect of social movements (discussed also in chapters 7 and 12). Habermas's account of the public sphere perhaps conforms too closely to the liberal bourgeois ideal in imagining it simply as a realm into which individuals bring their ideas and critiques. Both public discourse and democratic politics, however, seem crucially influenced by social movements. Such movements may be conceptualized as subsidiary publics, as Eley (chapter 12) does, or more stress may be placed on their attempts to use force to gain instrumental ends. In either case, movements are crucial to reorienting the agenda of public discourse, bringing new issues to the fore. The routine rational-critical discourse of the public sphere cannot be about everything all at once. Some structuring of attention, imposed by dominant ideology, hegemonic powers, or social movements, must always exist. The last possibility is thus crucial to democracy. Moreover, social movements are occasions for the restructuring not just of issues but of identities. Throughout the modern era, social movements have been in part occasions for the legitimation of new voices (by which I mean not just the inclusion of persons previously excluded but also changes in the identities from which included persons speak).[55] The absence of social movements from Habermas's account thus also reflects an inattention to agency, to the struggles by which the both public sphere and its participants are actively made and remade. Habermas approaches the public sphere and its transformations more as reflections of underlying developments in civil society and state.

Social movements are among the several possible sorts of subsidiary public spheres we might conceptualize if we break with the idea that there must be one public sphere for each state. Several writers in this book argue for a notion of multiple, sometimes overlapping or contending, public spheres (especially Eley, Baker, Garnham, and Fraser). Part of the background to this lies once again in Habermas's tendency to dichotomize public and private. This is too easily matched up with the similar dichotomy between state and civil society, which engenders the assumption that for any state there must be *one* public. It seems to me a loss simply to say that there are many public spheres, however, for that will leave us groping for a new term to describe the communicative relationships among them. It might be productive rather to think of the public sphere as involving a field of discursive connections. Within this network there might be a more or less even flow of communication. In nearly any imaginable case there will be clusters of relatively greater density of communication within the looser overall field. These clusters may be only more or less biased microcosms of the whole, as cities have their own public discourse within countries, and as neighborhoods within cities. But these clusters may also be organized around issues, categories, persons, or basic dynamics of the larger society. There is thus a sort of feminist public sphere, or counterpublic, and also a subsidiary public among lawyers. These are obviously different. For any such cluster we must ask not just on what thematic content it focuses but also how it is internally organized, how it maintains its boundaries and relatively greater internal cohesion in relation to the larger public, and whether its separate existence reflects merely sectional interests, some functional division of labor, or a felt need for bulwarks against the hegemony of a dominant ideology. This whole issue points not only to the importance of a more pluralistic, open approach to conceptualizing the public sphere but also to a need for analysis of its internal organization, something almost completely neglected in *Structural Transformation*. In the first half of the book, Habermas simply doesn't address the power relations, the networks of communication, the topography of issues, and the structure of influence of the public sphere except in very general terms of the existence of factions and parties.[56] In the second half of the book, these figure mainly in the account of degeneration. Yet whatever its qualities, any public sphere is necessarily a socially organized field, with characteristic lines of division, relationships of force, and other constitutive features.[57]

The most glaring and often cited instance of this issue is Habermas's decision that he could put the plebeian public sphere to one side as a derivative discourse during the eighteenth and nineteenth centuries. In one sense, Habermas here posited the existence of multiple public spheres, but this is somewhat deceptive, as he suggested that the plebeian public sphere was not only derivative but also "a variant . . . suppressed in the historical process" (p. xviii). Though it continued a submerged existence (kept alive by various social movements), it not only failed to attain dominance but oriented itself to the intentions of the bourgeois public sphere. Enough has been said about the unfairness of this characterization of the discourse of artisans, workers, and others. The point here is to note that this is more than just a simple omission. The lack of attention to the plebeian public sphere is also part of a failure to describe adequately the full field of force impinging on the bourgeois public sphere. Habermas is well aware, of course, though it is not a heavily developed theme, that the bourgeois public sphere was oriented not just toward defense of civil society against the state but also toward the maintenance of a system of domination within civil society. It is also the case, however, that throughout its existence the bourgeois public sphere was permeated by demands from below. These took the form not only of calls for broader inclusivity but also more basic challenges and the pushing of new issues forward on the agenda. Moreover, important parts of the struggle to establish some of the features Habermas describes as integral to bour-geois publicity, like freedom of the press, in fact were carried out largely by activists in the so-called plebeian public sphere. The hegemony of bourgeois publicity was always incomplete and exercised within a field constituted partly by its relation to other insurgent discourses.

9

Habermas's writing implies that the point of *Structural Trans-formation* is to show the degeneration of the public sphere and to argue that progress must lie in a democratic accommodation to the conditions of mass society rather than in their overthrow or a return to any golden age. Many readers have been most influenced by the book's critique of the twentieth-century mass public. But it seems to me that the most important part of the book is in fact the first half, in which Habermas constitutes the historical category of the public sphere and attempts to draw from it a normative ideal. For many commentators, this raises a basic question of how to identify the extent to which Haber-mas discusses theoretical ideals versus practical actualities of the bourgeois public sphere. This is clearly important as a matter of historical description. Theoretically, however, the precise balance between the two seems less significant. It is crucial that Habermas address both, for this not only enables his recovery of the ideal from flawed material practice, it enables the identification of the social foundations on which the ideal can be partially realized (and whose change must mean the structural transformation of the public sphere).

When he wrote *Structural Transformation,* Habermas still hoped that showing how a determinate set of sociohistorical conditions gave rise to ideals that they could not fulfill would provide motivation for the progressive transformation of those conditions. He has now rejected the tradition of ideology critique out of which his approach to historical reconstruction came. He sees it as undesirably linked to totalizing Marxist understandings of the relationship between base and superstructure, to a Hegelian dialectic of idea and reality, and to a notion of society that fails to grasp the substantial autonomy of systems of money and power. Nonetheless, Habermas has not surrendered the idea of immanent critique.[58] Rather, he has removed the immanence from specific historical conditions to universal characteristics of human communication. This allows him to ground his normative argument, to keep it from arbitrariness, but it removes it from any clear purchase on historical progress. That is, communicative ethics does a much better job of setting out a normative ideal than of indicating what is likely to make it persuasive to people at any particular point in time and how to make judgments about better or worse communication in circumstances far from the ideal. There remain, in other words, advantages to the historical specificity of *Structural Transformation* even if one does not keep to a strong Hegelian-Marxist faith.

Despite, or perhaps in a way because of, his moves away from critique of history and ideology, Habermas remains centrally engaged in the project of identifying the still-valuable normative ideals of modernity. Where he earlier took on a critique of the ideological contradictions of modernity, he now defends its unfinished project. That project involves a rationalization of society and of democratic will formation not far from that embodied in the notion of the political public sphere. The rehabilitation of formal democracy that thirty years ago was a crucial complement to Marxism now appears just as important in the struggle against the "new conservatives."[59] These people present themselves often as postmodernists and sometimes misleadingly as radicals or progressives. Though there are genuine insights in this tradition, at their worst, postmodernists reveal a cynicism and a relativism that together permit the normalization of evil; more generally, they throw out the criteria of progress along with the rigidities of utopia.

The Structural Transformation of the Public Sphere has a good deal to offer in this struggle. Its historical specificity, for example, should make it appealing where the neo-Kantian universalism of the theory of communicative action raises concerns. Though they are not always developed, *Structural Transformation* also offers much clearer openings to a political and social theory sensitive to issues of difference and identity. This is not to say that it solves the difficulties inherent in taking difference seriously while trying to avoid relativism and speak generally. But on this as on other issues, it offers a framework that should prove helpful to those who would develop it and use it in many different ways.

The most important destiny of Habermas's first book may prove to be this: not to stand as an authoritative statement but to be an immensely fruitful generator of new research, analysis, and theory. It is curious that it should do so in the English-speaking world nearly thirty years after its publication, but ironically the newly translated book seems enormously timely. Perhaps this is not only because of its theme but also because of the way in which it weaves economic, social-organizational, communicational, social-psychologial, and cultural dimensions of its problem together in a historically specific analysis. This multidimensional, interdisciplinary account is central to enabling Habermas to offer the richest, best developed conceptualization available of the social nature and foundations of public life. As scholars set out to make sense of the growing wealth of empirical research on the various specific topics related to this theme, this book will form an indispensable point of theoretical departure. It should also continue to inform a rich tradition of empirical work. We should be grateful that it has finally appeared in English.

It would perhaps be the nicest irony if this new reception of *Structural Transformation* should prove Habermas wrong, revealing that cynicism and exhaustion of utopian energies had not reached the point of rendering critique of ideology powerless. Certainly the book's resonance with so many discourses suggests that the recovery and extension of a strong normative idea of publicness is very much on the current agenda. No book is likely to help more than *The Structural Transformation of the Public Sphere*.

Notes

1. *Critique of Practical Reason* (New York, 1956), 250–251, quoted in Habermas, *The Structural Transformation of the Public Sphere*, trans. T. Burger and F. Lawrence (Cambridge, Mass., 1989), 106.

2. *Moral Consciousness and Communicative Action* (Cambridge, Mass., 1990; orig. 1983, 1988), p. 4; see also and "Law and Morality," in *The Tanner Lectures on Human Values*, vol. 8 (Salt Lake City and Cambridge, 1988), 217–299.

3. For example, O. Negt and A. Kluge, *The Public Sphere and Experience* (Minneapolis, forthcoming in translation; orig. 1973).

4. In chapter 17 Habermas notes his continuing appreciation for Abendroth but indicates that he now rejects most of Abendroth's Hegelian-Marxist optimism about total social transformation.

5. Negt and Kluge, *The Public Sphere and Experience;* Negt, "Mass Media: Tools of Domination or Instruments of Liberation? Aspects of the Frankfurt School's Communications Analysis," *New German Critique* 14 (1978): 61–80; see the more general discussion in Hohendahl, *The Institution of Criticism* (Ithaca, 1982). See also note 5 to chapter 17.

6. See especially H. Arendt, *The Human Condition* (Chicago, 1958); see also chapter 3.

7. See J. Cohen, "Why More Political Theory," *Telos* 40 (1979): 70–94, esp. pp. 74 ff.

8. References to *Structural Transformation* will be given simply by page numbers in the text.

9. Habermas's account of the modern public sphere is thus fundamentally at odds with the classical republican tradition (idealized by Arendt) not only in the instance of ancient Greece but also in that of the Renaissance (see J. G. A. Pocock, *The Machiavellian Moment*, Princeton, 1975).

10. Compare Wuthnow, *Communities of Discourse: Ideology and Social Structure in the Reformation, the Enlightenment, and European Socialism* (Cambridge, Mass., 1989), which refutes that more simplistic notion but does not take on Habermas's deeper conceptualization. Habermas, like Wuthnow, sees members of the state bureaucracies as the core of the "bourgeois" strata that occupied the central position in the new public sphere (pp. 22–23). "*Burgerliche*," it is also worth reminding ourselves, carries a less exclusively economic connotation than "bourgeois," reflects the transformation out of feudalism, and more clearly signifies urbanness.

11. This is why the plebeian public sphere was, in Habermas's view, derivative of the bourgeois, though I think that this is historically ambiguous; chapters 12 and 17 both discuss this further.

12. For a comment, from another angle, on the narrowing implicit in many invocations of civil society, see C. Taylor, "Modes of Civil Society," *Public Culture* 3, no. 1 (1990) pp. 95–118.

13. B. Anderson, *Imagined Communities* (London, 1982). Zaret (chapter 9) wants to go much further in making printing technology an independent causal factor in the analysis. This leads Kramer (chapter 10) to say that he favors a sort of technological determinism.

14. Charles Taylor (*The Sources of the Self*, Cambridge, Mass., 1989) has recently stressed the key role played in the making of the modern self by the "affirmation of ordinary life," which he traces especially to the era of the Protestant Reformation. This is a linked development inasmuch as it involves the same raising of the demands of ordinary existence—family, work, economy—to a level of primary value.

15. Chapter 7, "On the Concept of Public Opinion," is actually a very weak counterpart to chapter 4, "The Bourgeois Public Sphere: Idea and Ideology." It fits the scheme I suggested insofar as the "auxiliary science" of public-opinion research is a key ideological and intellectual reflection of what has become of the public sphere. It is, however, a much shallower treatment of twentieth century ideology of public life than its precursor is of seventeenth and eighteenth century ideology and political philosophy. Both before and after World War II there was a fairly large outpouring of literature on democracy and public life, some of which Habermas cites but the whole of which he never seriously addresses. He offers no consideration, for example, of John Dewey (e.g., *The Public and Its Problems*, New York, 1972) nor of early twentieth century American reformers or preachers of the social gospel.

16. It is remarkable that Habermas's account of how the family helped to give rise to a notion of "pure" and undifferentiated humanity does not betray any sense of the role of religion in helping to produce this result. Yet the tradition of interiority was pioneered by Augustine, and during the Protestant Reformation it was given decisive new form as something shared equivalently among all people.

17. In this connection, we can see in Habermas's discussion of the intimate sphere a prefiguration of his use of the lifeworld as a standpoint for critique of the "colonization" of systemic relations. Nancy Fraser has argued that this is a suspect standpoint for emancipatory critique because it involves an idealization, or an acceptance of the self-idealization, of the patriarchal family ("What's Critical about Critical Theory: The Case of Gender," in *Unruly Practices*, Minneapolis, 1990). Somewhat surprisingly, Habermas seems more attentive to this issue in *Structural Transformations* than in his later theory of communicative action (*Communication and the Evolution of Society*, trans. T. McCarthy, Boston, 1979; *The Structural Transformation of the Public Sphere*, trans. T. McCarthy, Boston, 1984 and 1988). Even in the earlier work, however, he approaches gender only in terms of equality (e.g., p. 56), not in terms of any more positive valuing of difference. See chapter 7 for a consideration of the seeming duality between a hierarchical recognition of difference and its suppression in the name of equality. See also chapter 18.

18. Salons were also distinctive in including, even being organized by, women. But this perhaps reflected their transitional nature, for the emerging bourgeois public sphere was firmly the province of patriarchal males (as were both coffee houses and table societies).

19. One of the criticisms of *Structural Transformation,* made as early as Negt and Kluge's *Public Sphere and Experience,* is that Habermas does not distinguish clearly enough between the ideal and the actuality of the bourgeois public sphere. See chapter 18.

20. "Intrinsic to the idea of a public opinion born of the power of the better argument was the claim to that morally pretentious rationality that strove to discover what was at once just and right" (p. 54).

21. This general legal capacity was linked to a progressive transformation in the idea of person. The simple qualification of property holder, for example, replaced various specific statuses based on family, urban freedoms, or feudal relations. Even that was but a way station, however, as the person was increasingly redefined as a natural category rather than a constructed category (see Taylor, *Sources of the Self*). It is no accident that the sort of economic reasoning that takes individual persons as uncritically given, and thus in no need of special theoretical construction, arose in the same period.

22. Here again, we see the later, even more neo-Kantian Habermas prefigured in *Structural Transformation.* He quotes Kant's *Critique of Pure Reason*: "The touchstone whereby we decide whether our holding a thing to be true is conviction or mere persuasion is therefore external, namely the possibility of communicating it and of finding it to be valid for all human reason" (p. 108).

23. Habermas (p. 115) finds two versions of Kant's political philosophy: in one the cosmopolitan order would emerge from natural necessity alone; in the other it had to be pushed along by moral politics as well.

24. Later liberals, especially the more economistic, have tended to succumb to equating capitalism with a natural basis for society, complete with a range of apparently objective, but in fact socially constructed, constraints.

25. In a sense, within the scheme of the book, described above, the discussion of Mill and Tocqueville would almost seem to belong in the last chapter (though that would disrupt the chronological flow of the book). Habermas seems to suggest that they present the basic theory of the posttransformation public sphere, much as Locke, the physiocrats, and Kant did for the classical bourgeois public sphere. Accordingly, it remains only to add the chapter on public-opinion research.

26. Habermas uses an excursis on law and legal norms to illustrate the loss of capacity to identify the general interest by loss of the formal universality that guaranteed "truth" (which now sounds antique as an attribute of laws): this truth "was only guaranteed as long as a public sphere, elevated in the parliament to an organ of the state, made it possible to discover, through public discussion, what was practically necessary in the general interest" (p. 178). As this idea of an objective, formally validated foundation was lost, the law not only suffered a potential loss of legitimacy but was changed internally. The distinction between general law and specific regulatory measure became blurred.

27. This resembles part of what Habermas would later call the "colonization of the lifeworld" (*The Theory of Communicative Action,* esp. vol. 2).

28. Rather surprisingly, perhaps, in a residual and narrow Marxism, Habermas treats leisure behavior as inherently apolitical because it is not tied to survival needs (p. 160).

29. Habermas rather confusingly talks about this being a result of "the private form of appropriation" (p. 163), when, of course, this is hardly unique to the new situation but in fact, on his own account, was essential to reading. A few pages later (p. 170)

Introduction

Habermas praises the private appropriation of the printed word for encouraging a distance from objects of appropriation that encourages critical thinking. I think the real point is that he does not see the new sort of private appropriation characteristic, for example, of television as coupled with a more rational-critical public exchange. Whether this is so, and if so, whether it has to do with media as such, can of course be debated. Habermas reflects here the orthodoxy of the critique of "mass culture"; this has been challenged, for example, by the so-called "new reception theory" and empirical studies purporting to show that people are much less passive recipients of mass-media messages than the mass culture critics had thought. See, e.g., S. Hall, "Cultural Studies and the Center: Some Problematics and Problems," in Hall et al., eds., *Culture, Media, Language* (London, 1980); R. Allen, ed., *Channels of Discourse* (Chapel Hill, 1986); J. Fiske, *Television Culture* (London, 1987); D. Kellner, *Television* (Boulder, 1990). Habermas acknowledges this issue in both his contributions to this book.

30. Habermas notes in chapter 17 that he underestimated the positive influence of expansion of formal schooling.

31. Here Habermas is on somewhat stronger ground with recent media scholars; see, e.g., J. Meyrowitz, *No Sense of Place* (New York, 1985).

32. See chapter 15 for an interesting perspective on this, stressing the importance of embodiment and abstraction from bodies—a theme that Habermas deals with minimally and weakly (though he acknowledges its significance in chapter 18).

33. See, however, chapter 15, where the implications of a consumer consciousness are given a broader reading.

34. It might be more accurate to say that no *text* attains such currency. Certainly news reports of certain public dramas, space shuttle explosions or hostage crises, for example, do attain thoroughly general currency and are, for a time, avidly discussed. Of course, these are not texts and generally do not involve communication or collective self-reflection of the same sort; I do not think any films or other sorts of communications manage to achieve a reception by the whole public rather than one or more of its subsections. This is one of the touchstones of contemporary criticism of public discourse, especially on the right, e.g., A. Bloom, *The Closing of the American Mind* (New York, 1987) and E. D. Hirsch, *What Every American Needs to Know* (New York, 1987), but also on the left, e.g., R. Jacoby, *The Last Intellectuals* (New York, 1988).

35. This is a special concern of Harry Boyte's; see chapter 13 and sources cited therein.

36. Here Habermas anticipates his later discussion (following Parsons and Luhmann) of the systemic integration necessary to modern large-scale societies but based on the nonlinguistic steering media of money and power and thereby always opposed to and distanced from the lifeworld (*The Theory of Communicative Action,* esp. vol. 2). As Habermas discusses in chapter 17, however, he later concluded that system and lifeworld must be seen not as aspects of a social totality but as separate parts of a two-tiered concept of society. He thus sees the conceptualization of *Structural Transformation* as flawed because it suggests a potential for internal democratization of the state apparatus and economy. He now sees these as "systematically integrated action fields" that cannot be transformed democratically from within. Instead of seeking transformation of the systems of administrative power and money, we should seek to prevent or limit their encroachment on the lifeworld by better boundary maintenance.

37. See the discussion in C. Calhoun, "Populist Politics, Communications Media, and Large Scale Societal Integration," *Sociological Theory* (1988): 219–241.

38. In what follows, I trace only a single thread in Habermas's social and political theory; I do not attempt to describe the whole of his voluminous work, which includes major writings on the philosophy of the social sciences, intellectual history, contemporary politics, and specific philosophical issues. In particular, I do not explore his attempt, especially during the remainder of the 1960s, to rethink the relationships between science and social life, theory and practice, though it clearly is closely related to the work discussed here, particularly in its development of a notion of rationalization. See *Theory and Practice* (London, 1974; orig. 1963–1971), *On the Logic of the Social Sciences* (Cambridge, Mass., 1988; orig. 1967), *Knowledge and Human Interests* (Boston, 1971; orig. 1968); and *Toward a Rational Society: Student Protest, Science, and Politics* (Boston, 1970; orig. 1968–1969).

39. *Legitimation Crisis*, trans. T. McCarthy (London, 1976). The discussion in D. Held, "Critical Theory and Political Transformation," *Media, Culture, and Society* 4 (1982): 153–160, is helpful and unusual in relating this to *Structural Transformation*.

40. This argument is central to *The Theory of Communicative Action*, which remains Habermas's fullest theoretical statement. It was developed earlier, however, especially in a pair of critical engagements with the work of other leading German scholars. Engaging Niklas Luhmann, Habermas sought to maintain a place for critical theory and normative engagement within functionalist sociology, and he rejected Luhmann's "methodological antihumanism." He thus accepted the bulk of Parsons and Luhmann's account of social systems but denied that an account of such systems was a full account of society, since it omitted the lifeworld. See J. Habermas and N. Luhmann, *Theorie der Gesellschaft oder Sozialtechnologie: Was leistet die Systemforschung?* (Frankfurt, 1971) and also the discussion and critique in T. McCarthy, "Complexity and Democracy, or the Seducements of Systems Theory," *New German Critique* 35 (1985): 27–53. Habermas has recently discussed Luhmann's appropriation of the philosophy of the subject in *The Philosophical Discourse of Modernity*, Cambridge, Mass., 1987, 368–385. Engaging Hans-Georg Gadamer, Habermas drew on hermeneutics to challenge the simplistic positivism of typical social science and was pushed toward the phenomenological notion of the lifeworld (for his more developed concept of which he draws on Schutz; see *The Theory of Communicative Action*, vol. 2, 119–152). Habermas contended, however, that hermeneutics (and phenomenology and what in English are called "interpretive sociologies") cannot offer an adequate account of the systemic dimensions of society and remain trapped within a context- and tradition-dependent point of view that is unable to ground the progressive and defensible development of norms and knowledge (see *The Logic of the Social Sciences*, Cambridge, Mass., 1989, orig. 1967, and also K.-O. Apel et al., *Hermeneutik und Ideologiekritik*, Frankfurt, 1971). Habermas initially relied on "ideology critique" to argue that subjective understanding is subject to systematic distortions. Abandoning the notion of ideology critique in his later work (see his discussion in chapter 17), Habermas nonetheless refused to accept the epistemological claims of Gadamer's *Truth and Method* (New York, 1975; orig. 1960) on the grounds that they are necessarily relativistic (Habermas, Review of *Truth and Method*, in F. R. Dallmayr and T. A. McCarthy, eds., *Understanding Social Inquiry*, South Bend, Ind., 1977). Habermas remained committed to the ideal of cumulative, perfectible, and especially universally valid knowledge and regarded sociology as a means for emancipation from tradition. Gadamer replied that no thinker can escape embeddedness in a tradition ("On the Scope and Function of Hermeneutic Reflection," in *Philosophical Hermeneutics*, Berkeley, 1976, orig. 1967). The exchange thus anticipated Habermas's continuing confrontations with so-called postmodernist thought.

41. Habermas's use of speech-act theory to develop his category of communicative action appear especially in volume 1 of *The Theory of Communicative Action*.

42. In a sense, his scheme remains Hegelian, positing an abstract communicative potentiality in all speech that is both challenged by instrumental use of language and (eventually) dialectically redeemable in a more fully developed form of social integration. Thus work like Kohlberg's theory of moral judgment was attractive to Habermas as a seeming empirical verification that there was some such process of cumulative gain in moral capacity at both the individual biographical level and the collective historical level. See Habermas, *Communication and the Evolution of Society, Moral Consciousness, and Communicative Action* and "Justice and Solidarity: On the Discussion Cocerning 'Stage 6'," *Philosophical Forum* 21 (1989–1990): 32–51. To the extent that Habermas no longer accepts and relies upon Kohlberg's theory (which has been subjected to widespread criticism), his own theory loses not only an empirical example but also an account of the development of the human individual that can locate the exercise of practical reasoning in a moral person.

43. See "Law and Morality." Habermas also remains committed to the close relationship between politics and morality and to the Kantian notion of the capacity of practical reason to bring these together. See *Moral Consciousness and Communicative Action* (Cambridge, Mass., 1990).

44. Chapter 17, sec. 3.

45. I do not mean that these are the only normative ideals addressed in Habermas's theory, only that they are central.

46. "The New Obscurity: The Crisis of the Welfare State and the Exhaustion of Utopian Energies," in *The New Conservatism: Cultural Criticism and the Historians' Debate* (Cambridge, Mass., 1989), 48–70.

47. In addition to the summary remarks above, see chapter 2 on the centrality in Habermas's theory of the attempt to discern a general interest.

48. Jean Cohen has similarly suggested that "both Habermas' early and late work, each in its own way, but neither on its own, are indispensable" for the task of grasping the gains and losses of modernity and the possibilities for emancipation and democracy. See "Why More Political Theory," p. 94.

49. See chapter 6.

50. See chapters 14 and 15; Nicholas Garnham, "The Media and the Public Sphere," in P. Golding, G. Burdock and P. Schlesinger, eds., *Communicating Politics: Mass Communications and the Political Process* (New York, 1986), 37–54; M. Warner, *The Republic of Letters* (Cambridge: Harvard University Press, 1991), and my "Populist Politics." As Ben Lee suggests, chapter 16, Habermas may also have inadequately grasped the distinctiveness of print media, understanding them implicitly as an extension of speech (contra Derrida). In any case, the question of what difference media make to communication in the later Habermasian theory remains open. The theory is clearly based on face-to-face communication, and its tenets may not be directly extendible to electronically mediated communication.

51. Habermas's discussion of literature as a basis for discourse about bourgeois subjectivity is an important exception to this, though it too is a relatively undifferentiated account.

52. It should be said that Habermas is far more attentive to cultural specificity in *Structural Transformation* than in any of his other major work. Chapter 17 gives an instance where Habermas might revise his work in the direction of greater attention

to cultural variation. With the transformations of Eastern and Central European postcommunist societies in mind, he comments, "A public sphere that functions politically requires more than the institutional guarantes of the constitutional state; it also needs the supportive spirit of cultural traditions and patterns of socialization, of the political culture, of a populace accustomed to freedom" (sec. 4).

53. The role played by the Catholic Church in Poland's recent democratization has brought this to widespread attention. But churches (and other religious institutions) have played crucial roles in other movements and public spheres, e.g., in sustaining the discourse about and struggle for civil rights in the United States during the 1950s and early 1960s, in the early twentieth-century preaching of the social gospel, in the British and American antislavery movements of the eighteenth and nineteenth centuries, and so forth. Thus Baker may be right that Zaret violates the strictures of historical specificity (and perhaps theoretical precision) in suggesting that Habermas should have treated early seventeenth-century religion and science as instances of the public sphere. But Zaret is no doubt right that these were significant precursors to and influences on the bourgeois public sphere. At least as important, religion remained an enduring constituent concern and institutional basis of the public sphere in many settings throughout the modern period. And religious claims were and are often made as part of a rational-critical public discourse, not simply to the religious conscience.

54. Rather surprisingly, Habermas does not consider the various provincial discourses on economic matters—e.g., in Edinburgh, Glasgow, and Manchester in the late eighteenth and early nineteenth centuries—as progenitors or subsidiaries of the public sphere. His account is focused exclusively on capital cities (as Ryan notes in chapter 11 in emphasizing the local state). He also perhaps overstates the prominence of a strictly literary public sphere in grounding the eventual political one.

55. This is a familiar theme of so-called new-social-movements theory. That theory suggests, however, that this is a recent change. It rather seems to me to have been a central part of the social movements throughout the modern era—of the early labor movement and the Second Great Awakening as much as of recent ecological or gay-rights activism.

56. Somewhat relatedly, having established that the ideology of the public sphere minimizes the importance of status distinctions, Habermas shows little interest in such factors as the occupational or regional identities of participants. He vaguely notes but does not consider, for example, the disproportionate involvement of members of the state bureaucracy itself in the early public sphere (on which see Robert Wuthnow, *Communities of Discourse*, Cambridge, Mass., 1989).

57. Pierre Bourdieu's approach to the analysis of such fields is perhaps the best developed but by no means the only one. See, e.g., *Homo Academicus* (Stanford, 1988) and P. Bourdieu and L. Wacquant, *An Invitation to Reflexive Sociology* (Chicago, 1991).

58. S. Benhabib, *Critique, Norm, and Utopia: A Study of the Foundations of Critical Theory* (New York, 1986) offers a clear discussion of this point.

59. J. Habermas, *The Philosophical Discourse of Modernity* (Cambridge, Mass., 1987); *The New Conservatism: Cultural Criticism and the Historians' Debate* (Cambridge, Mass., 1989).

I
Philosophical Models

2

Practical Discourse: On the Relation of Morality to Politics

Thomas McCarthy

From his earliest writings on the public sphere to his most recent writings on law, politics, and morality, Jürgen Habermas has been concerned to rethink the foundations of democratic theory.[1] Though there have been shifts in his conception of the appropriate political institutions and processes, his basic normative ideas have remained largely constant. Like Kant, he seeks to ground the principles of justice in notions of practical reason and autonomous self-legislation. Unlike Kant, he wants to do this without relying on supraempirical ideas of reason and autonomy, though he does retain a variant of the distinction between *Wille* (i.e., the rational general will) and *Willkür* (i.e., the aggregation of particular wills). And as with Kant, it is not possible to understand Habermas's legal and political theory without also examining his moral theory. They are, in fact, so closely interconnected that one might, with some justification, view his moral theory as a theory of "political morality"—of social justice rather than of moral virtue, character, feelings, and judgment, or of ethical life, community, and the good—and his political theory as being, at least at the core, a "moral politics"—as privileging strictly universal laws over the conflict and compromise of interests.

In what follows, I want to examine Habermas's conception of practical discourse with the aim of showing how a residue of the Kantian dichotomy between the phenomenal and the noumenal persists there in the form of a tension between situated reasoning and the transcendence of situatedness required by his model of rational consensus. I will then briefly indicate how that tension figures in his conception of the public sphere. Kant once wrote that the problem of a just political order could be solved for a race of devils, but only because a providential nature brought about the juridical condition that morality demanded. As Habermas does not rely on a providential nature, political justice can only be achieved for him through the discursive unification of empirical wills. The basis of political legitimacy becomes what all could will not as noumenal selves but as participants in practical discourse, whose adoption of the moral point of view enables them to transcend not only interest-oriented perspectives but also value-based perspectives. The question arises whether this is a realistic normative ideal for democratic theory.

I should make clear at the start that I will not be dealing with Habermas's attempt to ground his conception of procedural justice in universal pragmatic features of communication. Questions concerning his explication and justification of the moral point of view are bracketed in what follows.[2] My concern is only with whether his conceptions of practical discourse and rational consensus are appropriate models, however idealized, for political debate and collective decision making. It is also worth mentioning that I shall be pursuing a strategy of immanent critique. Rather than confronting Habermas's ideas with objections from competing theoretical traditions, I hope to bring out the tensions in those ideas themselves. In particular, I want to show that what he has to say about needs, interests, and values pulls against what he says about rational consensus, and it does so in ways that suggest a more flexible and politically serviceable conception of rationally motivated agreement.

1

In Habermas's discourse ethics, the rationally motivated consensus that expresses practical reason in the sphere of justice concerns the general acceptability of the anticipated consequences of a norm for the legitimate satisfaction of needs. If we are to understand more precisely the problems this approach faces, we shall have to take a close look at what he means by "needs." He is not referring to anything that can be attributed to individuals prior to or independently of social relations (in a way that society or the state could then be based on some form of contractual agreement to meet them). In his view, we have access to our needs only under culturally shared interpretations. Nor is he referring to needs in contrast to mere preferences, desires, feelings, or the like. He uses *Bedürfniße* in the very broad sense captured in the following passage:

Needs have two faces. They are differentiated on the volitional side into inclinations and desires, and on the other side, the intuitive, into feelings and moods. Desires are oriented toward situations of need satisfaction; feelings "perceive" situations in the light of possible need satisfaction. Needs are, as it were, the background of partiality that determines our subjective attitudes in relation to the external world. Such predilections express themselves both in the active striving for goods and in the affective perception of situations. The partiality of desires and feelings is expressed at the level of language in interpretations of needs, that is, in evaluations for which evaluative expressions are available. . . . These evaluative, need-interpreting expressions serve to make a predilection understandable . . . and at the same time to justify it, in the sense of making it plausible by appeal to general standards of evaluation that are widespread at least in our own culture. Evaluative expressions or standards of value have justificatory force when they characterize a need in such a way that addressees can, in the framework of a common cultural heritage, recognize in these interpretations their own needs.[3]

Thus the articulation of needs in practical discourse will draw upon existing standards of value; as interpreted, needs are internally related to, and thus inseparable from, cultural values.

At first sight, the implications of this for the possibility of rational consensus seem disastrous. If the evaluative expressions used to interpret needs have "justificatory force" only within "the framework of a common cultural heritage," how can we reasonably expect to arrive at universal (i.e., transcultural) agreements on the acceptability of the consequences of a norm for the legitimate satisfaction of needs? Or to bring the argument closer to our present concerns, how can we hope to achieve rational political consensus in a pluralistic society?

The first thing to note is that Habermas's understanding of "the general will," "the common interest," and the like has a Rousseauean strain. He is not talking of the aggregation of individual interests but of the transcendence of merely particular interests in a search for the common good. He differs from Rousseau, however, in stressing the *argumentative* nature of that search. The public deliberation that leads to the formation of a general will has the form of a debate in which competing particular interests are given equal consideration. It requires of participants that they engage in "ideal role-taking" to try to understand the situations and perspectives of others and give them equal weight to their own. This adoption of the standpoint of impartiality is what distinguishes an orientation toward justice from a concern merely with one's own interests or with those of one's group. And it is only from this standpoint, the moral point of view as Habermas reconstructs it, that we can draw a distinction between what is normatively required of everyone as a matter of justice and what is valued within a particular subculture as part of the good life.

In traditional societies the legal and political orders are interwoven with the tacit background certainties of an inherited form of life. Social institutions and intersubjectively binding norms belong to the taken-for-granted totality of the lifeworld. In modern societies the unquestioned validity of what is socially established becomes increasingly open to discussion. According to Habermas, when existing norms are subjected to examination from the standpoint of fairness, a key differentiation is introduced into the domain of social practice. On the one hand, there are matters of justice to be regulated by norms binding on all alike; on the other, there are questions of the good life, which are not susceptible of general legislation but have to be considered in connection with diverse life forms (*Lebensformen*) and life histories.[4] It is only after the specifically moral point of view has come to be distinguished from concrete forms of *Sittlichkeit*, or ethical life, that normative questions concerning what is right can be adequately distinguished from evaluative questions concerning what is good, which can *also* be rationally discussed but only within the context of a shared form of life.

How, then, are the two types of questions related? Valid norms, on Habermas's account, "claim to express, in relation to some matter requiring regulation, an interest common to all those affected" and thus "must be capable in principle of meeting with the rationally motivated approval of everyone involved."[5] The practical discourses in which such claims are examined will, then, have an internal relation to participants' interpretations of their interests and hence to their values.[6] So just as the analysis of needs led us to consider the values in terms of which needs are interpreted, the analysis of what is involved in ascertaining a common interest carries us in the same direction. But this means that discourse concerning the legitimacy of general norms, inasmuch as it concerns the acceptability of their consequences for the satisfaction of participants' needs and interests, will not admit of closure with respect to discussions of the appropriateness or adequacy of the value standards in the light of which needs and interests are interpreted. More generally, as Habermas acknowledges, it is in principle open to participants in practical discourse to call into question the language that frames debate, that is, the terms in which problems are identified and posed, data selected and described, reasons formulated and weighed, warrants proposed and assessed, and so forth.[7] Questioning the very terms of debate, particularly with regard to the adequacy or appropriateness of standards of value, is the sort of thing that regularly occurs in the political discourse of pluralistic societies. In such cases, normative disagreements turn on value disagreements. And, as Habermas realizes, we need not presuppose that rational agreement on values is possible: cultural values, though more or less widely shared, "do not count as universal"; they "can be made plausible only in the context of a particular form of life."[8]

The same can be said of the type of hermeneutical self-reflection that Habermas refers to as "ethical" (in contrast to "moral") deliberation. Pushed far enough, the discussion of "strong evaluations" can lead to a consideration of who we are and who we want to be, of what kind of life we want to lead. And these questions neither require nor permit the same distancing from the context of action that, according to Habermas, questions of justice do. In deliberating about who we are and examining the strong evaluations involved in our idea of the good life, "the roles of participant in argumentation and social actor overlap." We cannot "jump out of the particular life history or form of life in which [we] actually find [ourselves]" and with which our identities are "irrevocably bound up."[9]

If this meant that evaluative frames cannot be challenged and changed with reasons, that they have to be accepted as given in practical discourse, the orientation of the latter to universal validity would be an illusion. Thus, it is crucial for Habermas that value standards can be rationally criticized and revised. But the forms he envisages for such discussions again set them off from discourse: "critique" and "criticism" remain tied to the context of action and experience in ways that discourse does not.[10] One may challenge, for instance, the truthfulness of an agent's expression of desires, preferences, feelings, and so forth. When this goes beyond questions concerning insincerity, conscious deception, manipulation, or the like to questions of inauthenticity, self-deception, false consciousness, and the like, we may enter into a form of discussion whose paradigm case, in Habermas's view, is therapeutic critique. The aim of this mode of communication is to get an individual or group of individuals "to adopt a reflective attitude toward [their] own expressive manifestations," to "see through the irrational limitations" to which they are subject, to "clarify [their] systematic self-deception."[11] Of course, using psychotherapy as a model for the critique of false consciousness raises questions of its own, but I shall not consider them here. In the present context I am interested only in noting Habermas's acknowledgement that these modes of communication do not involve the idealizing presuppositions of practical discourse but remain closely tied to the context of action and experience.

The adequacy or appropriateness of standards of value can also be challenged in forms of communication for which aesthetic criticism serves as a paradigm. As Habermas understands it, this may involve an indirect challenge to our evaluative language by getting us to see a work or performance as "an authentic expression of an exemplary experience." Grounds or reasons serve here "to guide perception and to make the authenticity of a work so evident that this aesthetic experience can itself become a rational motive for accepting the standards" according to which it counts as such.[12] The general idea here seems to be that our wants, needs, feelings, emotions, attitudes, sentiments, and the like are not normally shaped *directly* by the force of arguments. But discussion can serve to "open our eyes" to the values disclosed or discredited in certain exemplary experiences. Habermas focuses on aesthetic experience, but a case could also be made for the transformative power of experiences of significant others, life crises, alien cultures, countercultures, nature, and the sacred, among other things. Modes of reflective discussion are, in these matters too, no substitute for experience but function to articulate and guide it. Thus they too remain bound to the context of action and experience in a way that, according to Habermas, discourses do not. But perhaps it is time now to examine this latter claim more closely.

2

It is fundamental to discourse ethics that rightness claims have cognitive and not merely volitional significance. Their validity, like the validity of truth claims, is based not on de facto acceptance but on the soundness of the reasons that can be offered in support of them. Warranted commands, like warranted assertions, require justification. Having insisted on this basic similarity between truth and rightness, Habermas is then at pains to point out some basic differences. For one thing, we do not conceive the normative order of society as existing independently of validity claims, as we do nature. Social reality is intrinsically linked to validity in a way that natural reality is not. "Consequently, the results of practical discourses in which it is demonstrated that the validity claim of de facto recognized rules cannot be vindicated . . . can stand in a critical relation to reality (i.e., the symbolic reality of society), while theoretical discourse can be directed not against reality itself (i.e., nature), but only against false assertions about it."[13] This is reflected in the types of argument and evidence relevant to the two cases. As we saw, the reasons advanced in practical discourse have to do with the anticipated consequences of proposed norms for the satisfaction of needs and interests. And this means that they will eventually refer to desires and feelings rather than to perceptions—which raises the question of whether desires and feeling can be standardized for purposes of normative consensus in the way that perceptions can (through measurement) for purposes of theoretical consensus. In terms of the previous discussion of values, the problems can be stated as follows. The backing for norms comes not in the form of demonstrative arguments but in the form of "casuistic evidence" regarding consequences for need satisfaction. The "cogency" or "consensus-generating power" of this kind of reason is, as we saw, inherently dependent on the sociocultural contexts in which they are mobilized.[14] Because of the diversification of ways of life in modern societies, which Habermas regards as irreversible, different sorts of reasons will obviously possess different degrees of cogency or power for different groups. What is more, the heightened individualism of modern life means that differences in individual temperament, experience, and situation can also translate into differences concerning the relative cogency of different sorts of reasons for action. In short, the selection and weighing of casuistic evidence for norms will itself reflect the pluralism and individualism of modern life. Furthermore, since Habermas cedes a certain privilege to subjects as regards the interpretation of their own needs, there can be no question of prescribing or dictating their needs to them.[15] We can at most try to convince others, by using arguments that run the spectrum from aesthetic to therapeutic, that their understanding of their own needs is inadequate, inauthentic, or what have you. But as we saw, these arguments themselves remain tied to specific contexts of action and experience and thus are not able wholly to transcend the struggle between Max Weber's warring gods and demons.

Habermas is aware of this situation and in fact conceives of discourse ethics as a *response* to it: "The fact that modern societies are differentiated into life forms and interest positions, and will increasingly be so, does not mean that action oriented to mutual understanding ceases to be effective. Our need to reach understanding increases to the same degree, and this need has to be met at higher and higher levels of abstraction.

Consequently, the norms and principles that we can agree upon become more and more general."[16] As a rule of argumentation, Habermas's universalization principle is meant precisely to bridge the gap between different individual and group wants and feelings, and norms whose validity everyone accepts on the grounds that they are in the general or common interest— the gap, that is, between the many particular wills and the general will. But how does this work if, in contrast to Rousseau, Habermas builds into his sociocultural starting point not only solidarity but also pluralism and individualism? His answer is, By argumentatively convincing everyone to accept the foreseeable consequences and side-effects that the general observance of a proposed norm can be expected to have for the satisfaction of each person's interests. But how do we do this if those interests are typically not only different but competing? It is of decisive importance for Habermas's political theory that he does not answer, by negotiating a compromise. This is not to say that he rejects bargaining and compromise as reasonable means for dealing with conflicts of interest. Quite the contrary. But as his debate with Ernst Tugendhat makes clear, he subordinates them to the achievement of consensus in practical discourse.[17] Compromise is, so to speak, a second-best alternative that we can turn to when discourse has shown there to be no common interest. Even if negotiated under conditions of a balance of power ensuring participants an equal opportunity to push their own interests, compromise fails to capture the core of our sense of justice: it "cannot account for an intuition that is very difficult to deny, the idea of impartiality, . . . of impartially judging the interests of all concerned."[18]

From the standpoint of impartiality, we seek not to maximize our own interests but to discover a general or common interest. There are two quite different ways of understanding this, and Habermas is not always clear about the difference. On the one hand, through discourse we may find or shape particular interests that are distributively shared by all participants. In this sense, for example, if security against violent attack turned out to be in each's own particular interest, then it could be said to be a common or shared or "generalizable" interest. But most of the matters that require regulation in complex, highly differentiated societies are not of this sort. They impinge on a diversity of life situations and life projects in a diversity of ways so that consequences are different for different individuals and groups. Discovering a general interest in such cases will require that participants distance themselves from particular "first-order" interests in a different sense from that required in the other case. This is why, according to Habermas, we can argumentatively agree on what is in the general interest only if every participant adopts an impartial standpoint from which his or her own particular interests count for no more nor less than those of any other participant. That is to say, "the impartial consideration of all interests affected already presupposes a moral standpoint. . . . We have to consider what general interest all those involved would agree upon if they were to adopt the moral standpoint of impartiality, taking into account all the interests affected."[19]

This is a lot to ask of participants in political debate, but it is not yet enough. For not only will the consequences differ among individuals and groups, the interpretation and assessment of those consequences will differ among them as well.[20] So the "ideal role taking" in which participants must engage will require each participant to put him- or herself in the place of every other participant in the very strong sense of coming to understand and appreciate the consequences from all of their interpretive and evaluative perspectives. Under ideal conditions this would be backed by the requirement that each have the opportunity to present his or her own point of view and to seek to make it comprehensible and plausible to others. Nevertheless, even if we outfit our good-willed participants with the intelligence and sensitivity to understand and appreciate the needs, interests, and points of view of others, we are still far from rationally motivated consensus. For one thing, participants' interpretations of their needs cannot simply be taken at face value. Though they have a "privileged access" to their own feelings and desires, they are by no means the sole and final arbiters regarding them. "Kant and the utilitarians . . . reduced the motives and aims of actions, as well as the interests and value orientations on which they depended, to inner states and private episodes. . . . In fact, however, motives and ends have something intersubjective about them; they are always interpreted in the light of a cultural tradition. . . . [Thus] the individual actor cannot be the *final* instance in developing and revising his interpretations of needs. Rather, his interpretations change in the context of the lifeworld of the social group to which he belongs; little by little, practical discourses can also gear into this quasi-natural process."[21] To the extent that this happens, the cultural interpretations in the light of which different participants understand their needs and values, interests and aims are also up for discussion. So consensus could be achieved only if all participants could come to agree on the authentic interpretation of each's needs, and they would have to do so from the very different hermeneutic starting points afforded by a pluralistic and individualistic culture. This would presumably entail criticizing and rejecting value orientations that are too self- or group-centered to permit the proper weighting of other participants' needs, as well as value orientations imbued with racism, sexism, ethnocentrism, homophobia, or any other less than universalistic outlook. In a word, only those value differences compatible with a postconventional moral orientation can survive practical discourse.

But we still have a way to go before we can arrive at rationally motivated consensus. For we now have somehow to "synthesize" all of the various consequences, variously interpreted and variously assessed, into one unified judgment of rightness or wrongness. We are, remember, dealing with the case in which particular "first-order" needs and interests are different. How, then, do we weigh x's feelings and desires against y's, or negatively affecting the intensely felt needs of a few against inconveniencing the less intensely felt needs of many, and so on? After hearing the arguments of everyone, each will have to judge for him- or herself which normative regulation seems fairest to all of the different–and differently interpreted, assessed, and weighted—interests involved. On what grounds should we suppose that everyone would, even under ideal conditions, agree in a judgment of this sort?[22]

The success of Habermas's universalization principle in getting from multifarious "I want"s to a unified "we will" depends on finding "universally accepted needs." The argument just sketched suggests that this may not be possible when there are fundamental divergences in value orientations. The separation of formal procedure from substantive content is never absolute: we cannot agree on what is just without achieving some measure of agreement on what is good. But practical discourse is conceived by Habermas to deal precisely with situations in which there is an absence of such agreement, that is, when there is a need to regulate matters concerning which there are conflicting interests and values, competing conceptions of the good.

3

In recent essays Habermas has proposed a multidimensional model of discourse in the democratic public sphere. It comprises a variety of types of "rational collective will-formation" in both the resolution of conflicts and the pursuit of collective goals.[23] What is common to these types is the neutralization of power differentials attached to conflicting interest positions or concealed in traditional value constellations. In addition to practical discourses in which laws and policies are justified as being in the general interest, the model includes deliberations in which general norms are applied to particular situations, ethical-political discussions concerning basic values and collective identity, the negotiation of compromises under fair bargaining conditions, and pragmatic discourses concerning the means of implementing policies and attaining goals. In a society organized along radical democratic lines, Habermas claims, this "whole web of overlapping forms of communication" would have to be effectively institutionalized.[24] But the institutionalization of practical discourses of justification remains central, for the integrity of the whole web depends on them: the conditions for negotiating fair compromises would have to be agreed to in practical discourse; the impartial application of general laws yields just results only if the laws themselves have stood the test of discursive justification; pragmatic discourses about means presuppose that we know what we want or should want; and ethical self-clarification itself cannot get us beyond the value differences that may result from it. Thus, despite these differentiations, the question still remains whether practical discourse is suitable as a normative ideal for discourse in the public sphere.

This question can be put in more concrete terms if we take a brief look at Habermas's account of the conditions of democratic politics.[25] He grants that large complex societies cannot do without markets and administrative bureaucracies and argues that the democratic ideal should be to bring these under the control of the will of the people as formed in open and public debate. For various reasons, which I shall not go into here, he does not think that this can be accomplished within the formal organizations of the economy and the state, or within formally organized political parties, interest and pressure groups, or the like. Having abandoned the hope that he earlier placed in the democratization of all governmentally relevant and publicly influential organizations, he now pursues the rather different line that locates rational collective will formation *outside* of formal organizations of every sort.[26] In this view, it is the variegated multiplicity of spontaneously formed publics engaged in informal discussions of issues of public interest that is the core of the democratic public sphere. The "nodal points" of this "web of informal communication" are voluntary associations that organize themselves and secure their own continued existence. "Associations of this kind concentrate on generating and disseminating practical convictions, that is, on discovering themes of relevance to society as a whole, contributing to the possible solution of problems, interpreting values, providing good reasons and discrediting others. They can only be effective in an indirect manner, that is, through changing the parameters of constitutional will-formation by way of widely influential changes in attitudes and values."[27]

I won't raise here the important question of how effective voluntary associations and social movements can be in monitoring and influencing the formal decision-making processes of a systemically integrated economy and state. I shall confine myself instead to pointing out that the tension between the reality of multiple value-perspectives and the ideal of rationally motivated consensus shows up in this account as well. Habermas acknowledges the sociostructural differentiation that goes along with a complex market economy and a bureaucratic state administration, and he welcomes the heightened pluralism of forms of life and individualism of personality structures characteristic of modern cultures. But the concomitant differences in background, situation, experience, training, and so forth regularly translate into basic differences in value orientation. And these differences get reflected in the voluntary associations and social movements that comprise the public sphere.[28] As a result, under the conditions specified in his model, the "democratic generalization of interests" and the "universalistic justification of norms" would encounter all the obstacles spelled out earlier in this essay.

Moreover, if judgments of the relative cogency of reasons that cite needs, interests, feelings, sentiments, and the like vary with interpretive and evaluative standpoints, and if there is no common measure by which to assess the relative weights of reasons articulated in different evaluative languages, then the distinction between argument and rhetoric, between convincing and persuading becomes less sharp than the discourse model allows. Habermas's interpretation of Freud holds out the promise of raising to consciousness unconscious determinants of behavior. This has to be understood in process terms, that is, not as an actually realizable state of affairs but as an orientation for what must always be an ongoing effort. The same can be said of the "cultural unconscious" that hermeneutics has unearthed and the "sociostructural unconscious" that systems theory tried to conceptualize. In all of these cases, even if we grant that it is possible in principle to bring any particular unconscious factor to consciousness, this by no means implies the possibility of making all of them conscious all at once. But this means that at every moment and in every situation, unconscious factors will play a role in shaping interpretive and evaluative perspectives and thus that the symbolic force of language will inevitably figure in judgments of cogency. As there is no Archimedean point from which to judge whether what democratic majorities regard as the better argument is really better, dissenters can only continue the debate. If minorities regularly fail to convince majorities or to be convinced by them, we may well conclude that judgements of better and worse in this domain are intrinsically susceptible to considerable variation, that unanimity on practical-political issues is not always attainable, and that democratic institutions should not be constructed on the supposition that it is.

4

Understanding why Habermas insists on the supposition that rational consensus be possible is the key to understanding his approach to practical reason. As he sees it, this supposition is not merely a normative or regulative *ideal* of argumentative discourse but one of its constitutive *presuppositions*. If participants in discourse did not make this supposition, if they were to assume instead that reaching agreement solely on the basis of reasons is impossible, their linguistic behavior would have a significance other than that of rational argumentation. More generally, if we were (*per impossible*) to drop the pragmatic presupposition that we could convince others of the validity of claims by offering good reasons in support of them, most of our rational practices would lose their sense, and this, it goes without saying, would entail far-reaching changes in our form of life. In Habermas's view, it would mean the elimination of our main alternative to violence, coercion, and manipulation as a means of conflict resolution and social coordination.

Be that as it may, I want to suggest that the participant's perspective, the underlying presuppositions of which Habermas's pragmatics aims to reconstruct, has to be consistently combined with the perspective of the observer. Assume for the sake of argument that the latter reveals something like the irreducible plurality of evaluative and interpretive standpoints that I sketched above. Assume further that this pluralism is found, from the observer's perspective, to be at the root of many intractable political disputes. Can we reconcile this finding with the participant's spontaneous supposition that rational agreement is possible? In dealing with similar situations, Habermas has introduced a notion of "reflective participation," of participants whose previously unreflective behavior comes to be informed by what they learn upon reflection to be the case. We might extend that notion here to participants in political discourse whose linguistic behavior is informed by the knowledge that irreducible value differences regularly give rise to intractable disagreements on normative questions. What pragmatic presuppositions might such participants bring to political discourse that would not simply transform it into more or less refined forms of symbolic manipulation? Or to bring this line of thought back to our original problem, is there a conception of public debate that is compatible both with this knowledge and with the supposition that some form of rationally motivated agreement, agreement based on good reasons, is possible?

I can do more here than to suggest a line of reasoning. To begin with, we have to modulate the idea of rationally motivated agreement beyond Habermas's basic distinction between a strategically motivated compromise of interests and an argumentatively achieved consensus on validity. If the ultimate *moral-political* significance of agreement based on reasons is to provide an alternative to open or latent coercion as a means of social coordination, there is room for more than these varieties. Here I shall only mention two additional types.

(a) Owing to differences in evaluative and interpretive perspective, well-intentioned and competent participants may *disagree about the common good* (e.g., in the multitude of situations where the preservation of traditional values conflicts with economic expansion). In this familiar case the dispute is not about competing particular interests but about what is "really" in the general interest. If the parties to the dispute want genuinely to debate the point, they will, as Habermas maintains, have to suppose that it is in principle possible to convince and be convinced by good reasons. As reflective participants, however, they may at the same time doubt that in the case at hand complete consensus is achievable. Being good-willed members of the same political community, they will also keep in mind that if their *experimentum argumentationis* does fail to produce a consensus, they will have to reach a reasoned agreement of another sort if they want to do more than simply to vote. If that agreement is to serve as a stable basis for social cooperation, it will have to be some form of compromise, not among strategically acting utility maximizers, but among community-minded consociates who want to live together in harmony even when they disagree about the common good. The point I am getting at is that *rationally motivated* agreement as a moral-political alternative to coercion may well involve elements of conciliation, compromise, consent, accommodation, and the like. Argument, including argument about what is in the general interest, can play a role in shaping any and all of them.[29] And thus the expectation that they will figure in the outcome of political debate, as well as consensus in Habermas's strict sense, can itself give sense to participants' argumentative practices. The only supposition that seems necessary for the genuine give and take of rational discourse is that the force of the better argument can contribute to the final shape of *whatever* type of agreement is reached.

(b) I was assuming in (a) that disagreement concerned only what was good for a particular political community and not what was right for human beings generally. In Habermas's terms, that could be called an "ethical-political" dispute in contrast to a "moral-political" one.[30] The second type of disagreement I want briefly to mention has to do with *norms that at least one party takes to be moral* in Habermas's sense, that is, to be binding on all human beings (e.g., in connection with abortion, euthanasia, pornography, animal rights). There are a number of subcases here. For example, what one party considers to be a moral issue, another party may regard merely as a pragmatic issue or as a question of values open to choice or as a moral issue of another sort, or the opposing parties may agree on the issue but disagree as to the morally correct answer. These types of disagreement are usually rooted in different "general and comprehensive moral views," to borrow a phrase from Rawls.[31] For instance, members of different religious communities may have conceptions of the significance and value of human life that differ from one another and from those of secular interpretive communities.[32] If not even moral philosophers have been able to agree on the nature and scope of morality, any realistic conceptualization of the democratic public sphere will have to allow for disagreement in this regard too. Furthermore, since political discourse always takes place under less than ideal conditions, it will always be open to dissenters to view any given collective decision as tainted by de facto limitations and thus as not acceptable under ideal conditions.[33] Disagreements of these sorts are likely to be a permanent feature of democratic public life. They are in general not resolvable by strategic compromise, rational consensus, or ethical self-clarification in Habermas's senses of these terms. All that remains in his scheme are more or less subtle forms of coercion, e.g., majority rule and the threat of legal sanctions.

But we might rescue a sense of "rationally motivated agreements" even for situations of this sort. Reflective participants will be aware of the "particularity" of general and comprehensible moral views, of their rootedness in particular traditions, practices, and experiences. If they are fallibilists and if they consider the basic political institutions and procedures of their society to be just, they may well regard collective decisions arising from them as legitimate, and hence as "deserving of recognition," even when they disagree.[34] That is, their background agreement with the operative political conception of justice may *rationally motivate* them to consent to laws they regard as unwise or unjust in the hope, perhaps, that they will be able to use the same resources eventually to change them. In such situations, arguments may be used to convince others of the justice or injustice of a norm, for example by getting them to adopt the view of human life from which its consequences appear acceptable or unacceptable. The expectation that *some* participants, perhaps even a majority, could be convinced by these means seems a sufficient basis for genuine debate.

None of these considerations is new to political theory. I mention them here only to show that Habermas's conception of practical discourse is too restrictive to serve as a model, even as an ideal model, of rational will formation and collective decision making in the democratic public sphere.[35] There are alternatives to coercion not captured by his notions of negotiated compromise and rational consensus, forms of reasoned agreement among free and equal persons that are motivated by good reasons in ways different from the way singled out by his strong conception of argumentation. In pursuit of such agreements, citizens may enter public debate with a variety of expectations, of which the possibility of unanimity is only one. And this diversity in types of agreement and expectation is reflected in the diversity of forms of political conflict resolution. A public sphere whose institutions and culture embodied this diversity would, I have wanted to suggest, be a more realistic ideal than one embodying, in however detranscendentalized a form, Kant's insufficiently contextualized notion of the rational will.

Notes

1. In addition to *The Structural Transformation of the Public Sphere*, see the studies in moral theory collected in *Moral Consciousness and Communicative Action* (Cambridge, Mass., 1990) and the two lectures "Law and Morality," in *The Tanner Lectures on Human Values*, vol. 8 (Salt Lake City and Cambridge, 1988), pp. 217–299. See also *Legitimation Crisis* (Boston, 1975), and "Legitimation Problems in the Modern State," in Habermas, *Communication and the Evolution of Society* (Boston, 1979), pp. 178–205.

2. For recent discussions of these questions see Stephen K. White, *The Recent Work of Jürgen Habermas* (Cambridge, 1988), Seyla Benhabib and Fred Dallmayr, eds., *The Communicative Ethics Controversy* (Cambridge, Mass., 1990), and Kenneth Baynes, *From Social Contract Theory to Normative Social Criticism* (Albany, 1991). See also the special issues of *Philosophical Forum* 21 (1989/1990), nos. 1–2, and *Philosophy and Social Criticism* 14 (1989), nos. 3–4.

3. *The Theory of Communicative Action*, vol. 1 (Boston, 1984), p. 92.

4. *Moral Consciousness and Communicative Action*, p. 177. "Ideas of the good life are not notions that simply occur to individuals as abstract imperatives; they shape the identities of groups and individuals in such a way that they form an integral part of culture and personality."

5. *The Theory of Communicative Action*, vol. 1, p. 19.

6. *The Theory of Communicative Action*, vol. 1, p. 20. "Values are candidates for interpretations under which a circle of those affected can, if the occasion arises, describe and normatively regulate a common interest."

7. See "Wahrheitstheorien," in Habermas, *Vorstudien und Ergänzungen zur Theorie des kommunikativen Handelns* (Frankfurt, 1984), pp. 127–183, here pp. 166–174.

8. *The Theory of Communicative Action*, vol. 1, p. 42.

9. "Individual Will-Formation in Terms of What Is Expedient, What Is Good, and What Is Just," paper read at Northwestern University, fall 1988, pp. 15, 17. See also *Moral Consciousness and Communicative Action*, pp. 177–178: "A person who questions the form of life in which his identity has been shaped questions his very existence. The distancing produced by life crises of that kind is of another sort than the distance of a norm-testing participant in discourse from the facticity of existing institutions."

10. See *The Theory of Communicative Action*, vol. 1, pp. 20–21, 40–42, and the table of types of argumentation on p. 23.

11. *The Theory of Communicative Action*, p. 21. Compare the interesting discussion by James Bohman, "Communication, Ideology, and Democratic Theory," *American Political Science Review* 84 (1990): 93–109.

12. *The Theory of Communicative Action*, p. 20. Following Albrecht Wellmer, Habermas has recently expanded his conception of the "illuminating power" of aesthetic experience. In addition to affecting our evaluative language, he now holds, it can also affect "our cognitive interpretations and normative expectations, and transform the totality in which these moments are related" ("Questions and Counterquestions," in R. B. Bernstein, ed., *Habermas and Modernity* [Cambridge, Mass., 1985], pp. 192–216, here p. 202). See also Albrecht Wellmer, "Truth, Semblence, Reconciliation: Adorno's Aesthetic Realization of Modernity," in Wellmer, *The Persistence of Modernity* (Cambridge, Mass., 1991), pp. 1–35.

13. "Wahrheitstheorien," p. 149. See also *Moral Consciousness and Communicative Action*, pp. 60–62.

14. Habermas ties the cogency or "consensus-producing power" of arguments to their capacity to provide "adequate motivation" for accepting a warrant as "plausible," in "Wahrheitstheorien," pp. 164–165. It seems obvious that this type of motivating force will not be the same in all contexts.

15. See *Moral Consciousness and Communicative Action*, pp. 67–68.

16. "A Philosophico-political Profile," in Peter Dews, ed., *Habermas: Autonomy and Solidarity* (London, 1986), pp. 149–189, here p. 174.

17. See *Moral Consciousness and Communicative Action*, pp. 68–76.

18. *Moral Consciousness and Communicative Action*, p. 72.

19. *The Theory of Communicative Action* (Boston, 1987), vol. 2, p. 94. Habermas's terminology tends to cover over the distinction in point. He uses "general interest," "generalizable interest," "common interest," "shared interest," and "equally good for all" as synonymous. But a fair general regulation need not be equally good for all or in the interest of all as regards its consequences for first-order needs.

20. I am focusing on differences in evaluative perspective, but an argument could be made with regard to differences in interpretive perspective generally. (The two are, in fact, connected.) Focusing on the hermeneutic dimension of interpretive social science and narrative history would make clear that not even the "facts of the matter" are beyond dispute in moral-political debates. In sociohistorical inquiry there is no agreed upon general interpretive framework that functions as, say, general theory does in physics. Hence, not only the assessment of consequences but their very description, not to mention their probability, will frequently be at issue.

21. *The Theory of Communicative Action*, vol. 2, pp. 95–96. For a discussion of this "transformative moment of practical discourse," see Seyla Benhabib, *Critique, Norm, and Utopia* (New York, 1986), pp. 313–316.

22. Compare Albrecht Wellmer, *The Persistence of Modernity*, pp. 168–182.

23. See especially "Volkssourveränität als Verfahren," *Merkur* 6 (1989): 465–477, and "On the Relationship of Politics, Law, and Morality," paper read at Northwestern University, fall 1988. An expanded version of the first essay appeared in *Die Ideen von 1789 in der deutschen Rezeption*, ed. by Forum für Philosophie, Bad Homburg (Frankfurt, 1989), pp. 7–36.

24. "On the Relationship of Politics, Law, and Morality," p. 11.

25. See *The Theory of Communicative Action*, vol. 2, esp. chap. 8; "The New Obscurity: The Crisis of the Welfare State and the Exhaustion of Utopian Energies," in Habermas, *The New Conservatism* (Cambridge, Mass., 1989), pp. 48–70; and "Volkssouveränität als Verfahren."

26. See my discussion of this shift in chap. 6 of McCarthy, *Ideals and Illusions*, (Cambridge, Mass., 1991).

27. "Volkssouveränität als Verfahren," p. 474.

28. Michael Walzer discusses the ways in which democratic theory and practice must adapt to processes of social differentiation in "Liberalism and the Art of Separation," *Political Theory* 12 (1984): 315–330. In *Spheres of Justice* (New York, 1985) he analyzes the differentiation of social goods, with different internal logics, that is part of such processes. For a discussion of the "politics of need interpretations" stressing their essential contestability and their connection to questions of social identity, see Nancy Fraser, *Unruly Practices* (Minneapolis, 1989), esp. chaps. 7 and 8.

29. For instance, when competing conceptions of the common good are at issue, arguments may serve to get others to see the authenticity or inauthenticity of core values and hence to give them the appropriate weight in shaping a political accord. In *this* respect, the constitutive suppositions of discussions of the common good may resemble those with which participants engage in what Habermas calls "critique and criticism": they need not assume that there is only one correct view. Compare Joshua Cohen's model of public deliberation on the common good in "Deliberation and Democratic Legitimacy," in A. Hamlin and P. Pettit, eds., *The Good Polity* (London, 1989), pp. 17–34. Cohen emphasizes the need to offer "reasons pursuasive to others" in making claims on social resources.

30. In his published works Habermas has not given this distinction the significance it deserves in *political* theory, as he has been chiefly concerned to elucidate and justify the *moral* point of view. In "On the Relationship between Politics, Law, and Morality," however, he adopts a tripartite scheme that distinguishes the "aggregate will" resulting from bargaining processes, the "common will" shaped in hermeneutic self-clarification, and the "general will" formed in universalizing moral discourse (p. 16). All three are treated as forms of "rational will formation" relying on argumentation of different types. But he is not always consistent in applying this distinction. For instance, in another unpublished manuscript entitled "Erläuterungen zur Diskursethik," he writes that morality, in contrast to ethics, has to do not with questions of the good life but with questions concerning "what norms we want to live by together and how conflicts can be resolved in the common interest" (p. 7). But normative questions and questions of the general interest arise already at the level of forming a common political will in a particular society. The distinction he needs here is not between values and norms but between binding social norms that are also moral norms and those that are not. Habermas uses the same model of discursively achieved consensus for both, but in one case the circle of potential participants includes the members of a political community and in the other all human beings. It should be noted that in his view there

Thomas McCarthy

can be no a priori determination of which issues are moral and which ethical. That too is a matter for discussion.

31. John Rawls, "The Idea of an Overlapping Consensus," *Oxford Journal of Legal Studies* 7 (1987): 1–25.

32. Habermas allows that philosophically based moral theories do not exhaust the "semantic potential" even of postmetaphysical religious discourse (see his *Nachmetaphysiches Denken*, Frankfurt, 1988, p. 60) and that as the latter is rooted in particular traditions, practices, and experiences, it comes in a variety of types ("Transzendenz von Innen, Transzendenz ins Diesseits: Eine Replik," ms., pp. 8 ff.). Precisely because of its highly formal nature, discourse ethics is compatible with different substantive conceptions of the meaning and value of life. Inasmuch as these differences figure in assessments of the general acceptability of anticipated consequences, they will play a role in deliberation about justice.

33. As the circle of potential participants in moral discourse trenscends all political boundaries, moral consensus will always be counterfactual, and hence contestable, in ways that political consensus need not be.

34. Rawls takes a similar track in "The Idea of an Overlapping Consensus." Of course, Habermas would view the basis of such consensus differently than Rawls. He discusses this issue under the rubric of "legality and legitimacy" in *Legitimation Crisis*, pp. 97–102, *The Theory of Communicative Action*, vol. 1, pp. 264–267, and "Wie ist Legitimität durch Legalität möglich?" *Kritische Justiz* 20 (1987): 1–16. His basic thesis is that formally correct procedures can legitimate decisions only if they are part of a legal-political system that is itself recognized as legitimate on grounds that all can rationally accept. (See note 35.)

35. As I indicated at the outset, I am not dealing here with the justification that Habermas offers for the basic rights and principles that define the public sphere. In contrast to Rawls's hermeneutic appeal to ideas implicit in our public political culture, Habermas argues that the basic structures of justice are themselves justified only if they are ones that free and equal persons could agree to in practical discourse. On this difference, see Kenneth Baynes, "The Liberal/Communitarian Controversy and Communicative Ethics," *Philosophy and Social Criticism* 14 (1989), nos. 3–4: 293–313. He explains how, on Habermas's view, civil and political rights, and some social rights as well, can be justified as necessary preconditions for free and equal participation in democratic will formation; as such, they could be *reflectively* agreed to in the very discourses they are meant to secure. I am indebted to Baynes for a discussion of the points in section 4 of this essay.

Models of Public Space: Hannah Arendt, the Liberal Tradition, and Jürgen Habermas

Seyla Benhabib

The art of making distinctions is always a difficult and risky undertaking. Distinctions can enlighten as well as cloud an issue. Also, one is always vulnerable to objections concerning the correct classification of the thought of certain thinkers. This essay will sidestep questions of historical interpretation and classification in order to delineate three different conceptions of public space that correspond to three main currents of Western political thought. The view of public space common to the "republican virtue" or "civic virtue" tradition is described as the "agonistic" view. Here the thought of Hannah Arendt will be my main point of reference. The second conception is provided by the liberal tradition, and particularly by those liberals who, beginning with Kant, make the problem of a "just and stable public order" the center of their political thinking. This I will name the "legalistic" model of public space, and it will be exemplified by Bruce Ackerman's conception of "public dialogue." The final model of public space is the one implicit in Jürgen Habermas's work. This model, which envisages a democratic-socialist restructuring of late-capitalist societies, will be name "discursive public space."

By situating the concept of public space in this context, my discussion is restricted from the outset to normative political theory. The larger sense of the term "Öffentlichkeit," which would include a literary, artistic, and scientific public, will not be of concern here; for whatever other applications and resonances they might have, the terms "public," "public space," "res publica" will never lose their intimate rootedness in the domain of political life. This approach will help highlight certain very significant differences among political theories, all of which on the surface appear to accord central place to public space or publicity in political life. Not only are there important differences among these three conceptions of public space; two of these views are severely limited in their usefulness for analyzing and evaluating political discourse and legitimation problems in advanced capitalist societies and possibly even in what is now being referred to as Soviet-style societies.[1] The strength of the Habermasian model, when compared with the Arendtian and liberal conceptions, is that questions of democratic legitimacy in advanced capitalist societies are central to it. Nevertheless, whether this model is resourceful enough to help us think through the transformation of politics in our kinds of societies is an open question. Taking the women's movement and the feminist critique of the public/private distinction as a point of reference, the final sections of this essay will probe the discourse model of public space from this point of view.

1 Hannah Arendt and the Agonistic Concept of Public Space

Without a doubt Hannah Arendt is the central political thinker of this century whose work has reminded us with great poignancy of the lost treasures of our tradition of political thought, and specifically of the loss of public space, of *der öffentliche Raum,* under conditions of modernity. Hannah Arendt's major theoretical work, *The Human Condition,* is usually, and not altogether unjustifiably, treated as an antimodernist political work. By "the rise of the social" Arendt means the institutional differentiation of modern societies into the narrowly political realm on the one hand and the economic market and the family on the other. As a result of these transformations, economic processes that had hitherto been confined to the "shadowy realm of the household" emancipate themselves and become public matters. The same historical process that brought forth the modern constitutional state also brings forth "society," that realm of social interaction that interposes itself between the household on the one hand and the political state on the other.[2] A century ago Hegel described this process as the development in the midst of ethical life of a "system of needs" (*System der Bedürfnisse*), of a domain of economic activity governed by commodity exchange and the pursuit of economic self-interest. The expansion of this sphere meant the disappearance of the universal, of the common concern for the political association, for the *res publica,* from the hearts and minds of men.[3] Arendt sees in this process the occluding of the political by the social and the transformation of the public space of politics into a pseudospace of interaction in which individuals no longer "act" but "merely behave" as economic producers, consumers, and urban city dwellers.

This relentlessly negative account of the "rise of the social" and the decline of the public realm has been identified as the core of Arendt's political antimodernism.[4] Indeed, at one level Arendt's text is a panegyric to the agonistic political space of the Greek *polis*. What disturbs the contemporary reader is perhaps less the high-minded and highly idealized picture of Greek political life that Arendt draws than her neglect of the following question: If the agonistic political space of the *polis* was only possible because large groups of human beings—like women, slaves, children, laborers, noncitizen residents, and all non-Greeks—were excluded from it while they made possible through their labor for the daily necessities of life that "leisure for politics" that the few enjoyed, then is the critique of the rise of the social, which was accompanied by the emancipation of these groups from the "shadowy interior of the household" and by their entry into public life, also a critique of political universalism as such? That is, is the "recovery of the public space" under conditions of modernity necessarily an elitist and antidemocratic project that can hardly be reconciled with the demand for universal political emancipation and the universal extension of citizenship rights that have accompanied modernity since the American and French Revolutions?[5]

Yet it would be grossly misleading to read Hannah Arendt only or even primarily as a nostalgic thinker. She devoted as much space in her work to analyzing the dilemmas and prospects of politics under conditions of modernity as she did to the decline of public space in modernity. If we are not to read her account of the disappearance of the public realm as *Verfallsgeschichte* (a history of decline), then how are we to interpret it? The key here is Arendt's odd methodology, which conceives of political thought as "story telling." Viewed in this light, her story of the transformation of public space is an exercise of thought. Such thought exercises dig under the rubble of history to recover those pearls of past experience, with their sedimented and hidden layers of meaning, so as to cull from them a story that can orient the mind in the future.[6] The vocation of the theorist as story teller is the unifying thread of Arendt's political and philosophical analyses from the origins of totalitarianism to her reflections on the French and American Revolutions, to her theory of public space, and to her final words to *Thinking*, the first volume of *The Life of the Mind*.

I have clearly joined the ranks of those who for some time now have been attempting to dismantle metaphysics, and philosophy with all its categories, as we have known them from their beginning in Greece until today. Such dismantling is possible only on the assumption that the thread of tradition is broken and we shall not be able to renew it. Historically speaking, what actually has broken down is the Roman trinity that for thousands of years united religion, authority, and tradition. The loss of this trinity does not destroy the past. . . .

What has been lost is the continuity of the past. . . . What you then are left with is still the past, but a *fragmented* past, which has lost its certainty of evaluation.[7]

Read in this light, Arendt's account of the "rise of the social" and the decline of public space under conditions of modernity can be viewed not as a nostalgic *Verfallsgeschichte* but as the attempt to think through human history, sedimented in layers of language. We must learn to identify those moments of rupture, displacement, and dislocation in history. At such moments language is witness to the more profound transformations taking place in human life. Such a *Begriffsgeschichte* is a remembering, in the sense of a creative act of "re-membering," that is, of putting together the members of a whole, of a rethinking that sets free the lost potentials of the past. "The history of revolutions . . . could be told in a parable form as the tale of an age-old treasure, which, under the most varied circumstances, appears abruptly, unexpectedly, and disappears again, under different mysterious conditions, as though it were a fata morgana."[8]

Nonetheless, Arendt's thought is not free of assumptions deriving from an *Ursprungsphilosophie,* which posits an original state or temporal point as the privileged source to which one must trace back the phenomena to capture their "true" meaning. As opposed to rupture, displacement, and dislocation, this view emphasizes the continuity between the past origin and the present condition and seeks to uncover at the origin the lost and concealed essence of the phenomena. There are really two strains in Hannah Arendt's thought: one corresponding to the method of fragmentary historiography and inspired by Walter Bejamin,[9] the other inspired by the phenomenology of Husserl and Heidegger and according to which memory is the mimetic recollection of the lost origins of phenomena as contained in some fundamental human experience. In accordance with this latter approach, reminders abound in the *Vita Activa* of "the original meaning of politics" or of the "lost" distinction between the private and the public.[10]

The concept that perhaps best illustrates Arendt's equivocation between fragmentary history and *Ursprungsphilosophie* is that of public space. This topographical figure of speech is suggested early on in her work, at the end of *The Origins of Totalitarianism,* to compare various forms of political rule. Constitutional government is likened to moving within a space where the law is like the hedges erected between the buildings and one orients oneself upon known territory. Tyranny is like a desert; under conditions of tyranny one moves in an unknown, vast, open space, where the will of the tyrant occasionally befalls one like the sandstorm overtaking the desert traveler. Totalitarianism has no spatial topology: it is like an iron band, compressing people increasingly together until they are formed into one.[11]

Indeed, if one reads Arendt's concept of public space in the context of her theory of totalitarianism, the term acquires a rather different focus than the one dominant in *The Human Condition.* The terms "agonistic space" and "associational space" can capture this contrast. According to the agonistic view, the public realm represents that space of appearances in which moral and political greatness, heroism, and preeminence are revealed, displayed, shared with others. This is a competitive space in which one competes for recognition, precedence, and acclaim. Ultimately it is the space in which one seeks a guarantee against the futility and the passage of all things human: "For the *polis* was for the Greeks, as the *res publica* was for the Romans, first of all their guarantee against the futility of individual life, the space protected against this futility and reserved for the relative permanence, if not immortality, of mortals."[12]

By contrast, the associational view of public space suggests that such a space emerges whenever and wherever, in Arendt's words, "men act together in concert."[13] On this model, public space is the space "where freedom can appear."[14] It is not a space in any topographical or institutional sense: a town hall or a city square where people do not act in concert is not a public space in this Arendtian sense. But a private dining room in which people gather to hear a *samizdat* or in which dissidents meet with foreigners become public spaces; just as a field or a forest can also become public space if it is the object and location of an action in concert, of a demonstration to stop the construction of a highway or a military air base, for example. These diverse topographical locations become public spaces in that they become the sites of power, of common action coordinated through speech and persuasion. Violence can occur in private and in public, but its language is essentially private because it is the language of pain. Force, like violence, can be located in both realms. In a way, it has no language, and nature remains its quintessential source. It moves without having to persuade or to hurt. Power, however, is the only force that emanates from action, and it comes from the mutual action of a group of human beings: once in action, one can make things happen, thus becoming a source of a different kind of force.

The distinction between the agonistic and the associational models corresponds to the Greek versus the modern experience of politics. The agonistic space of the *polis* was made possible by a morally homogenous and politically egalitarian but exclusive community in which action could also be a revelation of the self to others. Under conditions of moral and political homogeneity and lack of anonymity, the agonistic dimension, the vying for excellence among peers, could take place. But for moderns, public space is essentially porous; neither access to it nor its agenda of debate can be predefined by criteria of moral and political homogeneity. With the entry of every new group into the public space of politics after the French and American revolutions, the scope of the public gets extended. The emancipation of workers made property relations into a public political issue; the emancipation of women has meant that the family and the so-called private sphere became political issues; the attainment of rights by nonwhite and non-Christian peoples has put cultural questions of collective self and other representations on the public agenda. Not only is it the "lost treasure" of revolutions that eventually all can partake in public life, but equally, when freedom emerges from action in concert, there can be no agenda to *predefine* the topic of public conversation. The struggle over what gets included in the public agenda is itself a struggle for justice and freedom. The distinction between the social and the political makes no sense in the modern world, not because all politics has become administration and because the economy has become the quintessential public, as Hannah Arendt thought, but primarily because the struggle to make something public is a struggle for justice.

Perhaps the episode that best illustrates this blind spot in Hannah Arendt's thought is that of school desegregation in Little Rock, Arkansas. Arendt likened the demands of the black parents, upheld by the U.S. Supreme Court, to have their children admitted into previously all-white schools to the desire of the social parvenue to gain recognition in a society that did not care to admit her. This time around Arendt failed to make the final distinction and confused an issue of public justice, equality of educational access, with an issue of social preference, who my friends are or whom I invite to dinner. It is to her credit, however, that after the intervention of the black novelist Ralph Ellison, she had the grace to reverse her position.[15]

At the root of Arendt's vacillations on this issue lies another, and for my systematic purposes more important, problem, namely Arendt's phenomenological essentialism. In accordance with essentialist assumptions, "public space" is defined either as that space in which only a certain *type of activity,* namely action as opposed to work or labor, takes place, or it is delimited from other social spheres by reference to the *substantive content* of the public dialogue.

Both strategies lead to dead ends. It should be noted at the outset that the differentiation among action types and the principle of public space operate on different levels. Different action types, like work and labor, can become the locus of public space if they are reflexively challenged and placed into question from the standpoint of the asymmetrical power relations governing them. To give a few examples, productivity quotas in the workshop, how many chips per hour a worker should produce, can obviously become a matter of public concern if the legitimacy of those setting the quotas, their right to do so, their reasons for doing so are challenged. Likewise, as recent experience has shown us, even the most intricate questions of nuclear strategy, the number of nuclear warheads on a missile, the time required to diffuse them—all these issues can be reclaimed by a public under conditions of democratic legitimacy and become part of what our *res publica* is about. Arendt, by contrast, relegated certain types of activity like work and labor, and by extension all issues of economics and technology, to the private realm alone, ignoring the fact that these activities and relations too, insofar as they are based on power relations, could become matters of public dispute.

Likewise, the attempt to define "public space" by defining the agenda of public conversation is futile. Even on Arendtian terms, the effect of collective action in concert will be to put ever new and unexpected items on the agenda of public debate. Arendt herself in the associational model developed not a substantive but a *procedural* concept of public space, which is in fact compatible with this view. What is important here is not so much what public discourse is about as the way in which this discourse takes place: force and violence destroy the specificity of public discourse by introducing the dumb language of physical superiority and constraint and by silencing the voice of persuasion and conviction. Only power is generated by public discourse and is sustained by it. From the standpoint of this procedural model, neither the distinction between the social and the political nor the distinction among work, labor, and action are that relevant. At stake are the reflexive questioning of issues by all those affected by their foreseeable consequences and the recognition of their right to do so.

When compared to Hannah Arendt's reflections on these issues, the advantage of the liberal concept of public space is that the link between power, legitimacy, and public discourse is made most explicit by it. Yet this model is also more sterile than the Arendtian one in that it conceives of politics too closely on the analogy of juridical relations, thereby losing that emphasis on spontaneity, imagination, participation, and empowerment that Arendt saw to be the mark of authentic politics whenever and wherever it occurred.

2 The Liberal Model of Public Space as Public Dialogue

Although Bruce Ackerman's thought differs from that of John Rawls and Ronald Dworkin, who are usually considered the chief spokespersons for contemporary liberalism, in his model of liberal dialogue, Ackerman expresses certain fundamental assumptions of liberalism that would be shared by all. For Ackerman, liberalism is a form of political culture in which the question of legitimacy is paramount. In *Social Justice in the Liberal State* he writes, "Whenever anybody questions the legitimacy of another's power, the power holder must respond not by suppressing the questioner but by giving a reason that explains why he is more entitled to the resource than the questioner is."[16] Ackerman understands liberalism as a way of talking about power, as a political culture of *public dialogue* based on certain kinds of *conversational constraints*. The most significant conversational constraint in liberalism is *neutrality,* which rules that no reason advanced within a discourse of legitimation can be a good reason if it requires the power holder to assert that his conception of the good is better than that asserted by his fellow citizens, or that regardless of his conception of the good, he is intrinsically superior to one or more of his fellow citizens.[17]

Bruce Ackerman wants to base his case for public dialogue "not on some assertedly general feature of the moral life, but upon the distinctive way liberals conceive of the problem of public order."[18] His question is how different primary groups, about whom we only know that they do not share the same conception of the good, can "resolve the problem of mutual coexistence in a *reasonable* way."[19]

The way out is the path of "conversational restraint." When you and I learn that we disagree about one or another dimension of the moral truth, we should not search for some common value that will trump this disagreement; nor should we try to translate it into some putatively neutral framework; nor should we seek to transcend our disagreement by talking about how some unearthly creature might resolve it. We should simply say *nothing at all* about this disagreement and put the moral ideals that divide us off the conversational agenda of the liberal state. In restraining ourselves in this way, we need *not* lose the chance to talk to one another about our deepest moral disagreements in countless other, *more private, contexts.* . . . Having constrained the conversation in this way, we may instead use dialogue for pragmatically productive purposes: to identify normative premises all political participants find reasonable (or, at least, not unreasonable).[20] (My emphasis.)

The model of a public dialogue based on conversational restraint is not neutral, in that it presupposes a moral and political epistemology; this in turn justifies an implicit separation between the public and the private of such a kind as leads to the silencing of the concerns of certain excluded groups.

The liberal theorist of conversational restraint assumes that the primary groups to the conversation already know what their deepest disagreements are even before they have engaged in the conversation. These groups already seem to know that a particular problem is a moral, religious, or aesthetic issue, as opposed to an issue of distributive justice or public policy. While we can legitimately discuss the second, says the liberal theorist, let us abstract from the first. Take, however, issues like abortion, pornography, and domestic violence. What kinds of issues are they? Are they questions of justice or of the good life? The distinction between issues of justice and those of the good life cannot be decided by some moral geometry. Rather, it is the very process of unconstrained public dialogue that will help us define the nature of the issues we are debating. All those issues that participants in a practical discourse agree cannot be universalized and subject to legal norms constitute issues of the good life; the rest are issues of justice. This means that citizens must indeed feel free to introduce, in Bruce Ackerman's words, "any and all moral arguments into the conversational field." For it is only after the dialogue has been opened in this radical fashion that we can be sure that we have come to agree upon a mutually acceptable definition of the problem rather than reaching some compromise consensus that will silence the concerns of some.

An additional limitation of the liberal model of public space is that in it political relations are often conceived of far too narrowly along the model of juridical ones. The chief concern expressed by the idea of "dialogic neutrality" is that of the rightful coexistence of different groups in a pluralistic society, each with its different conception of the good. The just in modern societies, it is said, should be neutral vis-à-vis fundamental assumptions concerning the good life. Neutrality is indeed one of the fundamental cornerstones of the modern legal system: modern, promulgated law, unlike ancient and customary law, should not "ethically" mould character but should provide the space within which autonomous individuals can pursue and develop various conceptions of the good life. However, although the modern legal system must uphold neutrality, even under conditions of a modern, pluralistic, democratic society, politics is about something other than neutrality. Democratic politics challenges, redefines, and renegotiates the divisions between the good and the just, the moral and the legal, the private and the public. For these distinctions, as they have been established by modern states at the end of social and historical struggles, contain within them the result of historical power compromises. To illustrate, before the emergence of strong working-class movements and the eventual establishment of social-welfare measures in European countries and North America, questions relating to the health of workers in the workplace, problems of accidents on the job, and in our days, the harmful side effects of certain chemicals were frequently construed by employers as issues of "trade secrets" and "business privacy." As a result of political struggles the definition of these issues were transformed from trade secrets and private business practices to major issues of public concern. The principle of liberal neutrality is not helpful in guiding our thoughts on such matters. All it says is that once this redefinition and political renegotiation of the right and the good has occurred, then the law should be neutral, i.e., the Office of Safety and Health Administration should be neutral in applying this legislation to Chinese laundromats, Italian restaurants, and the Lockheed Corporation. But public dialogue is not about what all the Chinese laundromats, Italian restaurants, and the Lockheed Corporation know they agree to even before they have entered the public foray. Rather, public dialogue means challenging and redefining the collective good and one's sense of justice as a result of the public foray. The liberal principle of dialogic neutrality, while it expresses one of the main principles of the modern legal system, is too restrictive and frozen in application to the dynamics of power struggles in actual political processes. A public life conducted according to the principle of liberal dialogic neutrality would not only lack the agonistic dimension of politics, in Arendtian terms, but perhaps more severe, it would also restrict the scope of public conversation in a way that would be inimical to the interests of oppressed groups. All struggles against oppression in the modern world begin by redefining what had previously been considered private, nonpublic, and nonpolitical issues as matters of public concern, as issues of justice, as sites of power that need discursive legitimation. In this respect, the women's movement, the peace movement, the ecology movements, and new ethnic-identity movements follow a similar logic. There is little room in the liberal model of neutrality for thinking about the logic of such struggles.

By contrast and paradoxically, the chief virtue of the Habermasian "discourse model of public space" is its radical indeterminacy and openness. When compared to the Arendtian one, Habermas's model neither restricts access to public space nor sets the agenda for public debate. When compared to Ackerman's neutrality principle, the discourse model of public space is also distinctive in that it captures the dynamic and renego-

tiable aspects of such distinctions as that between the right and
the good. Admittedly, as will be explicated below, in his moral
theory of discourse ethics Habermas is quite close to the liberal
tradition represented by Ackerman among others, and like
them he proceeds from unquestioned distinctions between justice and the good life, the public and the private. However, the
discourse model of publicity and even the discourse model of
ethics, on my interpretation of them, do not permit an essentialist strategy in drawing these distinctions. To capture these
features of Habermas's discourse model of public space, it is
necessary to begin by discussing the principle of *Öffentlichkeit*
in the larger context of Habermas's theory of modernity.

3 The Discursive Model of Public Space

The defense of modernity in light of the principle of public
participation has been an essential aspect of Habermas's work
since *The Structural Transformation of the Public Sphere.*[21] Revers-
ing the pessimistic assessment of modernity as a "dialectic of
Enlightenment," Habermas has emphasized the extent to
which modernity not only signifies differentiation, individua-
tion, and bifurcation. The emergence of an autonomous public
sphere of political reasoning and discussion is also central to
the project of the moderns. Along with social differentiation
and the creation of independent value spheres, modernity
brings with it a threefold possibility.[22] In the realm of institutions, the consensual generation of general norms of action
through practical discourses moves to the fore. In the realm
of personality formation, the development of individual identities becomes increasingly dependent on the reflexive and critical attitudes of individuals in weaving together a coherent life
story beyond conventional role and gender definitions. Self-
definitions, who one is, become increasingly autonomous vis-
à-vis established social practices and fluid in comparison to
rigid role understandings. Likewise, the appropriation of cultural tradition becomes more dependent upon the creative
hermeneutic of contemporary interpreters. Tradition in the
modern world loses its legitimacy of being valid simply because
it is the way of the past. The legitimacy of tradition rests now

with resourceful and creative appropriations of it in view of the problems of meaning in the present.

Viewed in this threefold fashion, the principle of participation, far from being antithetical to modernity, is one of its chief prerequisites. In each realm—society, personality, and culture, that is, the functioning of institutional life, the formation of stable personalities over time, and the continuity of cultural tradition—the reflective effort and contribution of individuals becomes crucial.

This emphasis on political participation and the widest-reaching democratization of decision-making processes is one that Jürgen Habermas's critical theory shares with the tradition usually referred to as that of republican or civic virtue. The crucial distinction between the participatory vision of contemporary critical theory and that of the tradition of civic virtue is that thinkers of the latter tradition more often than not have formulated their views of participatory politics with express hostility toward the institutions of modern civil society, like the market. Virtue and commerce are thought to be antithetical principles.[23] Participatory politics is considered possible either for a land-based gentry with civil virtue or for the citizens of the Greek *polis*, but not for complex, modern societies with their highly differentiated spheres of the economy, law, politics, civil and family life.

In this broader context the meaning of participation is altered. The exclusive focus on political participation is shifted toward a more inclusively understood concept of discursive will formation. Participation is seen not as an activity only possible in a narrowly defined political realm but as an activity that can be realized in the social and cultural spheres as well. Participating in a citizen's initiative to clean up a polluted harbor is no less political than debating in cultural journals the pejorative presentation of certain groups in terms of stereotypical images (combating sexism and racism in the media). This conception of participation, which emphasizes the determination of norms of action through the practical debate of all affected by them, has the distinct advantage over the republican or civic-virtue conception that it articulates a vision of the political true to the realities of complex, modern societies.

This modernist understanding of participation yields a novel conception of public space. Public space is not understood *agonistically* as a space of competition for acclaim and immortality among a political elite; it is viewed democratically as the creation of procedures whereby those affected by general social norms and collective political decisions can have a say in their formulation, stipulation, and adoption. This conception of the public is also different than the liberal one, for although Habermas and liberal thinkers belive that legitimation in a democratic society can result only from a public dialogue, in the Habermasian model this dialogue does not stand under the constraint of neutrality but is judged according to the criteria, represented by the model of a "practical discourse." The public sphere comes into existence whenever and wherever all affected by general social and political norms of action engage in a practical discourse, evaluating their validity. In effect, there may be as many publics as there are controversial general debates about the validity of norms. Democratization in contemporary societies can be viewed as the increase and growth of autonomous public spheres among participants. As Jean Cohen has astutely observed, "Both the complexity and the diversity within contemporary civil societies call for the posing of the issue of democratization in terms of a variety of differentiated processes, forms, and *loci* depending on the axis of division considered. Indeed, there is an elective affinity between the discourse ethic and modern civil society as the terrain on which an institutionalized plurality of democracies can emerge."[24]

While the general intentions of Habermas's critical social theory of late-capitalist societies and the place of public participation within it are clear, in his later writings the "discourse model" has been less a part of his critical social and political theory of late capitalism, but has instead moved to the center of his moral theory of communicative or discourse ethics. There is almost a *décalage*, a rupture, here between the normative model and the social analysis, which seems to be already implicit in the *Strukturwandel der Öffentlichkeit*.

At first sight the message of the *Structural Transformation of the Public Sphere* is aporetic: the analysis traces the "transformation" of a "category of bourgeois society." However, this transformation is less an evolution than a "decline" of the public sphere. One senses the influence of the older Frankfurt School, and particularly of Adorno, in the depiction of the change of the public from a "reasoning" to a "consuming" one. At the end of this analysis, the normative principle of "free and unconstrained dialogue among reasoning individuals," which after all is the *principle of democratic legitimacy for all modern societies,* is left dangling without any anchoring in either institutions or the *Lebenswelt.* Despite this aporetic diagnosis, the fate of public life in late capitalism has never left the center of Habermas's concerns. It returns in a number of essays in the mid 1960s dealing with the *de jure* ideals of a democratic culture and the *de facto* imperatives of a scientific-technological civilization. In these essays, collected as *Towards a Rational Society,* the model of an unconstrained public dialogue among scientists, politicians, and the lay public is introduced as being the only one compatible with a democratic self-understanding. It is easy to locate the concepts of an "ideal speech situation" and "unconstrained dialogue," or "discourse," in these early essays.

Nonetheless, since the discourse model has been most explicitly worked out in recent years as a moral rather than a political or social theory, a number of distinctions are made in the former context that appear to me incompatible with the intentions, if not the details, of the general social diaognois of late capitalism. If the principle of publicity is to be interpreted as a principle of democratic participation, then a number of distinctions on which the moral model of a practical discourse rests are not tenable. The discourse model of ethics is said to be about norms as opposed to values, about "generalizable interests" as opposed to "culturally interpreted needs," about questions of "justice" as opposed to questions of the "good life." In some rough fashion the distinction between these pairs of opposites is also said to correspond to public matters of norms versus private questions of value, to "public issues of justice" as opposed to "private conceptions of the good life," to "public interests" as opposed to "private needs." My claim is that in his moral theory Habermas inherits a number of dubious distinctions from the liberal social-contract tradition that are at odds with the more critical and political intentions of his theory of late-capitalist societies.

I should note at the outset that the model of practical discourse developed in this ethical theory is a radically proceduralist one. It views normative dialogue as a conversation of justification taking place under the constraints of an "ideal speech situation."[25] The procedural constraints of the ideal speech situation are that each participant must have an equal change to initiate and to continue communication; each must have an equal chance to make assertions, recommendations, and explanations; all must have equal chances to express their wishes, desires, and feelings; and finally, within dialogue, speakers must be free to thematize those power relations that in ordinary contexts would constrain the wholly free articulation of opinions and positions. Together these conditions specify a norm of communication that can be named that of *egalitarian reciprocity*.[26]

Interpreted in this radically proceduralist fashion, the discourse model of public dialogue undermines the substantive distinctions between justice and the good life, public matters of norms as opposed to private matters of value, public interests versus private needs. If the agenda of the conversation is radically open, if participants can bring any and all matters under critical scrutiny and reflexive questioning, then there is no way to predefine the *nature* of the issues discussed as being ones of justice or of the good life itself prior to the conversation. Distinction between justice and the good life, norms and values, interests and needs are internal, and not external, to the process of discursive will formation. As long as these distinctions are renegotiated, reinterpreted, and rearticulated as a result of a radically open and procedurally fair discourse, they can be made in any of a number of ways.

Why is this a significant problem? Perhaps this is an issue in technical moral philosophy, but what implications could it have for a critical social and political theory?[27] From a feminist point of view, the answer is clear. In the tradition of Western political thought and down to our own days, these distinctions have served to confine women and typically female spheres of activity like housework; reproduction; nurture and care for the young, the sick, and the elderly to the "private" domain. These issues have often been considered matters of the good life, of values, of nongeneralizable interests. Along with their relegation, in Arendt's terms, to the "shadowy interior of the household," they have been treated, until recently, as "natural" and "immutable" aspects of human relations. They have remained prereflexive and inaccessible to discursive analysis. Much of our tradition, when it considers the autonomous individual or the moral point of view, implicitly defines this as the standpoint of the *Homo politicus* or *Homo economicus* but hardly ever as that of the female self.[28] Challenging the distinction of contemporary moral and political discourse, to the extent that they privatize these issues, is central to women's struggles, which intend to make these issues public.

In a recent article Habermas has responded to these criticisms. He writes, "Benhabib questions the restriction of moral argumentation to problems of justice alone, because she believes that the logical distinction between problems of justice and questions of the good life underlies the sociological distinction between public and private spheres or at least correspond to it. . . . All private relations and personal domains of life, which a patriarchal society first and foremost considers the women's sphere, would thereby be excluded per definitionem from the object domain of moral theory."[29] Habermas objects, however, that according to his theory, the conceptual distinction between issues of justice and those of the good life is different from the sociological distinction between the private and the public domains. I agree that in principle the distinction between justice versus the good life in moral theory and the categories of public versus private spheres in sociological theory need to be separated from each other. Yet I would maintain that in the modern social-contract tradition beginning with John Locke and including Rousseau, Kant, and in our days John Rawls, there has been a fundamental ambiguity governing the term "privacy" that has led to a silent conflation of these issues. To the extent that the discourse theory of ethics is indebted to this tradition, a similar ambiguity is also at work in Habermas's theory.

"Privacy," "privacy rights," and the "private sphere," as invoked by the modern tradition, have included at least three distinct dimensions. First and foremost, privacy has been understood as the sphere of moral and religious conscience. As a result of the historical compromise between church and state in Western European countries, and as a consequence of developments in modern philosophy and science, matters of ultimate faith concerning the meaning of life, the highest good, the most binding principles in accordance with which we should conduct our lives come to be viewed as rationally irresolvable and as matters about which individuals themselves should decide according to the dictates of their own consciences and worldviews.

In the emergence of Western modernity, a second set of privacy rights accompany the eventual establishment of the liberal separation of the church and state. These are privacy rights pertaining to *economic liberties.* The development of commodity relations in the market place and of capitalism means not only "the rise of the social," in Arendt's terms. Along with the socialization of the economy, that is, along with the decline of subsistence-type household economies and the eventual emergence of national markets, a parallel development establishing the privacy of economic markets takes place. In this context, "privacy" means first and foremost noninterference by the political state in the freedom of commodity relations, and in particular nonintervention in the free market of labor power.

The final meaning of "privacy" and "privacy rights" is that of the intimate sphere. This is the domain of the household, of meeting the daily needs of life, of sexuality and reproduction, and of care for the young, the sick, and the elderly. As Lawrence Stone's path-breaking study on the origins and transformations of the early bourgeois family shows, from the beginning there were tensions between the continuing patriarchal authority of the father in the bourgeois family and developing conceptions of equality and consent in the political world.[30] As the male bourgeois citizen was battling for his rights to autonomy in the religious and economic spheres against the absolutist state, his relations in the household were defined by nonconsensual, nonegalitarian assumptions. Questions of justice were from the beginning restricted to the public sphere, whereas the private sphere was considered outside the realm of justice.

To be sure, with the emergence of autonomous women's movements in the nineteenth and twentieth centuries, with women's massive entry into the labor force in this century, and with their gain of the right to vote, this picture has been transformed. Contemporary moral and political theory continues, however, to neglect these issues and ignores the transformations of the private sphere resulting from massive changes in women's and men's lives. While matters of justice and those of the good life are conceptually distinct from the sociological distinction between the public and private spheres, the conflation of religious and economic freedoms with the freedom of intimacy under the one ruberic of "privacy" or "private questions of the good life" has had two consequences. First, contemporary normative moral and political theory, Habermas's discourse ethics not excluded, has been gender blind, that is, these theories have ignored the issue of difference, the differences in the experiences of male versus female subjects in all domains of life. Second, power relations in the intimate sphere have been treated as though they did not even exist. The idealizing lens of concepts like intimacy does not allow one to see that women's work in the private sphere, like care for the young and the running of the household, has been unremunerated. Consequently, the rules governing the sexual division of labor in the family have been placed beyond the scope of justice. As with any modern liberation movement, the contemporary women's movement is making what were hitherto considered private matters of the good life into public issues of justice, by thematizing the asymmetrical power relations on which the sexual division of labor between the genders has rested. In this process the line between the private and the public, issues of justice, and matters of the good life are being renegotiated.

Certainly, a normative theory, and in particular a critical social theory, cannot take the aspirations of any social actors at face value and fit its critical criteria to meet the demands

of a particular social movement. Commitment to social transformation and yet a certain critical distance, even from the
demands of those with whom one identifies, are essential
to the vocation of the theorist as social critic. For this reason,
the purpose of these final considerations is not to criticize the
critical theory of Habermas simply by confronting it with the
demands of the women's movement. Rather, my goal is to point
to an area of conceptual unclarity and political contestation in
contemporary debates. Any theory of the public, public sphere,
and publicity presupposes a distinction between the public and
the private. These are the terms of a binary opposition. What
the women's movement and feminist theorists in the last two
decades have shown, however, is that traditional modes of
drawing this distinction have been part of a discourse of domination that legitimizes women's oppression and exploitation
in the private realm. But the discourse model, precisely because
it proceeds from a fundamental norm of egalitarian reciprocity
and projects the democratization of all social norms, cannot
preclude the democratization of familial norms and norms
governing the gender division of labor.[31] Once this is granted,
the distinction between matters of justice and those of the good
life, between generalizable interests and culturally intrepreted
needs, can be reconceptualized.[32]

Undoubtedly, our societies are undergoing a tremendous
transformation at the present. In existing Western democracies, under the impact of the mass media, growth of corpora-
tization, and of business-like political associations, like PACs
and other lobbying groups, the public sphere of democratic
legitimacy has shrunk. In the last U.S. presidential campaign
of 1988, the level of public discourse and debate, both in terms
of substance and style, had sunk so low that major networks
like CBS and ABC felt compelled to run sessions of self-reflec-
tive analysis on their own contributions as electronic media to
the decline of public discourse. The autonomous citizen, whose
reasoned judgment and participation was the sine qua non of
the public sphere, has been transformed into the "citizen consumer" of packaged images and messages or the "electronic
mail target" of large lobbying groups and organizations. This
impoverishment of public life has been accompanied by the

growth of the society of surveillance and voyeurism (Foucault) on the one hand and the "colonization of the lifeworld" (Habermas) on the other. Not only has public life been transformed, private life as well has undergone tremendous changes, only some of which can be welcomed for furthering the values of democratic legitimacy and discursive will formation.

As the sociologist Helga Maria Hernes has remarked, in some ways welfare-state societies are ones in which "reproduction" has gone public.[33] When, however, issues like child rearing; care for the sick, the young, and the elderly; reproductive freedoms; domestic violence; child abuse; and the constitution of sexual identities go public in our societies, more often than not a "patriarchal-capitalist-disciplianry bureaucracy" has resulted.[34] These bureaucracies have frequently disempowered women and have set the agenda for public debate and participation. In reflecting about these issues as feminists, we have lacked a *critical model of public space and public discourse*. Here is where as feminists we should not only criticize Habermas's social theory but also enter into a dialectcial alliance with it. A critical model of public space is necessary to enable us to draw the line between "juridification," "Verrechtlichung" in Habermas's terms, on the one hand and making public, in the sense of making accessible to debate, reflection, action, and moral-political transformation, on the other. To make issues of common concern public in this second sense means making them increasingly accessible to discursive will formation; it means to democratize them; it means bringing them under standards of moral reflection compatible with autonomous postconventional identities. As feminists, we have lacked a critical model that can distinguish between the bureaucratic administration of needs and collective democratic empowerment over them. More often than not, debates among feminists have been blocked by the alternatives of a legalistic liberal reformism (the NOW agenda, ACLU positions) and a radical feminism that can hardly conceal its own political and moral authoritarianism.[35]

For reasons I have already explored, some of the models of public space discussed in this essay are severely limited in their ability to help us cope with this task. Arendt's agonistic model is at odds with the sociological reality of modernity, as well as with modern political struggles for justice.[36] The liberal model of public space transforms the political dialogue of empowerment far too quickly into a juridical discourse about the right. The discourse model is the only one that is compatible both with the general social trends of our societies and with the emancipatory aspirations of new social movements, like the woman's movement. The radical proceduralism of this model is a powerful criterion for demystifying discourses of power and their implicit agendas. However, in a society where reproduction is going public, practical discourse will have to be "feminized." Such feminization of practical discourse will mean first and foremost challenging, from the standpoint of their gender context and subtext, unexamined normative dualisms as those of justice and the good life, norms and values, interests and needs.

Notes

1. See Andrew Arato, "Civil Society against the State: Poland 1980–81," *Telos* 47 (1981): 23–47; "Empire versus Civil Society: Poland 1981–82," *Telos* 50 (1981–1982): 19–48; Andrew Arato and Jean Cohen, *Civil Society and Political Theory* (Cambridge: MIT Press, forthcoming); John Keane, ed., *Civil Society and the State: New European Perspectives* (London: Verso, 1988); and John Keane, ed. *Democracy and Civil Society* (London: Verso, 1988).

2. H. Arendt, *The Human Condition* (Chicago, 1973, 8th ed.), pp. 38–49.

3. See G. W. F. Hegel, *Rechtsphilosophie* (1821), pp. 189 ff.; English translation by T. M. Knox, *Hegel's Philosophy of Right* (London: Oxford University Press, 1973 reprint), pp. 126 ff.

4. See Christopher Lasch, Introduction to the special Hannah Arendt issue of *Salmagundi*, no. 60 (1983): v ff.; Jürgen Habermas, "Hannah Arendt's Communications Concept of Power," in *Social Research: Hannah Arendt Memorial Issue*, no. 44 (1977): 3–24.

5. For a sympathetic critique of Arendt along these lines, see Hannah Pitkin, "Justice: On Relating Public and Private," *Political Theory* 9, no. 3 (1981): 327–352.

6. See Arendt, *Men in Dark Times* (New York: Harcourt, Brace and Jovanovich, 1968), p. 22; Preface to *Between Past and Future: Six Exercises in Political Thought* (Cleveland and New York: Meridian Books, 1961), p. 14. There is an excellent essay by David Luban that is one of the few discussions in the literature dealing with Hannah Arendt's

methodology of story telling. See D. Luban, "Explaining Dark Times: Hannah Arendt's Theory of Theory," *Social Research* 50, no. 1 (1983): 215–247. See also E. Young-Bruehl, "Hannah Arendt als Geschichtenerzählerin," In *Hannah Arendt: Materialien zu ihrem Werk* (München: 1979), pp. 319–327.

7. H. Arendt, *The Life of the Mind*, vol. 1, *Thinking* (New York, 1978), p. 212.

8. Arendt, *Between Past and Future*, p. 5

9. See Arendt's statement in note A appended to the English edition of Benjamin's "Theses on the Philosophy of History" (which Arendt edited in English): "Historicism contents itself with establishing a causal connection between various moments in history. But no fact that is cause is for that very reason historical. It became historical posthumously, as it were, through the events that may be separated from it by thousands of years. A historian who takes this as his point of departure stops telling the sequence of events like the beads of a rosary. Instead, he grasps the constellation which his own era has formed with a definite earlier one. Thus he establishes a conception of the present as the 'time of the now' which is shot through with chips of Messianic time." This appears in Walter Benjamin, *Illuminations*, ed. and with an intro. by H. Arendt (New York: Schocken Books, 1969).

10. Arendt, *Vita Activa*, pp. 23, 31 ff.

11. Arendt, *The Origins of Totalitarianism*, chap. 13, p. 466.

12. Arendt, *The Human Condition*, p. 56.

13. Hannah Arendt's persistent denial of the "women's issue" and her inability to link together the exclusion of women from politics and this agonistic and male-dominated conception of public space are astounding. The near absence of women as collective political actors in Arendt's theory (individuals like Rosa Luxemburg are present) is a difficult question, but to begin thinking about this means first challenging the private/public split in her thought, as this corresponds to the traditional separation of spheres between the sexes (men = public life; women = private sphere).

14. Arendt, *Between Past and Future*, p. 4.

15. See Arendt, "Reflections on Little Rock," *Dissent* 6, no. 1 (Winter 1959): 45–56; Ralph Ellison, in *Who Speaks for the Negro?* ed., R. P. Warren (New York, 1965), pp. 342–344; and Arendt to Ralph Ellison in a letter of 29 July 1965 as cited by Young-Breuhl in *Hannah Arendt: For Love of the World* (New Haven, Yale University Press, 1984), p. 316.

16. Ackerman, *Social Justice in the Liberal State* (New Haven, 1980), p. 4.

17. Ackerman, *Social Justice*, p. 11.

18. B. Ackerman, "Why Dialogue?" *Journal of Philosophy* 86 (1989): 8.

19. Ackerman, "Why Dialogue?" p. 9.

20. Ackerman, "Why Dialogue?" pp. 16–17.

21. Originally appeared as *Strukturwandel der Öffentilichkeit* (Luchterland: Darmstadt und Neuwied, 1962); English translation by Thomas Burger (Cambridge: MIT Press, 1989).

22. The following is a summary of the argument of the second volume of *The Theory of Communicative Action* and, in particular, of the chapter "Dialectics of Rationalization" (*The Theory of Communicative Action*, vol. 2, trans. by T. A. McCarthy (Boston: Beacon Press, 1985). I have dealt with this issue more extensively in "Autonomy, Modernity, and Community: Communitarianism and Critical Social Theory in Dialogue," in *Zwischenbetrachtungen im Prozess der Aufklärung*, ed. by A. Honneth, T. A. McCarthy, Claus Offe, and Albrecht Wellmer (Frankfurt: Suhrkamp, 1989), pp. 373–395; also forthcoming in S. Benhabib, *Situating the Self: Gender, Community, and Postmodernism in Contemporary Ethics* (New York: Routledge and Kegan Paul, 1992).

23. See J. G. A. Pocock, *The Machiavellian Movement* (1975) and *Virtue, Commerce, and History* (1985).

24. Jean Cohen, "Discourse Ethics and Civil Society," *Philosophy and Social Criticism* 14, no. 3/4 (1988): 328.

25. For a recent statement, see, "Diskursethik: Notizen zu einem Begründungsprogramm," in *Moralbewusstsein und kommunikatives Handeln*, pp. 53–127. English translation in Benhabib and Dallmayr, eds. *The Communicative Ethics Controversy* (Cambridge: MIT Press, 1990) and in J. Habermas, *Moral Consciousness and Communicative Action* (Cambridge: MIT Press, 1990).

26. Any proceduralist theory, unless it also clarifies the constraints on the procedure and tries to justify them, runs into a paradox that has been sharply formulated by Kenneth Baynes: "If there are no substantive constraints on what can be introduced into a practical discourse, what is to prevent the outcome from conflicting with some of our most deeply held moral convictions? What is to prevent the participants to agreeing to anything, or perhaps more plausibly, never reaching any general agreement at all?" in "The Liberal/Communitarian Controversy and Communicative Ethics," *Philosophy and Social Criticism* 14, no. 3/4 (1988), p. 304. I agree with Baynes that the way out of this dilemma is to clarify the "normative constraints" imposed on discourses and their constitutive role in the discourse, while one accepts that the constraints can be subject to discursive critique and clarification, even if they can never be wholly suspended. See also Benhabib, "In the Shadow of Aristotle and Hegel: Communicative Ethics and Recent Controversies in Practical Philosophy," in *Philosophical Forum* 21, nos. 1–2 (Fall 1989–Winter 1990): 1–31; also appeared as the afterword to *The Communicative Ethics Controversy*, ed. S. Benhabib and Fred Dallmayr (Cambridge: MIT Press, 1990), pp. 330–371.

27. For a fuller discussion of the ramifications of this issue for contemporary debates in practical philosophy, see Benhabib, "In the Shadow of Aristotle and Hegel."

28. See Benhabib, "The Generalized and the Concrete Other: The Kohlberg-Gilligan Controversy and Feminist Theory," in *Feminism as Critique*, ed. S. Benhabib and D. Cornell (University of Minnesota Press: Minneapolis, 1987), pp. 77–96.

29. Jürgen Habermas, "Transzendenz von innen, Transzendenz ins Diesseits: Eine Replik," ms., p. 22, forthcoming.

30. L. Stone, *The Family, Sex, and Marriage in England,* 1500–1800 (Harper and Row Publishers, abridged edition, 1979).

31. Nancy Fraser has raised these considerations pointedly in "What's Critical about Critical Theory? The Case of Habermas and Gender," in *Feminism as Critique*, ed. Benhabib and Cornell, pp. 31–56.

32. Faced with this claim, the liberal political theorist might respond that this solution invites the corrosion of rights of privacy and the total intrusion of the state into the domain of the individual. The issue, she will argue, is not that these distinctions must be reconceptualized but where the line between the private and the public will be situated as a result of the discursive reconceptualization. Put in more familiar terms, does discourse theory allow for a theory of individual rights, or is it simply a theory of democratic participation that does not respect the legal boundaries of individual liberty? Although so far a theory of rights has not been developed from discourse theory, in principle the discourse model is based upon a strong assumption of individual autonomy, and this respect for autonomy, together with the norm of egalitarian reciprocity, could be the basis for a theory of individual rights. I agree with Jean Cohen, who writes, "In point of fact, however, discourse ethics logically presupposes both clases of rights. By basing rights not on an individualistic ontology, as classical liberals have done, but on the theory of communicative interaction, we have strong reason to emphasize the cluster of rights of communication. . . . The rights of privacy would be affirmed because of the need to reproduce autonomous personalities without which rational discourse would be impossible. . . . From this point of view, the rights of communication point us to the legitimate domain for formulating and defending rights. The rights of personality identify the subjects who have the rights to have rights." See "Discourse Ethics and Civil Society," p. 327. Also see Baynes, "The Liberal/ Communitarian Controversy and Communicative Ethics," pp. 304 ff.

33. Helga Maria Hernes, *Welfare State and Woman Power: Essays in State Feminism* (London: Norwegian University Press, 1987).

34. See Nancy Fraser, *Unruly Practices: Power, Discourse, and Gender in Late-Capitalist Social Theory* (University of Minnesota Press, 1990); "Women, Welfare, and the Politics of Need Interpretation," *Hypatia: A Journal of Feminist Philosophy*, no. 2 (1987): 103–121.

35. For a very good example of the first trend, see Rosemarie Tong, *Women, Sex, and the Law* (Totowa, N.J.: Rowman and Littlefield, 1984). For the second trend, see Catharine MacKinnon's work and the amazing "return of the repressed" Marxist orthodoxy of the state and the law in her writings. See her early article "Marxism, Method, and the State: Toward Feminist Jurisprudence." *Signs* 8 (Summer 1983), pp. 645 ff. and the more recent *Feminism Unmodified: Discourses on Life and Law* (Cambridge: Harvard University Press, 1987).

36. In *The Reluctant Modernism of Hannah Arendt* (Sage publications, forthcoming) I shall argue that Arendt's "associational" model of public space, briefly mentioned in sec. 1, is very relevant for thinking about the experience of politics in all new social movements.

4

The Public Sphere: Models and Boundaries

Peter Uwe Hohendahl

The occasion for this symposium is the appearance of Jürgen Habermas's *Strukturwandel der Öffentlichkeit* in English, almost thirty years after its first publication in Germany. From the vantage point of the contemporary discussion in this country, it is not altogether easy to appreciate the exceptional impact of this study on younger West German intellectuals during the 1960s. *Strukturwandel* was received as a critical response to Horkheimer and Adorno's *Dialectic of Enlightenment* and the political pessimism of Adorno's writings during the 1950s and 1960s. Although Habermas remained in many ways indebted to his teachers, the book's positive assessment of the European Enlightenment, particularly its insistence on the democratic potential of the Enlightenment, was clearly not compatible with the radical critique of reason in the works of Horkheimer and Adorno. When we look back from Habermas's later theory, there is little doubt that *Strukturwandel* was a first attempt to map the project of modernity and, more specifically, to assess the chances of democracy in West Germany after the restoration of organized capitalism had been completed under Adenauer.

In 1962 Habermas made it quite clear that his study primarily dealt with the liberal tradition grounded in Western capitalism, while he treated the plebeian public sphere only as a nondominant variation. Yet in his discussion of Karl Marx he at least outlined the concept of a postbourgeois public sphere where participation does not depend on the institution of private property. In *Strukturwandel,* however, Habermas did not pursue the history of this counter model. Later, after his turn to a system-differentiation model, the Marxian solution and its legacy in the socialist tradition was not quite compatible any more with his own social theory. Still, the impetus to transcend the liberal model (since its classical form could not be restored under advanced capitalism) remained a significant element in Habermas's theory. Hence I want to argue that both the early work and the later theory are relevant for the purpose of our discussion. The concept of the public sphere can serve as a crucial category for a critical examination of the contemporary situation. Habermas's theory remains a provocative model for the discussion of contemporary issues.

It is noteworthy that both Thomas McCarthy and Seyla Benhabib focus their arguments on the recent work of Habermas, using *The Structural Transformation of the Public Sphere* only as a backdrop. This tendency is particularly explicit in McCarthy's essay, which refers to Habermas's early work only to underline the continuity of Habermas's position. Benhabib makes a similar point when she views Habermas's later work, especially *The Theory of Communicative Action,* as an attempt to come to grips with problems that remained unresolved in *Structural Transformation.* In either case the significant difference between Habermas's early study and his recent theory is either repressed (McCarthy) or played down (Benhabib). Within the present American debate, it seems, both Habermas's supporters and his foes have decided that the "real Habermas" begins to emerge around 1970, after the publication of *Knowledge and Human Interests,* and crystallizes in his magnum opus, *The Theory of Communicative Action.* This view, which probably coincides with the author's self-understanding, distances Habermas from his beginnings and deemphasizes his roots in the Frankfurt School. In America it has become increasingly more difficult to connect Habermas's work with the writings of Adorno and Benjamin. Moreover, the tendency expressed in McCarthy's and Benhabib's essays also reflects a theoretical and methodological shift in conceptualizing the public sphere. While the early Habermas, following the work of Horkheimer and Adorno, developed his theory of the public sphere on the basis of a historical narrative, Benhabib and McCarthy relegate history and historical questions to the background. History is no longer allowed a central position in the argument. There are, I think, two reasons for this shift in emphasis, and both of them are connected with the form of Habermas's recent theory. Unlike the early Habermas, neither Benhabib nor McCarthy believe that a theory of the public sphere can be grounded in history. Rather, for them the concept of the public sphere, as the space where questions of the common good can be negotiated and decided, has to be anchored in abstract principles. Again, McCarthy's essay stresses the systematic approach precisely by offering an immanent critique of Habermas's theory. Yet what he shares with the later Habermas is the overriding interest in a purely philosophical grounding of the public sphere, since historical references and arguments, which abounded in *Strukturwandel,* cannot assume general validity. By comparison, Benhabib stays closer to a historical understanding of Habermas's conception of the public sphere when she presents it as part of a typology by comparing Habermas to Hannah Arendt on the one hand and Bruce Ackerman on the other. Habermas's theory emerges as the superior solution to today's problems, although, according to Benhabib, it is still a deficient solution. In her account, history has still been reduced to the history of ideas, a conception that helps us to understand the philosophical and political argument. However, Benhabib's critique of Habermas brings much more clearly into the foreground why a historical approach is seen as less useful: The argument that women and their needs have been neglected in the public sphere points to a specific historical limitation that can be overcome only through a better and more complete theory of the public sphere. Hence this theory must not rely on historical arguments but secure the conception in abstract philosophical terms. In other words, the interest in norms that can serve as general guidelines for the structure of a public sphere reflects a situation where problems of gender, race, and class remain unresolved. The normative aspect of Habermasian theory, which was there from the beginning, gains almost complete priority; the validity of the argument depends exclusively on the strength of the theoretical grounding.

In this respect, McCarthy and Benhabib come to different conclusions. While Benhabib accepts Habermas's recent theory as valid to a large extent and therefore recommends only some recasting, McCarthy's criticisms, insofar as they are couched in the language of interpretation, go to the core. According to McCarthy, Habermas makes untenable claims because he forces what one might call the Rousseauian element of his theory, in contrast to the liberal. In either case the argument leads to the conclusion that the difference between the empirically existing public sphere(s) and the idea of a just and equitable democratic society cannot easily be bridged by Habermas's theory. The question arises of whether this aporia should not be taken as a hint that the search for a completely abstract definition of the public sphere could be part of the problem. Of course, as we have to remind ourselves, Habermas never attempted to rewrite the theory of the public sphere; he has formulated his recent moral and political theory in such a way that it is not bound to a specific culture. What Benhabib and McCarthy have attempted, then, is to sketch how the public sphere would be structured according to Habermas's recent theory. The following remarks will briefly summarize their reconstructions and then concentrate on their criticisms.

For Benhabib the problem of public participation is at the center of Habermas's recent work. Yet "public space is not understood *agonistically* as a space of competition for acclaim and immortality among a political elite; it is viewed democratically as the creation of procedures whereby those affected by general social norms and collective political decisions can have a say in their formulation, stipulation, and adoption" (chap. 3, sec. 3). This formulation emphasizes (much more than Habermas in *Structural Transformation*) the available procedures that facilitate the democratic process. Political discussion and debate, then, are expected to occur within the framework of generally accepted procedures that guarantee the public nature of these debates as well as equal access to and equal participation in the discussion. While Habermas defined the public space in *Strukturwandel* by excluding the family and the economy, Benhabib wants to keep the boundaries fluid. Public spheres have to be claimed and renegotiated when the need arises. There are two sets of questions that might encourage such a renegotiation: problems of justice and questions concerning the good life. By including the second realm, Benhabib seems to redraw the boundaries between public and private. At least she assumes that she is recasting Habermas's model, in which values are supposedly considered private. Yet it has to be noted that Habermas's distinction between public and private does not coincide with the norm/value distinction. In *Strukturwandel* Habermas had already discussed questions of taste and criticism under the rubric of "the literary public sphere," and he thereby recognized in principle the *public* nature of values without specific references to issues of race and gender. It is interesting to note that Benhabib's response to Habermas's criticism of her position uses *historical* arguments by pointing to the conflation of problems of the good life with the private realm during the eighteenth and nineteenth centuries. I shall come back to this point later.

McCarthy's reconstruction of Habermas's model works strictly with Habermas's theoretical categories and distinctions. He approaches the definition of the public sphere from the perspective of moral philosophy, specifically the problems of needs. By emphasizing the importance of cultural values for any definition of human needs, McCarthy highlights the problem of a functioning public sphere in a pluralistic society. He formulates the problem in the following way: "How can we hope to achieve rational political consensus in a pluralistic society?" (chap. 2, sec. 1). This concern is not identical with, but rather close to, the problems of gender addressed by Benhabib. In historical terms, both critics question the unquestioned aspects of the older liberal model, i.e., its patriarchal exclusion of women and its homogeneity in terms of class and shared cultural values. Once the existing pluralism has been acknowledged, for instance, in postwar America, the older liberal model becomes problematic indeed. One possible response to this situation is a new liberal model (for instance Ackerman) where value judgments are treated as problems than cannot be solved through general norms and therefore should be excluded from public debate.

For McCarthy, Habermas's distinction between moral theory (universal norms) and specific ethical discourses is crucial insofar as these two levels are separate but also linked. McCarthy argues that while the discussion about values and needs is informed by general norms, the opposite is also true: cultural communities will question the general norms that are supposed to frame the debate when these norms collide with human interests. "In such cases, normative disagreements turn on value disagreements" (sec. 1). However, when the point of view of criticism is that of values and concerns the good life rather than justice, this critique is culture-bound and consequently, as Habermas argues, not generalizable. Yet at the same time such judgments are supposed to be rational. We expect reasons for their soundness. This claim creates a strong tension between (general) norms and (particular) values. In the words of McCarthy, "The backing for norms comes not in the form of demonstrative arguments but in the form of 'casuistic evidence' regarding consequences for need satisfaction" (sec. 2). This argument leads McCarthy ultimately to a rejection of Habermas's position, as we will see. He does not share Habermas's belief that rational consensus can be achieved in the public sphere when conflicting needs and interests are concerned. When it comes to political conflicts, compromise is the only form of consensus that can be achieved if arguments should fail to persuade the other side.

Obviously, both Benhabib and McCarthy are not satisfied with Habermas's theory; they acknowledge the importance of the public sphere as a site of political and social debate, but at the same time they view Habermas's model as too inflexible for the concerns of a modern pluralistic society. I want to look at Benhabib's objections first and subsequently deal with McCarthy's more fundamental critique. Benhabib's criticism results in a curious way from her reading of Habermas's theory of communicative action. By stressing the procedural aspect of the public sphere, she also formalizes its structure: the ideal public sphere should be stripped of all those particular historical aspects that discriminate against individuals or groups in a given society. The ultimate norm of the public sphere is therefore egalitarian reciprocity. Measured against this standard, the existing public sphere is wanting. From a feminist point of view, for instance, the American public sphere is characterized by inequality not so much in terms of access as in terms of women's needs and interests, because, as Benhabib argues, the public sphere is constrained by the traditional distinction between public and private, which excludes concerns of women from public debate. Consequently, Benhabib wants to remove these traditional restrictions and broaden the public sphere in such a way that social and family issues concerning the good life come under public scrutiny. This means that Benhabib is less in disagreement with the theory of communicative action than with specific historical features of the liberal tradition (Kant, Rawls), namely its uncritical reliance on traditional European values in regard to the "intimate sphere."

In principle, Habermas's theory has no problems with making questions of the good life part of the public debate (among them questions of gender difference). The important point, however, is that these questions cannot be settled in the same manner as questions of justice, since values are culture-bound and cannot be generalized. Hence the insistence on procedural equality does not in and of itself solve problems of gender discrimination; it only enforces the admission of these problems to the realm of public debate. However, the crucial questions are, How can problems of gender discrimination be resolved within the public sphere? What mechanisms are available to reach a consensus? In this respect, I think, the reference to an ideal speech situation is less helpful than Benhabib assumes, because the substances of these issues are culture-bound and reflect the values of a particular community. Questions of the good life have to be argued and negotiated (as Habermas agrees) within a particular public space informed by specific cultural traditions. A theory of the public sphere must not lose this historical element as it defines and shapes the public space. In Habermas's early work this historical aspect was still taken for granted. Hence what Habermas conceptualized as *the* public sphere was in reality the public sphere of Western Europe. Benhabib makes a strong case for an extended public debate of "issues like child rearing; care for the sick, the young, and the elderly; reproductive freedoms;" etc. (sec. 3), but this debate will depend (in form and content) on the structure of the society involved, for instance, on the role of bureaucracies in advanced capitalist societies.

While Benhabib considers Habermas's discourse model as incomplete but basically sound, McCarthy takes a more skeptical view of its validity. His critique, strictly immanent, focuses on the question of rational consensus, using the distinction between demonstrative norms that can be derived from ultimate principles and norms the legitimacy of which depends on "the sociocultural contexts in which they are mobilized" (sec. 2). Following Habermas, he argues that most of the practical questions with which we are confronted in our lifeworlds cannot be solved through demonstrative arguments; instead, we have to reach a consensus through casuistic evidence. Still, Habermas's discourse ethics tries to transcend an unstable pluralism where individual needs and interests cancel each other. He wants to hold out the possibility of a consensus beyond a rationally negotiated compromise, i.e., a consensus based on the "impartial consideration of all interests affected."[1] For Habermas, McCarthy maintains, it is crucial that consensus (in regard to political or social problems) be grounded in an intersubjective understanding and assessment of needs (fairness). For McCarthy, this solution is not attainable, because there are, as Habermas concludes, no universally accepted standards of value. But like Habermas, McCarthy stresses the interdependence of norms and values, which means that "the separation of formal procedure from substantive content is never absolute" (sec. 2). This argument would certainly also subvert Benhabib's position, since her claim relies exclusively on formal procedures.

Practical discourse, McCarthy concludes, is not suitable as a normative ideal for discourse in the public sphere. Debates in the public sphere must not be expected to follow the logic of scientific or legal discourse. McCarthy's argument boils down to the fundamental distinction between values and demonstrative norms, between particular claims and general/universal considerations: a universalist justification of norms concerning political and social problems is not available, since these norms themselves are affected by cultural contexts. Consequently,

McCarthy has to redefine the conception as well as the function of the public sphere. In fact, for McCarthy, a discussion of *the* public sphere, as if it were a unified and homogeneous space, is no longer possible, because the procedures themselves do not guarantee a solution for the substantive issues. To put it differently, there is no *single* model of the public sphere, rather different societies have developed a variety of models with specific institutional and formal (procedural) features. In a roundabout way McCarthy's highly abstract argument coming out of Habermas' theory ultimately reintroduces history and historical particularities as the unavoidable context that cannot be eliminated by setting up formal procedures. The boundaries and the structure of the spaces where public debates of political and social issues take place are not stable; they have to be negotiated in accordance with the needs and values of the community.

This solution could be labeled "relativist," since it rejects the possibility of a demonstrative discourse for the solution of practical problems. In fact, this label itself might well serve as a (Habermasian) argument against McCarthy's position. In abandoning a model of the public sphere where conflicting interests and needs can be compared and evaluated through reason, McCarthy undercuts his own position, which makes use of rational arguments. To avoid irrational consequences, we have to define a level of rationality that allows us to transcend instrumental reason. Without rationality/reason as an Archimedian point, public debates seem futile. Hence an argumentative discourse is constitutive for the public sphere. Yet from McCarthy's point of view, this opposition between reason and irrationalism is problematic insofar as it underestimates local and particular rationality. This kind of rationality does not claim to provide a conclusive mechanism for creating a consensus, but it offers a comparative analysis of competing needs and values up to the point where a compromise can be negotiated. In other words, *rational* debate is possible without the presupposition of demonstrative universal norms. It seems to me that a weaker claim of rationality might ultimately be more fruitful for a highly pluralistic world where differences of race, class, and gender cannot be overlooked.

In *Strukturwandel* Habermas demonstrated the close connection between the political public sphere and the literary public sphere during the eighteenth and early nineteenth centuries. The debate in the literary public sphere (criticism), Habermas argued, prepared the discussion in the political public sphere. This cultural component is completely missing in Benhabib's and McCarthy's essays, since both of them come from Habermas's recent work on moral theory. In the case of Benhabib this omission is almost inevitable because cultural concerns cannot be generalized. In the case of McCarthy, on the other hand, the cultural component should come more into the foreground, since what Habermas used to call the "literary public sphere" is precisely the locus where problems of identity and difference have been articulated. National images and stereotypes, to give but one example, had been a significant part of the literary discourse of the eighteenth century before they entered the political discourse of the nineteenth and twentieth centuries. To emphasize the *public* nature of the cultural sphere is so important because political theorists tend to marginalize cultural (especially aesthetic) questions as private, personal, "nicht wahrheitsfähig" (not truth or false), and therefore ultimately irrelevant for the process of political decision making. A rigid distinction between the political and the cultural spheres, as it is reinforced by contemporary political institutions, will necessarily constrain our understanding of those concerns that come under the category the good life. In this context it is not accidental, therefore, that much of contemporary feminist theory has been developed within literary theory.

Note

1. Jürgen Habermas, *The Theory of Communicative Action* (Boston, 1987), vol. 2, p. 94. Quoted by McCarthy, sec. 2.

5

Rethinking the Public Sphere: A Contribution to the Critique of Actually Existing Democracy

Nancy Fraser

1 Introduction

Today in the United States we hear a great deal of ballyhoo about "the triumph of liberal democracy" and even "the end of history." Yet there is still quite a lot to object to in our own actually existing democracy, and the project of a critical theory of the limits of democracy in late-capitalist societies remains as relevant as ever. In fact, this project seems to me to have acquired a new urgency at a time when "liberal democracy" is being touted as the *ne plus ultra* of social systems for countries that are emerging from Soviet-style state socialism, Latin American military dictatorships, and southern African regimes of racial domination.

Those of us who remain committed to theorizing the limits of democracy in late-capitalist societies will find in the work of Jürgen Habermas an indispensable resource. I mean the concept of "the public sphere," originally elaborated in his 1962 book, *The Structural Transformation of the Public Sphere,* and subsequently resituated but never abandoned in his later work.[1]

The political and theoretical importance of this idea is easy to explain. Habermas's concept of the public sphere provides a way of circumventing some confusions that have plagued progressive social movements and the political theories associated with them. Take, for example, the longstanding failure in the dominant wing of the socialist and Marxist tradition to appreciate the full force of the distinction between the apparatuses of the state, on the one hand, and public arenas of citizen discourse and association, on the other. All too often it was assumed in this tradition that to subject the economy to the control of the socialist state was to subject it to the control of the socialist citizenry. Of course, that was not so. But the conflation of the state apparatus with the public sphere of discourse and association provided ballast to processes whereby the socialist vision became institutionalized in an authoritarian-statist form instead of in a participatory-democratic form. The result has been to jeopardize the very idea of socialist democracy.

A second problem, albeit one that has so far been much less historically momentous and certainly less tragic, is a confusion one encounters at times in contemporary feminisms. I mean a confusion that involves the use of the very same expression "the public sphere" but in a sense that is less precise and less useful than Habermas's. This expression has been used by many feminists to refer to everything that is outside the domestic or familial sphere. Thus "the public sphere" on this usage conflates at least three analytically distinct things: the state, the official economy of paid employment, and arenas of public discourse.[2] Now it should not be thought that the conflation of these three things is a merely theoretical issue. On the contrary, it has practical political consequences when, for example, agitational campaigns against misogynist cultural representations are confounded with programs for state censorship or when struggles to deprivatize housework and child care are equated with their commodification. In both these cases the result is to occlude the question of whether to subject gender issues to the logic of the market or of the administrative state is to promote the liberation of women.

The idea of "the public sphere" in Habermas's sense is a conceptual resource that can help overcome such problems. It designates a theater in modern societies in which political participation is enacted through the medium of talk. It is the space in which citizens deliberate about their common affairs, and hence an institutionalized arena of discursive interaction. This arena is conceptually distinct from the state; it is a site for the production and circulation of discourses that can in principle be critical of the state. The public sphere in Habermas's sense is also conceptually distinct from the official economy; it is not an arena of market relations but rather one of discursive relations, a theater for debating and deliberating rather than for buying and selling. Thus this concept of the public sphere permits us to keep in view the distinctions among state apparatuses, economic markets, and democratic associations, distinctions that are essential to democratic theory.

For these reasons I am going to take as a basic premise for this essay that something like Habermas's idea of the public sphere is indispensable to critical social theory and democratic political practice. I assume that no attempt to understand the limits of actually existing late-capitalist democracy can succeed without in some way or another making use of it. I assume that the same goes for urgently needed constructive efforts to project alternative models of democracy.

If you will grant me that the general idea of the public sphere is indispensable to critical theory, then I shall go on to argue that the specific form in which Habermas has elaborated this idea is not wholly satisfactory. On the contrary, I contend that his analysis of the public sphere needs to undergo some critical interrogation and reconstruction if it is to yield a category capable of theorizing the limits of actually existing democracy.

Let me remind you that the subtitle of *Structural Transformation* is "An Inquiry into a Category of Bourgeois Society." The object of the inquiry is the rise and decline of a historically specific and limited form of the public sphere, which Habermas calls the "liberal model of the bourgeois public sphere." The aim is to identify the conditions that made possible this type of public sphere and to chart their devolution. The upshot is an argument that under altered conditions of late-twentieth-century "welfare state mass democracy," the bourgeois or liberal model of the public sphere is no longer feasible. Some new form of public sphere is required to salvage that arena's critical function and to institutionalize democracy.

Oddly, Habermas stops short of developing a new, post-bourgeois model of the public sphere. Moreover, he never explicitly problematizes some dubious assumptions that underlie the bourgeois model. As a result, we are left at the end of

Structural Transformation without a conception of the public sphere that is sufficiently distinct from the bourgeois conception to serve the needs of critical theory today.

That, at any rate, is the thesis I intend to argue. To make my case, I shall proceed as follows: I shall begin in section 2 by juxtaposing Habermas's account of the structural transformation of the public sphere with an alternative account that can be pieced together from some recent revisionist historiography. Then I shall identify four assumptions underlying the bourgeois conception of the public sphere, as Habermas describes it, that this newer historiography renders suspect. Next in the following four sections I shall examine each of these assumptions in turn. Finally, in a brief conclusion I shall draw together some strands from these critical discussions that point toward an alternative, postbourgeois conception of the public sphere.

2   The Public Sphere: Alternative Histories, Competing Conceptions

Let me begin by sketching some highlights of Habermas's account of the structural transformation of the public sphere. According to Habermas, the idea of a public sphere is that of a body of "private persons" assembled to discuss matters of "public concern" or "common interest." This idea acquired force and reality in early modern Europe in the constitution of "bourgeois public spheres" as counterweights to absolutist states. These publics aimed to mediate between society and the state by holding the state accountable to society via publicity. At first this meant requiring that information about state functioning be made accessible so that state activities would be subject to critical scrutiny and the force of public opinion. Later it meant transmitting the considered "general interest" of "bourgeois society" to the state via forms of legally guaranteed free speech, free press, and free assembly, and eventually through the parliamentary institutions of representative government.

Thus at one level the idea of the public sphere designated an institutional mechanism for rationalizing political domination by rendering states accountable to (some of) the citizenry.

At another level, it designated a specific kind of discursive interaction. Here the public sphere connoted an ideal of unrestricted rational discussion of public matters. The discussion was to be open and accessible to all, merely private interests were to be inadmissible, inequalities of status were to be bracketed, and discussants were to deliberate as peers. The result of such discussion would be public opinion in the strong sense of a consensus about the common good.

According to Habermas, the full utopian potential of the bourgeois conception of the public sphere was never realized in practice. The claim to open access in particular was not made good. Moreover, the bourgeois conception of the public sphere was premised on a social order in which the state was sharply differentiated from the newly privatized market economy; it was this clear separation of society and state that was supposed to underpin a form of public discussion that excluded "private interests." But these conditions eventually eroded as nonbourgeois strata gained access to the public sphere. Then "the social question" came to the fore, society was polarized by class struggle, and the public fragmented into a mass of competing interest groups. Street demonstrations and back room, brokered compromises among private interests replaced reasoned public debate about the common good. Finally, with the emergence of welfare-state mass democracy, society and the state became mutually intertwined; publicity in the sense of critical scrutiny of the state gave way to public relations, mass-mediated staged displays and the manufacture and manipulation of public opinion.

Now let me juxtapose to this sketch of Habermas's account an alternative account that I shall piece together from some recent revisionist historiography. Briefly, scholars like Joan Landes, Mary Ryan, and Geoff Eley contend that Habermas's account idealizes the liberal public sphere. The argue that, despite the rhetoric of publicity and accessibility, the official public sphere rested on, indeed was importantly constituted by, a number of significant exclusions. For Landes, the key axis of exclusion is gender; she argues that the ethos of the new republican public sphere in France was constructed in deliberate opposition to that of a more woman-friendly salon culture that the republicans stigmatized as "artificial," "effeminate," and "aristocratic." Consequently, a new, austere style of public speech and behavior was promoted, a style deemed "rational," "virtuous," and "manly." In this way masculinist gender constructs were built into the very conception of the republican public sphere, as was a logic that led, at the height of Jacobin rule, to the formal exclusion of women from political life.[3] Here the republicans drew on classical traditions that cast femininity and publicity as oxymorons; the depth of such traditions can be gauged in the etymological connection between "public" and "pubic," a graphic trace of the fact that in the ancient world possession of a penis was a requirement for speaking in public. (A similar link is preserved, incidentally, in the etymological connection between "testimony" and "testicle."[4])

Extending Landes's argument, Geoff Eley contends that exclusionary operations were essential to liberal public spheres not only in France but also in England and Germany and that in all these countries gender exclusions were linked to other exclusions rooted in processes of class formation. In all these countries, he claims, the soil that nourished the liberal public sphere was "civil society," the emerging new congeries of voluntary associations that sprung up in what came to be known as "the age of societies." But this network of clubs and associations—philanthropic, civic, professional, and cultural—was anything but accessible to everyone. On the contrary, it was the arena, the training ground, and eventually the power base of a stratum of bourgeois men who were coming to see themselves as a "universal class" and preparing to assert their fitness to govern. Thus the elaboration of a distinctive culture of civil society and of an associated public sphere was implicated in the process of bourgeois class formation; its practices and ethos were markers of "distinction" in Pierre Bourdieu's sense, ways of defining an emergent elite, of setting it off from the older aristocratic elites it was intent on displacing on the one hand and from the various popular and plebeian strata it aspired to rule on the other.[5] Moreover, this process of distinction helps explain the exacerbation of sexism characteristic of the liberal public sphere; new gender norms enjoining feminine domesticity and a sharp separation of public and private spheres functioned as key signifiers of bourgeois difference from both higher and lower social strata. It is a measure of the eventual success of this bourgeois project that these norms later became hegemonic, sometimes imposed on, sometimes embraced by, broader segments of society.[6]

There is a remarkable irony here, one that Habermas's account of the rise of the public sphere fails fully to appreciate.[7] A discourse of publicity touting accessibility, rationality, and the suspension of status hierarchies is itself deployed as a strategy of distinction. Of course, in and of itself this irony does not fatally compromise the discourse of publicity; that discourse can be, indeed has been, differently deployed in different circumstances and contexts. Nevertheless, it does suggest that the relationship between publicity and status is more complex than Habermas intimates, that declaring a deliberative arena to be a space where extant status distinctions are bracketed and neutralized is not sufficient to make it so.

Moreover, the problem is not only that Habermas idealizes the liberal public sphere but also that he fails to examine other, nonliberal, nonbourgeois, competing public spheres. Or rather, it is precisely because he fails to examine these other public spheres that he ends up idealizing the liberal public sphere.[8] Mary Ryan documents the variety of ways in which nineteenth-century North American women of various classes and ethnicities constructed access routes to public political life, even despite their exclusion from the official public sphere. In the case of elite bourgeois women, this involved building a counter civil society of alternative, woman-only, voluntary associations, including philanthropic and moral-reform societies. In some respects, these associations aped the all-male societies built by these women's fathers and grandfathers, yet in other respects the women were innovating, since they creatively used the heretofore quintessentially "private" idioms of domesticity and motherhood precisely as springboards for public activity. Meanwhile, for some less privileged women, access to public life came through participation in supporting roles in male-dominated working-class protest activities. Still other women found public outlets in street protests and parades. Finally, women's-rights advocates publicly contested both women's exclusion from the official public sphere and the privatization of gender politics.[9]

Ryan's study shows that even in the absence of formal political incorporation through suffrage, there were a variety of ways of accessing public life and a multiplicity of public arenas. Thus the view that women were excluded from the public sphere turns out to be ideological; it rests on a class- and gender-biased notion of publicity, one which accepts at face value the bourgeois public's claim to be *the* public. In fact, the historiography of Ryan and others demonstrates that the bourgeois public was never *the* public. On the contrary, virtually contemporaneous with the bourgeois public there arose a host of competing counterpublics, including nationalist publics, popular peasant publics, elite women's publics, and working-class publics. Thus there were competing publics from the start, not just in the late nineteenth and twentieth centuries, as Habermas implies.[10]

Moreover, not only were there always a plurality of competing publics, but the relations between bourgeois publics and other publics were always conflictual. Virtually from the beginning, counterpublics contested the exclusionary norms of the bourgeois public, elaborating alternative styles of political behavior and alternative norms of public speech. Bourgeois publics in turn excoriated these alternatives and deliberately sought to block broader participation. As Eley puts it, "the emergence of a bourgeois public was never defined solely by the struggle against absolutism and traditional authority, but . . . addressed the problem of popular containment as well. The public sphere was always constituted by conflict."[11]

In general, this revisionist historiography suggests a much darker view of the bourgeois public sphere than the one that emerges from Habermas's study. The exclusions and conflicts that appeared as accidental trappings from his perspective become constitutive in the revisionists' view. The result is a gestalt switch that alters the very meaning of the public sphere. We can no longer assume that the bourgeois conception of the public sphere was simply an unrealized utopian ideal; it was also a masculinist ideological notion that functioned to legitimate an emergent form of class rule. Therefore, Eley draws a

Gramscian moral from the story: the official bourgeois public sphere is the institutional vehicle for a major historical transformation in the nature of political domination. This is the shift from a repressive mode of domination to a hegemonic one, from rule based primarily on acquiescence to superior force to rule based primarily on consent supplemented with some measure of repression.[12] The important point is that this new mode of political domination, like the older one, secures the ability of one stratum of society to rule the rest. The official public sphere, then, was, and indeed is, the prime institutional site for the construction of the consent that defines the new, hegemonic mode of domination.[13]

What conclusions should we draw from this conflict of historical interpretations? Should we conclude that the very concept of the public sphere is a piece of bourgeois, masculinist ideology so thoroughly compromised that it can shed no genuinely critical light on the limits of actually existing democracy? Or should we conclude rather that the public sphere was a good idea that unfortunately was not realized in practice but retains some emancipatory force? In short, is the idea of the public sphere an instrument of domination or a utopian ideal?

Well, perhaps both, but actually neither. I contend that both of those conclusions are too extreme and unsupple to do justice to the material I have been discussing.[14] Instead of endorsing either one of them, I want to propose a more nuanced alternative. I shall argue that the revisionist historiography neither undermines nor vindicates *the* concept of the public sphere *simpliciter*, but that it calls into question four assumptions that are central to the *bourgeois, masculinist* conception of the public sphere, at least as Habermas describes it. These are as follows:

• The assumption that it is possible for interlocutors in a public sphere to bracket status differentials and to deliberate *as if* they were social equals; the assumption, therefore, that societal equality is not a necessary condition for political democracy

• The assumption that the proliferation of a multiplicity of competing publics is necessarily a step away from, rather than toward, greater democracy, and that a single, comprehensive public sphere is always preferable to a nexus of multiple publics

• The assumption that discourse in public spheres should be restricted to deliberation about the common good, and that the appearance of private interests and private issues is always undesirable

• The assumption that a functioning democratic public sphere requires a sharp separation between civil society and the state

Let me consider each of these in turn.

3 Open Access, Participatory Parity, and Social Equality

Habermas's account of the bourgeois conception of the public sphere stresses its claim to be open and accessible to all. Indeed, this idea of open access is one of the central meanings of the norm of publicity. Of course, we know both from revisionist history and from Habermas's account that the bourgeois public's claim to full accessibility was not in fact realized. Women of all classes and ethnicities were excluded from official political participation on the basis of gender status, while plebeian men were formally excluded by property qualifications. Moreover, in many cases women and men of racialized ethnicities of all classes were excluded on racial grounds.

What are we to make of this historical fact of the nonrealization in practice of the bourgeois public sphere's ideal of open access? One approach is to conclude that the ideal itself remains unaffected, since it is possible in principle to overcome these exclusions. And in fact, it was only a matter of time before formal exclusions based on gender, property, and race were eliminated.

This is convincing enough as far as it goes, but it does not go far enough. The question of open access cannot be reduced without remainder to the presence or absence of formal exclusions. It requires us to look also at the process of discursive interaction within formally inclusive public arenas. Here we should recall that the bourgeois conception of the public sphere requires bracketing inequalities of status. This public sphere was to be an arena in which interlocutors would set aside such characteristics as differences in birth and fortune and speak to one another as if they were social and economic peers. The operative phrase here is "as if." In fact, the social inequalities among the interlocutors were not eliminated but only bracketed.

But were they really effectively bracketed? The revisionist historiography suggests they were not. Rather, discursive interaction within the bourgeois public sphere was governed by protocols of style and decorum that were themselves correlates and markers of status inequality. These functioned informally to marginalize women and members of the plebeian classes and to prevent them from participating as peers.

Here we are talking about informal impediments to participatory parity that can persist even after everyone is formally and legally licensed to participate. That these constitute a more serious challenge to the bourgeois conception of the public sphere can be seen from a familiar contemporary example. Feminist research has documented a syndrome that many of us have observed in faculty meetings and other mixed-sex deliberative bodies: men tend to interrupt women more than women interrupt men; men also tend to speak more than women, taking more turns and longer turns; and women's interventions are more often ignored or not responded to than men's. In response to the sorts of experiences documented in this research, an important strand of feminist political theory has claimed that deliberation can serve as a mask for domination. Theorists like Jane Mansbridge have argued that "the transformation of 'I' into 'we' brought about through political deliberation can easily mask subtle forms of control. Even the language people use as they reason together usually favors one way of seeing things and discourages others. Subordinate groups sometimes cannot find the right voice or words to express their thoughts, and when they do, they discover they are not heard. [They] are silenced, encouraged to keep their wants inchoate, and heard to say 'yes' when what they have said is 'no.'"[15] Mansbridge rightly notes that many of these feminist insights into ways in which deliberation can serve as a mask for domination extend beyond gender to other kinds of unequal relations, like those based on class or ethnicity. They alert us to the ways in which social inequalities can infect deliberation, even in the absence of any formal exclusions.

Here I think we encounter a very serious difficulty with the bourgeois conception of the public sphere. Insofar as the bracketing of social inequalities in deliberation means proceeding as if they don't exist when they do, this does not foster participatory parity. On the contrary, such bracketing usually works to the advantage of dominant groups in society and to the disadvantage of subordinates. In most cases it would be more appropriate to *unbracket* inequalities in the sense of explicitly thematizing them—a point that accords with the spirit of Habermas's later communicative ethics.

The misplaced faith in the efficacy of bracketing suggests another flaw in the bourgeois conception. This conception assumes that a public sphere is or can be a space of zero degree culture, so utterly bereft of any specific ethos as to accommodate with perfect neutrality and equal ease interventions expressive of any and every cultural ethos. But this assumption is counterfactual, and not for reasons that are merely accidental. In stratified societies, unequally empowered social groups tend to develop unequally valued cultural styles. The result is the development of powerful informal pressures that marginalize the contributions of members of subordinated groups both in everyday contexts and in official public spheres.[16] Moreover, these pressures are amplified, rather than mitigated, by the peculiar political economy of the bourgeois public sphere. In this public sphere the media that constitute the material support for the circulation of views are privately owned and operated for profit. Consequently, subordinated social groups usually lack equal access to the material means of equal participation.[17] Thus political economy enforces structurally what culture accomplishes informally.

If we take these considerations seriously, then we should be led to entertain serious doubts about a conception of the public sphere that purports to bracket, rather than to eliminate, structural social inequalities. We should question whether it is possible even in principle for interlocutors to deliberate *as if* they were social peers in specially designated discursive arenas when these discursive arenas are situated in a larger societal context that is pervaded by structural relations of dominance and subordination.

What is at stake here is the autonomy of specifically political institutions vis-à-vis the surrounding societal context. Now one salient feature that distinguishes liberalism from some other political-theoretical orientations is that liberalism assumes the autonomy of the political in a very strong form. Liberal political theory assumes that it is possible to organize a democratic form of political life on the basis of socioeconomic and sociosexual structures that generate systemic inequalities. For liberals, then, the problem of democracy becomes the problem of how to insulate political processes from what are considered to be nonpolitical or prepolitical processes, those characteristic, for example, of the economy, the family, and informal everyday life. The problem for liberals is thus how to strengthen the barriers separating political institutions that are supposed to instantiate relations of equality from economic, cultural, and sociosexual institutions that are premised on systemic relations of inequality.[18] Yet the weight of circumstance suggests that to have a public sphere in which interlocutors can deliberate as peers, it is not sufficient merely to bracket social inequality. Instead, a necessary condition for participatory parity is that systemic social inequalities be eliminated. This does not mean that everyone must have exactly the same income, but it does require the sort of rough equality that is inconsistent with systemically generated relations of dominance and subordination. *Pace* liberalism, then, political democracy requires substantive social equality.[19]

I have been arguing that the bourgeois conception of the public sphere is inadequate insofar as it supposes that social equality is not a necessary condition for participatory parity in public spheres. What follows from this for the critique of actually existing democracy? One task for critical theory is to render visible the ways in which societal inequality infects formally inclusive existing public spheres and taints discursive interaction within them.

4 Equality, Diversity, and Multiple Publics

So far I have been discussing what we might call "intrapublic relations," that is, the character and quality of discursive interactions within a given public sphere. Now I want to consider what we might call "interpublic relations," that is, the character of interactions among different publics.

Let me begin by recalling that Habermas's account stresses the singularity of the bourgeois conception of the public sphere, its claim to be *the* public arena, in the singular. In addition, his narrative tends in this respect to be faithful to that conception, since it casts the emergence of additional publics as a late development signaling fragmentation and decline. This narrative, then, like the bourgeois conception itself, is informed by an underlying evaluative assumption, namely, that the institutional confinement of public life to a single, overarching public sphere is a positive and desirable state of affairs, whereas the proliferation of a multiplicity of publics represents a departure from, rather than an advance toward, democracy. It is this normative assumption that I now want to scrutinize. In this section I shall assess the relative merits of a single, comprehensive public versus multiple publics in two kinds of modern societies: stratified societies and egalitarian multicultural societies.[20]

First, let me consider the case of stratified societies, by which I mean societies whose basic institutional framework generates unequal social groups in structural relations of dominance and subordination. I have already argued that in such societies, full parity of participation in public debate and deliberation is not within the reach of possibility. The question to be addressed here then is, What form of public life comes closest to approaching that ideal? What institutional arrangements will best help narrow the gap in participatory parity between dominant and subordinate groups?

I contend that in stratified societies, arrangements that accommodate contestation among a plurality of competing publics better promote the ideal of participatory parity than does a single, comprehensive, overarching public. This follows from the argument of the previous section. There I argued that it is not possible to insulate special discursive arenas from the effects of societal inequality and that where societal inequality persists, deliberative processes in public spheres will tend to operate to the advantage of dominant groups and to the disadvantage of subordinates. Now I want to add that these effects will be exacerbated where there is only a single, comprehensive public sphere. In that case, members of subordinated groups would have no arenas for deliberation among themselves about their needs, objectives, and strategies. They would have no venues in which to undertake communicative processes that were not, as it were, under the supervision of dominant groups. In this situation they would be less likely than otherwise to "find the right voice or words to express their thoughts" and more likely than otherwise "to keep their wants inchoate." This would render them less able than otherwise to articulate and defend their interests in the comprehensive public sphere. They would be less able than otherwise to expose modes of deliberation that mask domination by, in Mansbridge's words, "absorbing the less powerful into a false 'we' that reflects the more powerful."

This argument gains additional support from revisionist historiography of the public sphere, up to and including that of very recent developments. This historiography records that members of subordinated social groups—women, workers, peoples of color, and gays and lesbians—have repeatedly found it advantageous to constitute alternative publics. I propose to call these *subaltern counterpublics* in order to signal that they are parallel discursive arenas where members of subordinated social groups invent and circulate counterdiscourses to formulate oppositional interpretations of their identities, interests, and needs.[21] Perhaps the most striking example is the late-twentieth-century U.S. feminist subaltern counterpublic, with its variegated array of journals, bookstores, publishing companies, film and video distribution networks, lecture series, research centers, academic programs, conferences, conventions, festivals, and local meeting places. In this public sphere, feminist women have invented new terms for describing social reality, including "sexism," "the double shift," "sexual harassment," and "marital, date, and acquaintance rape." Armed with such language, we have recast our needs and identities, thereby reducing, although not eliminating, the extent of our disadvantage in official public spheres.[22]

Let me not be misunderstood. I do not mean to suggest that subaltern counterpublics are always necessarily virtuous. Some of them, alas, are explicitly antidemocratic and antiegalitarian, and even those with democratic and egalitarian intentions are not always above practicing their own modes of informal exclusion and marginalization. Still, insofar as these counterpublics emerge in response to exclusions within dominant publics, they help expand discursive space. In principle, assumptions that were previously exempt from contestation will now have to be publicly argued out. In general, the proliferation of subaltern counterpublics means a widening of discursive contestation, and that is a good thing in stratified societies.

I am emphasizing the contestatory function of subaltern counterpublics in stratified societies in part to complicate the issue of separatism. In my view, the concept of a counterpublic militates in the long run against separatism because it assumes a *publicist* orientation. Insofar as these arenas are *publics,* they are by definition not enclaves, which is not to deny that they are often involuntarily enclav*ed.* After all, to interact discursively as a member of public, subaltern or otherwise, is to aspire to disseminate one's discourse to ever widening arenas. Habermas captures well this aspect of the meaning of publicity when he notes that, however limited a public may be in its empirical manifestation at any given time, its members understand themselves as part of a potentially wider public, that indeterminate, empirically counterfactual body we call "the public at large." The point is that in stratified societies, subaltern counterpublics have a dual character. On the one hand, they function as spaces of withdrawal and regroupment; on the other hand, they also function as bases and training grounds for agitational activities directed toward wider publics. It is precisely in the dialectic between these two functions that their emancipatory potential resides. This dialectic enables subaltern counterpublics partially to offset, although not wholly to eradicate, the unjust participatory privileges enjoyed by members of dominant social groups in stratified societies.

So far I have been arguing that, although in stratified societies the ideal of participatory parity is not fully realizable, it is more closely approximated by arrangements that permit contestation among a plurality of competing publics than by a single, comprehensive public sphere. Of course, contestation among competing publics supposes interpublic discursive interaction. How, then, should we understand such interaction? Geoff Eley suggests that we think of the public sphere (in stratified societies) as "the structured setting where cultural and ideological contest or negotiation among a variety of publics takes place."[23] This formulation does justice to the multiplicity of public arenas in stratified societies by expressly acknowledging the presence and activity of "a variety of publics." At the same time, it also does justice to the fact that these various publics are situated in a single "structured setting" that advantages some and disadvantages others. Finally, Eley's formulation does justice to the fact that in stratified societies the discursive relations among differentially empowered publics are as likely to take the form of contestation as that of deliberation.

Let me now consider the relative merits of multiple publics versus a single public for egalitarian, multicultural societies. By "egalitarian societies" I mean nonstratified societies, societies whose basic framework does not generate unequal social groups in structural relations of dominance and subordination. Egalitarian societies, therefore, are societies without classes and without gender or racial divisions of labor. However, they need not be culturally homogeneous. On the contrary, provided such societies permit free expression and association, they are likely to be inhabited by social groups with diverse values, identities, and cultural styles, and hence to be multicultural. My question is, Under conditions of cultural diversity in the absence of structural inequality, would a single, comprehensive public sphere be preferable to multiple publics?

To answer this question, we need to take a closer look at the relationship between public discourse and social identities. *Pace* the bourgeois conception, public spheres are not only arenas for the formation of discursive opinion; in addition, they are arenas for the formation and enactment of social identities.[24] This means that participation is not simply a matter of being able to state propositional contents that are neutral with respect to form of expression. Rather, as I argued in the previous section, participation means being able to speak in one's own voice, and thereby simultaneously to construct and express one's cultural identity through idiom and style.[25] Moreover, as I also suggested, public spheres themselves are not spaces of zero-degree culture, equally hospitable to any possible form of cultural expression. Rather, they consist in culturally specific institutions, including, for example, various journals and various social geographies of urban space. These institutions may be understood as culturally specific rhetorical lenses that filter and alter the utterances they frame; they can accommodate some expressive modes and not others.[26]

It follows that public life in egalitarian, multicultural societies cannot consist exclusively in a single, comprehensive public sphere. That would be tantamount to filtering diverse rhetorical and stylistic norms through a single, overarching lens. Moreover, since there can be no such lens that is genuinely culturally neutral, it would effectively privilege the expressive norms of one cultural group over others and thereby make discursive assimilation a condition for participation in public debate. The result would be the demise of multiculturalism (and the likely demise of social equality). In general, then, we can conclude that the idea of an egalitarian, multicultural society only makes sense if we suppose a plurality of public arenas in which groups with diverse values and rhetorics participate. By definition, such a society must contain a multiplicity of publics.

However, this need not preclude the possibility of an additional, more comprehensive arena in which members of different, more limited publics talk across lines of cultural diversity. On the contrary, our hypothetical egalitarian, multicultural society would surely have to entertain debates over policies and issues affecting everyone. The question is, Would participants in such debates share enough in the way of values, expressive norms, and therefore protocols of persuasion to lend their talk the quality of deliberations aimed at reaching agreement through giving reasons?

In my view, this is better treated as an empirical question than as a conceptual question. I see no reason to rule out in principle the possibility of a society in which social equality and cultural diversity coexist with participatory democracy. I certainly hope there can be such a society. That hope gains some plausibility if we consider that, however difficult it may be, communication across lines of cultural difference is not in principle impossible, although it will certainly become impossible if one imagines that it requires bracketing of differences. Granted, such communication requires multicultural literacy, but that, I believe, can be acquired through practice. In fact, the possibilities expand once we acknowledge the complexity of cultural identities. *Pace* reductive, essentialist conceptions, cultural identities are woven of many different strands, and some of these strands may be common to people whose identities otherwise diverge, even when it is the divergences that are most salient.[27] Likewise, under conditions of social equality, the porousness, outer-directedness, and open-endedness of publics could promote intercultural communication. After all, the concept of a public presupposes a plurality of perspectives among those who participate within it, thereby allowing for internal differences and antagonisms and discouraging reified blocs.[28] In addition, the unbounded character and publicist orientation of publics allows people to participate in more than one public, and it allows memberships of different publics partially to overlap. This in turn makes intercultural communication conceivable in principle. All told, then, there do not seem to be any conceptual (as opposed to empirical) barriers to the possibility of a socially egalitarian, multicultural society that is also a participatory democracy. But this will necessarily be a society with many different publics, including at least one public in which participants can deliberate as peers across lines of difference about policy that concerns them all.

In general, I have been arguing that the ideal of participatory parity is better achieved by a multiplicity of publics than by a single public. This is true both for stratified societies and for egalitarian, multicultural societies, albeit for different reasons. In neither case is my argument intended as a simple postmodern celebration of multiplicity. Rather, in the case of stratified societies, I am defending subaltern counterpublics formed under conditions of dominance and subordination. In the other case, by contrast, I am defending the possibility of combining social equality, cultural diversity, and participatory democracy.

What are the implications of this discussion for a critical theory of the public sphere in actually existing democracy? Briefly, we need a critical political sociology of a form of public life in which multiple but unequal publics participate. This means theorizing about the contestatory interaction of different publics and identifying the mechanisms that render some of them subordinate to others.

5 Public Spheres, Common Concerns, and Private Interests

I have argued that in stratified societies, like it or not, subaltern counterpublics stand in a contestatory relationship to dominant publics. One important object of such interpublic contestation is the appropriate boundaries of the public sphere. Here the central questions are, What counts as a public matter? What, in contrast, is private? This brings me to a third set of problematic assumptions underlying the bourgeois conception of the public sphere, namely, assumptions concerning the appropriate scope of publicity in relation to privacy.

Let me remind you that it is central to Habermas's account that the bourgeois public sphere was to be a discursive arena in which "private persons" deliberated about "public matters." There are several different senses of "private" and "public" in play here. "Public," for example, can mean (1) state-related, (2) accessible to everyone, (3) of concern to everyone, and (4) pertaining to a common good or shared interest. Each of these corresponds to a contrasting sense of "private." In addition, there are two other senses of "private" hovering just below the surface here: (5) pertaining to private property in a market economy and (6) pertaining to intimate domestic or personal life, including sexual life.

I have already talked at length about the sense of "public" as open or accessible to all. Now I want to examine some of the other senses, beginning with (3), of concern to everyone.[29] This is ambiguous between what objectively affects or has an impact on everyone as seen from an outsider's perspective, and

what is recognized as a matter of common concern by participants. The idea of a public sphere as an arena of collective
self-determination does not sit well with approaches that would
appeal to an outsider's perspective to delimit its proper boundaries. Thus it is the second, participant's perspective that is
relevant here. Only participants themselves can decide what is
and what is not of common concern to them. However, there
is no guarantee that all of them will agree. For example, until
quite recently, feminists were in the minority in thinking that
domestic violence against women was a matter of common
concern and thus a legitimate topic of public discourse. The
great majority of people considered this issue to be a private
matter between what was assumed to be a fairly small number
of heterosexual couples (and perhaps the social and legal
professionals who were supposed to deal with them). Then
feminists formed a subaltern counterpublic from which we
disseminated a view of domestic violence as a widespread systemic feature of male-dominated societies. Eventually, after
sustained discursive contestation, we succeeded in *making* it a
common concern.

The point is that there are no naturally given, a priori boundaries here. What will count as a matter of common concern
will be decided precisely through discursive contestation. It
follows that no topics should be ruled off limits in advance of
such contestation. On the contrary, democratic publicity requires positive guarantees of opportunities for minorities to
convince others that what in the past was not public in the
sense of being a matter of common concern should now become so.[30]

What, then, of the sense of "publicity" as pertaining to a
common good or shared interest? This is the sense that is in
play when Habermas characterizes the bourgeois public sphere
as an arena in which the topic of discussion is restricted to the
"common good" and in which discussion of "private interests"
is ruled out. This is a view of the public sphere that we would
today call civic-republican, as opposed to liberal-individualist.
Briefly, the civic-republican model stresses a view of politics as
people reasoning together to promote a common good that
transcends the mere sum of individual preferences. The idea

is that through deliberation the members of the public can come to discover or create such a common good. In the process of their deliberations, participants are transformed from a collection of self-seeking, private individuals into a public-spirited collectivity, capable of acting together in the common interest. On this view, private interests have no proper place in the political public sphere. At best, they are the prepolitical starting point of deliberation, to be transformed and transcended in the course of debate.[31]

This civic-republican view of the public sphere is in one respect an improvement over the liberal-individualist alternative. Unlike the latter, it does not assume that people's preferences, interests, and identities are given exogenously in advance of public discourse and deliberation. It appreciates, rather, that preferences, interests, and identities are as much outcomes as antecedents of public deliberation; indeed, they are discursively constituted in and through it. However, the civic-republican view contains a very serious confusion, one that blunts its critical edge. This view conflates the ideas of deliberation and the common good by assuming that deliberation must be deliberation *about* the common good. Consequently, it limits deliberation to talk framed from the standpoint of a single, all-encompassing "we," thereby ruling claims of self-interest and group interest out of order. Yet, as Jane Mansbridge has argued, this works against one of the principal aims of deliberation, namely, to help participants clarify their interests, even when those interests turn out to conflict. "Ruling self-interest [and group interest] out of order makes it harder for any participant to sort out what is going on. In particular, the less powerful may not find ways to discover that the prevailing sense of "we" does not adequately include them."[32]

In general, there is no way to know in advance whether the outcome of a deliberative process will be the discovery of a common good in which conflicts of interest evaporate as merely apparent or the discovery that conflicts of interest are real and the common good is chimerical. But if the existence of a common good cannot be presumed in advance, then there is no warrant for putting any strictures on what sorts of topics, interests, and views are admissible in deliberation.[33]

This argument holds even in the best-case scenario of societies whose basic institutional frameworks do not generate systemic inequalities; even in such relatively egalitarian societies, we cannot assume in advance that there will be no real conflicts of interest. How much more pertinent, then, the argument is to stratified societies, which are traversed with pervasive relations of inequality. After all, when social arrangements operate to the systemic profit of some groups of people and to the systemic detriment of others, there are prima facie reasons for thinking that the postulation of a common good shared by exploiters and exploited may well be a mystification. Moreover, any consensus that purports to represent the common good in this social context should be regarded with suspicion, since this consensus will have been reached through deliberative processes tainted by the effects of dominance and subordination.

In general, critical theory needs to take a harder, more critical look at the terms "private" and "public." These terms, after all, are not simply straightforward designations of societal spheres; they are cultural classifications and rhetorical labels. In political discourse they are powerful terms frequently deployed to delegitimate some interests, views, and topics and to valorize others.

This brings me to two other senses of "private," which often function ideologically to delimit the boundaries of the public sphere in ways that disadvantage subordinate social groups. These are sense (5), pertaining to private property in a market economy, and sense (6), pertaining to intimate domestic or personal life, including sexual life. Each of these senses is at the center of a rhetoric of privacy that has historically been used to restrict the universe of legitimate public contestation.

The rhetoric of domestic privacy would exclude some issues and interests from public debate by personalizing and/or familializing them; it casts these as private, domestic or personal, familial matters in contradistinction to public, political matters. The rhetoric of economic privacy, in contrast, would exclude some issues and interests from public debate by economizing them; the issues in question here are cast as impersonal market imperatives or as "private" ownership prerogatives or as technical problems for managers and planners, all in contradistinction to public, political matters. In both cases, the result is to enclave certain matters in specialized discursive arenas and thereby to shield them from broadly based debate and contestation. This usually works to the advantage of dominant groups and individuals and to the disadvantage of their subordinates.[34] If wife battering, for example, is labeled a "personal" or "domestic" matter and if public discourse about it is channeled into specialized institutions associated with, say, family law, social work, and the sociology and psychology of "deviance," then this serves to reproduce gender dominance and subordination. Similarly, if questions of workplace democracy are labeled "economic" or "managerial" problems and if discourse about these questions is shunted into specialized institutions associated with, say, "industrial relations" sociology, labor law, and "management science," then this serves to perpetuate class (and usually also gender and race) dominance and subordination.

This shows once again that the lifting of formal restrictions on public-sphere participation does not suffice to ensure inclusion in practice. On the contrary, even after women and workers have been formally licensed to participate, their participation may be hedged by conceptions of economic privacy and domestic privacy that delimit the scope of debate. These notions, therefore, are vehicles through which gender and class disadvantages may continue to operate subtextually and informally, even after explicit, formal restrictions have been rescinded.

6 Strong Publics, Weak Publics: On Civil Society and the State

Let me turn now to my fourth and last assumption underlying the bourgeois conception of the public sphere, namely, the assumption that a functioning democratic public sphere requires a sharp separation of civil society and the state. This assumption is susceptible to two different interpretations, according to how one understands the expression "civil society."

If one takes that expression to mean a privately ordered, capitalist economy, then to insist on its separation from the state is to defend classical liberalism. The claim would be that a system of limited government and laissez-faire capitalism is a necessary precondition for a well-functioning public sphere.

We can dispose of this (relatively uninteresting) claim fairly quickly by drawing on some arguments of the previous sections. I have already shown that participatory parity is essential to a democratic public sphere and that rough socioeconomic equality is a precondition of participatory parity. Now I need only add that laissez-faire capitalism does not foster socioeconomic equality and that some form of politically regulated economic reorganization and redistribution is needed to achieve that end. Likewise, I have also shown that efforts to "privatize" economic issues and to cast them as off-limits with respect to state activity impede, rather than promote, the sort of full and free discussion built into the idea of a public sphere. It follows from these considerations that a sharp separation of (economic) civil society and the state is not a necessary condition for a well-functioning public sphere. On the contrary and *pace* the bourgeois conception, it is precisely some sort of interimbrication of these institutions that is needed.[35]

However, there is also a second, more interesting interpretation of the bourgeois assumption that a sharp separation of civil society and the state is necessary to a working public sphere, one that warrants more extended examination. In this interpretation, "civil society" means the nexus of nongovernmental or "secondary" associations that are neither economic nor administrative. We can best appreciate the force of the claim that civil society in this sense should be separate from the state if we recall Habermas's definition of the liberal public sphere as a "body of private persons assembled to form a public." The emphasis here on "private persons" signals (among other things) that the members of the bourgeois public are not state officials and that their participation in the public sphere is not undertaken in any official capacity. Accordingly, their discourse does not eventuate in binding, sovereign decisions authorizing the use of state power; on the contrary, it eventuates in "public opinion," critical commentary on authorized decision-making that transpires elsewhere. The public sphere, in short, is not the state; it is rather the informally mobilized body of nongovernmental discursive opinion that can serve as a counterweight to the state. Indeed, in the bourgeois conception, it is precisely this extragovernmental character of the public sphere that confers an aura of independence, autonomy, and legitimacy on the "public opinion" generated in it.

Thus the bourgeois conception of the public sphere supposes the desirability of a sharp separation of (associational) civil society and the state. As a result, it promotes what I shall call *weak publics*, publics whose deliberative practice consists exclusively in opinion formation and does not also encompass decision making. Moreover, the bourgeois conception seems to imply that an expansion of such publics' discursive authority to encompass decision making as well as opinion making would threaten the autonomy of public opinion, for then the public would effectively become the state, and the possibility of a critical discursive check on the state would be lost.

That, at least, is suggested by Habermas's initial formulation of the bourgeois conception. In fact, the issue becomes more complicated as soon as we consider the emergence of parliamentary sovereignty. With that landmark development in the history of the public sphere, we encounter a major structural transformation, since a sovereign parliament functions as a public sphere *within* the state. Moreover, sovereign parliaments are what I shall call *strong publics*, publics whose discourse encompasses both opinion formation and decision making. As a locus of public deliberation culminating in legally binding decisions (or laws), parliament was to be the site for the discursive authorization of the use of state power. With the achievement of parliamentary sovereignty, therefore, the line separating (associational) civil society and the state is blurred.

Clearly, the emergence of parliamentary sovereignty and the consequent blurring of the separation between (associational) civil society and the state represents a democratic advance over earlier political arrangements. This is because, as the terms "strong public" and "weak public" suggest, the force of public opinion is strengthened when a body representing it is empowered to translate such "opinion" into authoritative decisions. At the same time, there remain important questions about the relation between parliamentary strong publics and the weak publics to which they are supposed to be accountable. In general, these developments raise some interesting and important questions about the relative merits of weak and strong publics and about the respective roles that institutions of both kinds might play in a democratic and egalitarian society.

One set of questions concerns the possible proliferation of strong publics in the form of self-managing institutions. In self-managed workplaces, child-care centers, or residential communities, for example, internal institutional public spheres could be arenas both of opinion formation and decision making. This would be tantamount to constituting sites of direct or quasi-direct democracy, wherein all those engaged in a collective undertaking would participate in deliberations to determine its design and operation.[36] However, this would still leave open the relationship between such internal public spheres cum decision-making bodies and those external publics to which they might also be deemed accountable. The question of that relationship becomes important when we consider that people affected by an undertaking in which they do not directly participate as agents may nonetheless have a stake in its *modus operandi;* they therefore also have a legitimate claim to a say in its institutional design and operation.

Here we are again broaching the issue of accountability. What institutional arrangements best ensure the accountability of democratic decision-making bodies (strong publics) to *their* (external, weak, or, given the possibility of hybrid cases, weak*er* publics?[37] Where in society are direct democracy arrangements called for, and where are representative forms more appropriate? How are the former best articulated with the latter? More generally, what democratic arrangements best institutionalize coordination among different institutions, including coordination among their various coimplicated publics? Should we think of central parliament as a strong superpublic with authoritative discursive sovereignty over basic societal ground rules and coordination arrangements? If so, does that require the assumption of a single weak(er) external superpublic (in addition to, not instead of, various other smaller publics)? In any event, given the inescapable global interdependence manifest in the international division of labor within a single shared planetary biosphere, does it make sense to understand the nation-state as the appropriate unit of sovereignty?

I do not know the answers to most of these questions, and I am unable to explore them further in this essay. However, the possibility of posing them, even in the absence of full, persuasive answers, enables us to draw one salient conclusion: any conception of the public sphere that requires a sharp separation between (associational) civil society and the state will be unable to imagine the forms of self-management, interpublic coordination, and political accountability that are essential to a democratic and egalitarian society. The bourgeois conception of the public sphere, therefore, is not adequate for contemporary critical theory. What is needed, rather, is a postbourgeois conception that can permit us to envision a greater role for (at least some) public spheres than mere autonomous opinion formation removed from authoritative decision making. A postbourgeois conception would enable us to think about strong *and* weak publics, as well as about various hybrid forms. In addition, it would allow us to theorize the range of possible relations among such publics, which would expand our capacity to envision democratic possibilities beyond the limits of actually existing democracy.

7 Conclusion: Rethinking the Public Sphere

Let me conclude by recapitulating what I believe I have accomplished in this essay. I have shown that the bourgeois conception of the public sphere as described by Habermas is not adequate for the critique of the limits of actually existing democracy in late-capitalist societies. At one level, my argument undermines the bourgeois conception as a normative ideal. I have shown first that an adequate conception of the public sphere requires not merely the bracketing, but rather the elimination, of social inequality. Second, I have shown that a multiplicity of publics is preferable to a single public sphere both in stratified societies and egalitarian societies. Third, I have shown that a tenable conception of the public sphere must countenance not the exclusion, but the inclusion, of interests and issues that bourgeois, masculinist ideology labels "private" and treats as inadmissible. Finally, I have shown that a defensible conception must allow both for strong publics and for weak publics and that it should help theorize the relations among them. In sum, I have argued against four constitutive assumptions of the bourgeois conception of the public sphere; at the same time, I have identified some corresponding elements of a new, postbourgeois conception.

At another level, my argument enjoins four corresponding tasks on the critical theory of actually existing democracy. First, this theory should render visible the ways in which social inequality taints deliberation within publics in late-capitalist societies. Second, it should show how inequality affects relations among publics in late-capitalist societies, how publics are differentially empowered or segmented, and how some are involuntarily enclaved and subordinated to others. Next, a critical theory should expose ways in which the labeling of some issues and interests as "private" limits the range of problems, and of approaches to problems, that can be widely contested in contemporary societies. Finally, the theory should show how the overly weak character of some public spheres in late-capitalist societies denudes "public opinion" of practical force.

In all these ways the theory should expose the limits of the specific form of democracy we enjoy in late-capitalist societies. Perhaps it can thereby help inspire us to try to push back those limits, while also cautioning people in other parts of the world against heeding the call to install them.

Acknowledgments

I am grateful for helpful comments from Craig Calhoun, Joshua Cohen, Nancy J. Hirschmann, Tom McCarthy, Moishe Postone, Baukje Prins, David Schweikart, and Rian Voet. I also benefitted from the inspiration and stimulation of participants in the conference on "Habermas and the Public Sphere," University of North Carolina, Chapel Hill, September 1989.

Notes

1. Jürgen Habermas, *The Structural Transformation of the Public Sphere: An Inquiry into a Category of Bourgeois Society*, trans. Thomas Burger with Frederick Lawrence (Cambridge: MIT Press, 1989). For Habermas's later use of the category of the public sphere, see Jürgen Habermas, *The Theory of Communicative Action*, vol. 2, *Lifeworld and System: A Critique of Functionalist Reason*, trans. Thomas McCarthy (Boston: Beacon Press, 1987). For a critical secondary discussion of Habermas's later use of the concept, see Nancy Fraser, "What's Critical About Critical Theory? The Case of Habermas and Gender," in Fraser, *Unruly Practices: Power, Discourse, and Gender in Contemporary Social Theory* (University of Minnesota Press, 1989).

2. Throughout this paper I refer to paid workplaces, markets, credit systems, etc. as *official*-economic institutions so as to avoid the androcentric implication that domestic institutions are not also economic. For a discussion of this issue, see Nancy Fraser, "What's Critical about Critical Theory? The Case of Habermas and Gender."

3. Joan Landes, *Women and the Public Sphere in the Age of the French Revolution* (Ithaca: Cornell University Press, 1988).

4. For the "public"/"pubic" connection, see the *Oxford English Dictionary* (2nd ed., 1989), entry for "public." For the "testimony"/"testicle" connection, see Lucie White, "Subordination, Rhetorical Survival Skills, and Sunday Shoes: Notes on the Hearing of Mrs. G.," *Buffalo Law Review* 38, no. 1 (Winter 1990): 6.

5. Pierre Bourdieu, *Distinction: A Social Critique of the Judgment of Pure Taste* (Cambridge: Harvard University Press, 1979).

6. Geoff Eley, "Nations, Publics, and Political Cultures: Placing Habermas in the Nineteenth Century," in *Habermas and the Public Sphere*, ed. Craig Calhoun. See also Leonore Davidoff and Catherine Hall, *Family Fortunes: Men and Women of the English Middle Class, 1780–1850* (Chicago: University of Chicago Press, 1987).

7. Habermas does recognize that the issue of gender exclusion is connected to a shift from aristocratic to bourgeois public spheres, but, as I argue below, he fails to register its full implications.

8. I do not mean to suggest that Habermas is unaware of the existence of public spheres other than the bourgeois one; on the contrary, in the Preface to *Structural Transformation* (p. xviii) he explicitly states that his object is the liberal model of the bourgeois public sphere and that therefore he will discuss neither "the plebeian public sphere" (which he understands as an ephemeral phenomenon that existed "for just one moment" during the French Revolution) nor "the plebiscitary-acclamatory form of regimented public sphere characterizing dictatorships in highly developed industrial societies." My point is that, although Habermas acknowledges that there were alternative public spheres, he assumes that it is possible to understand the character of the bourgeois public by looking at it alone in isolation from its relations to other, competing publics. This assumption is problematic. In fact, as I shall demonstrate, an examination of the bourgeois public's relations to alternative publics challenges the bourgeois conception of the public sphere.

9. Mary P. Ryan, *Women in Public: Between Banners and Ballots, 1825–1880* (Baltimore: John Hopkins University Press, 1990) and "Gender and Public Access: Women's Politics in Nineteenth Century America," in *Habermas and the Public Sphere*, ed. Craig Calhoun.

10. Geoff Eley, "Nations, Publics, and Political Cultures."

11. Geoff Eley, "Nations, Publics, and Political Cultures."

12. I am leaving aside whether one should speak here not of consent *tout court* but rather of "something approaching consent," "something appearing as consent," or "something constructed as consent" in order to leave open the possibility of degrees of consent.

13. The public sphere produces consent via circulation of discourses that construct the common sense of the day and represent the existing order as natural and/or just, but not simply as a ruse that is imposed. Rather, the public sphere in its mature form includes sufficient participation and sufficient representation of multiple interests and perspectives to permit most people most of the time to recognize themselves in its discourses. People who are ultimately disadvantaged by the social construction of consent nonetheless manage to find in the discourses of the public sphere representations of their interests, aspirations, life problems, and anxieties that are close enough to resonate with their own lived self-representations, identities, and feelings. Their consent to hegemonic rule is secured when their culturally constructed perspectives are taken up and articulated with other culturally constructed perspectives in hegemonic sociopolitical projects.

14. Here I want to distance myself from a certain overly facile line of argument that is sometimes made against Habermas. This is the line that ideological functions of public spheres in class societies simply undermine the normative notion as an ideal. This I take to be a non sequitur, since it is always possible to reply that under other conditions, say, the abolition of classes, genders, and other pervasive axes of inequality, the public sphere would no longer have this function but would instead be an institutionalization of democratic interaction. Moreover, as Habermas has often pointed out, even in existing class societies, the significance of the public sphere is not entirely exhausted by its class function. On the contrary, the idea of the public sphere also functions here and now as a norm of democratic interaction that we use to criticize the limitations of actually existing public spheres. The point here is that even the revisionist story and the Gramscian theory that cause us to doubt the value of the public sphere are themselves only possible because of it. It is the idea of the public sphere that provides the conceptual condition of possibility for the revisionist critique of its imperfect realization.

15. Jane Mansbridge, "Feminism and Democracy," *The American Prospect*, no. 1 (Spring 1990): 127.

16. In *Distinction* Pierre Bourdieu has theorized these processes in an illuminating way in terms of the concept of "class habitus."

17. As Habermas notes, this tendency is exacerbated with the concentration of media ownership in late-capitalist societies. For the steep increase in concentration in the United States in the late twentieth century, see Ben H. Bagdikian, *The Media Monopoly* (Boston: Beacon Press, 1983) and "Lords of the Global Village," *The Nation* (June 12, 1989). This situation contrasts in some respects with countries with television owned and operated by the state. But even there it is doubtful that subordinated groups have equal access. Moreover, political and economic pressures have recently encouraged privatization of media in several of these countries. In part, this reflects the problems of state networks having to compete for "market share" with private channels airing U.S.-produced mass entertainment.

18. This is the spirit behind, for example, proposals for reforms of election-campaign financing aimed at preventing the intrusion of economic dominance into the public sphere. Needless to say, within a context of massive societal inequality, it is far better to have such reforms than not to have them. However, in light of the sorts of informal effects of dominance and inequality discussed above, one ought not to expect too much from them. The most thoughtful recent defense of the liberal view comes from someone who in other respects is not a liberal. See Michael Walzer, *Spheres of Justice: A Defense of Pluralism and Equality* (New York: Basic Books, 1983). Another very interesting approach has been suggested by Joshua Cohen. In response to an earlier draft of this essay, he argued that policies designed to facilitate the formation of social movements, secondary associations, and political parties would better foster participatory parity than would policies designed to achieve social equality, since the latter would require redistributive efforts that carry "deadweight losses." I certainly support the sort of policies that Cohen recommends, as well as his more general aim of an "associative democracy." The sections of this paper on multiple publics and strong publics make a case for related arrangements. However, I am not persuaded by the claim that these policies can achieve participatory parity under conditions of social inequality. That claim seems to me to be another variant of the liberal view of the autonomy of the political, which Cohen otherwise claims to reject. See Joshua Cohen, "Comments on Nancy Fraser's 'Rethinking the Public Sphere' " (unpublished manuscript presented at the meetings of the American Philosophical Association, Central Division, New Orleans, April 1990).

19. My argument draws on Karl Marx's still unsurpassed critique of liberalism in section 1 of "On the Jewish Question." Hence the allusion to Marx in the title of this essay.

20. My argument in this section is deeply indebted to Joshua Cohen's perceptive comments on an earlier draft of this paper in "Comments on Nancy Fraser's 'Rethinking the Public Sphere.' "

21. I have coined this expression by combining two terms that other theorists have recently effectively used for purposes consonant with my own. I take the term "subaltern" from Gayatri Spivak, "Can the Subaltern Speak?" in *Marxism and the Interpretation of Culture,* ed. Cary Nelson and Larry Grossberg (Chicago: University of Illinois Press, 1988), pp. 271–313. I take the term "counterpublic" from Rita Felski, *Beyond Feminist Aesthetics* (Cambridge: Harvard University Press, 1989).

22. For an analysis of the political import of oppositional feminist discourses about needs, see Nancy Fraser, "Struggle over Needs: Outline of a Socialist-Feminist Critical Theory of Late-Capitalist Political Culture," in Fraser, *Unruly Practices.*

23. Geoff Eley, "Nations, Publics, and Political Cultures." Eley goes on to explain that this is tantamount to "extend[ing] Habermas's idea of the public sphere toward the wider public domain where authority is not only constituted as rational and legitimate, but where its terms are contested, modified, and occasionally overthrown by subaltern groups."

24. It seems to me that public discursive arenas are among the most important and underrecognized sites in which social identities are constructed, deconstructed, and reconstructed. My view stands in contrast to various psychoanalytic accounts of identity formation, which neglect the formative importance of post-Oedipal discursive interaction outside the nuclear family and which therefore cannot explain identity shifts over time. It strikes me as unfortunate that so much of contemporary feminist theory has taken its understanding of social identity from psychoanalytic models, while neglecting to study identity construction in relation to public spheres. The revisionist

historiography of the public sphere discussed earlier can help redress the imbalance by identifying public spheres as loci of identity reconstruction. For an account of the discursive character of social identity and a critique of Lacanian psychoanalytic approaches to identity, see Nancy Fraser, "The Uses and Abuses of French Discourse Theories for Feminist Politics," *boundary 2*, 17, no. 2 (Summer 1990): 82–101.

25. For another statement of this position, see Nancy Fraser, "Toward a Discourse Ethic of Solidarity," *Praxis International* 5, no. 4 (January 1986): 425–429. See also Iris Young, "Impartiality and the Civic Public: Some Implications of Feminist Critiques of Moral and Political Theory" in *Feminism as Critique*, ed. Seyla Benhabib and Drucilla Cornell (Minneapolis: University of Minnesota Press, 1987), pp. 56–76.

26. For an analysis of the rhetorical specificity of one historical public sphere, see Michael Warner, *The Letters of the Republic: Publication and the Public Sphere in Eighteenth Century America* (Cambridge: Harvard University Press, 1990).

27. One could say that at the deepest level, everyone is *mestizo*. The best metaphor here may be Wittgenstein's idea of family resemblances, or networks of crisscrossing, overlapping differences and similarities, no single thread of which runs continuously throughout the whole. For an account that stresses the complexity of cultural identities and the salience of discourse in their construction, see Nancy Fraser, "The Uses and Abuses of French Discourse Theories for Feminist Politics." For accounts that draw on concepts of *métissage*, see Gloria Anzaldua, *Borderlands: La Frontera* (1987) and Françoise Lionnet, *Autobiographical Voices: Race, Gender, Self-Portraiture* (Ithaca: Cornell University Press, 1989).

28. In these respects, the concept of a public differs from that of a community. "Community" suggests a bounded and fairly homogeneous group, and it often connotes consensus. "Public," in contrast, emphasizes discursive interaction that is in principle unbounded and open-ended, and this in turn implies a plurality of perspectives. Thus, the idea of a public can accommodate internal differences, antagonisms, and debates better than that of a community. For an account of the connection between publicity and plurality, see Hannah Arendt, *The Human Condition* (Chicago: University of Chicago Press, 1958). For a critique of the concept of community, see Iris Young, "The Ideal of Community and the Politics of Difference," in *Feminism and Postmodernism*, ed. Linda J. Nicholson (New York: Routledge, Chapman and Hall, 1989), pp. 300–323.

29. In this essay I do not directly discuss sense (1), state-related. However, in the next section of this essay I consider some issues that touch on that sense.

30. This is the equivalent in democratic theory of a point that Paul Feyerabend has argued in the philosophy of science. See Feyerabend, *Against Method* (New York: Verso, 1988).

31. In contrast, the liberal-individualist model stresses the view of politics as the aggregation of self-interested, individual preferences. Deliberation in the strict sense drops out altogether. Instead, political discourse consists in registering individual preferences and in bargaining, looking for formulas that satisfy as many private interests as possible. It is assumed that there is no such thing as the common good over and above the sum of all the various individual goods, and so private interests are the legitimate stuff of political discourse.

32. Jane Mansbridge, "Feminism and Democracy," p. 131.

33. This point, incidentally, is in the spirit of a strand of Habermas's recent normative thought, which stresses the procedural, as opposed to the substantive, definition of a democratic public sphere; here the public sphere is defined as an arena for a certain type of discursive interaction, not as an arena for dealing with certain types of topics and problems. There are no restrictions, therefore, on what may become a topic of deliberation. See Seyla Benhabib's account of this radical proceduralist strand of Habermas's thought and her defense of it as the strand that renders his view of the public sphere superior to alternative views: Benhabib, "Models of Public Space: Hannah Arendt, the Liberal Tradition, and Jürgen Habermas," in *Habermas and the Public Sphere*, ed. Craig Calhoun.

34. Usually, but not always. As Josh Cohen has argued, exceptions are the uses of privacy in *Roe v. Wade*, the U.S. Supreme Court decision legalizing abortion, and in Justice Blackmun's dissent in *Bowers*, the decision upholding state antisodomy laws. These examples show that the privacy rhetoric is multivalent rather than univocally and necessarily harmful. On the other hand, there is no question but that the weightier tradition of privacy argument has buttressed inequality by restricting debate. Moreover, many feminists have argued that even the "good" privacy uses have some serious negative consequences in the current context and that gender domination is better challenged in this context in other terms. For a defense of privacy talk, see Joshua Cohen, "Comments on Nancy Fraser's 'Rethinking the Public Sphere.'"

35. There are many possibilities here, including such mixed forms as market socialism.

36. I use the expression "quasi-direct democracy" to signal the possibility of hybrid forms of self-management involving the democratic designation of representatives, managers, or planners held to strict standards of accountability through, for example, recall.

37. By "hybrid possibilities" I mean arrangements involving very strict accountability of representative decision-making bodies to their external publics through veto and recall rights. Such hybrid forms might be desirable in some circumstances, though certainly not all.

6

Was There Ever a Public Sphere? If So, When? Reflections on the American Case

Michael Schudson

Critiques of American politics and culture are sometimes posed as if contemporary life represents a decline from some great and golden age. Christopher Lasch, for instance, bemoans "the transformation of politics from a central component of popular culture into a spectator sport." What once existed but has been lost, in Lasch's view, is "the opportunity to exercise the virtues associated with deliberation and participation in public debate." What we are seeing is "the atrophy of these virtues in the common people—judgment, prudence, eloquence, courage, self-reliance, resourcefulness, common sense."[1] Different images of the good old days appear without consensus about just when the good old days happened. George Anastaplo, among many others, has blamed much of the recent decline on television, and he successively offered two datings of the golden age. First, impressed that people would stand in the hot sun for several hours listening to "tight, tough arguments," he suggests the Lincoln-Douglas debates as a contrast to the TV era. He argues that the trouble with TV is not only that it fails to inform but also that it deceives people into believing they are informed. In contrast, "a generation ago"—not, I note, an era when people listened to hours of tight, tough argument in any forum—"you would know that if you had not read certain things, you were not able to talk about issues properly, and you might defer to those who had taken the trouble to inform themselves."[2]

If liberals see atrophy, so too do conservatives. Allan Bloom is the most celebrated to discuss a straight-line decline of civility in an age characterized by lack of character, lack of seriousness, lack of discipline, lack of nerve by those in positions of authority, the advance of a superficial and relativistic democratic ethos ultimately inimical to a good society. Both liberals and conservatives often see television as the cause, or at any rate the chief symptom, of the decline of a public sphere. It is an almost reflexlike, parenthetical explanatory catchall, as in the claim of *New York Times* media and politics reporter Michael Oreskes that "the first generation raised with television is a generation that participates less in the democracy than any before it."[3]

In fact, Oreskes is referring to the second generation raised with television, not the first, and he is wrong that it participates less in the democracy than any before it. Voting rates were just as miserable in 1920 as in 1984, and were worse in the 1790s. But let me offer as the main foil for this discussion an observation in the very important and influential research of American political scientist Walter Dean Burnham. In a 1974 essay he offers the example of the Lincoln-Douglas debates as evidence of the character of the mid nineteenth century American voter. He infers, from the fact that rational campaigners seeking election would engage in what seem to us unusually sophisticated and erudite debates on national issues before rural publics and the fact that party newspapers with similar rational inclinations to advance the interests of their candidates would reprint these debates in their entirety, that mid-nineteenth-century voters were literate, attentive, and interested in issues of transcendent importance.[4]

Are these safe inferences to make? I do not think so. Burnham himself all but declares them faulty in his next paragraphs. For he goes on to hold that nineteenth-century American politics was characterized by what he terms "political confessionalism." That is, mid-nineteenth-century Americans were devoutly attached to political parties. They tended to live in "island communities" surrounded by other people like themselves. Ethnic and religious communities provided the basis for political allegiances and very often were closely connected to the ideological content of political parties.[5] Political campaigns were, in a sense, more religious revivals and popular entertainments than the settings for rational-critical discussion. It is true that the voters who attended or read of the Lincoln-Douglas debates in their party newspapers were literate. It is true that they attended, but it is not at all apparent what in those debates they attended to. It is true that they participated, but it is not clear that they were "interested in issues of transcendent importance" (or that even if they were in 1858, a moment of particularly heightened political conflict, this has any bearing on their political interests in 1848 or 1868).

A point of comparison may help clarify this. Lawrence Levine has shown that Shakespearean drama was enormously popular in nineteenth-century America. But do we know from this how audiences related to it? No. What Levine's research suggests is that audiences enjoyed Shakespeare because they could read him as a creator of just the sorts of melodramas to which they were most partial. They saw Macbeth or Lear as rugged individualists up against the dangers of time and nature, warring against fate with all the larger-than-life energy Americans liked to see on the stage. Audiences saw Shakespeare's plays as a set of moral lessons: Thomas Jefferson saw *Lear* as a study of the importance of filial duty; Abraham Lincoln saw *Macbeth* as a study of tyranny and murder; John Quincy Adams saw *Othello* as a tale cautioning against interracial marriage. In popular American ideology and in the Shakespeare that Americans enjoyed, the individual bore responsibility for his own fate; if he failed, it was only through lack of inner discipline and control. All of these lessons came draped in the kind of expansive oratory that Americans liked in both their theater and their politics.[6]

What does this say of Lincoln-Douglas? It reminds us, as does a great deal of contemporary literary theory, that what the audience receives from the texts it approaches is not obviously encoded in the texts themselves. Did the Lincoln-Douglas audiences attend the debates because they sought to rationally and critically follow the arguments? Did they attend because they were thinking through the questions of slavery and states' rights? Were they out for a good time? Were they connoisseurs of oratory who admired the effectiveness of Lincoln and Douglas at skewering each other but lacked much concern for whether their arguments were right or wrong? Did they simply enjoy the spectacle of solitary combat? Had they already made up their political minds and come out only to show support for their man?

The longing of contemporary critics of our political culture to stand in the sun for three hours to listen to political speeches is selective. If there is nostalgia for the Lincoln-Douglas debates (not that they left any words, phrases, or ideas anyone can recall), there is no hankering for dramatic readings of Edward Everett's hours-long address at Gettysburg. Instead, it is Abraham Lincoln's sound-bite-length address that has left a lasting impression. (As it happens, not long ago people did listen to literally hours of political address, interspersed with music, at antiwar rallies in the 1960s. If it is any measure, I can say from personal experience that there is a big difference between attending a rally and actually listening to the speeches.)

This is not to deny that the Lincoln-Douglas debates were an impressive exercise of democracy. But it is well to remember that they were strikingly unusual even in their own day. The idea that a public sphere of rational-critical discourse flourished in the eighteenth or early nineteenth century, at least in the American instance, is an inadequate, if not incoherent, notion. Its empirical basis, in the American case, seems to me remarkably thin. When we examine descriptions of what public life was actually like, there is not much to suggest the rational-critical discussion Jürgen Habermas posits as central to the public sphere. Perhaps more distressing, for some periods there is not much to indicate even very general interest, let alone participation, in public affairs.

What I want to focus on in the rest of this paper are two defining features of the political public sphere. First, what is the level of participation in the public sphere: who is legally eligible for political activity and what portion of those eligible actually participate? Second, to what extent is political participation carried out through rational and critical discourse? This is a vital part of the concept of the public sphere as Habermas has presented it. No plebiscitary democracy, for instance, would qualify for Habermas as having a functioning public sphere; not only does participation need to be widespread, but it must be rational. One of the great contributions of the concept of a public sphere is that it insists that an ideal democratic polity be defined by features beyond those that formally enable political participation. It is not only the fact of political involvement but its quality that the concept of the public sphere evokes. There are, certainly, other conditions or preconditions of a public sphere, but these two are undoubtedly central, and I will limit my discussion in this paper to these alone.[7] This discussion is inspired by Habermas more than it is directly responsive to his work. That is, I am not engaged in criticizing the historical evidence he adduces for the emergence (and later disintegration) of a public sphere. His historical account concerns European affairs, and I do not presume the American case either confirms or contradicts European developments. I am concerned with Habermas's model of the public sphere not so much as "a paradigm for analyzing historical change," as Peter Hohendahl put it, but more as "a normative category for political critique."[8] That is, I think historians should examine as a central question of political history the rise or fall, expansion or contraction (the appropriate metaphor is not clear) of a public sphere or, more generally, what the conditions have been in different periods that encourage or discourage public participation in politics and public involvement in rational-critical discussion of politics.

1 Citizen Participation in Politics

The more people participate as citizens in politics, the closer one comes to the ideal of a public sphere. By this criterion, in American history the period since 1865 is an improvement upon all prior periods, with the enfranchisement of Negroes; the period since 1920 is better than any prior period, with the enfranchisement of women; and the period since 1965 is better still with the civil rights laws that made the Fifteenth Amendment a substantial reality.

But the question is not only what segments of the population are legally eligible to participate in politics (I am taking the franchise as a reasonable, though certainly incomplete, index of inclusion in the political world but also what percentages of those groups actually exercise their political rights. Contemporary commentators regularly observe that present voting participation rates are significantly lower than they were in the mid nineteenth century. This is so. There was a sharp decline in voter turnout from the 1880s to a low in the 1920s; during the New Deal and after, voting rates increased, but there has been a striking decline again from 1960 to the present. This should be viewed, however, in the longer perspective of American history.

Jane Mansbridge found in her study of a New England town meeting in the 1970s that only some 35 percent of eligible voters turned out to this archetype of democratic decision making. How did this compare, she asked, to the New England town meetings of the seventeenth and eighteenth centuries? In Dedham, Massachusetts, where records are quite complete for the mid seventeenth century, attendance varied. From 1636 to 1644, 74 percent of eligible voters typically attended meeting. While this turnout is much higher than in town meetings today, its significance is mitigated by the fact that every inhabitant lived within one mile of the meeting place, there were fines for lateness to town meeting or absence from town meeting, a town crier visited the house of every latecomer or absentee half an hour into the meeting, and only some sixty men were eligible in the first place. In Sudbury, a town that did not impose fines, attendance averaged 46 percent in the 1650s. In many towns for which we have good evidence, attendance in the eighteenth century was lower still. Mansbridge estimates that 20 to 60 percent of potential voters attended meeting in eighteenth-century Massachusetts. The figures for the nineteenth century are similar except for periods of particularly intense conflict, when turnout rose to as high as 75 percent. In the town she studied, ninteenth-century attendance was 30 to 35 percent while in the current period it is around 25 percent or as high as 66 percent in times of special conflict.[9]

John Adams told a friend while visiting Worcester in 1755, "This whole town is immersed in politics." Yet as historian Robert Zemsky concludes, "The average provincial seldom engaged in political activity. He had little desire to hold office; his attendance at town meetings and participation in provincial elections was sporadic; and when he did join in political campaigns, he rarely lent more than his moral support to the cause."[10] In revolutionary America, 10 to 15 percent of white adult males voted at the beginning of the Revolution, 20 to 40 percent during the 1780s.[11] In Massachusetts the first Congressional elections of 1788 and 1790 brought out 13 percent and 16 percent of eligible voters. The high point of turnout in state elections in the decade came in 1787 after the "near civil war" of Shays Rebellion—a 28 percent turnout.[12]

In eighteenth-century New England, the most democratic culture in colonial North America, people participated in politics occasionally at best. "Apathy prevailed among citizens until they perceived a threat to their immediate interests," according to historian Ronald Formisano's analysis of eighteenth-century Massachusetts.[13] The nineteenth century, before party mobilization began in the 1840s, was no better. "In the 1820s the vast majority of citizens had lost interest in politics. They had never voted much in presidential elections anyway, and now they involved themselves only sporadically in state and local affairs."[14] There is not much to be said in favor of any time in America's past before the 1840s in terms of political participation and political interest. William Gienapp characterizes American political life before the 1820s as follows: "Previously deference to social elites and mass indifference characterized the nation's politics; despite suffrage laws sufficiently liberal to allow mass participation, few men were interested in politics, and fewer still actively participated in political affairs. Politics simply did not seem important to most Americans."[15]

With the rise of mass-based political parties in the Jacksonian era, political participation took a new turn. Voting rates shot up dramatically. For example, the percentage of the potential electorate that voted in Connecticut was 8 percent in 1820 and 15 percent in 1824. By 1832 this rose to 46 percent and by 1844 to 80 percent.[16] Turnout figures of around 80 percent were common outside the South until the turn of the century, when they began to decline, reaching a lower point in the 1920s than at any time since before Andrew Jackson. If we take voter turnout as the measure (and it seems to me a good one), there is no question that in terms of political participation, there *was* a golden age of American political culture, the period from 1840 to 1900. This period, then, merits close consideration. What was the character of political culture in this period? What was the nature of political discourse? What features of the era supported mass political involvement? And was this involvement of a type or quality we might reasonably long for, or at least learn from, today?

2   Rational-Critical Political Discourse

It is difficult enough to know voter turnout rates for the nineteenth century. To try to learn how eighteenth- or nineteenth-century voters conceived of politics, came to political views, and arrived at political choices and actions is substantially harder. There is so much here we would need to know and that we never will know in any complete way. Did people talk about politics in their homes? Was the talk of politics at taverns or coffeehouses "rational-critical," or was it gossipy, incidental background to sociability rather than its center? What connection did people feel to politics? Was voting a proud act of citizenship or a deferential act of social obligation to community notables? When people read about politics, what did they look for? What frameworks of meaning did they possess for absorbing new information? Did they have coherent ideologies or patchwork sets of beliefs with little connection among the pieces? None of this is easy to discover. Still, there are some important clues available. For purposes of exposition, I will distinguish between the internal resources of citizens for participation in political discourse and the external resources available for their use—specifically, parties, the press, and electoral procedures.

Internal Resources of Citizens

American colonists of the eighteenth century were not well read. If they owned a book at all, it was the Bible. If they owned a second book, it was likely to be a collection of sermons or possibly John Bunyan's Christian allegory, *Pilgrim's Progress,* or some other religious work. Where we have comprehensive inventories of communities, even in New England 50 to 70 percent of households owned no books at all. The most active bookseller in Virginia in the mid eighteenth century sold books to 250 customers a year in a colony with a white population of 130,000.[17] In New England, where literacy rates were somewhat higher than elsewhere in the colonies, popular reading was severely restricted and was almost exclusively religious. Works of science or literature reached only a small audience made up almost entirely of the very small group of people who were college graduates.[18]

The one class of deeply literate people, the clergy, almost exclusively read religious literature and played relatively minor roles (judging, for instance, from their insignificance at the Constitutional Convention) in the great political debates of their time.[19] That Benjamin Franklin and Thomas Jefferson read widely in contemporary philosophy is not a trait they shared with many contemporaries. That Franklin read books at all was itself a social calling card; he reports in his autobiography that when he first journeyed to Philadelphia, he met a physician at an inn who "finding I had read a little" became sociable and friendly. Readers were relatively rare birds, not participants in a broad, ongoing, and institutionalized rational-critical discourse. The best-seller success of Thomas Paine's pamphlet *Common Sense* in 1776 was due, in Paine's own estimation, not only to its being issued at a time of intense political conflict but also to its being addressed to the common republican reader. Political pamphlet literature in the colonies was ordinarily addressed to the small, educated elite and was written in a florid style full of classical references that had meaning only to a few. Paine purged his writing of the classics, used as reference primarily the Biblical tradition, and sought "language as plain as the alphabet."[20]

In the nineteenth century the intellectual resources of the population expanded. Literacy shifted from being intensive to being extensive, schooling became much more accessible, and the secularization of culture, along with the democratization of religion, spread a wider range of ideas to more and more people. This is not to say that the growth of literacy and the growing market for printed literature, including political literature, was necessarily a force for liberation at each moment. Harvey Graff, among others, has argued that literacy was equally a form of social control designed to keep people in their place and that it was often successful in its aim.[21] Still, nineteenth-century Americans were more educationally equipped for participation in a public sphere than their eighteenth-century forebears. And despite concerns about a "decline" in American educational achievement in recent years (a decline that, by the measure of test scores, began in the 1960s and ended by the early 1980s), basic literacy skills and educational attainment have become more widely available in the twentieth century than in the nineteenth.[22] All of this is a relatively poor measure of the internal resources of American citizens for political participation. The notion of internal resources may, in any event, be one that cannot be taken very far. At least, however, this thumbnail sketch suggests little reason for nostalgia about the educational qualifications of any prior era in American history.

External Resources of Political Culture

The Press

One critical feature of the bourgeois public sphere is the availability of public media for carrying on and informing public discussion. There is a distinction to be made between "carrying on" and "informing." Habermas distinguishes between an early press devoted to political controversy and a later, commercial press that pursues the commodification of news. While the commercial press is not without its virtues, actively engaging the public in political debate is not one of them. In the terms of James Carey, there has been a shift from a "conversation" model to an "information" model of the press, and it has been an unhappy shift at that.[23] James Lemert has shown that the contemporary mainstream commercial American press in a sense prevents the political activity of its readers. It avoids publishing what Lemert calls "mobilizing information." That is, it will report about a political demonstration but it will not announce it the day before and provide a phone number or other information on how to reach the organizers. Where there is a celebration or demonstration that unites the community (the Fourth of July parade), in contrast, "mobilizing information" is ready at hand, with parade routes and locations for watching fireworks.[24] Tocqueville's notion of a newspaper as a creator of associations accurately described the reform journals of the 1830s and 1840s, has some application to the party papers that remained strong into the late nineteenth century, and also describes a large number of newsletters of voluntary associations even today. But the commercial model of journalism that dominates general, public discourse today and grew out of the penny press of the 1830s seeks a market, not an association or a community. The leading early editor of a penny paper, James Gordon Bennett, boasted that his press was "subservient to none of its readers—known to none of its readers—and entirely ignorant who are its readers and who are not."[25] This market ideal of the new journalism is the antithesis of association or community.

That journalism shifted toward a more and more fully commercial model during the nineteenth century should not lead us to romanticize the conversation model of the early press or to assume that it dominated uniformly in the era before the modern commercial newspaper pushed it to the sidelines. As Stephen Botein has argued, the colonial newspaper scrupulously avoided controversy on almost all occasions up to the decade before the Revolution, when the printers were dragged, sometimes kicking and screaming, into taking sides with the loyalists or the patriots.[26] When news was printed, it was generally chosen because it avoided controversy. The beginnings of the information press, in a sense, lie far back in the eighteenth century, when news was self-consciously regarded as a safe alternative to political debate and polemic. In fact, the more remote the news, the better. News of other colonies was more useful, because it was regarded with greater indifference, than news of one's own colony; news of European affairs were better still, because they had even less connection to local affairs.

So the colonial press was not, generally speaking, a press of political conversation except as political drama dragged it into the arena. Politics sometimes made of newspapers and pamphlets a public forum, but it was rare indeed that editors of their own volition created a public forum that stimulated political action. This is not to diminish the importance of the press at moments of heightened political activity, as during the Stamp Act crisis of 1765 or in the years leading up to the Revolution. But the colonial press was not a permanent resource for political discussion; its politicization was a sometime thing. By the early nineteenth century the politicalness of the American press receded just as party competition evaporated in the Era of Good Feelings. The relevance of the press to political discourse rose and fell with the fortunes of formal political organization, close electoral competition, and intense community conflict.

In any case, there were limits to what the press could provide. Eighteenth-century colonial assemblies conducted much of their business in secret. In Massachusetts the House began publishing a journal of its proceedings annually in 1715, though it was published twice a week after 1717. But the journal only rarely published roll-call votes (17 between 1739 and 1756), which made it difficult to know the policy stands of one's own representative. Any newspaper or other commentator who revealed business of the House not printed in the journal was subject to fine. Boston's half-dozen newspapers and its pamphleteers therefore usually just paraphrased what the journal already published. In times of crisis, enough information might percolate out to enable rational voting; in ordinary times, this was rarely the case.[27] One could reasonably argue that Massachusetts towns were homogeneous enough so that the legislator "ordinarily voiced his community's aspirations and grievances because he shared its prejudices."[28] If this was democracy, it was nonetheless far from a democracy based on rational-critical discussion. And Massachusetts was not unusual. From the 1740s to the Revolution, the New York Assembly regularly restated its right to prohibit the publication of its proceedings. Only two state constitutions drafted in the years after the Revolution opened the doors of the legislature to the public.

Through the 1780s, historian Thomas Leonard has written, "when Americans found a speech in their newspapers it was more likely to have been made in the Parliament of the kingdom they had rejected than in the assemblies of the new nation they had joined."[29] In Congress, reporters were forbidden until 1800. Even when reporters gained access, few newspapers took advantage. Until the 1820s no newspaper outside Washington maintained a regular Washington correspondent.[30]

In contrast, the press of the heyday of American political participation, from 1840 to 1900, was of a different color altogether. Somewhere between the world of conversation and the world of information, these papers were typically loyal to political parties; they served as information-promoting boosters of a particular political organization. American politics saw its highest level of participation begin just as party organizations moved self-consciously away from ideological stances. As Richard Hofstadter documents, from the 1840s on, political parties shifted from ideological institutions within an elite to organizational combat units competing for masses of voters.[31] They sought voter loyalty on the basis of program but even more on the basis of social and communal solidarity. American politics in this era has been described as divided along ethnocultural lines—people voted in solidarity with their ethnic and religious communities, not in allegiance to a political theory or philosophy and not with careful discussion or consideration of alternatives. People did not normally choose a political party or political philosophy any more than they chose a religion. On election day, most voters did not conceive of their having a choice between alternatives any more than the Methodist imagined he had a choice Sunday morning between the Methodist Church and the Congregational Church across the street. (If people had sought to make rational choices among parties, it would not have been an easy matter. Parties in the nineteenth century showed relatively little ideological consistency. By the 1890s, Ballard Campbell reports, the most consistent separation of Republicans and Democrats on the state level in Midwestern legislatures was over the liquor issue. This was the kind of "quasi-confessional" matter, to recall Burnham's terms, that parties did clearly represent with some consistency, but no

major party represented a coherent political program or philosophy.[32])

Correspondingly, newspapers boosted the parties they represented. The press, in Michael McGerr's terms, "imposed a
coercive cultural uniformity" on its readers. The press encouraged citizens to see politics in partisan terms. While this helped
citizens to understand politics, it also helped them to see politics
in the most simplified light: "By reducing politics to black-and-
white absolutes, the press made partisanship enticing. The
committed Republican or Democrat did not need to puzzle
over conflicting facts and arguments; in his paper he could
find ready-made positions on any candidate and every issue."[33]
Later, when more than one position could be found in a single
newspaper, editors feared readers would find this bewildering.
In the median political paper for the mid nineteenth century,
if one can imagine such a thing, a one-sided view of the political
battleground was maintained not only by attacking the opposition party and its candidates but, for the most part, by failing
to mention them altogether. The aggregate of political newspapers, read side by side, might well have approximated some
form of rational-critical discourse, or at least the kind of cari-
catured, zany "Point/Counterpoint" that "Saturday Night Live"
used to lampoon. But there is nothing to indicate that papers
were read in this way, no more than one would expect the
Baptist to peruse the church newsletter of the Presbyterian.

Party
In any event, without some way of limiting debate, defining
issues, and restricting alternatives, no debate can be rational.
To be sensible, political debate cannot be a set of simultaneous
equations that only a computer could handle. It has to be a
small set of identifiable, branching alternatives that can be
examined reasonably enough one at a time. The party helped
make that possible. "Parties," as Maurice Duverger put it, "create public opinion as much as they express it; they form it
rather than distort it; there is dialogue rather than echo. Without parties there would be only vague, instinctive, varying tendencies dependent on character, education, habit, social
position and so on."[34] Parties do not distort raw opinion but

make possible real opinion. Critics, as Duverger wrote, "fail to realize that raw opinion is elusive, that formed opinion alone can be expressed, and that the method of expression necessarily imposes on it a frame which modifies it."[35] If this is so, then modern democracies owe a great deal not only to the bourgeoisie in general but to the United States in particular for its invention of the mass-based party in the 1840s.

At the same time, party politics does not necessarily mean rational, informed voting. In William Gienapp's description of politics from 1840 to 1860 there is more evidence of participation than of serious discussion. Gienapp notes the widespread popularity of campaign songs whose purpose was to "provide entertainment and generate enthusiasm while lampooning the opposition."[36] Political barbeques were popular in Western states, and politics provided relief from social isolation. Was this good political education? That would be harder to affirm. "Campaign hoopla generated popular interest, but at times this pageantry took precedence over the dissemination of political information."[37] If that is the kind of politics as popular culture that Christopher Lasch fondly looks back on, not all contemporaries felt the same. Edward Everett Hale, for one, complained that the 1856 Republican campaign with a tent, traveling blacksmith orator, and glee club "is putting politics on just the level of Circus Riding."[38]

It should be noted that the Lincoln-Douglas kind of campaign had its critics in Lincoln's day. Hale felt stump speaking "one of the downward tendencies" of the age, favoring the young and able-bodied over more seasoned, and presumably wiser, leaders and giving too much room to mere adventurers.[39] In an era suspicious of television, and suspicious in part because television seems to favor certain superficial traits of good looks and the ability to invent a catchy sound bite, it is important to remember that an era of oratory had related problems. To be a winning public speaker was no guarantee that one could be a wise leader in office. The public speech before a live audience uses a "medium" with special properties just as much as the interview before a camera. (As it happens, live public speeches by the candidates were not very common, at least in presidential campaigns, in the nineteenth century.

The campaign of 1888, for instance, had an incumbent president, Grover Cleveland, who made exactly one speech, to accept his nomination, and a challenging candidate, Benjamin Harrison, who gave quite a number of speeches, but every one of them from the front porch of his home in Indiana.) In any event, it is also true that in a day of intensely strong party loyalties, the people who listened to Lincoln and Douglas were not listening to make up their minds. They were there to rally for their candidate, whatever he might say. It was neither a personality contest nor a debate whose winner would be declared by people weighing the best arguments.

Electoral Procedures
Stanley Kelley wrote in a 1960 study of political campaigning that the basic assumption of his work is that "campaign discussion should help voters make rational voting decisions."[40] That seems a useful assumption. Can we characterize when over American history campaign discussion most closely approximated that ideal?

Michael McGerr examines this subject in *The Decline of Popular Politics*. McGerr examines political campaigning in the American North from the middle of the nineteenth century through the 1920s. In short, he chronicles campaigning from the era of the greatest participation of citizens in American politics through its rapid decline to low levels in the 1920s that it had not reached since before 1840 and would not reach again until the 1970s. While McGerr recognizes a variety of factors that contributed to the decline of voter turnout, he draws attention to the influence of a conception of politics among an elite of reformers that decried the party-dominated and emotionally extravagant campaign of the Civil War era. These reformers decried "spectacular" politics and sought to replace it with "educational politics." Pamphlets, not parades, was their idea of the rational way to run a campaign. Perusing, not parading, is what they sought to encourage.

In the spectacular style of politics, local party organizations created special clubs, marching groups, and civic organizations that engaged in parades, demonstrations, picnics, and other outdoor forms of political entertainment. These forms were widely participatory, more so than any other form of American politics before or since, but this does not mean they were altogether democratically participatory. Members of the upper class held the most important local offices, and parades, as Michael McGerr observes, "stopped at the homes of the wealthy to serenade them and to hear their wisdom."[41] The spectacle of nineteenth-century politics helped establish, McGerr argues, "the upper class's right to rule."[42]

Politics, then, was more a communal ritual than an act of individual or group involvement in rational-critical discussion. This extended all the way to the ballot box. Ballots were drawn up by parties, not by a common state agency, and voters would very often deposit them in separate ballot boxes. Until the late nineteenth century there was no secret ballot in the United States, and the act of balloting was relatively public. Your neighbors knew not only if you voted but also which party you voted for. The party-printed ballots made it difficult for individuals to split their tickets; they also made it easy for bribery to be effective, since the party leaders could determine whether the bribed voter did or did not follow through on his voting pledge. The election, as a form of political communication, was itself a very different experience than it is today. It was organized much less with the rational choice of the individual voter in mind. The voter, in a sense, was not conceived of as an individual but as an entity enveloped in and defined by social circumstance and party affiliation. The transformation of the election campaign from a communal ritual to a political marketplace, a transformation that took place primarily in the period 1880 to 1920, was in part a self-conscious effort of reformers to root out the corruption of the party system— bribery and multiple voting—and to improve upon the election as a voice of people rationally seeking their interests on the basis of informed judgment. The reformers promoted what they called "educational" campaigns that replaced parades with pamphlets and replaced outdoor rallies with in-home newspaper reading. The reformers, who were remarkably successful as McGerr tells their story, helped to create the electoral campaign as an institution that pictures as the ultimate object of its efforts the isolated individual, gathering information from different sides, rationally evaluating it, and conscientiously making up his mind. The irony about contemporary longing for nineteenth-century politics is that it seeks the realization of an ideal that itself was formulated only on the funeral pyre of participatory, communal, ritualistic politics.

3 Conclusion

It does not appear that in any general sense rational-critical discussion characterized American politics in the colonial era. The politically oriented riot was a more familiar form of political activity than learned discussion of political principles. If some contemporary authors write with fondness of the spontaneity of such political expression,[43] others shed doubt that these riots were very often spontaneous at all.[44] In the nineteenth century, when political participation increased substantially, political discourse did not become markedly more rational and critical. To infer eighteenth-century politics from the fact that the Federalist papers appeared in the newspapers or to infer nineteenth-century politics from the Lincoln-Douglas debates would be something like characterizing American politics of the 1970s by the fact that the impeachment debates in the House Judiciary Committee in 1974 were broadcast live on television and discussed widely and fervently among people of all walks of life. All these events were extraordinary; none of them represents the normal political discourse of its era.

I find the concept of a public sphere indispensable as a model of what a good society should achieve. It seems to me a central notion for social or political theory. I think it is also enormously useful as a model that establishes a set of questions to ask about politics past and present. What I have tried to do here is just that and, in the process, to raise questions about how well a model of the public sphere was approximated in earlier periods of American history. Obviously, this essay is more a provocation than a settled position; it relies on the judgments of other scholars more than it carves out its own comprehensive position. If I have used my questions more as a club than a beacon, I have done so to dispel the retrospective wishful thinking that beclouds too much contemporary political and cultural analysis. Our place in the world is different from that of eighteenth-century or nineteenth-century Americans, but not, I think, fallen. Thinking through the conditions and possibilities for more rational and critical, fair and fair-minded, political practices in our own day will not profit from maintaining illusions about the character of the public sphere in days gone by.

Notes

1. Christopher Lasch, "A Response to Joel Feinberg," *Tikkun* 3 (1988): 43.

2. George Anastaplo, "Education, Television, and Political Discourse in America," *Center Magazine*, July–August 1986, p. 21.

3. *New York Times*, January 31, 1988, p. IV-5.

4. Walter Dean Burnham, "Theory and Voting Research," in Walter Dean Burnham, *The Current Crisis in American Politics* (New York: Oxford University Press, 1982) p. 83.

5. Burnham, "Theory and Voting Research," pp. 84–86.

6. Lawrence Levine, *Highbrow/Lowbrow: The Emergence of Cultural Hierarchy in America* (Cambridge: Harvard University Press, 1988).

7. Other dimensions of the public sphere would focus on the extent to which a legal or constitutional framework exists to preserve rational-critical discussion and citizen participation; the degree to which public-mindedness is encouraged in the ethnic and value system of public servants; the extent to which relative economic equality prevails or to which a political system prevents the undue influence of the wealthy; the extent to which social life (family, church, and private associations) is imbued with a democratic, rather than deferential, spirit that would socialize individuals into readiness for public participation.

8. Peter Hohendahl, "Critical Theory, Public Sphere, and Culture: Jürgen Habermas and His Critics," *New German Critique* 6 (1979): 92.

9. Jane Mansbridge, *Beyond Adversary Democracy* (New York: Basic Books, 1980) pp. 130–131.

10. Robert Zemsky, *Merchants, Farmers, and River Gods: An Essay on Eighteenth-Century American Politics* (Boston: Gambit, 1971) p. 37.

11. J Morgan Kousser, "Suffrage," in Jack Greene, ed. *Encyclopedia of American Political History*, vol. 3 (New York: Charles Scribner's, 1984).

12. Ronald Formisano, *The Transformation of Political Culture: Massachusetts Parties, 1790s–1840s* (New York: Oxford University Press, 1983) p. 30

13. Formisano, *Transformation of Political Culture*, p. 27.

Michael Schudson

14. Formisano, *Transformation of Political Culture,* p. 17.

15. William Gienapp, "'Politics Seem to Enter into Everything': Political Culture in the North, 1840–1860," in Stephen E. Maizlish and John J. Kushma, eds., *Essays on American Antebellum Politics, 1840–1860* (College Station, Texas: Texas A&M Press, 1982) p. 15.

16. Walter Dean Burnham, *The Current Crisis in American Politics* (New York: Oxford, 1982) p. 129.

17. David Hall, "The Uses of Literacy in New England, 1600–1850," in David Hall, ed., *Printing and Society in Early America* (Worcester: American Antiquarian Society, 1983) pp. 27–28.

18. Harry S. Stout, *The New England Soul* (New York: Oxford University Press, 1986) p. 87.

19. From 1790 to 1830 evangelical Christianity became a powerful force for a democratic culture. In 1776 or 1787, however, the democratic revolution in the churches had not matured. See Nathan O. Hatch, *The Democratization of American Christianity* (New Haven: Yale University Press, 1989).

20. Quoted in Eric Foner, *Tom Paine and Revolutionary America* (New York: Oxford University Press, 1976).

21. Harvey Graff, *The Literacy Myth* (New York: Academic Press, 1979).

22. Lawrence C. Stedman and Carl F. Kaestle, "Literacy and Reading Performance in the United States, from 1880 to the Present," *Reading Research Quarterly* 22 (1987): 8–46.

23. James Carey, "The Press and Public Discourse," *Center Magazine* 20 (1983): 4–16.

24. James Lemert, "News Context and the Elimination of Mobilizing Information: An Experiment," *Journalism Quarterly,* 1984, 243–249, 259.

25. Quoted in Michael Schudson, *Discovering the News: A Social History of American Newspapers* (New York: Basic Books, 1978) p. 21. For a discussion of the model of journalism as the center of an association of readers, see David Nord, "Tocqueville, Garrison, and the Perfection of Journalism," *Journalism History* 13 (1986): 56–63.

26. Stephen Botein, "'Meer Mechanics' and an Open Press: The Business and Political Strategies of Colonial American Printers," *Perspectives in American History* 9 (1975) pp. 127–228.

27. Robert Zemsky, *Merchants, Farmers, and River Gods,* pp. 239–241.

28. Robert Zemsky, *Merchants, Farmers, and River Gods,* p. 252.

29. Thomas Leonard, *The Power of the Press: The Birth of American Political Reporting* (New York: Oxford University Press, 1986) p. 65.

30. Leonard, *The Power of the Press,* p. 70.

31. Richard Hofstadter, *The Idea of a Party System* (Berkeley: University of California Press, 1972).

32. Ballard Campbell, *Representative Democracy: Public Policy and Midwestern Legislatures in the Late Nineteenth Century* (Cambridge: Harvard University Press, 1980), p. 92.

33. Michael McGerr, *The Decline of Popular Politics* (New York: Oxford University Press, 1986), p. 21.

34. Maurice Duverger, *Political Parties* (London: Methuen, 1954), p. 378.

35. Duverger, *Political Parties,* p. 380.

36. Gienapp, "'Politics Seems to Enter into Everything,'" p. 33.

37. Gienapp, "'Politics Seems to Enter into Everything,'" p. 35.

38. Gienapp, "'Politics Seems to Enter into Everything,'" p. 35.

39. Gienapp, "'Politics Seems to Enter into Everything,'" p. 40.

40. Stanley Kelley, Jr., *Political Campaigning: Problems in Creating an Informed Electorate* (Washington, D.C.: The Brookings Institution, 1960), p. 3.

41. McGerr, *The Decline of Popular Politics,* p. 31.

42. McGerr, *The Decline of Popular Politics,* p. 32.

43. Benjamin Ginsberg, *The Captive Public* (New York: Basic Books, 1986).

44. Gary Nash, "The Transformation of Urban Politics, 1700–1765," *Journal of American History* 60 (1973): 605–632.

7

Political Theory and Historical Analysis

Moishe Postone

1

The question of the relation between political theory and social and historical analysis is raised in important ways by Jürgen Habermas's *Structural Transformation of the Public Sphere* as well as by Michael Schudson's "Was There Ever a Public Sphere?" and Nancy Fraser's "Rethinking the Public Sphere." Habermas's recently translated book is an inquiry into the conditions and possibilities of democracy in contemporary capitalist societies presented in the form of an investigation into the historical constitution and subsequent decline of the liberal public sphere. The book contains a double argument. First, Habermas argues that an essential condition of democracy in large-scale industrial capitalist societies is the existence of a functioning public sphere, that is, a sphere at the intersection of political and social life, outside of the formal state apparatus, yet not immediately identical with civil society; it is constituted by citizens engaged in critical public debates. In a society characterized by a functioning public sphere, public opinion is formed in the course of such debates and influences the formal governmental apparatus. Within this framework, public opinion is not simply the aggregation of individual opinions as revealed by market research or opinion polls but is actively created by people.

Habermas's second basic thesis in this work is that the nature of a public sphere and the conditions of its possible existence must be understood historically. He analyzes the constitution of the liberal public sphere in Western Europe with reference to the differentiation of state and civil society that accompanied the development of liberal capitalism in the seventeenth and eighteenth centuries, and he traces its decline in terms of the far-reaching social, economic, political, and cultural transformations associated with the late-nineteenth-century transition from the liberal to the state-interventionist form of capitalist society.

In his examination Habermas notes the exclusionary and ideological character of the liberal public sphere; he also argues that the entrance of the masses into the political arena and the structural changes constituting the transition to state-interventionist (or organized) capitalism not only undermined the liberal public sphere but also rendered it inadequate as a direct model for democracy today. Nevertheless, the liberal public sphere was the first functioning example of a public sphere, according to Habermas. Investigating the historical conditions of its development and decline can help illuminate the possible conditions for a functioning public sphere and hence for democracy today.

Democracy, for Habermas, cannot be grasped in purely quantitative terms, for example, in terms of the relative proportion of the population that is enfranchised. Rather, democracy is related to self-determination, to the possibility of greater collective control by people over the political, social, and economic circumstances of their lives. One of the apparent paradoxes of modern capitalist development described by Habermas is that increased formal political inclusion of previously excluded segments of the population has not necessarily led to greater democracy in this sense. Indeed, what has precisely characterized capitalist development is that, although the franchise has been extended and the standard of living of most of the population has been raised, more and more aspects of life have become molded by and subject to the control of abstract anonymous forces over which citizens exercise very little control.

Habermas does not focus primarily on the general structural conditions that would allow for collective self-determination (although this theme does indirectly enter his investigation in his analysis of the transition from liberal to state-interventionist capitalism). His major concern in this book is to draw attention to the central importance for any functioning democracy of the public sphere as a sort of extrainstitutional institution. His book does, however, implicitly indicate that these two sorts of conditions for democracy are related; his exposition suggests that a contemporary theory of democracy must take cognizance of the historical changes that undermined the liberal public sphere. Democratic political theory, in other words, is inseparable from social and historical analysis. It is primarily with reference to this central theme that I shall consider the papers by Michael Schudson and Nancy Fraser and reflect on Habermas's own approach.

2

In his richly informative paper on aspects of American political life and discourse in the eighteenth and nineteenth centuries, Michael Schudson takes issue with positions that, in criticizing the nature of political discourse in the United States today, compare it unfavorably with the level of politics of an earlier era.

Schudson demonstrates that there was no "golden age" of American political participation and argues that illusions about the past can hinder serious consideration of the conditions and possibilities for more rational political practices. His analysis of voter participation in the late eighteenth century and of the press and political parties in the nineteenth century cautions against glorifying the character of past political discussion and participation in the United States. The only form of politics in America that could be characterized as rational, according to his account, was the "educational politics" introduced by an elite group of reformers between 1880 and 1914, which was directed against the party-centered form of politics of the mid nineteenth century and which treated citizens as well-informed, completely isolated individuals. The immediate effect of this more "rational" form of politics, however, was a precipitous drop in political participation rather than an increase in critical political discourse.

Although Schudson's article is not intended as a direct response to Habermas, it does seem to imply a critique of the latter's notion of the decline of the liberal public sphere, as well as his conception of the public sphere as constituted by rational-critical discourse. As a critique of Habermas, however, Schudson's argument is not entirely fair. Habermas's notion of rational political discourse refers not simply to the intellectual level of discussion but also to the conditions of a situation in which the outcome of political debate is not structurally predetermined, for example, by unequal relations of power. It points to the necessity of elucidating those conditions and, as such, has a structural moment. Whatever its problematic aspects, such a conception of rational politics does not refer to learned discourse.

Moreover, Habermas's analysis of the decline of the liberal public sphere does not mourn the passing of a golden age. As mentioned above, he is clearly aware of the exclusionary and ideological character of the bourgeois public sphere. The problem Habermas addresses is why the new role of the masses in politics and the growth of formal democracy in the second half of the nineteenth century did not result in an expanded, functioning public sphere. That the actual transformation of political life was considerably more negative than many had expected resulted not simply from the entry of the masses into the political arena according to Habermas but from the circumstance that the entry was associated with other social and economic processes that can be described in terms of the transition from liberal to organized capitalism. Habermas, then, is not simply concerned with treating the liberal public sphere as a normative standard by which to judge contemporary public life but seeks to elucidate the social, economic, and cultural conditions for an effective public sphere and hence democracy.

In some respects, however, Habermas's position is in tension with the implications of his own historical approach. He apparently presupposes that a democratic order today would realize the ideals expressed, in ideological form, in the bourgeois public sphere. In my view, we no longer can take for granted the notion, whose ultimate source is the early socialist tradition, that an emancipated society would entail the realization of the universalistic ideals of the bourgeois revolution and that the only problem with those ideals is that they were deformed in practice by the particularistic character of bourgeois class domination. Such a conception must either attribute transcendental status to historically constituted ideals or seek ontologically to ground those ideals in the nature of social life. Both approaches break with a consistent historical approach and entail various historical-theoretic problems that I cannot elaborate here.

It should be noted, furthermore, that many contemporary social movements, such as feminism, have begun to call into question the Enlightenment notion of universality itself. They do so not only because its practical application has been exclusionary but also because the nature of that universality is such that it negates difference. Such criticisms are of a determinate form of universality rather than of universality per se. They suggest that the values of the Enlightenment should be grasped within the framework of an opposition between an abstract universalist position that seeks to abolish hierarchy by negating difference, and positions that recognize difference but grasp it hierarchically. The new social movements have raised the issue of whether it is possible to get beyond this Enlightenment antinomy itself. Rather than seeking to realize the form of abstract universality that is only one pole of this antinomy, they point toward a newer form of universality that can encompass difference. In so doing, they have implicitly shown the Enlightenment antinomy to be historically determinate and socially constituted and have historically relativized the early socialist conception of emancipation, thereby suggesting a more consistently historical political theory of democracy.

Michael Schudson's paper also stresses the importance of analyzing the conditions for more rational forms of politics. His implicit critique of Habermas, however, shifts the focus of the analysis of the public sphere away from such considerations. Although Schudson approvingly notes that Habermas's conception of the public sphere refers to the quality of political participation, what is meant by "quality" is quite different.

Habermas's primary concern is to investigate the structure of the public sphere in relation to its historical context. Schudson's is to debunk the notion of a golden age of political participation. He therefore focuses his discussion of the quality of political participation on the level of rationality and sophistication of political discourse. The problem with this shift is not that it is unfair to Habermas but that it is not fully adequate to the richness of the materials presented in Schudson's paper itself; it deflects attention from further consideration of the historical structuring of precisely those aspects of American political life that Schudson presents.

In his treatment of pre-Jacksonian politics, for example, Schudson draws attention to the relatively low level of voter participation and political interest and cautions us not to exaggerate the degree to which the press, prior to the introduction of the commercial model of journalism, engaged in "carrying on" discussion, as opposed to merely "informing" its readers.

What structural and historical conclusions are we to draw from the material presented? Because Schudson's focus is to debunk the notion of a golden age, his argument does not elaborate the relation of historical conditions and the nature of political life. It is not clear, for example, whether he thinks that a sphere of extragovernmental political discourse did exist in late eighteenth and early nineteenth century America but its effectiveness and extension were quite limited, or he thinks that, as a result of conditions specific to America, such a sphere never really did come into being, or, finally, he is calling into question the effective existence of a liberal public sphere anywhere.

If Schudson's account leaves uncertain the status of the pre-Jacksonian public sphere, his discussion of American politics after 1840 parallels, on one level, Habermas's discussion of the decline of the liberal public sphere in the second half of the nineteenth century. It too indicates that greater political inclusion and participation does not necessarily signify a greater degree of democracy. Yet here also one would have wished more consideration of the specific structuring characteristics of the American situation. Why did the entrance of the masses onto the political stage in the United States find expression in parties organized along ethnocultural lines and not along class lines? What influence did this circumstance have on the nature of partisan political discourse in this country?

These, of course, are time-honored questions. They are raised implicitly by Michael Schudson's discussion of American politics but at the same time are bracketed as a result of the focus of his argument.

The issue of class indirectly raised by Schudson's description of the rise of mass politics in the United States also draws our attention to the absence of any extensive discussion of the role of social movements, in particular of the working class movement, in Habermas's discussion of the transition from liberal to organized capitalism. Such movements may ultimately have been defeated or integrated. Yet in Europe they were certainly constitutive of new forms of public discourse at the end of the nineteenth century and the beginning of the twentieth century and, it could be argued, were engaged in a struggle to reconstitute the public sphere.

Consideration of such movements would have enriched and deepened Habermas's discussion of the transformation of the public sphere in the transition to state-interventionist capitalism. Moreover, the question of the relationship between social movements and their context is an important aspect of any consideration of the conditions and possibilities of a public sphere today.

3

Consideration of the relationship between social movements and the character of a public sphere today strongly inform Nancy Fraser's timely paper on the limitations of liberal conceptions of democracy. At the center of her inquiry is Habermas's notion of the public sphere. She regards that notion to be of crucial importance for a critical theory that would seek to uncover the limits of democracy in late-capitalist society and point toward alternative democratic forms. However, the specific way in which Habermas elaborates this idea must be rethought, according to Fraser, inasmuch as it remains too bound to the liberal form of the public sphere. For although Habermas traces the rise and decline of that form, he does not develop a new, postbourgeois conception of the public sphere.

Fraser begins rethinking the notion of the public sphere by criticizing the ideals of liberal conceptions of democracy on the basis of an alternative account of the public sphere that she constructs from recent revisionist historiographic accounts. She thereby calls into question Habermas's contention that the utopian potential of the liberal public sphere, which was not realized historically, could serve as the basis for a democratic public sphere. Fraser does not reject the concept of the public sphere itself. Rather, she attempts to critically appropriate Habermas's concept by criticizing four central assumptions that characterize the liberal conception of the public sphere and, in her view, render its ideals ideological ("bourgeois-masculinist"). In this way Fraser separates the concept of the public sphere from its liberal form and uses it as the basis for a critique of actually existing democracy and for an approach to a postbourgeois model of the public sphere that is clearly informed by the experiences, needs, and worldviews of the new social movements of recent decades.

Fraser begins by calling into question the assumption that social equality is not a necessary condition for political democracy. Relying primarily on feminist research, she points out that the attempt to bracket social inequalities in settings of formal equality frequently serves to mask and reproduce domination, and she argues that a democratic public sphere would require eliminating, rather than bracketing, social inequality.

She then questions the assertion that a comprehensive public sphere is always preferable to a multiplicity of competing publics, arguing that the latter are to be preferred both in modern stratified societies as well as in (hypothetical) egalitarian multicultural societies.

The third issue Fraser addresses is that of the appropriate scope of publicity in relation to privacy. She argues that the boundaries dividing what is considered to be a matter of common concern (and hence political) and what is not (and hence private) are not naturally given but are decided through discursive contestation. For that reason, according to Fraser, a democratic public sphere must countenance inclusion, rather than a priori exclusion, of issues and concerns that are labeled private by the dominant ideology.

Finally, Fraser calls into question the idea that a functioning democratic public sphere requires a sharp separation between civil society and the state. Indeed, she argues that the forms of self-management, interpublic coordination, and political accountability essential to a fully democratic society can only be adequately constituted when the line separating civil society (understood in terms of public associations) and the state is blurred.

Fraser's sophisticated and suggestive critical analysis of these central assumptions underlying the liberal model of the public sphere is an important contribution to critical political theory. Nevertheless, in spite of its power, her critique does not fully address a central dimension of Habermas's approach to the public sphere, namely the relation between political form and historical context.

As noted above, Habermas analyzes the nature and structural transformation of the bourgeois public sphere historically, with reference to the development of liberal, and then state-interventionist, capitalism. Fraser's criticism that he only traces the rise and decline of the bourgeois public sphere and neglects to develop a new, postbourgeois model of the public sphere, as well as her critique of his notion that the ideals of the liberal public sphere can serve as the basis for a democratic public sphere, seems to imply an analysis that is more consistently historical than that of Habermas. Yet this dimension of her argument—her notion of the structuring principles and dynamic trajectory of the historical context—remains underdeveloped. Instead, her critique of the limits of the liberal public sphere focuses almost entirely on social relations among groups—on relations of domination and exclusion, on issues of equality, diversity, and contested definitions of publicity—to the exclusion of the historical dimension of those relations. Capitalism is dealt with only as a form of structural social inequality, that is, in an essentially static manner.

Fraser's argument that liberal theory brackets the social dimension is very well taken. However, because she deals with that dimension in terms of social groupings and their interactions alone, without considering the structuring of their historical context, the approach she outlines does not fully address a number of important problems raised by her discussion itself. I shall briefly discuss several of these problems in order to indicate the importance of extending her discussion of the social conditions of a democratic public sphere in a more historical direction as well.

When Fraser argues, for example, that democratic politics are better served by a multiplicity of publics than by a single, comprehensive public sphere, she conceptually embeds those multiple publics within a larger setting. Thus, she speaks of a single structural setting that advantages some people and disadvantages others in stratified societies, and of a comprehensive arena in egalitarian societies in which members of different publics talk across lines of cultural diversity. Fraser does not, however, thematize the structuring of, and historical conditions for, those two sorts of political metaspaces.

Relatedly, in criticizing the assumption that a functioning democratic public sphere requires a sharp separation of civil society and the state, Fraser argues convincingly that this condition could not refer to a privately ordered capitalist economy, inasmuch as the latter does not foster the conditions needed for democracy. She also develops the very interesting argument that if civil society is understood in terms of public associations, the blurring of the line separating state and civil society does not undermine democracy but actually represents a democratic advance. She does not, however, address the general issue of the way in which the changing interrelation of state and economy affects the structure of the larger public sphere as well as of the multiplicity of publics.

Similarly, when Fraser discusses discursive struggles over what is considered to be public and what private, she does so without raising the question of whether shifts in the boundaries separating what are classified as political, economic, and domestic spheres of life in capitalism can be explained completely in terms of those discursive struggles, or whether those struggles themselves do not also have to be understood with reference to other changes in the structuring of their historical context.

Another weakness of arguments that attempt to deal with the structuring of society in terms of the structuring of social groupings alone is that they cannot adequately deal with the relation of society and ideology. Such approaches tend to approach ideology either in a functionalist manner (e.g., as means of legitimating emergent class rule) or in a manner that tacitly privileges conscious agency in the construction of ideology (e.g., as a discourse that is deployed as a strategy). In either case, the relation of the content of the ideology to its historical context is rendered random. A theory of the structuring mediations and trajectory of the social context (and this can only be alluded to here) could allow for an approach to the relatedness of meaning and social life that is not available to theories of society focused entirely on social groupings and their practices. Such a theory, then, could allow social critiques of liberal conceptions of democracy to avoid the antinomy of functionalism and conscious construction when dealing with ideologies.

Finally, the most important issue raised by Fraser's discussion is that of the limits to democracy imposed by determinate social conditions. When Fraser addresses that issue, she does so exclusively in terms of problems of social inequality and exclusion. The fundamental problem for democracy posed by capitalism, however, is not only one of the unequal distribution of wealth and power. It is also that of the quasi-objective constraints imposed by the structure of capital itself, as populations living in the East and in the West, in the North and in the South, have been experiencing.

In her critique of liberal conceptions of democracy, Fraser argues that the ideal of formal inclusion does not go far enough in delineating the conditions of democracy if the issue of substantive inequality is bracketed; a democratic polity requires substantive equality. As important and timely as her argument is, I would like to extend it by suggesting that, although its emphasis on substantive equality and diversity goes far beyond the limits of liberal democratic theory, the conditions of democracy it proposes are also insufficient if it brackets the severe constraints imposed on any sort of democratic decision-making process by the imperatives of capital accumulation with their enormous social, political, economic, ecological, and geographic effects—imperatives that appear to be quasi-natural, unavoidable features of modern life.

These observations do not detract in any way from the importance and insightfulness of Fraser's arguments. Nevertheless, they do suggest that, however powerful are critiques of liberal conceptions of democracy that focus on existing relations of exploitation, domination, and exclusion, such critiques must also consider the structuring of the historical context if important aspects of the problematic of democracy are not to be bracketed.

4

I would like to conclude by turning briefly to the question of our historical context.

One of the central tenets of Habermas's *Structural Transformation of the Public Sphere* is that liberal capitalism proved to be a historical phase of developed capitalist society that ended about 1873, and that an adequate contemporary democratic theory must take cognizance of the enormous social, economic, political, and cultural changes involved in the transformation of that society into a state-interventionist, or organized, form. Such a theory, then, must be aware of its historical context.

I would like to suggest that we now can see that the state-interventionist form of postliberal capitalism has also proved to be a phase, one that ended about 1973. Since then we have been entering a still newer historical phase. The contours of this newest phase are not yet fully clear, but it is apparently characterized by the weakening and partial dissolution of the institutions and centers of power that had been at the heart of the state-interventionist mode: national state bureaucracies, industrial labor unions, and physically centralized, state-dependent capitalist firms. Those institutions have been undermined in two directions: by the emergence of a new plurality of social groupings, organizations, movements, parties, regions, and subcultures on the one hand and by a process of globalization and concentration of capital on a new, very abstract level that is far removed from immediate experience and is apparently outside of the effective control of the state machinery on the other.

This analysis suggests that one of the most pressing tasks of democratic political theory today is to come to an understanding of the parameters of this new situation in order better to understand the conditions and possibilities of democracy. In so doing, such theory cannot afford to remain bound to assumptions and presuppositions regarding historical context that now can be seen to have been limited to the state-interventionist phase of capitalism. (For example, one no longer can simply assume that problems of the capitalist economy can be effectively regulated by state intervention.)

One of the many weaknesses of orthodox Marxist theories was that they fixed their critical gaze exclusively on the conditions of nineteenth-century capitalism. They therefore did not recognize that, although the concentration of state power provided a possible means of abolishing private ownership of the means of production, it did not necessarily represent a positive political development. Today a variety of approaches exist whose critiques remain fixated on the concentrated, rationalized, state-centered modes of integration that characterized twentieth-century state-interventionist capitalism, that is, on what we can now see was another secular phase of capitalist development. If such approaches simply welcome the weakening of the older forms of integration without taking cognizance of the newer, more abstract, and global forms of domination that, at least for the moment, are not mediated by state policies, they may also find themselves celebrating as emancipatory what is probably one dimension of a more complex process of global restructuring.

However, any critical theory that, like the French General Staff, prepares for future battles by planning to win the previous war may all too easily find itself outwitted by what apparently can still be characterized as the cunning of history.

Acknowledgment

I would like to thank Ruth Slavin for transcribing my oral presentation at the conference, which helped considerably in creating this written version.

II
Historical Publics

8

Defining the Public Sphere in Eighteenth-Century France: Variations on a Theme by Habermas

Keith Michael Baker

For English readers interested in the origins and character of democratic political culture, the publication of a long-awaited translation of *Strukturwandel der Öffentlichkeit* is a welcome event. It is at least appropriate that it finally appear during the period of the bicentennial of the French Revolution, a time when scholarly and public attention has been redirected to the nature, implications, and dynamics of that revolutionary eighteenth-century transformation of the public sphere so central to the themes explored in Habermas's book.

Interestingly enough, the book is perhaps more relevant now to current research on the Old Regime and the French Revolution than when it was written. Indeed, it is fascinating to remark the extent to which topics central to Habermas's analysis of the phenomenon he calls the bourgeois public sphere—as to the earlier research of Reinhart Koselleck, to whom Habermas acknowledges a substantial debt[1]—have been taken up by other scholars in recent years. Multivolume studies of the history of private life and of changing practices of reading, writing, and publishing have developed our knowledge of the constitution of the literary public as a distinctive feature of eighteenth-century society.[2] The institution of criticism in the name of that public has been recognized as profoundly reshaping the practice of literature, painting, music, and the theater.[3] Publicity and "public opinion" have been reconsidered as fundamental categories of the transformed political culture of the Old Regime.[4] The dynamics of the political struggle to control competing definitions of the public sphere have moved to the heart of current research on the French Revolution.[5] English readers interested in these developments, among many others, will find much of interest in Habermas's first book.

Though it differs considerably in scope, focus, and emphasis, my more modest research on the idea of public opinion in prerevolutionary France owes much to the stimulation of an encounter with Habermas's early work. I am therefore grateful for the opportunity this volume affords to look once again at his definition of the bourgeois public sphere as it applies to eighteenth-century France and to consider how my understanding of the emergence of public opinion as a fundamental political category in the prerevolutionary period might differ from, or perhaps qualify, his. Given the importance of feminist scholarship in directing renewed attention to questions regarding the political and social construction of the public sphere, and to the significance of Habermas's work in this respect, I shall also take the opportunity to offer some remarks concerning one of the most interesting recent works on this theme, Joan Landes's *Women and the Public Sphere in the Age of the French Revolution*.[6]

1 Habermas on the Eighteenth-Century Public Sphere

It might be useful to begin by emphasizing several features of Habermas's account of the bourgeois public sphere. First, he insists upon the *historical specificity* of the phenomenon he is describing. The bourgeois public sphere, he argues, appeared at a particular moment in the development of civil society in Europe. "We conceive [the] bourgeois public sphere as typical of an epoch. It cannot be abstracted from the unique developmental history of that 'civil society' (*bürgerliche Gesellschaft*) originating in the European High Middle Ages; nor can it be transferred, idealtypically generalized, to any number of historical situations that represent formally similar constellations" (p. xvii).[7] Thus *The Structural Transformation of the Public Sphere* offers an account of a particular "historical constellation" (p. xviii) by analyzing the conditions under which the category of the bourgeois public sphere emerged in the eighteenth century and disappeared in the nineteenth.

Second, there is a profound ambiguity built into Habermas's definition of the public sphere as a category of bourgeois society. This "public of private people making use of their reason" (p. 51) can be understood either as a discursive category expressing a normative ideal or as an actually existing social reality. Indeed, the great interest of Habermas's book (and perhaps part of the difficulty of coming to terms with it) is that it presents the appearance of a bourgeois public sphere simultaneously in two registers: as the emergence of a normative ideal of rational public discussion from within the distinctive social formation of bourgeois civil society and as the realization, or rather the fleeting, partial realization, of this ideal within that society. Habermas's later work, as I understand it, has involved precisely the effort of disengaging more explicitly the notion of the rational public sphere, as normative ideal, from the historical social formation in which it was first embedded: reformulating it more abstractly in terms of the theory of communicative rationality; and asking how and how far it might now be recovered (having lost its even partial realization) in the political and social practice of late-capitalist society.

As a discursive category, then, the new eighteenth-century concept of "the public" that Habermas describes expressed the ideal of communicative rationality among free and equal human beings. (I use quotes to indicate that I am discussing the status of "the public" as a concept rather than as an existing reality.) Participants in this modern public sphere were to be conceived not as citizens of an ancient polis assembling together to engage in the common exercise of political will but as the dispersed members of "a society engaged in critical public debate" (p. 52). "Public opinion," the ultimate source of authority in this sphere, was construed as the universal reason of the generality of thinking individuals continuously engaged in open discussion. Under its aegis, power and domination in human life were to give way to free acceptance of the enlightened order of human rationality.

This normative ideal, Habermas insists, was embedded historically in the particular conditions of the development of bourgeois civil society. The subjectivity of the private individuals comprising the new public originated in the "intimate sphere" of the bourgeois family, a zone created "to the degree to which commodity exchange burst out of the confines of the household economy [and] the sphere of the conjugal family became differentiated from the sphere of social reproduction" (p. 28). Here, apparently free from dependence upon economic activity, privatized individuals could view themselves as "persons capable of entering into 'purely human' relations with one another" (p. 48). Thus bourgeois subjectivity was essentially intersubjective (Habermas calls it "audience oriented"). Privatized individuals stepped from their living rooms into the salons; they defined their inner consciousness in letters to others; they explored the new domain of subjectivity in that expansion of the epistolary form that was the novel, the great mirror of the eighteenth-century soul. In this way, Habermas argues, reading became an intimate, subjective experience; the shared world of readers and authors a domain of "intimate mutual relationships between privatized individuals who were psychologically interested in what was 'human,' in self-knowledge, and in empathy" (p. 50). The intimate sphere of the conjugal family was thus expanded into, and completed by, the literary public sphere: "The public sphere of a rational-critical debate in the world of letters within which the subjectivity originating in the interiority of the conjugal family, by communicating with itself, attained clarity about itself" (p. 51).

But this literary public sphere, "the public sphere in the world of letters," also had its own economic foundations. Its existence depended upon the commercialization of culture in a capitalist society. Private persons could be constituted as a reading public, Habermas maintains, only through the postal services, periodicals, and other communications systems that had grown in regularity with a market society; their individual access to the printed word could be sustained only insofar as it fed the commercial expansion of the printing and publishing trades; their personal taste for culture could be satisfied only in the coffee houses, salons, reading societies, theaters, museums, and concert halls opened to them in the urban centers of a bourgeois society; their collective judgment could be informed only by the new class of writers and critics whose livelihood now depended upon the production of culture as a commodity. The literary public sphere was constituted by the market institutions of bourgeois civil society.

Habermas also sees the literary public sphere as profoundly implicated in the defense of those institutions. For through the forms of the public sphere in the world of letters, he suggests, "the experiential complex of audience-oriented privacy made its way into the political realm's public sphere. The representation of the interests of the privatized domain of a market economy was interpreted with the aid of ideas grown in the soil of the intimate sphere of the conjugal family" (p. 52). In the domain of politics, the needs of civil society were now articulated—against the absolutist, mercantilist state—as the collective judgment of the generality of private individuals making use of their reason. Publicity, the essential condition for rational discussion, was now opposed to the secrecy shrouding the mysteries of absolute sovereignty. Reason—abstract, universal, constant reason—was invoked against the disordered commands of arbitrary will. The rights of thinking humanity were counterposed against the traditional prerogatives of power. The social benefits of free market mechanisms were weighed against the evils of mercantilist regulation. Abstractness, universality, rationality—these became the attributes imputed to that tribunal of "public opinion" before which civil society now summoned the state to judgment; these became the criteria of the enlightened reforms and rigorous codifications by which rule was to be brought into convergence with reason. These, finally, became the legal principles of the constitutional states through which bourgeois civil society eventually secured its interests in the early nineteenth century.

These rational criteria of generality and abstractness, Habermas insists, also "had to have a peculiar obviousness for privatized individuals who, by communicating with each other in the public sphere of the world of letters, confirmed each other's subjectivity as it emerged from their spheres of intimacy" (p. 54). Indeed, they simply restated and expanded upon the norms of openness and inclusiveness by which the bourgeois public sphere was in principle accessible to all individuals regardless of their statuses. But they rested ultimately on the essential ambiguity of the identification of *bourgeois* and *homme*, the male property owner and the individual human being.

For within the intimate sphere of the bourgeois family, Habermas emphasizes, individuals were by no means free from the constraints of the market, nor were they equal in legal and social status. Bound by emotional ties of intimacy, they nonetheless remained subject to the laws of patriarchy and property necessary to sustain the family as an essential institution for the reproduction of capital. The bourgeois head of family was simultaneously "owner of goods and persons and one human being among others" (p. 55). Habermas finds this same ambiguity also operating within the public sphere. The functioning of that sphere depended, of course, upon a relationship between property and education that excluded the great majority of the population from effective participation in it. Moreover, it obscured the essential slippage between the public of privatized individuals communicating in the world of letters (which included women and dependents) and the public of male property owners articulating the needs and interests of civil society in the political public sphere, eventually secured by the creation of the bourgeois constitutional state. "The fully developed bourgeois public sphere was based on the fictitious identity of the two roles assumed by the privatized individuals who came together to form a public: the role of property owners and the role of human beings" (p. 56). This fiction could be maintained as long as, but no longer than, it served the positive function of emancipating civil society from mercantilist rule and absolutist regimentation. "Because it turned the principle of publicity against the established authorities, the objective function of the public sphere in the political realm could initially converge with its self-interpretation derived from the categories of the public sphere in the world of letters; the interest of the owners of private property could converge with that of the freedom of the individual in general" (p. 56).

Third, then, Habermas describes the category of the bourgeois public sphere as resting on an ideological fiction. "Class interest," he argues, "was the basis of public opinion" (p. 87).

But as long as the principle of universal access was maintained, "as long as publicity existed as a sphere and functioned as a principle, what the public itself believed to be and to be doing was ideology and simultaneously more than mere ideology" (p. 88). The formation of the bourgeois public sphere was ideological to the extent that it secured the domination of one class over another but more than merely ideological to the degree that it constituted the normative ideal of the dissolution of domination into the consensual rule of reason through the mechanisms of open discussion and debate. Only in the nineteenth century, as changing social and political conditions subverted the separation between state and civil society, thereby eroding the structure of the bourgeois public sphere, did it become clear that in the name of publicity the bourgeoisie had founded a "political order . . . whose social basis did not make domination superfluous at all" (p. 88).

Thus it is a fourth essential feature of Habermas's account, and perhaps the most paradoxical, that the *public* sphere he is describing took form within the *private* realm of civil society. "The bourgeois public sphere evolved in the tension-charged field between state and society," he argues. "But it did so in such a way that it remained itself a part of the private realm" (p. 140). This conception of the public sphere is therefore quite different from the conventional distinction between the public (as the domain of political power) and the private (as the domain of social reproduction). And it is altogether antithetical to the classical republican conception of the public political realm as the domain in which independent citizens participate in the common exercise of a sovereign, political will, whether that be understood in the terms of the early-modern discourse of classical republicanism, best studied by J. G. A. Pocock,[8] or of the more idealized philosophical reworking of that conception by Hannah Arendt.[9] The creation of the public sphere that Habermas describes was understood as a distinctive feature of modern society rather than a recovery of the model of the ancient polis. Its members were construed as private individuals dispersed throughout society, not as citizens of a republic gathered in common in a political forum; they participated in the critical discussion leading to the formulation of a rational, consensual judgment, not in the agonistic struggle for the formation of a common will.

Given the historical specificity of Habermas's account; the ambiguity of its definition of the bourgeois public sphere as normative ideal, ideological fiction, and social form; and the unusual relationship it bears to the conventional distinction between public and private; efforts to extend his analysis to (or test it against) other times and places necessarily become somewhat problematic. In their chapters for this volume, Michael Schudson and Mary Ryan, for example, consider a very different kind of polity, one operating with quite different definitions of the public sphere. Schudson throws strong doubt on the actual existence of a public sphere of rational-critical discourse in eighteenth- and nineteenth-century America, but his empirical demonstration loses force to the extent that Habermas presents the bourgeois public sphere, even in its European manifestation, more as normative ideal (or ideological fiction) than as fully actualized social reality. And Ryan clearly tells a very different story of American life, revolving around women's contestation of their relegation to the domain of the private and their exclusion from a public political sphere of republican citizenship conceived in quite other terms than Habermas's rational public sphere. Both chapters suggest, in effect, how specifically Habermas's conception of the public sphere is tied to the institutional and cultural history of eighteenth- and early nineteenth-century Europe.

The same might also be said of David Zaret's claims (in his chapter for this volume) for the importance of public opinion as already a crucial feature of English political and religious life in the middle of the seventeenth century. For the phenomenon Zaret is describing is not the appeal to "public opinion" as an explicit category of rational authority but the invocation of a quite different notion of collective judgment, the conscience of the godly, which he translates as the equivalent of public opinion. It may indeed be true, as Zaret suggests, that the constitution of a discursive community in protestant terms was more important than Habermas allows in preparing the later emergence of a discursive community constituted in more secular terms as a rational public sphere. But it seems to be a mistake to equate the reason of Milton's "members of the church" with "public opinion" as if they meant exactly the same thing or were simply different terms for the same sociological referent. Appeals to a wider community or public constitute that entity precisely in the choice of the terms they use; "publics" are always to that extent differentiated political and cultural constructions rather than a common social phenomenon bearing a variety of names. A public constituted in terms of will, for example, may have a very different political resonance than one constituted in terms of reason; nor are invocations of the public voice necessarily equivalent to claims about the public spirit.[10] Indeed, the notion of the "public" is almost always a highly contested notion, claimed and reclaimed for a great variety of purposes and susceptible of a considerable variety of constructions. From this point of view, although he occasionally conflates such different constructions as "public voice," "public spirit," and "public opinion" as if they referred necessarily to the same social-structural development of the bourgeois public sphere, Habermas's basic emphasis on the *distinctive* characteristics of the eighteenth-century conception of the public sphere remains one of the most important and valuable aspects of his work.

2   The French Case

How clearly, then, can the particular historical constellation described in *The Structural Transformation of the Public Sphere* be found in eighteenth-century France? It must be acknowledged from the outset that Habermas's discussion of eighteenth-century French developments is relatively sketchy. Eighteenth-century Britain, which he sees as the more advanced capitalist economy, is presented as the "model case" of the development of the bourgeois public sphere; France appears (with Germany) only as one of the "continental variants." This in itself presents a problem to the extent that the bourgeoisie and the social and political institutions sustaining the new public sphere are presented as more fully developed in England, while the theories of publicity and public opinion providing the rationale for the bourgeois public sphere (as a defense of civil society against the absolute state) are seen to emerge most explicitly in France (with the physiocrats) and Germany (with Kant). In this formulation the conception of the bourgeois public sphere is largely produced by blending the sociology of Britain with the philosophy of the Continent.

As France appears in *The Structural Transformation of the Public Sphere,* its bourgeoisie is too weak and isolated, its nobility too far removed from dynamic economic activity, to offer the social basis for the developed political journalism and parliamentary institutions seen across the Channel. For these reasons, Habermas suggests, the literary public sphere of the Enlightenment remained more closely tied to aristocratic society, while the development of a public sphere in the political realm remained relatively rudimentary for much of the century. Only in the 1780s did Necker abruptly breach the absolutist principle of secrecy by opening the mysteries of state debt to public discussion. Only then, "brought into life, with the help of intellectuals who had risen socially, in the womb of a parasitic, economically and politically functionless, yet socially eminent nobility," did "the sphere of a public that eventually also engaged in a critical debate of political issues now definitely [become] the sphere in which civil society reflected on and expounded its interests" (p. 69). The subsequent convening of the Estates General finally brought about a revolution that "created in France overnight, although with less stability, what in Great Britain had taken more than a century of steady evolution: the institutions, which until then had been lacking, for critical public debate of political matters" (p. 70).

Recent research has done much to revise these characterizations in ways that would make England and France more similar in the eighteenth century than Habermas's analysis allows. Many social historians would now wish to stress the growth of the eighteenth-century French economy, the active participation of the nobility in that growth, and the appearance of a relatively open and progressive elite of wealth and title, fostered by the activities of a modernizing state.[11] Historians of political culture, in their turn, could point to the extent to which the traditional politics of absolutism had already been transformed, from the 1750s on, by conflicts between the crown and the judicial magistrates of the parlements.[12] These conflicts extended to an entire range of religious, fiscal, economic, and administrative issues—and ultimately to the question of the essential nature of the French constitution itself. And as they escalated, so the French moved much closer to the politics of contestation they associated with their neighbor across the Channel than has often been realized—much closer, indeed, than many of them found comfortable. In the last decades of the Old Regime, parlementary remonstrances denouncing royal despotism circulated (albeit illegally) in large numbers; pamphlets proliferated on all sides, as writers were recruited and put to work by the government and its critics alike; magistrates and ministers jockeyed for coverage in the relatively independent international press; radical journalists, writing in albeit precarious journals, began to hone the techniques of revolutionary denunciation. Despite the lack of fully representative political institutions, or perhaps precisely because of that lack, the entire conduct of the French state was brought into question before the tribunal of "the public." In the course of this process, "public opinion" emerged as the defining concept of a new political space quite different from the traditional political culture of an absolute monarchy.

In some ways, then, eighteenth-century France might appear today to be less like a "Continental variation" and more like the English model of the emerging public sphere than it seemed to Habermas almost thirty years ago. But there are several respects in which the fuller picture of French political culture we now have still seems to resist his categorization. Certainly it has been achieved at the cost of a growing skepticism regarding the utility of the notion of the bourgeoisie as a category to illuminate eighteenth-century French social and political life. The new public politics that appeared in France in the latter part of the century clearly assumed such features of a developing market society as literacy, printing, and communications; and there can be little doubt that it eventually came to revolve around the essential issues of taxation and representation posed by the problems of the state debt. But it seems difficult to characterize the new public space as a specifically bourgeois phenomenon or to see "public opinion" as the device by which a specifically bourgeois civil society sought to defend its needs and interests against the absolute state.

In my own work I have tended to put more emphasis on the concept of "public opinion" as a political invention appearing in the context of a crisis of absolute authority in which actors within an absolutist political system appealed to a "public" beyond as a way of reformulating institutional claims that could no longer be negotiated within the traditional political language. Little seems to be gained by attempting to analyze these political developments in the conventional Marxist terms of class used by Habermas in 1962. These terms seem too vague, on the one hand, to characterize the political actors contending within the traditional system, actors whose purposes and goals can be described and differentiated much more precisely in terms of their competing institutional positions within an increasingly contradictory regime. They seem too concrete, on the other hand, to characterize the new "public" to which these actors appealed as their conflicts escalated, for "the public" was much more an abstract political category than it was a sociological one, and once put into play, it could be deployed in the service of a wide variety of social and political interests.

It follows that notions such as "the public" and "public opinion" remained constantly contested and subject to competing claims. Habermas certainly recognizes the existence of different inflections upon these terms in prerevolutionary French debate. But at the same time, because he assumes they have an ultimate sociological referent in relation to the needs and interests of bourgeois civil society, he also tends to assimilate their different meanings. He recognizes, for example, that the physiocrats' rationalistic conception of *opinion publique* is no less antithetical to Rousseau's definition of the same term—the first being an outcome of critical public discussion, the second the unreflective force of common assumptions and beliefs—than it is to his voluntaristic conception of the *volonté générale*. He also acknowledges that this latter notion implied the repudiation of the assumptions of the bourgeois public sphere in favor of "the unbourgeois idea of an intrusively political society in which the autonomous private sphere, that is, civil society emancipated from the state, had no place" (p. 97). Yet he is nevertheless able to conclude that these apparently antithetical notions ultimately represented two complementary functions of public opinion within the bourgeois public sphere that were brought together by the French Revolution.

The physiocrats spoke out in favor of an absolutism complemented by a public sphere that was a place of critical activity; Rousseau wanted democracy without public debate. Both sides lay claim to the same title: *opinion publique.* Hence the meaning of the latter became particularly polarized in prerevolutionary France. However, the Revolution itself combined the two functions of public opinion, the critical and the legislative. (P. 99)

Habermas brings us close here to a telelogical conception in relation to which opposing notions of the public must be seen to be ultimately reconcilable as representing different aspects of the developing bourgeois public sphere. In the context of eighteenth-century political theory, however, the rationalist conception of public opinion and the voluntaristic conception of the general will belonged to radically different political discourses. They grounded quite different assumptions about the nature of social and political order and implied competing conceptions of the public sphere that might replace or transform the traditional absolutist regime. Rousseau combined a formidable critique of modern society with a profound nostalgia for the lost political community of the ancients; his paradoxical ideal was the recovery of individual freedom and social community through the operation of a general will in a reconstituted polis. But this reworking of classical republicanism, obsessed with replacing arbitrary particular wills with the general will of the entire body of citizens, was quite antithetical to the physiocratic theory of modern society grounded on the principles of the rights of man and the division of labor, with its impulse to exorcise political will entirely through the general rule of reason. As Enlightenment reworkings of the languages of classical republicanism and natural jurisprudence, the Rousseauian general will and the physiocratic rule of reason already offered, in effect, that radical choice between the "liberty of the ancients" and the "liberty of the moderns" that Benjamin Constant identified as so fateful for the French Revolution.

From this perspective, the revolutionaries did not simply bring together hitherto sundered aspects of a single conception; they made tragic choices and combinations, with unforeseen consequences, among competing conceptual and political possibilities.

Among the earliest of such possibilities to be discarded in 1789 was the public politics of a system of distributing and balancing competing powers, exemplified by the English constitution—a system given its clearest theoretical formulation by Delolme's *Constitution de l'Angleterre* as the best modern alternative to Rousseau's idealization of the direct democracy of the ancients. In France the disorder and incoherence entailed in such a system of political contestation and compromise was often invoked to discredit efforts of the parlementary magistrates to resume a more active political role, as public representatives of the nation, in checking arbitrary monarchical government. And it was in contradistinction to parlementary claims construed in the light of the dangerous English model, no less than to the political voluntarism inherent in Rousseauian republicanism, that the physiocrats developed their conception of the public rule of reason. Since Habermas attributes to the physiocrats the first explicit formulation of the notion of "public opinion as the expression of reason" (p. 54), it will be useful to consider their doctrine in this respect somewhat more fully.

In Habermas's account, the physiocrats, hoping thereby "to bring rule into convergence with reason," first "declared that *opinion publique* alone had insight into and made visible the *ordre naturel*" (p. 55), upon which an enlightened monarch should base his action. "Only when the physiocrats ascribed it to the *publique éclairé* itself," he later says, "did *opinion publique* receive the strict meaning of an opinion purified through critical discussion in the public sphere to constitute a true opinion" (p. 95). In fact, the physiocratic conception of *opinion publique* seems more ambiguous than these passages might suggest. The physiocrats were unanimous that the surest guarantee against abuse of authority lay in public knowledge of the natural and essential principles of the social order, but they did not claim that these principles were made evident only by public opinion or owed the certainty of their truth directly to its authority. In their view, on the contrary, the public had to be instructed in these truths before its judgment could properly constitute an *enlightened* public opinion. Only then, on the one hand, could its judgment limit abuses of power. Only then, on the other, would it be responsive to those measures of rational administration through which the exercise of power would be transformed into the rule of reason.

In this way the notion of public opinion could be reworked as a counteroppositional notion, legitimating the transformation of the absolute monarchy through administrative decentralization, while evading the claims of the parlements to check royal power as representatives of the nation acting with public support. Explaining the proposal for a hierarchical system of assemblies of property holders developed during Turgot's term as Controller-General, Condorcet argued that it was intended to substitute a rational expression of the national interest for "that public opinion [that is] a kind of obstacle common to all absolute governments in the conduct of affairs, the resistance of which is less constant, but also less tranquil, often as powerful, sometimes harmful, and always dangerous." The system he described would therefore be introduced gradually, with consultation at the national level delayed until participation at the local levels had "subjugated public opinion" and created the conditions for informed consent.[13]

A similar argument was made by Le Trosne, another advocate of the physiocratic idea of decentralizing administration through the creation of provincial assemblies.[14] General diffusion of the principles of the natural social order would be far better in limiting abuses of power than a system of "counterforces" distributing and balancing competing powers, he argued in *De l'ordre social,* since it "would direct public opinion without division."[15] It would also provide a sound basis for rational administration. For what can the most beneficent administration do, Le Trosne demanded, if error and ignorance cause resistance to the most salutary operations; "if ancient mistakes find a support in public opinion; if society itself, complicit in its own misfortunes, shows only indifference regarding its condition, and is ignorant equally of what is favorable, and what fatal, to it?"[16] Thus Le Trosne does not yet identify public opinion with rational collective judgment. "It is public opinion that must be directed above all," he argues; "generally, it governs men more than reason."[17] Before it can be appealed to, enlightened public opinion must be brought into being by an enlightening government.

To master and transform men is therefore a matter only of knowing how to direct opinion; and if dangerous opinions contrary to their interest and happiness can win such a violent attachment from them, why couldn't truth, reason, and justice inspire in them the same conviction, the same courage, the same devotion, especially when these ideas are divorced from abstractions and bound to palpable and evident interests?[18]

Le Trosne understands the task of reform as bringing civil society into self-conscious existence as a condition for the rationalization of administration and the transformation of power. Once the true nature and interests of society are understood by all, he believes, the unitary authority of reason will replace the unitary political will of the monarch.

But it is not among the physiocrats that one finds the fullest development of the notion of a rational public opinion in prerevolutionary France. For that one must look to one of their principal rivals among reforming administrators, Jacques Necker, the Swiss banker who eventually replaced the ousted Turgot as minister of finances and ultimately led the government into its meeting with the Estates General in 1789. Necker too sought to outmaneuver parlementary opposition by appeals to the public and by making publicity the key to the political strategy of the monarchy. Dismissed from the ministry but already preparing the way for his return to power with public support, he offered a dramatic appeal to public opinion in his *De l'administration des finances de la France,* published in 1784. And the characterization of *opinion publique* he offered in that work was quickly taken up by Jacques Peuchet, the editor of the volumes of the *Encyclopédie méthodique* devoted to public administration. In these works, "public opinion" was clearly presented as a characteristic of a specifically modern society, the fruit of that social progress and rational communication that had made the enlightened Europe of the eighteenth century so different from the political world of the ancients.[19] "This word designates in a general manner the sum of all social knowledge [*lumières sociales*]," Peuchet argues, "or rather the result of this knowledge, considered as grounds for the judgments made by a nation on the matters submitted to its tribunal."[20]

But if "public opinion" now emerges in this conceptualization as the ultimate authority inherent in modern society, one of its most striking features is the extent to which it remains imbued with the characteristics hitherto attributed to absolute monarchy. "Very slow to take form," Peuchet insists, public opinion alone "can oppose a dike to the torrent of disorders."[21] Long synonymous with fickleness and flux, "opinion" has now been stabilized by the procedures of publicity, taking on the order and stability of *la chose publique* in absolutist discourse. At the same time, these very characteristics have become the criteria by which true public opinion is to be distinguished from false. "It is necessary to avoid confusing public opinion, as I have described it here, with those ephemeral movements that often pertain only to certain societies and certain circumstances," Necker argues. "It is not before such judgments that the man capable of conducting a great administration should prostrate himself. On the contrary, it is necessary to know how to disdain them, in order to remain faithful to that public opinion whose characteristics are all authoritative [*imposants*] and which reason, time, and the universality of sentiments alone have the right to consecrate."[22]

The profound imprint left by the historical experience and theoretical claims of absolutism upon French social and political life has often been remarked. It is clearly perceptible in the conception of rational public opinion developed as it was by the administrative theorists of the reforming absolute monarchy. That conception ascribed to public opinion—understood as the rational consensus achieved by open procedures of public discussion and criticism—the universality and rationality, order and objectivity, that absolutist theorists had once claimed as the hallmark of monarchical rule. It implied acceptance of a politics of open public discussion on the one hand, but it was seen as an alternative to a politics of contestation and compromise on the other. Public opinion was endowed with the rationalized characteristics of absolute power; unitary authority was transformed and transposed to the critical judgment of the public.

From this perspective, the disagreements surfacing at this conference over whether Habermas's conception of rational public deliberation requires only the postulate of radical proceduralism or depends upon other conditions for the possibility of consensus may be seen historically as a continuing exploration of the ambiguity of the notion of the rational public sphere in its eighteenth-century formulation, an ambiguity that derives from its historical relationship to the experience and claims of absolutism.

3 Women and the Public Sphere

One of the most interesting efforts to engage Habermas's conception of the public sphere in understanding the political culture of eighteenth-century France is Joan Landes's *Women and the Public Sphere in the Age of the French Revolution*. Landes sets out to offer "significant revisions" of Habermas's argument, which she regards as insufficiently attentive to the gendered aspects of the eighteenth-century public sphere.[23] As we have seen, Habermas does indeed emphasize the extent to which the conceptual universality of the public sphere was still an ideological fiction for women, deriving as it did from an intimate domestic sphere in which they remained subjected to male authority.[24] He nevertheless understands the universalistic conception of humanity inherent in the notion of the public sphere as entailing a logic of female emancipation from existing constraints; indeed, he identifies this as "the element of truth that raised bourgeois ideology above ideology itself, most fundamentally in that area where the experience of 'humanity' originated: in the humanity of the intimate relationships between human beings who, under the aegis of the family, were nothing more than human" (p. 48).

But Landes offers a more radical argument. Her aim is to demonstrate that the bourgeois public sphere was "essentially,

not just contingently, masculinist."[25] Far from pointing out that
the logic of universality and reason defining the bourgeois
public sphere was not extended to the inclusion of women in
the public sphere, she contends that it was the essential function of these norms of universality and reason to exclude
women from that sphere. Under the Old Regime, she maintains, women still retained some possibilities for public speech
and action, despite criticisms that associated their prominence
with the decline of traditional institutions. But women were to
be expelled from the bourgeois public sphere as it was given
conceptual form by the Enlightenment and institutional realization by the French Revolution. In the new logic the distinctions between universal and particular, natural and artificial,
transparent and masked, were aligned with the distinction between male and female. "The symbolic politics of the emerging
bourgeois public sphere was framed from the very outset by
masculinist interests and assumptions."[26]

Landes finds the key to this masculinist strategy in "the ideology of republican motherhood,"[27] invented by Rousseau.
"Amiable and virtuous countrywomen, the fate of your sex will
always be to govern ours," declaimed the Citizen of Geneva in
the dedication of his *Second Discourse.* "It is fortunate when
your chaste power, exercised solely in conjugal union, makes
itself felt only for the glory of the state and public happiness.
. . . Therefore always be what you are, the chaste guardians of
morals and the gentle bonds of peace; and continue to exploit
on every occasion the rights of the heart and of nature for the
benefit of duty and virtue."[28] In Rousseau's imagination, all
the disorders of modern civilization were condensed into the
practice of wet-nursing, which is to say women's abandonment
of their maternal role. Their public ostentation being emblem-
atic of all that was theatrical, artificial, and corrupt in the Old
Regime, women were to be banished to a newly textualized
world of private intimacy. The transparent order of reason
and nature could be restored and virtue recovered only by
returning women to that sweet domesticity required as a strict
corollary of their gender. Rousseau's philosophy therefore entailed a radical new theory of sexual differentiation making
men and women essentially incommensurate in their natures

and hence in their social and political roles.[29] The natural man could not exist in society without the natural woman, who would complement and sustain his existence, nor could the virtuous republican citizen reappear without that social reproduction of civic life that was the duty of the virtuous wife and mother.

In Landes's analysis, the Rousseauian ideology of republican motherhood became the basis for the exclusion of women from the bourgeois public sphere when it was institutionalized by the French Revolution. In essence, she argues, this ideology was the expression of a male anxiety about women's participation in public political life that became increasingly hysterical as a succession of women activists sought to claim, on behalf of their sex, the rights of humanity apparently held out to them by the universalistic language of 1789. Not surprisingly, then, it received one of its most impassioned formulations as this anxiety culminated, in October 1793, in the suppression of the Society of Revolutionary Republican Women. "Each sex is called to the kind of occupation which is fitting for it," insisted André Amar in justifying the repression of women's popular societies on behalf of the Committee of General Security. "To begin educating men, to prepare children's minds and hearts for public virtues, to direct them early in life toward the good, to elevate their souls, to educate them in the political cult of liberty: such are [women's] functions after household cares." For Amar, active participation in popular politics could only divert women's cares from these essential duties. Worse still, it would inevitably introduce disorder and error into public affairs:

Let us add that women are disposed by their organization [i.e., the constitution of their physical and moral being] to an over-excitation which would be deadly in public affairs and that interests of state would soon be sacrificed to everything which ardor in passions can generate in the way of error and disorder. Delivered over to the heat of public debate, they would teach their children not love of country but hatreds and suspicions.[30]

Accomplished with the Terror, this expulsion of women from the public to the private domain was not reversed when the

Terror came to an end. To the contrary, Landes points out, it was extended after Thermidor and made all the more systematic by the provisions of the Civil Code.

The ideology of republican motherhood therefore proved a powerful instrument for the repression of women's revolutionary expectations. Indeed, Landes seems to suggest, this ideology was so profoundly inscribed within the bourgeois public sphere that it fatally crippled feminist arguments themselves. Even Condorcet, that "most impassioned liberal defender of women," appears in her analysis as someone who "worries that, once emancipated, women will neglect their (feminine) duties," who "subscribes to the republican—ultimately, Rousseauist—demand for a reform of domestic habits," and who "is made nervous by overly ambitious public women."[31] And Mary Wollstonecraft appears in this light as the author of a self-defeating "feminist version of the ideology of republican motherhood."[32] In Landes's interpretation, Wollstonecraft's *Vindication of the Rights of Woman* was intended to demonstrate that women must necessarily be admitted equally to the political public sphere to qualify them to raise citizens fit to participate in it. But Landes sees the argument of that work as profoundly undermined by Wollstonecraft's own "fears about woman's capacity to illegitimately displace power"[33] and by the gendered view of women's nature underlying the republican ideology that she embraced. Ultimately, she insists, "Wollstonecraft finds it difficult to deny the central presumption of her age, that women possess natures different from men's."[34]

This is a challenging argument but not an altogether convincing one. It seems clear that Rousseau did indeed articulate a radical theory of natural sexual difference and that his reworking of classical republican themes rested on a strict separation between the male (public) and female (domestic) spheres. In this respect, then, the revolutionary republican ideology that drew upon Rousseauian inspiration was indeed "essentially, not contingently, masculinist." But it does not follow that the entire eighteenth-century notion of the public sphere, and with it the entire philosophy of the French Revolution, was essentially masculinist. In developing her argument, Landes simply identifies Rousseauian republican ideology with the public sphere described by Habermas, altogether disregarding the fact that the central terms of Habermas's "public of private people making use of their reason" do not correspond at all to the distinction between public (political) and private (domestic), around which her own work (and republican ideology) is organized. Moreover, Landes fails to grasp the extent to which republican and rationalist conceptions of the public sphere derive from radically competing discourses in the eighteenth-century context. Rousseau's reworking of the discourse of classical republicanism, fundamentally concerned with the recovery of sovereignty by a community of autonomous citizens, was couched in quite different terms than the rationalist discourse of the social, grounded on notions of the rights of man, the division of labor, and the apolitical rule of reason. This latter conception of the public sphere was contingently masculinist to the extent that it admitted contingent grounds for denying women (and others) full and immediate participation in the exercise of universal individual rights, but it was not essentially masculinist in the sense that women were excluded from the exercise of such rights by definition of their very nature.

To demonstrate that this is so, we need look no further than Condorcet's defense of women's political rights and their equal access to education. There is nothing in his writings on these topics to suggest that Condorcet "worries that, once emancipated, women will neglect their (feminine) duties" or "is made nervous by overly ambitious public women" in the manner Landes suggests. He does indeed address the concern that granting political rights to women would take them away from "those duties that nature *seems* [my emphasis] to have reserved for them."[35] But he does so only after stating categorically that "the rights of men result simply from the fact that they are sentient beings, capable of acquiring moral ideas and of reasoning concerning these ideas. Women, having these same qualities, must necessarily possess equal rights."[36] The objection that women's political involvement would detract from the exercise of their domestic responsibilities is thus immediately invalidated as a merely pragmatic one, based on an appeal to "utility, which cannot outweigh a true right" (and which has "too often served as the pretext and excuse of tyrants").[37]

Nevertheless, answering this objection "in order to leave no argument unanswered," Condorcet rejects it as ill-founded on the grounds that "women would be torn from their homes no longer than agricultural laborers from their plows, or artisans from their workshops."[38] He then adds a further observation, particularly revealing in the present context. The principal cause of the fear that women will abandon domestic concerns for political affairs, he argues, is "the idea that every person admitted to the rights of citizenship immediately thinks of nothing but governing others." But this is a revolutionary overinvestment in the political characteristic of "a time when the constitution is being established," which "can scarcely prove durable." The interests of society, in other words, must necessarily reassert themselves, and with them the customary social division of labor. "And so it is unnecessary to believe that because women could become members of national assemblies, they would immediately abandon their children, their homes, and their needles. They would be only the better fitted to educate their children and to rear men."[39] That Condorcet assumes the majority of women will indeed continue to carry out these domestic functions seems clear, but he sees no basis in women's nature to confine them to these functions, to exclude them from active participation in political life, or to deny them full access to the public instruction upon which rational politics and the progress of society must depend. Condorcet does not need, then, to extract arguments for women's emancipation from the recalcitrant lode of republican discourse. He finds them abundantly available in the competing discourse of rational social progress underlying his entire philosophy.

And so does Mary Wollstonecraft. Her work certainly plays on some of the traditional themes of classical republicanism, most notably in its comparison of the vices forced upon women by male oppression with those acquired by the members of a standing army, that most baneful of institutions in republican eyes. Nor is it entirely free of the ideology of republican motherhood. But Wollstonecraft does not draw her feminism primarily from a republican spring. To the contrary, her most fundamental arguments are derived from the Enlightenment discourse of rational social progress, particularly in the secularized theological version favored in England by such writers as Price and Priestley. *A Vindication of the Rights of Woman* therefore begins with a defense of the progress of reason and civilization against Rousseau's denunciations. "To assert that a state of nature is preferable to civilization, in all its possible perfection," Wollstonecraft insists, "is . . . to arraign supreme wisdom."[40] The perfectibility of human reason, that "stamen of immortality,"[41] could not be denied without refusing the providential design of a deity who had "thought fit to call into existence a creature above the brutes, who could think and improve himself."[42] Rousseau, then, had simply identified as "consequences of civilization" the effects of those "vestiges of barbarism" still plaguing human existence—not the least of these vestiges being the domination of kings and priests, which served as the keystone of male oppression.

It is the pestiferous purple which renders the progress of civilization a curse, and warps the understanding, till men of sensibility doubt whether the expansion of intellect produces a greater portion of happiness or misery. But the nature of the poison points out the antidote; and had Rousseau mounted one step higher in his investigation, or could his eye have pierced the foggy atmosphere, which he almost disdained to breathe, his active mind would have darted forward to contemplate the perfection of man in the establishment of true civilization, instead of taking his ferocious flight back to the night of sensual ignorance.[43]

For women to participate in the benefits of that progress required that they share in the same rational human nature as men. Thus Wollstonecraft explicitly repudiates Rousseau's claim that women's nature is radically different from men's. "If women are by nature inferior to men," she argues, "their virtues must be the same in quality, if not in degree, or virtue is a relative idea."[44] Wollstonecraft is therefore willing to admit *hypothetically* that women might be naturally inferior to men, but she does this only as a way of excluding the far more radical argument that the sexes differ so profoundly that their virtue and knowledge are simply incommensurate. Her rhetorical stance is to disclaim the "wish to invert the order of things" and to grant that "from the constitution of their bodies, men *seem* [my emphasis] to be designed by Providence to attain a greater degree of virtue," but these disclaimers lead directly to a denial of any "shadow of a reason to conclude that their virtues should differ in respect of their nature."[45] Similarly, she declares herself willing to "allow that bodily strength *seems* [my emphasis] to give man a natural superiority over woman; and this is the only solid basis on which the superiority of the sex can be built," only to insist that "not only the virtue, but the *knowledge* of the two sexes should be the same in nature, if not in degree, and that women, considered not only as moral, but rational creatures, ought to endeavor to acquire human virtues (or perfections) by the *same* means as men, instead of being educated like a fanciful kind of *half* being—one of Rousseau's wild chimeras."[46]

In arguing that Wollstonecraft "finds it difficult to deny the central presumption of her age, that women possess natures different from men," Landes therefore seems to me to have misconstrued the central rhetorical thrust of the *Vindication*. Wollstonecraft specifically repudiates the claim that women's nature is qualitatively different from men's by admitting the hypothetical possibility that, while similar in nature, the two sexes might differ in degree. But even as she admits the hypothesis that women might be inferior to men (though similar in nature), Wollstonecraft works to undermine its plausibility. The female characteristics invoked to justify women's subjection are themselves the result of that subjection, she argues; men placed in similar circumstances exhibit similar traits. Since the causes that have degraded women have had the same effect on men, the question of whether women are indeed inferior must remain radically open. These causes, Wollstonecraft argues, "all spring from want of understanding. Whether this arise from a physical or accidental weakness of faculties, time alone can determine . . . ; I only contend that the men who have been placed in similar situations, have acquired a similar character."[47]

Thus Wollstonecraft challenges men to find out whether women are really not capable of acting as rational creatures by treating them as if they are. "Frankly acknowledging the inferiority of women *according to the present appearance of things*" (my emphasis), she claims only "that men have increased that inferiority till women are almost sunk below the standard of rational creatures." But how far this inferiority is natural, how far acquired, simply remains to be established. Human capacity for progress is such that "it is difficult for us purblind mortals to say to what height human discoveries and improvements may arrive when the gloom of despotism subsides." All that is possible is to put the presumption of equality to the test. "Let [women's] faculties have room to unfold, and their virtues to gain strength, and then determine where the whole sex must stand in the intellectual scale."[48] Reason is the "simple power of improvement. . . . More or less may be conspicuous in one being or another." But time alone will tell how far it may be differentially distributed among men and women. In the meantime, women have not only been denied the power of understanding; it has been declared inconsistent with their sexual nature. "Let men prove this," Wollstonecraft challenges, "and I shall grant that woman only exists for man."[49]

Gradually, then, Wollstonecraft shifts from admitting the hypothetical possibility of women's natural inferiority to inviting men to prove it in the only way possible: by admitting women fully to the rational public sphere. Men are challenged to put their claims at risk by testing them against the postulate of a common human rationality. A test of this kind can have only two possible outcomes: men must either abandon their domination altogether or see it transformed by the free rule of reason, which would amount to the same thing. "I love man as my fellow; but his sceptre, real, or usurped, extends not to me, unless the reason of an individual demands my homage; and even then the submission is to reason, and not to man. In fact, the conduct of an accountable being must be regulated by the operations of its own reason; or on what foundation rests the throne of God?"[50]

This is not a crippled feminist inflection on the ideology of republican motherhood but a daring appeal for the realization of women's rights within the contrary discourse of the progress of modern society through the cultivation of individual human reason. "Till women are more rationally educated," Wollstonecraft insists, "the progress of human virtue and improvement in knowledge must receive continual checks."[51] Like Condorcet, Wollstonecraft imagines a society progressing through the differentiation of occupations and professions exercised by individuals, who remain equal in their rights even as they may differ in their rational abilities and social responsibilities. "Speaking of women at large," she argues, "their first duty is to themselves as rational creatures." If "the next in point of importance, as citizens, is that which includes so many, of a mother,"[52] this role cannot be fulfilled without the full cultivation of a woman's rational talents and abilities. Nor is it the only role to which these talents and abilities may be productively applied. "How many women thus waste life away the prey of discontent, who might have practised as physicians, regulated a farm, managed a shop, and stood erect, supported by their own industry . . . ?"[53]

Wollstonecraft, like Condorcet, therefore derived her fundamental arguments for women's emancipation from the rationalist discourse of the social, which Habermas was essentially describing under the category of the "bourgeois public sphere." Their arguments were unsuccessful, at least in the short run, but their ability to formulate these arguments as implications of the basic assumptions of individual rights and social progress shows that this discourse was far from being "essentially, not just contingently, masculinist." The republican discourse that Landes characterizes in these latter terms was not identical with the rationalist discourse of the social but a competing definition of the social and political space imagined as an alternative to the Old Regime. In 1789 the revolutionaries were offered several conceptual possibilities, several competing visions of a new order. The political choices they made in 1789 and thereafter ultimately privileged the republican discourse of political will, which found its fullest expression in the Terror. But the rationalist discourse of the social submerged by the Terror became the basis for the "liberty of the moderns," rediscovered by Benjamin Constant, among others, after Thermidor. Still unfulfilled, its principles held out that open-ended promise of individual emancipation for all in a rational, democratic society, which continues now more than ever to define the modern political agenda.

Notes

1. Reinhart Koselleck, *Kritik und Krise: Eine Studie zur Pathogenese der bürgerlichen Welt* (Freiburg, 1959); English translation, *Critique and Crisis: Enlightenment and the Pathogenesis of Modern Society* (Cambridge, Mass., 1988). A French translation appeared in 1979.

2. See Philippe Ariès and Georges Duby, eds., *Histoire de la vie privée*, 5 vols. (Paris, 1982–1985), especially volumes 3–4; Henri-Jean Martin, Roger Chartier, Jean-Pierre Vivet, eds., *Histoire de l'édition française*, 4 vols. (Paris, 1982–1986). Other important works on literacy, printing, and practices of reading include François Furet and Jacques Ozouf, *Lire et écrire: L'alphabétisation des Français de Calvin à Jules Ferry* (Paris, 1977); Elizabeth Eisenstein, *The Printing Press as an Agent of Social Change: Communications and Cultural Transformations in Early-Modern Europe*, 2 vols. (Cambridge, 1979); Roger Chartier, ed., *Pratiques de la lecture* (Paris, 1985) and *Les usages de l'imprimé (XV–XIXe siècle)* (Paris, 1987).

3. See especially Thomas E. Crow, *Painters and Public Life in Eighteenth-Century Paris* (New Haven, 1985).

4. See Keith Michael Baker, "Politics and Public Opinion under the Old Regime: Some Reflections," in Jack R. Censer and Jeremy D. Popkin, eds., *Press and Politics in Prerevolutionary France* (Berkeley, 1987), pp. 204–246, revised version reprinted in Baker, *Inventing the French Revolution* (Cambridge, 1990), 167–199; Mona Ozouf, "Opinion publique," in Keith Michael Baker, ed., *The French Revolution and the Creation of Modern Political Culture*, vol. 1, *The Political Culture of the Old Regime* (Oxford, 1987), pp. 419–434 (an English translation by Lydia Cochrane has appeared as "'Public Opinion' at the End of the Old Regime," *Journal of Modern History* 60 suppl. [1988]: 3–21); Sarah Mazah, "Le tribunal de la nation: Les mémoires judiciaires et l'opinion publique à la fin de l'ancien régime," *Annales: ESC* 47 (1987): 75–90. The issue is also taken up in Roger Chartier, *Cultural Origins of the French Revolution* (Durham, N.C., 1991).

5. In this respect the influence of François Furet, *Interpreting the French Revolution*, trans. Elborg Forster (Cambridge, 1981, originally published in 1978), has been fundamental. Recent works exploring this theme include Mona Ozouf, *Festivals and the French Revolution*, trans. Alan Sheridan (Cambridge, Mass., 1988, originally published in 1976); Lynn Hunt, *Politics, Culture, and Class in the French Revolution* (Berkeley, 1984); Baker, ed., *The French Revolution and the Creation of Modern Political Culture*, vol. 1, *The Political Culture of the Old Regime*; Colin Lucas, ed., *The French Revolution and the Creation of Modern Political Culture*, vol. 2, *The Political Culture of the French Revolution* (Oxford, 1988); François Furet and Mona Ozouf, eds., *The French Revolution and the Creation of Modern Political Culture*, vol. 3, *1795–1848*; François Furet and Mona Ozouf, eds., *Critical Dictionary of the French Revolution*, trans. Arthur Goldhammer (Cambridge, Mass., 1989).

6. Joan B. Landes, *Women and the Public Sphere in the Age of the French Revolution* (Ithaca, 1988).

7. Parenthetical page references are to Jürgen Habermas, *The Structural Transformation of the Public Sphere: An Inquiry into a Category of Bourgeois Society,* trans. Thomas Burger and Frederick Lawrence (Cambridge, Mass., 1989).

8. J. G. A. Pocock, *The Machiavellian Moment* (Princeton, 1975).

9. Hannah Arendt, *The Human Condition* (Chicago, 1958). For a comparison of Arendt's conception of the public sphere and Habermas's, see the chapter by Seyla Benhabib in this volume.

10. In France, for example, the latter was frequently an administrative term applied to the state of mind of a subject population, without any connotations of public initiative or consent.

11. See, for example, Guy Chaussinand-Nogaret, *The French Nobility in the Eighteenth Century: From Feudalism to Enlightenment,* trans. William Doyle (Cambridge, 1985).

12. On this point, see the essays in Baker, ed., *The Political Culture of the Old Regime.*

13. M.-J.-A.-N. Caritat de Condorcet, *Œuvres,* ed. F. Arago and A. Condorcet-O'Connor, 12 vols. (Paris, 1847–1849), 5:123–124; see also Baker, *Inventing the French Revolution,* pp. 162–163.

14. See Guillaume François Le Trosne, *De l'administration provinciale et de la réforme de l'impôt* (Basel, 1779).

15. Le Trosne, *De l'ordre social* (Paris, 1777), p. 258.

16. Le Trosne, *De l'ordre social,* p. 4.

17. Le Trosne, *De l'ordre social,* p. 295.

18. Le Trosne, *De l'ordre social,* p. 296.

19. The following discussion of these works draws on Baker, *Inventing the French Revolution,* pp. 190–197.

20. Jacques Peuchet, Discours préliminaire, in *Encyclopédie méthodique: Jurisprudence,* vol. 9, *Police et municipalités,* p. ix.

21. Peuchet, Discours préliminaire, pp. lxxx–lxxxi.

22. Necker, *Œuvres complètes,* ed. A.-L. de Staël-Holstein, 15 vols. (Paris, 1820–1821), 4:56.

23. Landes, *Women and the Public Sphere,* p. 7.

24. "The independence of the property owner in the market and in his own business was complemented by the dependence of the wife and children on the male head of the family; private autonomy in the former realm was transformed into authority in the latter and made any pretended freedom of individuals illusory" (p. 47).

25. Landes, *Women and the Public Sphere,* p. 7.

26. Landes, *Women and the Public Sphere*, p. 40.

27. Landes, *Women and the Public Sphere*, p. 129.

28. Rousseau, *The First and Second Discourses*, trans. Roger D. Masters and Judith R. Masters (New York, 1964), p. 89; quoted in Landes, *Women and the Public Sphere*, pp. 69–70.

29. The radical character of Rousseau's argument concerning sexual differentiation, as compared with earlier notions, is well brought out in Thomas Laqueur, *Making Sex: Body and Gender from the Greeks to Freud* (Cambridge, Mass., 1990).

30. André Amar, speech to the National Convention (30 October 1793), in Darline Gay Levy, Harriet Branson Applewhite, and Mary Durham Johnson, eds., *Women in Revolutionary Paris, 1789–1795: Selected Documents* (Urbana, 1979), pp. 216–217; quoted in Landes, *Women and the Public Sphere*, p. 144. My interpolation.

31. Landes, *Women and the Public Sphere*, pp. 116–117.

32. Landes, *Women and the Public Sphere*, p. 138.

33. Landes, *Women and the Public Sphere*, p. 134.

34. Landes, *Women and the Public Sphere*, p. 130.

35. Condorcet, "On the Admission of Women to the Rights of Citizenship," in *Condorcet: Selected Writings*, ed. Keith Michael Baker (Indianapolis, 1976), p. 101.

36. Condorcet, "On the Admission of Women to the Rights of Citizenship," p. 98.

37. Condorcet, "On the Admission of Women to the Rights of Citizenship," p. 101.

38. Condorcet, "On the Admission of Women to the Rights of Citizenship," p. 101.

39. Condorcet, "On the Admission of Women to the Rights of Citizenship," p. 102.

40. Mary Wollstonecraft, *A Vindication of the Rights of Woman*, ed. Mrs. Henry Fawcett (London, 1891), p. 42.

41. Wollstonecraft, *A Vindication of the Rights of Woman*, p. 94.

42. Wollstonecraft, *A Vindication of the Rights of Woman*, p. 42.

43. Wollstonecraft, *A Vindication of the Rights of Woman*, p. 48; cf. p. 44.

44. Wollstonecraft, *A Vindication of the Rights of Woman*, p. 58.

45. Wollstonecraft, *A Vindication of the Rights of Woman*, p. 59.

46. Wollstonecraft, *A Vindication of the Rights of Woman*, p. 75.

47. Wollstonecraft, *A Vindication of the Rights of Woman*, p. 127.

48. Wollstonecraft, *A Vindication of the Rights of Woman*, pp. 69, 70.

49. Wollstonecraft, *A Vindication of the Rights of Woman*, p. 96.

50. Wollstonecraft, *A Vindication of the Rights of Woman*, p. 72.

51. Wollstonecraft, *A Vindication of the Rights of Woman*, p. 77.

52. Wollstonecraft, *A Vindication of the Rights of Woman*, p. 218.

53. Wollstonecraft, *A Vindication of the Rights of Woman*, p. 223.

9

Religion, Science, and Printing in the Public Spheres in Seventeenth-Century England

David Zaret

1   Introduction

Critical commentary enjoys an unfair advantage when it is directed at historical and sociological scholarship published nearly thirty years ago. The advantage is greater where the work in question analyzes the rise of some significant aspect of modern society, as Habermas does in *The Structural Transformation of the Public Sphere.*[1] In such cases perfunctory criticism all too often follows advances in historical scholarship as they sharpen our sensitivity to historical anachronism and, oddly enough, also diminish it to historical novelty. Critical commentary thus reveals either that the significant aspect of modernity did not exist or existed well before its alleged point of origin. The dilemma, then, is to assess Habermas's account of the origins of the public sphere in the light of nearly three decades of subsequent scholarship, without invoking that scholarship in a facile critique that displays little more than hypersensitivity to anachronism or a diminished sense of novelty in history.

To that end I treat Habermas's model of the public sphere as an ideal type, a limiting case against which existent practices and presuppositions can be measured. I see no other way of thinking about the notion of a public body of citizens conferring in an unrestricted manner about public issues. Both the social distribution of this activity and the extent to which it is unrestricted exhibit considerable variation, but in no historical case will its distribution or unrestricted character be complete.

In this view, Habermas's account is not challenged by the observation that many of the inhabitants of early modern England or France had little contact with the activities that constitute the public sphere. Under this set of premises, Habermas's book can be said to outline an extremely important aspect of modernization that cannot be dismissed either with references to anachronism or prior precedent. Something resembling a public sphere did begin to coalesce in parts of early modern Europe, and the practices that constituted this sphere represent radically new assumptions about knowledge, social authority, and individual rights.

That *The Structural Transformation of the Public Sphere* should not be dismissed in a facile manner does not make it immune to all criticism. Taking early modern England as my case, I argue that the rise of a public sphere was indeed an important development but that Habermas's analysis of it is flawed by errors of omission. Though the analysis is magisterial in its deft use of a diverse set of historical and philosophical materials, it leads to a greatly truncated account of the public sphere because of its close adherence to a Marxist framework. To be sure, Habermas, in *The Structural Transformation,* relies on a version of Marxism, critical theory, that is less doctrinaire than others and is more sensitive to complexities inherent in empirical historical research. Even so, it is unequal to the task of providing a compelling account for the emergence of the liberal model of the public sphere in the political realm.

The following discussion identifies several empirical and theoretical problems in an analysis that associates the rise of the public sphere too narrowly with economic forces and issues. Foremost among the empirical problems is the virtual neglect of religion, science, and printing in England. Aside from a few scattered references in the text and in a long footnote,[2] Habermas's account glosses over the relevance of religion for the emergence of a public sphere in politics at a time when religious discourse was a, if not the, predominant means by which individuals defined and debated issues in this sphere. Equally neglected are the implications of the printing and scientific revolutions for new views on public reason that were incorporated in political appeals to a reasoning public. While Habermas refers implicitly to the printing revolution in his discussion of the rise of a reading public, he regards it narrowly as a means for disseminating and sharing ideas and not as an independent causal factor that shaped new modes of thought.[3]

Consideration of the joint effects of developments in religion, science, and printing on the rise of the public sphere leads to a theoretical issue central to Habermas's account. This concerns the idea that the activities proper to the public sphere—the rational and critical discourse of enlightened persons—exist by virtue of its isolation from the exigencies of everyday life in early modern Europe. "The rational-critical debate of private people in the *salons,* clubs, and reading societies was not directly subject to the cycle of production and consumption, that is, to the dictates of life's necessities."[4] This argument reiterates an old theme that in revised form became a key feature in early twentieth-century sociology and in the critical theory that guides Habermas's account of the public sphere: the opposition between civilization and culture as realms respectively of necessity and freedom. Modern versions of this theme can be found in writings by Alfred Weber and by the first generation of critical theorists. According to critical theory, the institutional separation of high culture from material civilization ensured the survival of critical ideas that were contradicted by the exploitative structures in material life.[5] Yet it is precisely this notion of an encapsulated culture that, for both popular and learned culture, has been demolished by early modern historians who trace the impact of printing on new modes of thought. In describing printing's impact on learned culture, Darnton and Eisenstein call attention to the capitalist organization of printing; for popular culture, Chartier and Davis show, "This new relationship with the printed word cannot be separated from the social relations that lay at the heart of all forms of popular sociability—work-connected, religious, or festive."[6]

These empirical and theoretical issues are far too broad to be adequately documented in a single article. My intent, then, is to call attention to the relevance of religion, science, and printing for understanding how public opinion came to acquire its authority in seventeenth-century England, and to consider how this relevance undermines an encapsulated model of the cultural practices that appear in the public sphere. Abandoning the overemphasis on economic factors in the rise of the public sphere reduces the need to isolate critical discourse from civilization. More critical, rational modes of reflection on matters of collective social interest can be situated in their social context when developments in religion, science, and printing are taken into account. These developments produced more critical habits of thought based on appeals to public reason, which subsequently became conflated with explicitly political issues. The critical rationality in an emergent public sphere of politics was not a superstructural appendage of economic life; it was a feature of many noneconomic processes that in the seventeenth century were propelling England into the modern world.

2 The English Revolution and the Public Sphere

Habermas's account of the liberal model of the public sphere traces its origins to structural transformations wrought by early capitalism. In the rise of the absolutist state, the decline of the parcelized sovereignty that characterized feudalism occurred alongside the attenuation of conditional constraints on property rights.[7] As seignorial property ceased to be a source of juridical authority, it was also emancipated from conditions of fealty and respect for manorial custom. Thus the rise of unconditional property rights proceeded with the assumption of an indivisible sovereignty by the absolutist state. Of course, the absolutist state was not truly absolute—corporate groups continued to mediate between sovereign and subject—and interference with property rights persisted in fiscal feudalism, e.g., wardships. But the significance of this juncture for critical discourse, as Mannheim observed,[8] is that political philosophers presumed sovereignty, however vested, to be absolute and property rights to be inviolate. The liberal model of the public sphere presupposes this separation between a private sphere dominated by commodity production and a public realm of sovereign authority.

Not only did capitalist development create this structural opposition between private life and public authority; it also

supplied the primary actors in the public sphere (the bourgeoisie) as well as the issues that initially dominate this sphere.
According to Habermas, the "protection of a commercial economy" impels the bourgeoisie to constitute the public sphere.
"The bourgeois public sphere may be conceived above all as
the sphere of private people come together as a public; they
soon claimed the public sphere regulated from above against
the public authorities themselves, to engage them in a debate
over the general rules governing relations in the basically privatized but publicly relevant sphere of commodity production
and social labor."[9] Because "the regulations of mercantilist policy" had consequences that reverberated throughout the economy, "broad strata of the population" were drawn into the
debates taking place in the public sphere. The hallmark of this
public sphere was more rational, critical habits of thought,
which made it "a sphere of criticism of public authority." "The
medium of this political confrontation was peculiar and without
historical precedent: people's public use of their reason."[10] The
overriding emphasis on economic issues is moderated a bit by
Habermas's references to critical intellectual habits cultivated
in a public sphere of the world of letters and to religion's role
in the creation of the private sphere.[11] But the broad outlines
of this analysis follow the familiar Marxist argument that democracy is an ideological superstructure that rests on an economic foundation built by the rising historical fortunes of the
bourgeoisie. Habermas generally locates the development of
the political public sphere in England, the "model" case, at the
end of the seventeenth century.

Perhaps the most startling feature of this account as it applies
to England is the omission of nearly all of the seventeenth
century. At "the turn of the eighteenth century," writes Habermas, "forces endeavoring to influence the decisions of state
authority appealed to the critical public in order to legitimate
demands before this new forum."[12] Yet precisely this forum,
public opinion, was the center stage for many major events in
the midcentury English Revolution, beginning with the Civil
Wars between King Charles and Parliament (1642–1648), the
Regicide (1649), the creation of the Republic (1649–1653) and

Cromwell's Protectorate (1653–1658), and the Restoration (1660).

This aspect of the Revolution has been thoroughly documented by Christopher Hill, Brian Manning, David Underdown, and other historians who describe the development of more democratic patterns of debate and dissent in the English Revolution. In Parliament and the more radical groups outside its walls, revolutionary leadership depended less on charismatic qualities perceived in leaders than on popular appraisals of their adherence to tenets of a belief system that lay claim to universal validity. Symptomatic of this new style of dissent is the central place of debates over the propriety of Parliament's appeals to public opinion in protestations and remonstrances and of popular petitions presented to Parliament. "With or without the author's consent, speeches by MPs in the House were printed and circulated, thereby violating the convention that parliamentary proceedings should not be publicised, yet very few complaints of breaches of privilege ensued."[13] This last comment understates the degree to which this development was contested. One member of the House of Commons explained in 1643 why, in spite of his prior opposition to the fiscal and religious policies of the monarchy, he had resigned from Parliament. Referring to his support for the opposition in earlier sessions of Parliament, he asks, "In all those Parliaments did we ever see any declarations of both Houses against the King, or of one House against the other, printed and published to the people? . . . Did we ever see when anything had been proposed to and rejected by the House of Lords, the House of Commons notwithstanding proceed in it, and express their minds of it to the people?" At about this time another parliamentarian who also opposed fiscal and religious policies of the Stuart Monarchy, Sir Edward Dering, complained, "I did not dream that we should remonstrate downward, tell stories to the people, and talk of the King as a third person."[14]

At issue was not simply a clash between contrary views on religious and political life, for example, between Episcopal and Presbyterian models of the church. The propriety and (to some) threatening implications of popular participation in debates on these issues and appeals to public opinion by competing elites in Parliament were also topics of debate. Conservative observers unhappily discerned in the popular "contempt of Episcopal government . . . how multitudes of the baser sort even in the streets assume unto themselves a vote . . . for the utter ruin of that sacred and apostolical institution." "Religion is now become the common discourse and table-talk in every tavern and alehouse."[15] It was printing that brought Parliamentary debates on religion and politics into the streets, and printing also presented Parliament with popular views on these topics. A contemporary description of this process emerges in a preface to a pamphlet that provided readers with the background to the specific issue it proposed to debate: "A petition for peace is presented to the Parliament by some thousands of citizens; the petition finds a peaceable answer; and that answer (as I shall now set forth) is opposed by an unpeaceable reply." The novelty of this development was apparent not only to those distressed by it, as is evident in some of the comments quoted above, but also to those who approved of the expanding opportunities for participating in the formation of public opinion. At the bottom of the title page to a pamphlet that attacked the Royalist side appears not simply its date of publication but the following proclamation: "Printed in the year when men think what they list, and speak and write what they think." Two years earlier, in 1641, a utopian account of the Kingdom of Macaria, where the free play of ideas occurs before the Great Council of the Kingdom, predicted that in the rest of the world "the art of printing will so spread knowledge that the common people, knowing their own rights and liberties, will not be governed by way of oppression."[16]

Another sign of new democratic patterns of dissent is the process of progressive polarization and radicalization within the revolutionary movement. The new conditions imposed on dissent by the appeal to public opinion made divergent interpretations of ideological systems a factor of central importance in shaping the inner development of revolutionary movements. Expression of grievance in the English Revolution were ideological; they were defined and justified by dissident elites in terms of abstract beliefs that seemed applicable to all, regardless of social or economic division. But printing's dissemination of the ideology, the universalism of that ideology, and the different interest situations of elite and mass components of the revolutionary movement combined to create different interpretations of the ideology.

The doctrines of natural right that justified opposition to Charles I penetrated to Parliament's rank-and-file support as it filtered through the popular press in newspapers such as *Mercurius Britannicus* and printed copies of speeches and sermons by MPs and Puritan preachers.[17] In the Long Parliament, natural law justified rule by the propertied classes, but for Levellers in the New Model Army, "every man born in England cannot, ought not, neither by the Law of God nor the Law of Nature . . . be exempt from the choice of those who are to make laws for him."[18] These divergent interpretations of a shared ideology point to new patterns of dissent that emerge from appeals to public opinion. Intellectual dependency no longer characterizes the rank-and-file supporters of dissident politics as they adopt critical views of the policies and pronouncements of their ostensible leaders. Levellers' arguments on behalf of the freedom of the press relied explicitly on a liberal model of the public sphere. Levellers demanded of Parliamentarians "that you will precisely hold yourselves to the supreme end, the freedom of the people; as in other things, so in that necessary and essential part of speaking, writing, printing, and publishing their minds freely." Ultimately, the rationale for this position on the press is that it is necessary for the government "to hear all voices and judgments, which they can never do but by giving freedom to the press."[19] The same point appears in Milton's *Areopagitica* (1644), which holds that sound decisions in politics would be the result of a free and open exchange of ideas in a public forum.

Additional evidence suggests that the idea of a public sphere in the English Revolution was not entirely novel. Political discourse in the reign of Elizabeth referred rarely to members of Parliament as public persons, but beginning in the reign of James I (1603–1625) there appeared a new "emphasis on the fact of representation." By 1640, just prior to the Revolutionary era, elections were more likely to be contested affairs, tripling in number between 1604 and 1624 and then doubling by 1640, in which gentlemen standing for election appealed to an electorate that "was gradually coming to think in terms of national issues."[20] The same evidence suggests that the end of the Revolutionary era, in 1660, did not bring with it an end to political contests that took place in the forum of public opinion: "More general elections and more contests at these elections, took place between 1689 and 1715 than for the rest of the eighteenth-century."[21]

These reflections on the English Revolution point to three problems in Habermas's account of the rise of the public sphere. First, that development antedates the eighteenth-century period assigned to it; indeed, the public sphere appears to have been larger and stronger in the last half of the seventeenth century than in the next century. Second, the increased importance attached to public opinion as the arbiter of politics had intimate links with initiatives in a more popular social milieu than in the learned culture that is the focus of Habermas's account. Finally, the connection to religious issues becomes obvious when the events and consequences of the English Revolution are taken into consideration. These last two points are connected. The development of the English Reformation has been exhaustively studied in terms of a shifting balance between cleric and layperson that steadily favored popular intellectual initiatives in religious life.[22] In promoting the public use of more critical, rational habits of thought, this popular initiative in religion had profound implications for political discourse.

3 The Reformation and Lay Initiative

The term "Puritan Revolution" has become unfashionable because of growing recognition of the importance of nonreligious factors that precipitated and shaped the English Revolution. Scholars today are less likely than in the past to describe liberal democratic ideology as a secular extension of Protestant theology, liberalism as Protestantism without God.[23] While this is a welcome development, it does not justify perfunctory dismissal of the relevance of religion for the creation of a public sphere in the political realm. At this time Protestant doctrines with any degree of orthodoxy short of deism displayed an unremitting hostility to a liberal model of the public sphere in politics. However, popular developments in Protestantism created a public sphere in religion that cultivated nearly the same critical, rational habits of thought that Habermas locates in the public spheres of politics and letters.

This development is obscured by Habermas's focus on the privatizing effects of the Reformation. These effects are certainly important: the Protestant emphasis on interior dimensions of faith and on conscience as its arbiter justifies the claim that "religion . . . became a private matter."[24] The same point applies more generally to contemporary views of reason: "Reason was now regarded less as a communal property than as an individual capacity."[25] Yet this description of the shift from Catholicism to Protestantism, or from Hooker to Hobbes, is too narrow, for it ignores the *public* dimension of both developments. Faith and reason were now held to be attributes of individuals, but they were defined, defended, and debated in arguments that appealed explicitly to public opinion.

In England the progress of the Reformation, from the initial reception of Lutheran doctrines under Henry VIII to the subsequent rise of Puritanism, can be measured in terms of the growth of a public sphere in religious life. Encouragement of popular participation in religious debates was both a means for disseminating reformed doctrine and a principal topic of controversy that divided the reformers from religious conservatives. Early tracts denouncing the Catholic mass boldly appealed to public opinion: "Reade me first from toppe to toe / And afterward judge me a friend or a foe." To support arguments about the idolatry of the mass, these pamphlets invoked the ultimate ground of individual judgment: "& if you will not believe us herein, search these scriptures following," with a list of appropriate references.[26] This appeal to lay judgment constituted a public sphere by breaking the clerical monopoly on religious discourse. Fed by a vernacular religious literature, lay religious intellectualism pointed to a future in which a rough equality between cleric and layman would replace traditional lay subservience in religious matters. This was already evident to contemporaries at the onset of the English

Reformation. As one of Thomas Cromwell's proteges boasted in 1539, "The people begin to know what they that be curates ought to preach." Stephen Gardiner, a leading conservative opponent to early religious reform, asked in 1546 why the laity would defer to the clergy if, as the reformers held, truth lay in scriptures, available to all in vernacular form. This fear was put into the words of a priest in a satirical dialogue that attacked the religious conservatives: "If these hobbes and rusticals be suffered to be thus busy in reading of English heresy and to dispute after this manner with us which are spiritual men, we shall be fain to learn some other occupation, or else we are like to have but a cold broth."[27] By the turn of the seventeenth century the unanticipated consequences of the reformers' encouragement of lay initiative were evident: it had developed to the point where even the Puritan ministry, along with the ungodly bishops and their clerical supporters, found their authority and conduct under attack from separatists, heretics, and even broad groups within the Puritan mainstream.[28] By midcentury this initiative propelled a lay insurgency from the pews that demanded democratic control by sectarian congregations over religious matters.

In stressing the relevance of Puritanism, I do not mean to suggest that it led directly to political democracy. Rank-and-file Puritans were more directly and deeply concerned with asserting democratic control over their congregations than with ecclesiological disputes in Parliament over Episcopal versus Presbyterian models of the Church. Hence demands for subordinating kingly prerogative to Parliamentary control may have followed in the wake of demands for democracy in the local parishes. Yet it is also true that popular aspirations to participate in politics may have stimulated desires for religious democracy.[29] According to John Milton, in politics there is knowledge of "the general reason of that government to which . . . subjection is required; how much more ought the members of the church . . . seek to inform their understanding in the reason which the church claims to have over them."[30] In this connection, politics as a precedent for democratic ideas in religion also appears in Puritan remarks on Adam and Christ as "public persons." Discussion of the representative nature of their actions as public persons presupposed lay familiarity with the secular political precedent. In speaking of Christ in these terms, one cleric observed, "The notion of a public representative to do acts that in law are counted as theirs whom he represents, is common among all nations."[31]

It thus seems unlikely that the relevance of religious developments for the subsequent rise of a public sphere in politics lies in a simple transformation of religious ideas on spiritual equality into democratic models of political life. Rather, this relevance can be found in the creation of a public sphere in religious life that initially legitimated the reasonableness of public opinion as a forum and arbiter for criticism and debate. Not simply Protestantism but its lay initiative created the first body of public opinion, the public sphere of religion, whose participants saw it in terms of "critical reflections of a public competent to form its own judgments"—to use Habermas's description of the political sphere that appeared in the next century.[32] *Pace* Habermas, it was not in the identification of opinion with conscience that Protestantism abetted the rise of the public sphere.[33] Here again the emphasis is on the inward, privatizing effects of the Reformation. But the crucial point is that conscience and opinion were both associated with public reason, whose use was thought to be accessible to the common lay person.

This argument requires one important qualification. The public sphere in religion created by lay initiative in Puritanism did not achieve the same level of rationality or universality as in the liberal model of the public sphere. In line with the broad Protestant tradition laid down by Luther and Calvin, Puritanism stressed the corruption of reason, and hence limited its role in religion, as a consequence of its abiding sense of human depravity.[34] This not only set limits to reason but also restricted its exercise to the godly. At the same time, Puritanism developed in ways that minimized these irrational elements by focusing attention on the public dimensions of God's word as revealed in scriptures. One such tendency was Puritan covenant theology, whose importance was first noted fifty years ago by Perry Miller.[35] In place of the austere and mysterious God of Calvin there appeared the heavenly contractor who, accord-

ing to Bacon, "condescends to the weakness of our capacity
. . . , inoculating, as it were, his revelations into the notions
and comprehensions of our reason." Since reason on earth led
individuals to use contracts to deal with each other, God instituted a heavenly contract of salvation whose terms are publicly
announced in the covenant of grace.[36]

A second tendency, unlike covenant theology, moved beyond
orthodoxy to a wholesale rejection of nearly every major doc-
trinal tenet in the reformed tradition laid down by Luther and
Calvin. This way led to deism and natural religion, where the
rationality intuited in public opinion was no longer limited by
a pessimistic sense of the innate corruption of human nature.
From this development came new ideas on the public spheres
in religion and politics that mark the beginning of classical
liberalism.

4 Natural Religion and Public Reason

The liberal model of the public sphere emerged in England as
an elite response to the radicalism and sectarianism that flourished during the English Revolution. These problems arose in
a religious public sphere governed by the Puritan admixture
of rational and irrational principles. Appeals to a universally
valid reason legitimated popular participation that extended
to the humblest social groups, the emphasis on inward faith
precluded intersubjective controls on judgments of conscience,
and the result was an explosion of sectarian activity in which
the tenets and practices of any one group were seen by others
as further instances of the worldliness that oppressed the saints.
In this context, sectarianism was a fertile ground for social
radicalism, which developed as a charismatic revolt against
those worldly institutions—including the church, the law, the
universities, and the state—that were held to be impediments
to the creation of a holy commonwealth.

These developments led to a collective response by several
elite groups to tame the public sphere of religion by replacing
revelation with public reason.[37] This response led to the removal of the limits, discussed above, that Protestantism im-

posed on the public sphere of religion. There could be nothing in religion that was not compatible with reason—so argued leading members of the Royal Society, the Latitudinarian Churchmen, and the Cambridge neo-Platonic philosophers. So did the Whig ideologues, such as Locke, Shaftesbury, and Sidney, who had complex ties to the scholars and scientists. Not all proponents of natural religion were Whig theorists, but nearly all of the latter supported some version of natural religion.[38] Proponents of these views constituted a cohesive group within the high cultural establishment, united not only by their ideas but also by social origins and networks. They reached adulthood during the Revolutionary era and had attended Oxford or Cambridge. Most grew up in Puritan families, but all rejected Calvinist theology and the sectarian ideal of a holy commonwealth.

In arguing that nothing in religion was incompatible with reason, these thinkers referred to a public reason that derived from experience. This reason was vested in the individual by nature, not grace. Religion, argued Benjamin Whichcote (1609–1683), "is no stranger to human nature," a point commended to the public by the Earl of Shaftesbury.[39] Hence the pessimistic doctrines about innate sin and the corruption of reason went out the window. Natural reason was sufficient in itself to reveal the existence of Providence and its design in the universe. It is, said Chillingworth, "a public and certain thing."[40] Religious fanaticism and intolerance were inevitable, in this view, when religion rejected reason in favor of private revelation. Locke argued that "to this crying up faith in opposition to reason, we may, I think, in good measure ascribe those absurdities that fill almost all the religions which possess and divide mankind." Revelation's danger was that it legitimated irrationality in religion. "If such groundless thoughts as these concern ordinary matters, and not religion . . . , we call it raving and everyone thinks it a degree of madness, but in religion men accustomed to the thoughts of revelation make a greater allowance to it."[41]

This appeal to public reason in natural religion had immediate consequences for the formation of a public sphere in

politics. Banishing revelation from religion made divinity irrelevant to political discourse. The appeal to reason led to a
rejection of nearly every key tenet of Puritanism, including
covenant theology and predestination. Equally neglected was
"the central doctrine of Christianity, the mediation of Jesus to
redeem man," and "instead of religiosity," natural religion provided "a code of social conduct."[42] Beyond the existence of
providence and an afterlife, the core tenets of natural religion
constituted a utilitarian creed with a few ethical maxims, such
as the golden rule. "The laws of God," said Archbishop Tillot-
son (1630–1694), "are reasonable, that is, suitable to our nature
and advantageous to our interest." Bishop Wilkins (1614–1672)
thought it was "not possible for us to contrive any rules more
advantageous to our own interest than those which religion
does propose."[43] This is the outlook of the Enlightenment,
where the union of morality and utility creates this best of all
possible worlds. In this context, natural religion became irrelevant to politics because it held that utility, not revelation,
should guide political discourse. To be sure, magistracy is an
institution ordained by God, but "God having in the institution
of magistracy, confined such as shall be chosen rulers, within
no other limits in reference to our civil concerns, save that they
are to govern for the good of those over whom they come to
be established, it remains free and entire to the people . . . to
prescribe and define what shall be the measure and boundaries
of the public good."[44]

The public sphere in politics initially delineated by the early
Whig theorists relied on natural religion for a confident appraisal of human nature that made revealed religion superfluous. This is the source of the "liberal confidence" that separates
Puritanism from Lockean liberalism.[45] But from whence derived this confident appraisal of public reason? So far we have
seen how reason was championed at the expense of revelation
in a revolutionary era where religious enthusiasm generated a
good deal of conflict and social radicalism. The negative response to these popular developments by thinkers drawn from
relatively elite backgrounds led them to proclaim the priority
of tolerance over revelation as a precondition for the pluralist

pursuit of utility. Yet more than a negative response to religious enthusiasm was at work, for that alone hardly explains the tremendous confidence expressed in public reason when, in place of religious rationales for political discourse, Whig ideologues put at the center of politics the adjudication of empirical claims to utility. The explanation emerges when we turn our attention to the implications of printing and experimental science for new conceptions of reason and public opinion in the mid seventeenth century.

5 Printing, Science, and Opinion

The communications revolution wrought by printing and the progress of experimental science must be key factors in explaining how public opinion acquired its social authority. Otherwise, it becomes difficult to show why there was growing confidence in the idea that the advance of reason requires critical and open debate in a public forum. We have seen how religious developments created a public sphere that initially legitimated a right to participate in critical public debates. But the expectation that public use of reason will lead to good ends is another matter. This derived principally from well-publicized triumphs of experimental science,[46] which emerged in a public sphere that was self-reflectively understood by its participants as a model for rational discourse in both religion and politics. Other contemporary developments, and not only experimental science, also fueled the unbridled "confidence in human abilities" of this era.[47] The growing sophistication of historical and philological criticism enabled scholars reliably to assess the sources and validity of legal, religious, and philosophical documents. Increasing mastery over the physical environment produced a flood of proposals for reforming England's agrarian and economic life. All these developments relied on the impact of the printing revolution not only for advertising their accomplishments but also for achieving these accomplishments in the first place. But experimental science was clearly the most important for reshaping the more general views of reason and public opinion that made plausible the liberal model of the public sphere.

Proponents of the Royal Society, such as Thomas Sprat (1635–1713), regarded knowledge produced by experimental science to be "public knowledge" and they so represented it to the world.[48] Yet the service rendered by printing to science went beyond publicity, in advertising science's accomplishments, to the very existence of a public forum in which the experimental findings of science were produced and validated. The printing revolution created the experimental laboratory as a public space. Printing transformed the idiosyncratic practices and results of individual experiments: it surmounted limits, in scribal modes of transmission, to reliably communicating vast stores of information on empirical data, designs of scientific instruments used to collect that data, and mathematical tables for data analysis.[49] The objectivity of experimental science ultimately derived from the implications of printing for putting laboratory practices in the public sphere:

> Experimentalists like Boyle and his Royal Society colleagues in the 1660s were engaged in a vigorous attack on the privacy of existing forms of intellectual practice. The legitimacy of experimental knowledge, it was argued, depended upon a public presence at some crucial state. . . . If experimental knowledge did indeed have to occupy public space during part of its career, then its realization as authentic knowledge involved its transit to and through a public space.[50]

Laboratories linked by printing constituted this public space, the public sphere of science, in which reason's reign over opinion was held to be complete. The deficiency of other intellectual communities, wrote Sprat, lay in the social restrictions they imposed on free thought. No such restrictions were, he thought, to be found in the experimental laboratory. Hence the older

> seats of knowledge, have been for the most part heretofore, not *Laboratories* . . . but only *Scholes*, where some have taught, and all the rest subscribed. The very inequality of the titles of teachers and scholars does very much suppress and tame men's spirits; which though it should be proper for discipline and education, yet it is by no means consistent with a free philosophical consultation. It is undoubtedly true that scarce any man's mind is so capable of thinking

strongly in the presence of one whom he fears and reverences; as he is when that restraint is taken off.[51]

Referring to his colleagues in the "Invisible College" of the 1640s, Boyle noted their abhorrence of the scholasticism they associated with "school-philosophy," for they would rather learn from "the meanest, so he can but plead reason for his opinion."[52]

The rule of reason over opinion in the kingdom of science was often cited as a model for religious and political discourse. The significance of this precedent for the liberal model of the public sphere becomes clearer if we recall the point, made earlier, about the complex networks that linked members of the Royal Society to the proponents of natural religion and to the Whig theorists. Proponents of science observed that the free play of reason in science was capable of leading all persons to perceive the unity of providential design in the universe. This amiable idea led to the claim that "the proper study of nature bridges religious and political divisions among men."[53] This is the source of confidence in the public use of reason expressed by early Whig proponents of the liberal model of the public sphere in politics. Yet it was not so much the substantive findings of scientific inquiry, e.g., providence in nature, or even its methodological commitment to mathematical representations of the universe,[54] but the public use of reason to shape opinion that was the key issue. Thus Isaac Barrow (1630–1677), a mathematician, Latitudinarian Churchman, and teacher of Newton, held that the same principles govern religious and scientific discourse: when religion "has to the satisfaction of a man's mind, with solid reason made good its principles, it then enjoins men to surcease further scruple . . . , which is a proceeding most reasonable and conformable to the method used in the strict sciences."[55] Still, infallibility was not attributed to opinion molded by the free play of ideas in the public forum of science. Joseph Glanvill (1636–1680) argued that skepticism should always qualify "confidence in opinion."[56] This view was reinforced by growing reliance at this time on statistics in actuarial calculations and in experimental science.[57] Paradoxically, this development provided "opinion" with added authority. In England before the mid seventeenth century "'knowledge' and 'science' were rigidly distinguished from the category 'opinion.' . . . English experimentalists of the mid seventeenth century and afterwards took the view that all that could be expected of physical knowledge was 'probability,' thus breaking down the radical distinction between 'knowledge' and 'opinion.'"[58]

6 Conclusion

In too brief a space this essay has surveyed developments in religion, science, and printing as they relate to the liberal model of the public sphere in politics. The implications of these developments go beyond merely pushing back in time the origins of this model or asserting the importance of noneconomic factors. Beyond that, they call into question the assumption that more critical, rational habits of thought were successfully institutionalized in a public sphere because they were isolated from the brute realities of material civilization. The assumption is plausible enough in historical accounts of the public sphere—such as the one in Habermas's analysis—that focus on economic factors. It becomes less plausible with the recognition that there were several public spheres in which a free and open exchange of ideas flourished. These developed in both popular and learned cultures that were woven into the fabric of social life and reflected its broader pattern. Indeed, activities within these spheres left their imprint on that broader pattern. Thus the liberal model of the political public sphere can best be described as a historical accretion of print culture, lay bible reading, actuarial calculations, experimental science, and capitalist enterprise. The social authority of public opinion gained strength from the importance variously attached at different times to all these activities. This would have been a far feebler authority had it derived chiefly from economic activities, from Marx's "noisy sphere" of exchange relations.[59]

This account of the origins of the liberal model of the public sphere has optimistic implications for its subsequent development. If the authority of public use of more critical, rational habits of thought developed as part of, and not in isolation from, the larger civilization, it would appear that these intellectual habits may not necessarily be threatened today by the contaminating effects of that civilization. Arguments about the danger to a public sphere posed by the commodification of cultural production in advanced-capitalist society become less forceful in view of the fact that this sphere was in its origins and early development a representation of a larger civilization in which capitalism was—along with printing, bible reading, and science—a dominant element. Whatever else may be said about Enlightenment discourse in early modern England and France, it was not conducted by talk in isolation from the broader texture of social life. Darnton's wry observation about the monumental achievement of the *philosophes*—"Nothing could have been more cutthroat and capitalistic than the *Encyclopedie* as an enterprise, but the audience of the *Encyclopedie* did not consist of capitalists"—applies to the corresponding achievement of the Royal Society in England: "The *Transactions* encouraged signed contributions and attracted authors even from abroad with the lure of fame. Its editors took measure to ensure the protection of intellectual property rights by dating contributions and adjudicating priority disputes."[60] These observations certainly contradict the self-image cultivated by inhabitants of the early-modern public sphere. They regarded critical, rational thought as an activity in regal isolation from society, as did Montaigne in describing his library when he wrote, "There is my throne. I try to make my authority over it absolute, and to withdraw this one corner from all society, conjugal, filial, and civil."[61] But we should not conflate self-image and reality. Critical habits of thought were not antithetical to the baser motives in life. The liberal model of the public sphere always had close links to capitalism, religion, science, and printing, yet this does not imply that the critical, rational habits of thought in that sphere were any more capitalist than they were religious or scientific in nature. The social authority of opinion in this sphere derived from a way of life framed simultaneously and paradoxically by capitalism, religion, and science. Hence the current prospects and future of the public sphere seem reasonably secure in a world that continues to be shaped by these three forces.

David Zaret

Notes

1. Jürgen Habermas, *The Structural Transformation of the Public Sphere: An Inquiry into a Category of Bourgeois Society* (Cambridge: MIT Press, 1989). This is a translation of *Structurwandel der Öffentlichkeit* (Neuwied: Luchterhand, 1962).

2. *Structural Transformation*, p. 265.

3. This is the theme of several important studies, including Roger Chartier, *The Cultural Uses of Print in Early Modern France* (Princeton, 1987), p. 145, and Elizabeth Eisenstein, *The Printing Press as an Agent of Change* (Cambridge, 1980), passim.

4. *Structural Transformation*, p. 160.

5. "By virtue of its remoteness from the world of socially necessary labor . . . because of its separation from the daily struggle for existence, culture could create and preserve the mental space in which critical transgression, opposition, and denial could develop," Herbert Marcuse, "Remarks on a Redefinition of Culture," in G. Holton, ed., *Science and Culture* (Boston, 1967), p. 223. I discuss this point at greater length in "Critical Theory and the Sociology of Culture," *Current Perspectives in Social Theory* (forthcoming).

6. Chartier, *Cultural Uses of Print*, p. 180. See also Robert Darnton, *The Business of Enlightenment* (Cambridge, Mass., 1979); Natalie Z. Davis, *Society and Culture in Early Modern France* (Stanford, 1976), pp. 209–226; Eisenstein, *The Printing Press as an Agent of Change*, passim.

7. This theme is discussed in Perry Anderson, *Lineages of the Absolutist State* (London, 1974), p. 20; Immanuel Wallerstein, *The Modern World System* (New York, 1974), p. 114.

8. Karl Mannheim, *Essays on Sociology and Social Psychology* (London, 1953), p. 170.

9. *Structural Transformation*, pp. 52, 27.

10. *Structural Transformation*, pp. 24, 51, 27.

11. "The so-called freedom of religion historically secured the first sphere of private autonomy," *Structural Transformation*, p. 11.

12. *Structural Transformation*, p. 57. In later writings Habermas continues to locate the origins of the public sphere in the eighteenth century. See *Theory and Practice* (London, 1974), p. 77; *Communication and the Evolution of Society* (Boston, 1979), p. 192. Habermas's views on this development are evident in Zygmunt Bauman, *Legislators and Interpreters* (Ithaca, 1987), and Norman Birnbaum, *The Crisis of Industrial Society* (Oxford, 1970), pp. 121–122.

13. Keith Lindley, "London and Popular Freedom in the 1640s," in R. C. Richardson and G. M. Ridden, *Freedom and the English Revolution* (Manchester, 1986), p. 112. See also Sheila Lambert, "The Beginning of Printing for the House of Commons," *Library*, 6th series, 3 (1981): 43–61.

14. Anon., *A Letter from a Grave Gentleman Once a Member of This House of Commons* (Oxford, 1643), p. 5; Christopher Hill, *Change and Continuity in Seventeenth-Century*

Religion, Science, and Printing in the Public Spheres of England

England (London, 1974), p. 193. See also Edward Hyde, *The History of the Rebellion and Civil Wars in England* (Oxford, 1849), vol. 1, pp. 279, 441.

15. John Theyer, *Aerio-Mastix, Or, A Vindication* (Oxford, 1642), sig. *4; anon., *Religions Enemies . . . Presuming to Tosse Religion in a Blanquet* (London, 1641). Direct evidence in support of these claims can be found in Paul S. Seaver, *Wallington's World: A Puritan Artisan in Seventeenth-Century London* (Stanford, 1985).

16. Anon., *Accomodation Cordially Desired* (London, 1643), p. 1; anon., *One Argument More against the Cavaliers* (London, 1643); [Gabriel Platte], *A Description of the Famous Kingdome of Macaria* (London, 1641), pp. 13–14.

17. In 1644 "any Londoner who wanted to read his newspaper in English had a dozen to choose from. On Monday he could select *A Perfect Diurnall, Certaine Informations,* or *Aulicus.* . . . Tuesday he had *The Kindomes Weekly Intelligencer;* Wednesday, *The Weekly Account* or the newly revived *A Continuation* . . . and Thursday a choice between *Britanicus* and *Civicus.* Friday brought forth three papers. . . . On Saturday the reader either acquired *The True Informer* or went newspaperless. On Sunday he rested," Joseph Frank, *The Beginnings of the English Newspaper, 1620–1660* (Cambridge, Mass., 1961), pp. 56–57. See also Seaver, *Wallington's World,* p. 156.

18. A. S. P. Woodhouse, ed., *Puritanism and Liberty: Being a Record of the Army Debates, 1647–49* (London, 1938), p. 56.

19. D. M. Wolfe, ed., *Leveller Manifestoes of the Puritan Revolution* (New York, 1967), pp. 328–329.

20. Derek Hirst, *The Representative of the People?* (Cambridge, 1975), pp. 8, 111, 153. See also John Gruenfelder, *Influence in Early Stuart Elections* (Columbus, 1981), pp. 183–202. For similar developments in municipal politics, see John T. Evans, *Seventeenth-Century Norwich: Politics, Religion, and Government* (Oxford, 1979), pp. 66–70, 105–107.

21. J. H. Plumb, *The Growth of Political Stability in England* (Harmondsworth, 1967), pp. 10–11.

22. Three outstanding examples of this work are Patrick Collinson, *The Elizabethan Puritan Movement* (London, 1967); A. G. Dickens, *Lollards and Protestants in the Diocese of York, 1509–1558* (Oxford, 1959); Christopher Hill, *Society and Puritanism in Prerevolutionary England* (New York, 1967).

23. See David Zaret, "Religion and the Rise of Liberal-Democratic Ideology in Seventeenth-Century England," *American Sociological Review* 54 (1989), pp. 163–179.

24. *Structural Transformation,* p. 11. See also p. 265.

25. Robert Eccleshall, *Order and Reason in Politics* (Oxford, 1978), p. 169.

26. Quoted in David Zaret, *The Heavenly Contract: Ideology and Organization in Prerevolutionary Puritanism* (Chicago, 1985), p. 56.

27. Zaret, *Heavenly Contract,* p. 58.

28. Zaret, *Heavenly Contract,* pp. 90–127.

29. Brian Manning, "Puritanism and Democracy," in D. Pennington and K. Thomas, *Puritans and Revolutionaries* (Oxford, 1978), p. 140.

30. John Milton, *Complete Prose Works* (New Haven, 1953), vol. 1, p. 747.

31. Christopher Hill, *Collected Essays* (Amherst, 1986), vol. 3, p. 305.

32. *Structural Transformation*, p. 90.

33. This identification freed opinion "from its polemically devalued associated with pure prejudice," *Structural Transformation*, pp. 91–92.

34. John Morgan, *Godly Learning: Puritan Attitudes toward Reason, Learning, and Education, 1560–1640* (Cambridge, 1986), pp. 43–61.

35. Perry Miller, *The New England Mind: The Seventeenth Century* (Cambridge, Mass., 1939). See also Christopher Hill, *Collected Essays* (Amherst, 1986), vol. 3, pp. 300–324.

36. Zaret, *Heavenly Contract*, pp. 167–168.

37. I have developed this thesis in "Religion and the Rise of Liberal-Democratic Ideology."

38. See Richard Ashcraft, *Revolutionary Politics and Locke's Two Treatises of Government* (Princeton, 1986).

39. Benjamin Whichcote, *Works* (Aberdeen, 1751), vol. 3, pp. 5–7, 181.

40. Cited in Hill, *Change and Continuity*, p. 120.

41. John Locke, *An Essay Concerning Human Understanding* (Oxford, 1894), vol. 2, p. 246; *The Correspondence of John Locke* (Oxford, 1976), vol. 2, p. 500.

42. Richard Westfall, *Science and Religion in Seventeenth-Century England* (New Haven, 1958), pp. 118–125, 134, 157, 161.

43. John Tilotson, *Works* (London, 1728), vol. 1, p. 57; John Wilkins, *Of the Principles and Duties of Natural Religion* (London, 1675), p. 393.

44. Robert Ferguson, *A Representation of the Threatening Dangers* (London, 1689), p. 6. See also Thomas Hunt, *The Great and Weighty Consideration* (London, 1680), p. 8; James Tyrrell, *Patriarcha non monarcha* (London, 1681), p. 243.

45. Michael Walzer, *The Revolution of the Saints* (Cambridge, Mass., 1965), p. 302.

46. See Margaret C. Jacob, *The Newtonians and the English Revolution, 1689–1720* (Ithaca, 1976), and Charles Webster, *The Great Instauration: Science, Medicine, and Reform, 1626–1660* (New York, 1976).

47. Westfall, *Science and Religion in Seventeenth-Century England*, p. 7. See also Keith Thomas, *Religion and the Decline of Magic* (Harmondsworth, 1973), pp. 774–785.

48. Eisenstein, *The Printing Press as an Agent of Change*, pp. 668–670. This assertion glosses over different views on the topic (e.g., Boyle versus Hobbes). See Steven Shapin and Simon Schaffer, *Leviathan and the Air Pump: Hobbes, Boyle, and the Experimental Life* (Princeton, 1985).

49. Eisenstein, *The Printing Press as an Agent of Change*, pp. 520–574.

50. Steven Shapin, "The House of Experiment in Seventeenth-Century England," *Isis* 79 (1988): 384.

51. Shapin, "The House of Experiment," p. 397.

52. Webster, "The Great Instauration," p. 60.

53. James Jacob, *Robert Boyle and the English Revolution* (New York, 1977), pp. 117–118. See also Shapin and Shapiro, *Leviathan and the Air Pump*, p. 301.

54. See John Redwood, *Reason, Ridicule, and Religion: The Age of Enlightenment in England* (Cambridge, Mass., 1976), p. 215.

55. Isaac Barrow, *Theological Works* (Cambridge, 1859), vol. 3, p. 399. See also Joseph Glanvill, *The Vanity of Dogmatizing* (London, 1661), pp. 229–231.

56. Glanvill, *The Vanity of Dogmatizing*, passim.

57. See Thomas, *Religion and the Decline of Magic*, pp. 781–785. See also Barbara Shapiro, *Probability and Certainty in Seventeenth-Century England* (Princeton, 1983).

58. Shapin and Shapiro, *Leviathan and the Air Pump*, pp. 23–24.

59. Karl Marx, *Capital* (New York, 1970), vol. 1, p. 176.

60. Darnton, *Business of Enlightenment*, p. 527; Eisenstein, *The Printing Press as an Agent of Change*, p. 667.

61. Michel de Montaigne, *Essays* (Stanford, 1958), p. 629.

10

Habermas, History, and Critical Theory

Lloyd Kramer

Specific books and specific authors become important in intellectual history when they begin to define a common paradigm for cultural analysis among groups of people who otherwise pursue widely divergent professional, political, and intellectual interests. By this criterion of importance, the works of Jürgen Habermas might already be compared to the books of Rousseau, Hegel, Marx, Nietzsche, Freud, and Foucault, all of whom challenged and helped to transform the ways in which modern people understood past and contemporary societies. Habermas's themes and objectives clearly differ in various respects from those of his influential predecessors, but he shares their exceptional ability to cross the inherited boundaries of nationalities and intellectual disciplines, challenge the dominant ideas of modern cultures and institutions, analyze the systemic patterns of modern states and economies, and develop the conceptual paradigms that sustain empirical research in the humanities and social sciences. English-language readers of *The Structural Transformation of the Public Sphere* will find all of these tendencies of Habermas in this book, though they will inevitably choose to pursue the themes that come closest to their own interests and priorities.

The essays of Keith Michael Baker and David Zaret exemplify the process of reader reception in a group that can draw much insight from *The Structural Transformation*: historians and historical sociologists. In fact, as Baker notes in his essay, Habermas's concept of the public sphere has already influenced recent American and English studies of eighteenth-century European political culture, and the English translation of *Strukturwandel der Öffentlicheit* will begin to influence other historians who want to explain the emergence of Western political cultures and democracies or who study similar transformations in other places and eras. Habermas offers historians a complex model of historical development—we can call it a paradigm— within which or against which they can extend their empirical research in political, economic, social, and intellectual history. It is not surprising that historians like Baker and Zaret should find problems with Habermas's account when they apply its broad arguments to their specific research. What remains, however, is a conceptual framework that sets the agenda for research. Like other productive paradigms, Habermas's description of the "structural transformation of the public sphere" in Europe can be exploited for articles, books, and dissertations on a wide range of research projects. This expanding research will surely push Habermas's original project in directions that differ from his own goals and interests and that obscure his own models of historical analysis. Although historians might extract several important analytical models from *The Structural Transformation*, I would like to focus on only two of the possible ways in which this book can inform their work.

Historians can refer to Habermas's book on one level as a model account of the processes in European history that led to the conception and partial realization of a modern public sphere in culture and politics. This use of Habermas's work draws on his argument for examining particular events (e.g., revolutions), testing particular hypotheses (e.g., Did bourgeois families in, say, eighteenth-century Edinburgh read novels?), defining particular research projects (e.g., Was a democratic public sphere present in times or places that Habermas ignores?), or studying particular groups in past societies (e.g., How were women admitted to or excluded from the public sphere?). Responding to Habermas on the level of empirical study, historians can redefine old research problems, develop new areas of research, and debate the meaning of their research by debating the implications of Habermas's work, which is of greatest relevance to historians of early modern Europe.

Historians can also draw on Habermas's book in a second way, one that does not refer so specifically to the transformations of early modern Europe. On this second level Habermas provides the model of a historically informed, critical theorist who sees historical study as a method for challenging and transforming the present as it rediscovers and reinterprets the past. Most historians may be willing to deal with Habermas's work on the first, empirical level, but it seems clear that his own interest in history relates more to this second, critical level. He believes that historical analysis should contribute to the search for a critical social theory and enter critically into the public culture of the present era. Thus the analysis of a "bourgeois public sphere" in eighteenth-century Europe acquires its real significance as it exposes the flaws and contradictions in contemporary social, cultural, and political life. This kind of historical study does not become propoganda, but it does set out self-consciously to provoke reflection and action in our own society. I want to propose that this second, critical level in Habermas's work should come into the historians' debate, along with his hypotheses about eighteenth-century European culture.

The interesting, informative essays of Baker and Zaret engage Habermas's book almost exclusively on the level of empirical analysis. They develop limited critiques of Habermas as a historian through detailed discussions of significant themes that he deemphasizes, simplifies, or ignores in his book. Their criticisms show how careful empirical scholarship expands our knowledge of past cultures, broadens our understanding of historical causality, and revises our categories of historical interpretation. Yet in taking the historical fruits from Habermas's labor, they shy away from the critical roots and tree that are so important for Habermas himself. It is not simply a coincidence that Baker and Zaret focus on the first half of Habermas's book (which describes the historical emergence of a public sphere) and ignore the second half (wherein Habermas describes the breakdown of the public sphere since the early nineteenth century). In part this emphasis reflects the research specialities of the authors, but I suspect that it also reflects the problem that almost all academic historians will face if they want to assimilate the wider, critical themes of Habermas's work. The problem for these authors (and for myself) might be posed as a question: How can historians research and write about the past within the disciplinary constraints of their profession and also develop the critical engagement with the present that Habermas's work calls for and demonstrates? This open-ended question frames my own response to Baker's and Zaret's essays, which I want to discuss by looking at their reception of Habermas as a historian and as a critical theorist.

1 Habermas as Historian

Baker and Zaret are both aware of the intersecting levels of Habermas's work, but they do not give much attention to the links between the empirical and critical dimensions of the argument. Baker notes the "profound ambiguity" in Habermas's tendency to use the term "public sphere" as both a description of social reality and a "normative ideal"; Zaret sees Habermas's book as an account of one "important aspect of modernization," which must nevertheless be read as "an ideal type" rather than as an actually existing historical case. After evoking the critical implications of such terms as "normative ideal" and "ideal type," however, both historians go on to the main points of their essays: the analysis of how Habermas simplifies or excludes important aspects of the historical development of the public sphere in early modern Europe. Their revisions and extensions of Habermas's book clearly assume the utility of the categories public sphere and public opinion, but they introduce other ways to describe the emergence and meaning of these concepts, and they develop several shared divergences from Habermas's own approach to history.

First and perhaps most conspicuous, both authors reject Habermas's Marxist explanations of economic causality and his emphasis on the *bourgeois* public sphere. Habermas is by no means an orthodox Marxist, but *The Structural Transformation* often relies on the classical Marxist view of a dynamic bourgeoisie that rose to power over the eighteenth century and achieved its greatest victory in the French Revolution of 1789. This view has been widely challenged and revised since the 1960s, so both Baker and Zaret express the strong contemporary skepticism toward most Marxist models and categories.[1] In fact, for the present generation of historians, it is probably the residue of Marxist historical assumptions in *The Structural Transformation* that makes the book seem most out of date. The preferred categories and models of historical transformation now refer more to culture than to economics.

This preference for cultural categories over economic forces is a second similarity in the revisions that Baker and Zaret propose for Habermas's work. Although the cultural emphasis picks up on themes that Habermas develops in his discussion of literary journals, the press, and salons, Baker and Zaret want to push the analysis much further into our expanding conceptions of what constitutes culture: the role of language and rhetoric, the definitions of gender, the influence of religion and science, and the circulation of knowledge. *The Structural Transformation* points repeatedly to the importance of cultural factors in history, but recent historians, influenced especially by literary theory and anthropology, have increasingly come to emphasize (again?) the autonomy and even the causal force of nonmaterial culture in the historical process.

Finally, the essays of Baker and Zaret share another characteristic that reflects the structuring presuppositions of most contemporary historical studies and separates them from the work of Habermas. Each author focuses on the historical development of one nation, whereas Habermas carries his bold comparative approach from England to France to Germany. I do not make this point to criticize Baker and Zaret (who have written papers rather than books), and yet I think it is worth noting that the empirical response of most historians to Habermas's wide-ranging argument will most likely follow the example of these essays in focusing on a single national context. This division of labor along national boundaries derives partly from the institutional structure of historical studies, and it suggests a significant contrast between modern historiography and modern critical theory.

Although each of the shared tendencies in the essays of Baker and Zaret could be used to discuss the complexities of assimilating Habermas to contemporary historical studies, I want to address the issue that enters most fully and self-consciously into their revisionary critiques: the attempts to expand the cultural meaning of the early-modern European public sphere. At this point the differences between Baker and Zaret become more important than the similarities.

Baker acknowledges Habermas's stimulating influence on his own historical research and provides a thoughtful, careful summary of what "bourgeois public sphere" means in Habermas's account. He brings out key themes in the description of the public sphere, including the influence of the new market economy, the links between domestic and public life, the importance of "communicative rationality," the originality of a "public" sphere composed of "private" persons, and the distinctiveness of the eighteenth-century "conception of the public sphere." This helpful summary conveys Baker's agreement with much of Habermas's argument, especially the historicist theme that emphasizes its applicability to a unique time and place.

Yet Baker also finds certain problems in Habermas's analysis of eighteenth-century France that expose the differences between Habermasian history and the cultural approach that Baker develops as an alternative. The critique begins with some discussion of the similarities in English and French political cultures that Habermas may have overlooked and some criticism of Habermas's Marxist class vocabulary, but Baker's most significant criticism focuses on Habermas's understanding of how such terms as "the public" and "public opinion" function in a political culture. Specifically, he argues that Habermas connects these terms to "an ultimate sociological referent in relation to the needs and interests of bourgeois civil society" and thereby loses sight of the multiple meanings and interests that such terms could support. Baker's analysis of "public" or "public opinion," by contrast, stresses that " 'the public' was much more an abstract political category than it was a sociological one, and once put into play, it could be deployed in the service of a wide variety of social and political interests." Drawing implicitly on the lessons of recent literary criticism, Baker assumes that the same words develop very different meanings as they are used in various interpretive traditions, social groups, and political contexts. People might say the same words, but they do not give these words the same meaning. Baker's criticism therefore questions Habermas's desire to reconcile or combine the meanings of certain words whose meanings always remain variable and contested.

A major example of this problem for Baker appears in the term *opinion publique*. Habermas seems to follow a "teleological conception" of the "bourgeois public sphere" by suggesting that contestation over the meaning of *opinion publique* ended in the French Revolution's reconciliation of competing prerevolutionary antiabsolutist political traditions. In fact, Baker explains, the crucial differences between the rationalist, physiocratic definitions of public opinion (or the social system) and the radical republican, Rousseauian definitions of public opinion (or the social system) persisted throughout the revolutionary era and sustained an enduring conflict in French political culture. For Habermas, a term such as "public opinion" in the era of the "bourgeois revolution" comes to have a common meaning for the active, communicating participants in the "bourgeois public sphere." For Baker, however, "the rationalist conception of public opinion [descending from physiocrats] and the voluntaristic conception of the general will [descending from Rousseau] belonged to radically different political discourses. They grounded quite different assumptions about the nature of social and political order and implied competing conceptions of the public sphere that might replace or transform the traditional absolutist regime." The difference between these contending "discourses," which Baker (following Benjamin Constant) distinguishes as the "liberty of the moderns" and the "liberty of the ancients," did not disappear, despite the temporary, tragic attempt of the Reign of Terror to impose one definition of liberty (the ancient, Rousseauian one) on everyone in the society.

The apparently minor difference over the multiple or unified meaning of the term *opinion publique* during the French Revolution exemplifies the cultural twist that Baker brings to Habermas's work. Habermas's emphasis on a developing consensus of "communicative rationality" in a specific sociological reality (the bourgeois class) differs significantly from Baker's emphasis on competing discourses that carry the linguistic nuances of different interpretive traditions rather than a specific sociological reality (e.g., the bourgeoisie). Baker's analysis of "public" and "public opinion" leads us from a dialectical struggle between relatively coherent social groups to a realm of floating signifiers whose meanings shift and conflict *within* and *across* the social groups (and individuals) that constitute a political culture.[2] This latter view stresses the variable meaning of Habermas's key terms, questions the possibility of a consensus on linguistic usage, and pushes Habermas's historical account in directions that Habermas the theorist would probably dispute.

Baker's discussion of "public opinion" also poses questions about the kind of conceptual transformation that actually occurred in eighteenth-century French culture. The writings of Jacques Necker and Jacques Peuchet, for example, suggest some remarkable continuities between traditional conceptions of authority in the absolute monarchy and the new conception of a "public opinion" that was to provide the order and objectivity that had formerly come from kings. "Public opinion," Baker explains, "was endowed with the rationalized characteristics of absolute power; unitary authority was transformed and transposed to the critical judgment of the public." Here, then, is another variation on the problem of linguistic meaning. New words come into usage, but they can be used to reaffirm familiar aspects of old traditions. The historical problem, as Baker describes it, therefore lies in discerning the continuities and discontinuities of political cultures in which linguistic meanings are never entirely stable, never entirely fixed.

Baker takes up similar problems of linguistic meaning in his concluding analysis of Joan Landes's critical use of Habermas's concepts in her recent book *Women and the Public Sphere in the Age of the French Revolution.* The discussion of gender introduces another theme that many historians will want to push beyond Habermas's own passing references to the issue in *The Structural Transformation,* and Landes shows how a revisionist, feminist critique alters the historical significance of the late-eighteenth-century public sphere. According to Baker, though, this critique repeats Habermas's analytic mistake by failing to recognize the irreconcilable difference between the classical "republican discourse" of Rousseau and the "rationalist discourse" of Condorcet and Wollstonecraft (who extended the earlier physiocratic tradition). He agrees with Landes's charge that republican discourse and practice excluded women from the public sphere through the theoretical claim that they were *by nature* different from men, but he also stresses that this naturalist argument against women did not appear in the rationalist discourse of Condorcet and Wollstonecraft ("the liberty of the moderns"). Calling again for a careful examination of language and competing interpretive traditions, Baker develops his own persuasive analysis of gender themes in rationalist discourse. Ironically, the criticism of Landes leads Baker to a defense of Habermas because he concludes that Habermas's account of the public sphere refers "essentially" to the "rationalist discourse of the social" rather than to Rousseau's classical "republican discourse." Baker therefore reestablishes for Habermas the theoretical, linguistic distinction of meanings that he earlier finds Habermas himself abandoning in his account of the conception of public opinion during the French Revolution. From Baker's perspective, one could perhaps argue that Landes makes her mistake in following Habermas's account of the revolution too closely. In both cases, however, Baker directs our attention back to the complex language of competing, theoretical traditions.

Baker's response to Habermas thus raises two prominent themes in recent cultural history that problematize certain aspects of Habermas's book for contemporary historians: the variability of linguistic meanings and the historical meanings of gender. It seems obvious that Habermas's conception of the public sphere can become a productive analytical category for cultural and feminist historians (the work of Baker and Landes offers two excellent examples), but Habermas's original project and assumptions are likely to be transformed as they are appropriated (Baker and Landes also offer examples of possible transformations).

David Zaret's essay moves the cultural critique of Habermas's work from language and gender into the historical spheres of religion, science, and technology. Although he shares Baker's desire to free Habermas's "public sphere" from its links to the bourgeoisie and a stage of capitalist development, he adopts a more polemical tone in attacking what he sees as the "constricted" Marxist framework of *The Structural Transformation*. Zaret wants to revise Habermas by showing that Protestantism, science, and the printing press played decisive roles in shaping the English public sphere that actually emerged in the seventeenth century rather than in the eighteenth century. The specific question of dating England's early public sphere points to a wider, unexamined problem in Zaret's paper. On the one hand, he argues that Habermas's "public sphere" is an "ideal type" that could never actually exist; on the other hand, however, he argues that Habermas fails to see how the modern public sphere was already operating in seventeenth-century England. The theme of ideal types drops away as Zaret develops his main criticism that Habermas ignores an actually existing public sphere of debate and contestation in early modern England.

This flaw in Habermas's work exemplifies for Zaret the dangers of a Marxism that privileges economic forces over cultural phenomena, such as religion or science. In opposition to an economic emphasis, Zaret's critique takes us back toward Max Weber's account of Protestantism and the rise of capitalism. The debate here focuses on the rise of a modern public sphere, but Zaret implicitly draws on Weber's interest in the formative contribution of Protestantism to the emergence of modernity. His conception of culture, though, draws explicitly on contemporary historians who rely more on modern anthropology than on Weber's sociology. Anthropology encourages historians to see that cultural or political debates of social elites are always embedded in a wider cultural system and that the literate "public sphere" should not be described without reference to the popular culture that surrounds it. Zaret is interested in what historians of early modern societies like to call *mentalité*, and in seventeenth-century England this deep, cultural *mentalité* referred constantly to religion. According to Zaret, therefore, when every Puritan believer becomes an interpreter of scripture and a public advocate of truth, we already have a public sphere in action, though Habermas cannot acknowledge this new reality because of his economic blinders and his assumptions about the privatism of Protestantism.

Zaret's account of religious conflicts develops an important theme that deserves more attention (and attention in other national contexts) than Habermas provides, and yet it seems apparent that the public debates over scripture were not entirely comparable to Habermas's conception of the new public sphere. Habermas stresses the decisive, organizing theme of reason in the public sphere, whereas the seventeenth-century Puritans were debating the meaning of revelation. The contrasting emphasis on reason and revelation suggests that Zaret's essay describes something different from Habermas's "bourgeois public sphere," as Zaret himself seems to concede after making his case for the importance of Puritan religious debates. "The public sphere in religion created by lay initiative in Puritanism," he writes, "did not achieve the same level of rationality or universality as in the liberal model of the public sphere." Zaret thus recognizes certain problems in the way he tries to integrate Habermas's argument into his account of seventeenth-century English Puritans. However, there are other problems or tensions in his critique, which he does not acknowledge and which ultimately undermine the force of his own argument. Although I agree with Zaret on the need to extend the cultural meaning of Habermas's public sphere, I think that any such extension must proceed with more consciousness of its own possible contradictions.

Among the various criticisms of Habermas that appear in Zaret's essay, I want to isolate three examples of the tensions or contradictions that weaken his critique. He stressed (1) that Habermas ignores the role of the Puritan Revolution in shaping the early public sphere, (2) that Habermas can only make his argument by separating elite culture from popular culture, and (3) that Habermas relies too much on economic determinism to explain historical change. Setting aside the question of whether these criticisms accurately describe what Habermas does in his book, I think the problem in Zaret's critique lies in its tendency to replicate each of the analytic patterns that he criticizes as mistakes in Habermas's history. Curiously enough, the replication of Habermas's three alleged mistakes emerges somewhat systematically in the three guiding themes of Zaret's essay: religion, science, and printing.

Despite his insistence on the importance of Puritanism in an emerging public sphere, Zaret eventually argues that the real origins of the "liberal model" of the public sphere (presumably the model of communicative rationality that interests Habermas) can be found in the new "natural religion" of seventeenth-century England. This religion rejected "nearly every key tenet of Puritanism" and established its claims to truth on reason rather than on revelation. It expressed remarkable confidence in what human beings could do for themselves (using reason), fostered early Whig political theory, and "made revealed religion superfluous." It also had the practical consequence of separating religion from politics "because it held that utility, not revelation, should guide political discourse." As Zaret describes it, this natural religion was obviously closer than Puritanism to modern conceptions of the public sphere, which might explain why Habermas could ignore the Puritans in his history. If the Puritans played a role in shaping new conceptions of the public sphere, it was the role of a negative referent: a sectarian tradition that the advocates of natural religion wanted to discredit and replace with the rationality of science.

The history of natural religion thus leads Zaret into seventeenth-century science and the problematic distinction between elite and popular cultures that he finds at the center of Habermas's argument. Zaret's critique of these elite/popular distinctions seems questionable, given Habermas's extensive discussion of the links between elite, literary culture and the new bourgeois family, the new marketplace, the new reading public, and the daily existence of consumers.[3] Whether or not Habermas actually makes the radical cultural distinctions for which he is criticized, however, it is clear that Zaret himself relies on elite/popular dichotomies in his own historical account. The defenders of natural religion were all from the elite sphere, educated at Oxford or Cambridge, and closely connected to the new science. Zaret's emphasis on the contribution of experimental science to the emerging model of reason in the public sphere offers a persuasive addition to Habermas's argument, but it does not challenge Habermas's alleged dichotomy of elite and popular culture. On the contrary, the distinction becomes even more important because the elite sphere of experimental science was surely more removed from popular culture than were the coffeehouses and literary markets in which Habermas locates the emerging European public sphere. Yet Zaret argues that the new science stands apart from other intellectual and institutional developments of the era as "the most important for reshaping the more general views of reason and public opinion that made plausible the liberal model of the public sphere."

Science resembled all other forms of intellectual life, though, in that its assumptions entered the new public culture via the printing press. This third theme of Zaret's argument replaces the much-criticized economic determinism of Habermas's account with a kind of technological determinism in which the printing press becomes the fundamental precondition for a public sphere in culture, politics, or science. "All these developments," writes Zaret, "relied on the impact of the printing revolution not only for advertising their accomplishments but also for achieving these accomplishments in the first place." Habermas's capitalist marketplace thus gives way to print technology, and science offers the best example of how this technology shaped the historical transformations of public culture. "The printing revolution created the experimental laboratory as a public space. . . . The objectivity of experimental science ultimately derived from the implications of printing for putting laboratory practices in the public sphere." Zaret's discussion of print technology adds another important, explanatory theme to the historical account of the developing public sphere in early modern Europe. What he apparently overlooks, however, is the tendency of the printing press to assume ultimate causal functions that come surprisingly close to what he criticizes as the ultimate economic causality in Habermas's conception of history.

I have noted some problematic aspects of Zaret's critique in order to point out the difficulties that can develop for historians who utilize and criticize Habermas in the analysis of their own historical concerns. His essay offers valuable suggestions and evidence for expanding Habermas's account of the emerging public sphere into the histories of religion, science, and the printing press. Indeed, this cultural search for the shaping historical influences on early conceptions of the public sphere could well be extended into other European intellectual movements and social institutions that helped to develop new standards of truth, authority, and public communication. But Zaret's essay also suggests that extensions of Habermas's work can easily run into conflict with parts of the specific argument and that revisionary critiques can easily replicate at least part of what they set out to reject.

Like all other historical accounts, *The Structural Transformation* will be challenged and revised by historians who know about historical events, people, institutions, or empirical information that Habermas does not discuss. It is nevertheless striking that historians can find so much stimulation in a work written thirty years ago by a social theorist and philosopher (to draw some disciplinary boundaries) rather than a professional historian. Baker and Zaret show us how Habermas's historical paradigm opens new problems and interpretations for empirical research. Their qualifications of his argument and their attention to other forms of cultural history indicate some of the ways in which contemporary historians might revise Habermas's work. At the same time, their various attempts to assimilate Habermas's arguments suggest some of the formidable challenges that will face other historians who bring Habermas into their research projects. If we assume, though, that professional historians can draw creatively on Habermas as a historian (Baker and Zaret confirm this assumption), what can they do with Habermas as a critical theorist?

2 Habermas as Critical Theorist

The imaginative, detailed historical argument in *The Structural Transformation* might cause some readers to lose sight of the critical, theoretical concerns that inform all of Habermas's historical work. History demands our attention, according to Habermas, because of what it tells us about our contemporary society and because of how it shapes the way we understand ourselves. This emphasis on the historical links between past societies or events and our own social problems or disputes appears whenever Habermas writes about history, from the early arguments of *The Structural Transformation* to recent books such as *The Philosophical Discourse of Modernity* and *The New Conservatism: Cultural Criticism and the Historians' Debate*.[4] In each of these books Habermas discusses historical realities and ideas (e.g., the eighteenth-century public sphere, the emergence of modern conceptions of time and subjectivity, the destructive policies of Nazi Germany) whose implications continue to be important for the historical moment in which he is writing. Thus *The Structural Transformation* moves from the Enlightenment to a critical discussion of advertising and German political campaigns in the late 1950s; *The Discourse of Modernity* moves from Hegel to a critical discussion of such contemporary theorists as Jacques Derrida and Michel Foucault; *The New Conservatism* moves from Nazi genocide at Auschwitz to a critical discussion of contemporary historians who want to revise previous interpretations of the Nazi era. Habermas's histories, in short, always lead to the present, and this feature of his historical work poses the greatest challenge to professional historians.

The responses of Baker and Zaret to the critical, present-centered aspect of Habermas's work might well exemplify the typical reactions of most professional historians. As I noted earlier, both authors acknowledge the "normative" or "ideal-type" dimensions of *The Structural Transformation,* but they both focus on only the first part of the book (pre-1800) and address specific issues in early modern European culture. It is significant, however, that insofar as these essays engage the critical Habermas, they both tend to defuse at least some of the critical implications in his argument. Their responses to Habermas's critical argument nevertheless differ, much as their responses to the empirical argument also differ.

Baker's essay partly reduces Habermas's critical impact by stressing that Habermas's account of the public sphere refers to a very specific European historical era. He therefore suggests that attempts to apply the historical concept to other places or times simply do not work, and he argues that "Habermas's basic emphasis on the *distinctive* characteristics of the eighteenth-century conception of the public sphere remains one of the most important and valuable aspects of his work." In my opinion, Baker's eagerness to historicize Habermas's view of the public sphere diverts his reader from the universal aspects of that "conception of the public sphere" (e.g., its rationality, equality, openness, democracy) that Habermas clearly sees as relevant for a critique of our own societies. The stress on the distinctiveness of this "conception of the public sphere" in another time and culture leaves us with less appreciation for its relevance to ourselves and hence with less of its possible critical force. Having developed this strong, historicist theme, however, Baker eventually comes to a concluding paragraph that seems to embrace the critical, normative, still-relevant perspective that Habermas himself draws from the eighteenth century's "rationalist discourse of the social." Indeed, Baker takes up this critical, Habermasian argument most explicitly in his final sentence on the modern, rationalist conception of liberty: "Still unfulfilled, its principles held out that open-ended promise of individual emancipation for all in a rational, democratic society, which continues now more than ever to define the modern political agenda." The possibility of political connections with a distinctive past era is thus partially restored as Baker uses his last words (where historians feel most comfortable with such statements) to affirm his own apparent support for Habermas's universal theme.

Where Baker diffuses part of the critical Habermas by emphasizing a historicist interpretation of the eighteenth-century public sphere, Zaret responds to Habermas's critical analysis by stressing the public sphere's remarkable continuity in modern societies. For Zaret, the historical realities that created the "liberal model of the public sphere" in seventeenth-century England (religion, science, printing, capitalism) are still present today, and so we need not worry much about the alleged collapse or commodification of public culture, which attracts the critical attention of Habermas. Pessimistic arguments about the "structural transformation" of the modern public sphere mostly disappear when we keep our eyes on the "larger civilization" and when we see the historical continuity of modern culture. "If the authority of public use of more critical, rational habits of thought developed as part of, and not in isolation from, the larger civilization," writes Zaret (Habermas would agree), "it would appear that these intellectual habits may not necessarily be threatened today by the contaminating effects of that civilization" (Habermas's critical argument loses its relevance). In fact, after warning against Montaigne's mistake of isolating rational thought from society—Montaigne seems to be a strange substitute for Habermas—Zaret offers his own concluding historical lesson for would-be pessimists. "The social authority of opinion in this [early-modern public] sphere derived from a way of life framed simultaneously and paradoxically by capitalism, religion, and science [and printing?]. Hence the current prospects and future of the public sphere seem reasonably secure in a world that continues to be shaped by these three forces." Readers who come upon Zaret's optimistic conclusion after reading Habermas may find some comfort in this diagnosis if they can assume that our economy, religions, and science are currently fostering a public exchange of communicative rationality. In any case, the significant theme here suggests that historians can use Habermas without pursuing the critical contemporary implications of his work.

Baker and Zaret therefore provide two contrasting approaches to Habermas's critical methodology. Baker stresses the importance of historical discontinuities (or differences), and Zaret stresses the importance of historical continuities (or similarities). The first approach reduces the universalist, critical theme in Habermas's work by which he argues that certain normative ideals can and should cross from one historical era to another. The second approach reduces the historically specific, critical theme in Habermas's work by which he argues that dynamic, transformative social processes can and should compel each historical generation to create new institutions and new ideas. It is the simultaneous emphasis on continuity and discontinuity that gives Habermas's historical work its critical force. I think that Baker is more sensitive than Zaret to the two sides of Habermas's writing (historical, critical) and to the intricate connection between continuity and discontinuity in Habermas's conception of history. Baker's conclusion, for example, takes up the possibility of normative, universal values that much of his paper seems to question, whereas Zaret never really considers the possibility of significant transformations in the early modern public sphere that his paper describes. In their different ways, however, and with varying degrees of self-consciousness, both essays reveal the difficulty of integrating the critical Habermas into contemporary historical studies.

Fortunately, Habermas's historical and critical insights will more than repay the efforts of historians who take up the challenge of understanding his work on its various levels. *Structural Transformation* leads readers to these levels by developing comprehensive historical and critical arguments and by pointing to themes of discontinuity and continuity that bring the levels of argumentation together. The historical reality of discontinuity receives detailed attention in the second half of the book as Habermas describes the social-structural transformation of an earlier bourgeois public sphere into the modern realm of commodified mass culture. On this level of analysis the force of historical change seems to overwhelm all possibilities of historical continuity:

The world fashioned by the mass media is a public sphere in appearance only [Habermas writes in his account of contemporary culture]. . . . Indeed, the public sphere becomes the sphere for the publicizing of private biographies, so that the accidental fate of the so-called man in the street or that of systematically managed stars attain publicity, while publicly relevant developments and decisions are garbed in private dress and through personalization distorted to the point of unrecognizability. . . .

For the criteria of rationality are completely lacking in a consensus created by sophisticated opinion-molding services under the aegis of a sham public interest. Intelligent criticism of publicly discussed affairs gives way before a mood of conformity with publicly presented persons or personifications. . . . Publicity once meant the exposure of political domination before the public use of reason; publicity now adds up the reactions of an uncommitted friendly disposition. (*Structural Transformation*, pp. 171–172, 195)

This description of a transformed public sphere strongly challenges Zaret's optimistic view of cultural continuities across time; in fact, the profound historical discontinuities seem to suggest the futility of all efforts to draw normative standards from an earlier historical era such as the Enlightenment.

Yet Habermas refuses to let go of what he finds essential, even utopian, in the normative aspirations of the eighteenth-century conception of the public sphere. Instead, he wants to reaffirm those aspirations and extend their meaning into our own time (he recognizes, of course, that the specific institution-alization of such ideals will differ from the practices of an earlier society). On this level of analysis the possibility of historical continuities seems to overcome all despair about radical discontinuities.

The two conditions for a public sphere to be effective in the political realm—the objectively possible minimizing of bureaucratic decisions and a relativizing of structural conflicts of interest according to the standard of a universal interest everyone can acknowledge—can today no longer be disqualified as simply utopian. The dimension of the democratization of industrial societies constituted as social-welfare states is not limited from the outset by an impenetrability and indissolubility . . . of irrational relations of social power and political domination. The outcome of the struggle between a critical publicity and one that is merely staged for manipulative purposes remains open; the ascendancy of publicity regarding the exercise and balance of political power mandated by the social-welfare state over publicity merely staged for the purpose of acclamation is by no means certain. But unlike the idea of the bourgeois public sphere during the period of its liberal development, it cannot be denounced as an ideology. If anything, it brings the dialectic of that idea, which had been degraded into an ideology, to its conclusion. (*Structural Transformation*, p. 235)

This proposal for reviving and revising the earlier rational ideal of the bourgeois public sphere to meet new historical conditions points to the critical importance of certain continuities in historical development. In fact, Habermas's interest in the critical functions of such continuities challenges the historicist tendency (as it appears, for example, in Baker's essay) to stress the particularity or otherness of eighteenth-century culture. To be sure, this reconstituted public sphere could only develop through a new, critical understanding of the institutions that have transformed Western societies since the eighteenth century: the media, capitalist corporations, welfare-state governments, and others. But amid the vast changes of the last two centuries there remains for Habermas a valid, rational conception of the democratic public sphere that emerged in the eighteenth century and might now be brought "to its conclusion."

The task of describing both the discontinuities and the continuities in our society falls especially (though by no means exclusively) to historians, and the critical influence of this task pushes the apparently obscure labor of historical research toward the center of public culture. Indeed, a good Habermasian historian would view the interpretation of history as one of the key intellectual approaches to the disputed territory of our much-diminished contemporary public sphere. Historical writing for Habermas is not simply of antiquarian or professional interest, because it shapes national identities and describes the traditions within which our public cultures must inevitably evolve. This insistence on the public dimension of historical writing and teaching takes Habermas's historical model far beyond the culture of early modern Europe and reminds historians that their research and interpretations always carry implications for the social-political world in which they live.

Habermas's broad conception of the role of historical scholarship in public culture appears in *The Structural Transformation*, but it has become more prominent in his recent debates with German historians who are attempting to redefine and even normalize the events of the Nazi era and World War II in Germany. According to Habermas, this revisionist historical analysis (which downplays or destroys the exceptionalism of Nazi totalitarianism and genocide by drawing comparisons to repressive regimes in other places) undermines a critical understanding of national history, alters the public definitions of what is acceptable in a society, and "affects the political morality" of a German state that was founded in opposition to Nazi policies and ideas.[5] In every case the consequences of historical interpretation pass directly into the political public sphere, even if the historians ignore or deny the political ramifications of their work. Arguing against the politics that may lie hidden (or exposed) in this kind of historiography, Habermas urges historians to recognize their own involvement and responsibility in contemporary public culture and to understand that their connection with the political context is never merely passive or inconsequential: "In the public process of transmitting a culture we decide which of our traditions we want to continue and which we do not. The debate on this rages all the more intensely the less we can rely on a triumphal national history, on the unbroken normality of what has come to prevail, and the more clearly we become conscious of the ambivalence in every tradition" (*New Conservatism*, p. 263). Habermas thus warns historians that reassuring, "triumphal" national histories cannot sustain democratic public cultures in our era. At the same time, though, he insists that a critical understanding of our complex national histories (the contribution of historians) remains essential for the active democratic public sphere that he advocates throughout his political, historical, and theoretical works.

To say that historians must enter critically into the public sphere does not mean that they must follow the ideas and methods of Jürgen Habermas. The engagement with public culture requires an open debate on all ideas that may appear in public discourse, including, of course, the many ideas of Habermas himself. A critical examination of his own ideas, for example, should generate some pointed questions about the epistemological status of reason (What is the relation between rational and nonrational forms of knowledge?) or the extreme preoccupation with Western culture (What could critical theory learn from non-Western cultures?) or the pervasive seriousness of his theoretical texts (Must we exclude Nietzschean laughter from the realm of history and theory?). Such questions will come as no surprise to Habermas. His theory and his practice assume that critical debate is at the heart of all intellectual activity and every healthy public sphere, and it is clear that he expects his own writing to face the criticisms and contestations with which he regularly confronts his opponents.

I am therefore entirely willing to follow Baker, Zaret, and other historians in bringing Habermas to the English-language historical debates of our time. But I would like to see Habermas's insights brought to bear on both the empirical and the critical levels that appear in *The Structural Transformation* and that might push historians toward more critical interaction with our contemporary public culture. An engagement with Habermas's critical theory no doubt poses greater problems than does the response to his empirical arguments, and yet the dialogue between historians and theorists enlivens history and criticism alike. Indeed, the work of Habermas shows how creative the dialogue can be. Drawing on the long tradition of *philosophes* and critical theorists that precedes him, Habermas suggests that historical understanding might help to change the world as it interprets the past. This emphasis on possible transformations leads to the concluding sentence of Habermas's provocative, first book, which (since I have cited the last words of Baker and Zaret) it seems only fair to cite here. "In the case of the structural transformation of the bourgeois public sphere," he concludes, "we can study the extent to which, and manner in which, the latter's ability to assume *its* proper function determines whether the exercise of domination and power persists as a negative constant, as it were, of history—or whether as a historical category itself, it is open to substantive change" (*Structural Transformation*, p. 250). Historians who accept the challenge of this last statement may eventually find themselves thinking and acting differently in their daily lives as well as their historical research.

Notes

1. One sign of Habermas's provocative influence on historical studies appears in the ironic fact that a work based on traditional Marxist assumptions about the bourgeois French Revolution has become a key conceptual source for the entire revisionist interpretation of that revolution. As the work of Keith Baker and many others suggests, Habermas's concept of the emerging public sphere has become a decisive theoretical stimulus for the anti-Marxist developments in French and American historiography of late eighteenth-century France. This anti-Marxist appropriation of a book with significant Marxist perspectives (including an emphasis on the economy) would be an interesting intellectual process to analyze in detail.

2. Baker has given a fuller account of how he views the evolution of political language in a book he has edited on eighteenth-century French political culture. In such a culture, he explains, "heterogeneous discourses frequently overlap and changing practices are frequently superimposed one upon another, coexisting in everyday life as in the consciousness of individuals. . . . While these many political language games (taken in the Wittgensteinian sense) often overlap in complicated ways, they are not neces-

Lloyd Kramer

sarily unitary or homogeneous." See Keith Michael Baker, ed., *The French Revolution and the Creation of Modern Political Culture,* vol. 1, *The Political Culture of the Old Regime* (Oxford, 1987), pp. xii–xiii.

3. Habermas analyzes various links between the emerging public sphere and the early-modern social-economic world in *The Structural Transformation of the Public Sphere: An Inquiry into a Category of Bourgeois Society,* trans. Thomas Burger with the assistance of Frederick Lawrence (Cambridge, Mass., 1989), pp. 14–56. This analysis of connections between social and cultural life could obviously be expanded, but Habermas at least has looked at how the various levels of culture were embedded in a social world.

4. Jürgen Habermas, *The Philosophical Discourse of Modernity: Twelve Lectures,* trans. Frederick Lawrence (Cambridge, Mass., 1987), and *The New Conservatism: Cultural Criticism and the Historians' Debate,* ed. and trans. Shierry Weber Nicholsen (Cambridge, Mass., 1989).

5. Habermas, *The New Conservatism,* pp. 237–240; quotation on p. 240.

11

Gender and Public Access: Women's Politics in Nineteenth-Century America

Mary P. Ryan

In the twenty-five years since *The Structural Transformation of the Public Sphere* was written, public life has shifted, convulsed, and been transformed anew. With those changes the political and intellectual project that the book inaugurated has become more crucial than ever. The word "public" has long served as the placemarker for the political ideal of open, inclusive, and effective deliberation about matters of common and critical concern. Early in the 1960s such a public discourse was hardly audible in the United States amid the manipulative communications of consumer culture and consensus politics. Before that decade ended, however, the staid surfaces of welfare-state mass democracy had been fractured. The civil rights and antiwar movements disturbed the equanimity and passivity of public discourse, shattered consensus, and revitalized a conception of politics based on participatory democracy. Those movements and student activism around the globe opened a narrow wedge in entrenched political structures and permitted their participants to experience, however briefly, a more commodious public space.

In that same historical moment, a rekindled feminism ignited the consciousness of that sex whose relationship to the public had been most tenuous and ever problematic. The illumination that the women's movement cast over public life exposed the gendered limits on participation in the public sphere and at the same time gave new urgency to the ideals that the term encapsulated. The strictures of gender were quickly discerned as among the tightest, oldest, most categorical restrictions on public access. Women were patently excluded from the bourgeois public sphere, that ideal historical type that Habermas traced to the eighteenth century, and were even read out of the fiction of the public by virtue of their ideological consignment to a separate realm called the private. The subsequent historical transformation of the public did little to accommodate women, who were constrained just as tightly within mass welfare-state democracy. Their sex was the special target of consumer culture, yet they were poorly represented among those who wielded power in both the state and the capitalist sectors. Accordingly, the appropriate feminist stance toward the public seemed deceptively simple: to position women and their political concerns for a direct assault upon that hallowed sphere to which they had been so long denied access. Public access held many promises for women: escape from manipulative media of consumerism (called the "feminine mystique" by Betty Friedan), recognition of the unwaged, unrewarded labors of social reproduction for Marxist-feminists, some taste of efficacy and power to those like the members of the National Organization for Women intent on entering the "mainstream" of American public life. The new feminists were not simply demanding admission to the public; they also placed a multitude of specific issues, often drawn from their "private" experience, on the public agenda. Finally, as feminists made haste to construct theoretical guidelines for their political activism, they located the structural underpinnings of gender inequality along the private-public axis. Michelle Rosaldo's hypothesis that neither biology nor reproductive functions but the denial of access to the public realm was the basic underpinning of women's secondary status became a classic postulate of feminist theory.[1]

Through the first decade of the new feminism the significance of the public was assumed more than articulated or examined. The first task of feminist scholars and activists was to dredge through their personal lives and women's everyday experience for those issues that required publicity. Having found the substance of women's politics in the family, sexuality, and the relations of reproduction, feminists took their grievances directly into the public arena through any pragmatic avenue available, be it an arm of the state (courts and legislative bodies) or any media of communication (from street demonstrations to scholarly journals to TV talk shows). To this day much of feminist theory is still occupied on the private side of this political project, debating the notion of gender identity as it takes form in the private spaces of the psyche, infant development, and the family. Two decades of feminist practice, however, has left a well-marked trail through the public sphere itself, a record of women in public that feminist theorists have begun to address forthrightly.[2]

Locating women in the theory of the public is not a simple task, especially for American feminists. The intellectual guardians of that sphere have not provided a very legible map of this august territory. Certainly the mountains of voting studies and administrative analyses compiled by political scientists are not of ready use to feminist theorists. Even a political philosopher like Hannah Arendt, who characterized the public in more compelling terms, constructed that realm along its classic boundary with household concerns and thereby seemed to banish women. In this theoretical void Habermas's "The Public Sphere: An Encyclopedia Article" began to circulate among feminist scholars, and it's compact and yet capacious outline of the concept became a key text in a search for women in public.[3]

Habermas's construction of the public sphere had a singular advantage for feminists: it freed politics from the iron grasp of the state, which, by virtue of the long denial of the franchise to women and their rare status as public officials, effectively defined the public in masculine terms. The concept of the public sphere was suffused with a spirit of openness that feminists found inviting. (The second sentence of the encyclopedia article read, "Access is guaranteed to all citizens.") The public for Habermas, writing in 1964, was centered in a wide, diffuse, open field: "Citizens behave as a public body when they confer in an unrestricted fashion—that is, with the guarantee of freedom of assembly and association and the freedom to express and publish their opinions—about matters of general interest." Not only could women find access to a sphere so constructed, but once there, they seemed to be promised a hearing, whatever their concerns. In other words, Habermas's enunciation of the public sphere, as I first read it, was formulated in such a magnanimous way that female subjects and their opinions were a legitimate part of the common good.

When in 1989 English-speaking feminists turn to *The Structural Transformation of the Public Sphere* for a more elaborate blueprint of this inviting territory, their vision will be refracted through theoretical developments that long postdate its German publication. It is not surprising to find that Habermas was not so clairvoyant as to foresee the full agenda of feminist concerns that accumulated in the twenty-five years after its writing. Nor could he anticipate the fundamental critiques that feminism, in combination with postmodernism, would level against key elements in his model and his history, especially his confidence in abstract rationality and his tendency to construe the conjugal family as a natural reservoir of pure subjectivity. At the same time, to the extent to which the reader of the 1990s can place herself back in the intellectual climate of the early 1960s, she might be impressed by Habermas's cognizance of the historical malleability of the border between private and public as well as his recognition of the patriarchal caste of the bourgeois family.

1 An American Setting for the Public Sphere

I do not intend to enter the discussion on this theoretical plane, however, and will leave it to others to identify the gendered assumptions that underwrite public philosophy from Aristotle through Habermas.[4] Rather, I will engage the subject of women and the public sphere on the ground of history. From the vantage point of a historian of the United States, I will sketch a counternarrative to Habermas's depiction of the chronological decline from an idealized bourgeois public sphere. Starting at approximately the same time and place where Habermas commences his story of the eviscerating transformation of the public sphere (Western republics in the eighteenth and nineteenth centuries), feminist historians plot out the ascension of women into politics. This discrepancy cannot be ironically dismissed with the painful observation that when women finally won the franchise and official access to the public, they found themselves the conquerers of a hollow fortress. Although female suffrage did not swiftly lead to gender equality, it did remove a major constitutional impediment to public access and in the process undermined a gender division that had both hamstrung women as political subjects and blemished the whole doctrine of the public sphere. Moreover, in a critical slice of history that postdates the writing of *Structural Transformation*, the new women's movement injected considerable feminist substance into public discourse, articulating concerns once buried in the privacy of one sex as vital matters of public interest. Even the barest outlines of women's political history are sufficient to call into question a characterization of the last century as a blanket, undifferentiated decline of public life. I propose to outline in a very sketchy and condensed way how this feminist-inspired history of the public deviates from Habermas's account. From a woman's perspective this history starts out from different premises, evolves through a different and more problematic relationship to the public sphere, and presents a distinctive projectory into the future.

The geographical location and temporal parameters of my abbreviated history, the United States between 1825 and 1880, introduce additional contrasts with Habermas's model, based largely in Western Europe. The public as built on American soil in the nineteenth century was structured around different political possibilities and challenges. The relatively painless and rapid expansion of suffrage to adult white males circumvented the intense, abrasive encounter between the bourgeois public sphere and French revolutionaries or English Chartists. Subsequently the American polity was divided more fractiously by ethnic, racial, and sectional differences than on the continent. These divisions, along with more mottled class differences, were organized swiftly and bipolarly into two mass political parties. Perhaps most decisive of all, the American Republic, stepchild of the parliament of Great Britain, was not born in a ferocious struggle against absolutism, nor in close conjunction with a strong mercantilist state. The limited government of confederated states endured through the Civil War. As Stephen Showronek has recently pointed out and as Tocqueville observed long ago, antebellum public life was intensely focused

at the local and municipal level. It is at this historical site that
I (drawing evidence especially from New York, New Orleans,
and San Francisco) have based my search for women in public.[5]

Since I share Habermas's premise that no prototype of the
public sphere can be "abstracted to any number of historical
situations that represent formally similar constellations," my
search for an American public spotlights different times, institutions, forms, and locations as the markings of the public.
First of all, from my historical vantage point the most robust
expressions of American publicness date from the 1820s and
1830s, not the eighteenth century. Second, this public spirit
flourished in distinctive spaces, not primarily in literary and
political clubs and in the culture of print but in outdoor assem-
blages, in open, urban spaces, along the avenues, on street
corners, and in public squares. Third, American citizens enacted publicness in an active, raucous, contentious, and unbounded style of debate that defied literary standards of
rational and critical discourse. Fourth, the practice of publicness in nineteenth-century America took shape in a distinctive
class and social context. Although elite merchants dominated
local public offices, convened their own public meetings, set
up their own literary clubs, and were treated deferentially in
the public press, this American garden variety of the bourgeoisie was not the major staging ground of public politics.
Nor could the most exuberant public formations of Jacksonian
America be characterized as plebian. Rather, this urban public
found its social base in amorphous groupings of citizens ag-
gregated according to ethnicity, class, race, pet cause, and party
affiliation. These widespread, diverse, and intersecting political
conventions were a popular enactment of the principle of open
access to public debate on matters of general interest. Not the
ideal bourgeois public sphere but this variegated, decentered,
and democratic array of public spaces will be the setting of my
story and serve as my historical standard of publicness.

Although this pivot of my history is quite remote from the
starting point of Habermas's chronology, it provides the best
American approximation of the optimal function of the public
sphere as he presents it: "a process in which the exercise of
social power and political domination is effectively subjected

to the mandate of democratic publicity." Moreover, these social, political, and cultural practices of the American public resemble Western European publicness in critical ways. On both sides of the Atlantic publicness is premised on and propelled by a normative allegiance to open discussion of matters of general concern, and yet every Western republic was founded on the exclusion of the female sex and the elision of gender difference. So in chronicling the American history that proceeded from these premises, I will be detouring away from Habermas's text in two ways: by simultaneously presenting a different historical construction of the public sphere and a distinct experience, that of women citizens.

2   The Republican Public circa 1825

My history starts early in the nineteenth century when citizens walked the compact spaces of the small port cities of New York and New Orleans in the proud demeanor of republicans. They did not, however, exercise very public modes of politics. Most American municipalities were private corporations, vesting in the officers of the city corporation the privileges of collecting a few taxes and adjudicating the disputes brought by individual petitioners. Election days brought little popular excitement and elevated elite merchants to a position of public stewardship. Political clubs like New York's Tammany Hall added faction and fervor to this representative politics but seldom challenged the social hierarchy, which deferentially linked voters to elite officials. Given the limited public business, there was little local conflict capable of disturbing the republican premise that virtuous public-spirited citizens could oversee a transcendent common good. Maintaining public consensus did require, however, something akin to that display of reputation calculated to elicit popular acclamation of authority that Habermas found in both absolutist and modern democratic states. The elite officers of the city corporation demonstrated their superior civic stature by giving public dinners, leading processions through the streets, and organizing public festivals.[6]

Women, largely absent from all the institutional sites of the public—from polling places, city councils, public offices, the newspaper rooms, and political clubs—were an extreme case of the social exclusions of early American republicanism. Unlike those barred from citizenship on the basis of age, lack of property, or color of skin, however, some women had a particularly honored place in the ceremonial representations of the public. The "ladies" were toasted at public dinners and honored at civic celebrations, like those that marked the completion of the Erie Canal in New York harbor and the visit of Lafayette to New Orleans in 1825. Female symbols, like the goddess of liberty and Columbia, were favored emblems of civic virtue carried in procession by merchants, artisans, and students alike. As a symbol or goddess, as a consort of the elite on ceremonial days, or as a sexual pariah in public houses, women bore the mark of either ornament or outcast in public life. This negative relationship between women and the ruling political circles of the early-nineteenth-century city betokens the severe social limits of the bourgeois public sphere. It indicates as well that it was not beneath the dignity of the bourgeois custodians of the commonweal to make use of provocative yet seemingly superfluous symbols, in particular gratuitous references to femininity, to ornament their public identities.

But women constituted far more than just a quiescent population awaiting the structural changes or liberal reforms that would bring them directly into public life. The same stroke that inscribed gender differences on the public as a principle of exclusion placed a mark of selective social identity on citizenship in general. Republican ideology held that the female sex embodied those uncurbed human passions that inevitably subverted the self-control and rationality required of citizens. This rationale for gender boundaries on the public sphere inspired toasts to the ladies at public dinners, such as this pithy philosophy of gender heard in New Orleans in 1825: "The fair sex—Excluded by necessity from participation in our labours: we profess equality, the presence of woman would make us slaves, and convert the temple of wisdom into that of love." The converse gender logic made "manliness" the standard of republican character and "effeminancy" the most debilitating political malady. As historians of the early republic and feminist political theorists have amply demonstrated, the universal citizen was not genderless but a male. As such he carried a con-stricted notion of the general interest into public discourse. He, no less than a twentieth-century lobbyist, was the repre-sentative of a private interest group.[7]

From the first the American public sphere was constructed in the shadow of both gender restrictions and an emerging private sector of social life. This relationship was expressed in the eighteenth-century notion of the republican mother. This now familar prescription that women's stake in the polity was the private nurturance of infant citizens was more than a ra-tionalization of misogynist politics. It invested the social prac-tices of bourgeois wives and mothers with public significance. Sequestered from the developing market economy and barred from public politics, wives of merchants and professionals took up the practice of socializing children with alacrity, devising methods of moral education that placed particular stock in maintaining a buffer of privacy between future (male) citizens and the corrupting influence of the city. In other words, the same structural transformation that gave definition to a public realm designated women a second species of citizens and marked out around them a social space called the private. The public sphere of bourgeois America was moored in a private and gendered social geography, built, that is, on a fragile foun-dation.

3   Toward a Democratic Public, 1830–1860

The mantle of publicness in American cities nonetheless pro-vided ample room for expanding the public jurisdiction be-yond its vanguard class of commercial elites. The steady expansion of the franchise and rapid growth of the urban population had significantly enlarged and diversified the American citizenry by the second quarter of the nineteenth century. This process agitated everyday public life with partic-ular force in the 1830s, when a popular penny press attuned for the first time to local political issues broadcast calls for public assemblies with head-spinning regularity. By the 1840s the dailies labeled densely packed columns of newsprint with the words "Public Meetings." These public notices invited citizens to assemble to discuss a wide range of special issues, like the public school, relief during a severe winter, erecting a public building, providing a public service, or organizing a public celebration. The political parties were a mainstay of public culture; workingmen and nativists, as well as Whigs and Jacksonians, met weekly. Sometimes these proliferating public groupings met at merchants' exchanges, mechanics halls, grand hotels, or neighborhood saloons. Often the meeting spilled out into the streets. Just as often the designated spot for assembly was a public thoroughfare, street corner, or town square. Wherever their location, these invitations to popular assemblies were steeped in a language of publicness. The notices read "Great Public Meeting," "Mass Meeting of the Citizens," "Great Meeting of the People," "Great Democratic Republican Meeting." When in 1849 a collection of gold miners and fortune hunters gathered along San Francisco Bay, determined to constitute themselves a public, they simply issued a notice in the local press inviting every inhabitant to assemble in the central square to draw up blueprints for self-government. San Francisco used the public living room of Portsmouth Plaza again a few years later to select delegates to the constitutional convention of the State of California. Those delegates were instructed that "all political power is inherent in the people," whose inalienable rights included that of "public assembly."[8]

These homespun democratic theorists were also careful to prescribe the procedures for maintaining public sovereignty. Invitations to public assemblies were regularly rescinded when it was discovered that a private, vested interest had contrived them. One such meeting was aborted in New Orleans in 1837 on the grounds that it was not based in "an understanding among the citizens generally." One of the most conspicuous political events in Jacksonian America, the creation of the Locofoco Party in New York in 1835 (which set the radical and antibank platform of the Democrats) erupted into being when party leaders were found tampering with the democratic procedures for convening the meeting and choosing its officers. The public meetings held to a rough-hewn standard of parliamentary procedure, raised upwards of 3,000 hands to vote on scores of resolutions, and employed the device of literally "dividing the hall"—yeahs to the front and nays to the rear—to resolve their disputes. This is not to say that the meticulous efforts to insure open, democratic expression made for a contemplative and sedate style of public discourse. Public meetings were rowdy (erupting in shouting matches and fist fights), festive (spiced with drink and riddled with laughter), and fiercely partisan (sometimes culminating in an assault on the polling place of the opposition).

This cacophonous style of politics might appear as a symptom of the descent of the public sphere from the height of logical-critical discourse. The Jacksonians were more rambunctious than rational in style of debate and militantly asserted the identities and interests of specific sectors of the population. But the same evidence can also be read as an effective means of fulfilling the public promise to openly challenge political domination. Once public access had been translated into popular ideology, harnessed to a machinery of public communication, and regularly practiced in the open spaces of the city, a larger citizenry could contribute to the historical construction of the public good. Furthermore, in such democratized public spaces with citizens mobilized on so many fronts, the pretense of one indivisible and transcendent common good lost credibility. No incident exposed this bourgeois fiction more dramatically than the action of the vigilance committee of San Francisco in the 1850s. When the Vigilantes hung two unsavory citizens without benefit of trial in 1856, they posed as "the people in their sovereign capacity." In fact, the "people" were merchants, Protestants, and Republicans defying a local government with an Irish, Catholic, Democratic, and plebeian composition.[9] This clash of interests was one unseemly manifestation of a muscular democratic public. This unruly incident and many others like it were set in a political climate of vigorous publicity and broad, active citizenship, which might be read as a moment of democratic possibility that coincided with the relative decline of bourgeois political hegemony.

The proliferation of publics—convened around concrete, localized, and sometimes "special" interests—also opened up new political possibilities for women. In the 1830s women first joined in the public meetings convened by men and then gathered publicly among themselves. The first order of going public was the least likely to insert female interests in the public good. The failure of this strategy was dramatically demonstrated by the public appearances of Fanny Wright in New York City. Wright's radical opinions, as well as her gender, provoked catcalls, sexual epithets, and stink bombs and led to her prompt exile from the major public halls of the city. The prominence of women among abolitionists lead to similar conclusions: riotous attacks on promiscuous antislavery meetings and a shift in antislavery tactics to focusing on the masculine method of electoral politics. Women's participation in the meetings of workingmen also led only so far: to the incorporation of women's interests into appeals for a family wage, paid, of course, to husbands, fathers, or sons. The sorry story of a Madam Ranke, who addressed a meeting of unemployed men camped in New York City's Thompkins Square in 1857, records this stalemated attempt to desegregate the male public. When Madam Ranke took the public podium, she was greeted by cries like "Don't listen to a woman," or alternatively, "Damn it, don't interrupt a woman." The female voice was neither easily blended nor distinctly heard in the embattled sectors of the male public sphere, and Madam Ranke was escorted from the square under a protective escort of women.[10]

This did not mean, of course, that male-dominated public spaces were gender blind. They were riddled with gender distinctions: masculine definitions of a legitimate public actor and a profusion of newly feminized symbols of political identity. The democratic constituents of the Jacksonian public were perhaps more inveterately masculine than ever. They organized primarily around male roles: the voter, the worker, the militiaman. It was around these same male roles that democrats performed their own ritual representation of the political order, the all-American parade. Formed into units of the chamber of commerce, craftsmen, laborers, Democrats, and Whigs, citizens took manly strides through the streets on July 4 and a score of annual anniversaries, giving a masculine embodiment to the diverse components of the polity. The putative universality of the public now inhered less in the civic virtue of the bourgeoisie and more in the gender characteristics of males. This more plebian and democratic era seemed no more receptive to women than its bourgeois, republican predecessor.[11]

This new configuration of the public did draw on the female and private sphere, not for members or issues, but for a symbolic reinforcement of the legitimacy of different segments of the male public. In the 1840s the mass parties took the lead in deploying these cultural cues of political status, inviting "the ladies" to the rallies that ratified party nominees and posing their feminine supporters as badges of their respectability. Ethnic brotherhoods were quick to employ the same tactic, mounting Goddesses of Liberty and Maids of Erin on their banners, thereby pointedly demonstrating that ethnic identity was rooted in kinship bonds and imbricated both sexes. Temperance associations, yet another segment of the urban public activated in the 1840s, were steeped in the feminized symbols that linked politics to the private sphere of sobriety and domestic tranquility. Local political squabbles also dredged up issues from the usually private domain of sexuality. The vitriol of nativist fights in the 1850s was often churned up by images of the sexual license of the foreign-born, which tarnished civic reputation and defiled true womanhood. Campaigns to control prostitution, which figured prominently in the rhetoric of local politics during the 1850s, were largely a smoke screen for economic interests and partisan differences. However much the Know-Nothings of New Orleans or the Vigilantes of San Francisco posed as the protectors of female purity or the bane of prostitutes, they failed to represent the interests of women citizens and declined to invite females to participate in open public debate. The increasingly elaborate feminine symbols of antebellum politics lured women closer to the public sphere, but along duplicitous, dependent, and manipulative avenues, and then only to a center of discourse still dominated by men.[12]

At the same time the democratic expansion of publicness in the decades before the Civil War also created space in which women could politically organize in their own behalf. The first conventions of an embryonic women's rights movement date from this era but remained scattered, ad hoc, and ill-attended public affairs. Another public convention of women had earlier origins, more forceful impact on the local political scene, and more sustained organization. Female Moral Reform Societies, which garnered full publicity in northeastern cities in the 1830s, demonstrate the possibilities and the limitations of opening a female space in a democratic public. First activated by male evangelicals who were outraged by the ugly blemishes of sexual immorality on the civic countenance, moral reform brought women flocking to public meetings early in the 1830s. Soon women took over the campaign for sexual reform, transposed its political agenda into a woman's crusade, and even succeeded in changing the law as well as public opinion. Construing sexual immorality as acts of male seduction, New York's Female Moral Reform Society pushed through a state statute that inflicted stiff fines or jail sentences on men guilty of these private transgressions.[13]

Despite this success in the heart of the public sector, female moral reform was buffeted by a contrary political wind, wafting in the direction of privacy. Before 1850 female moral reformers had left the public stage to practice their campaign of purification in more secluded domains. They worked away from the spotlight of newspaper publicity and public meetings in the quieter female vistas of the church and family visits and in their own private institutions for the rehabilitation of prostitutes. Most crucially, they came to rest their hopes for moral regeneration not on public action but in the ministrations of women to their children and husbands in the privacy of their homes. Soon the organ of their movement was converted into a general mothers' magazine trafficking in advice on how to rear sons to more exacting standards of sexual purity.

The retreat of female reformers was typical of the more secluded channels favored by women social activists during the antebellum period. While menfolk flocked to public meetings, American women, especially of the urban middle classes, worked just as franticly to infuse the home with social functions, giving new definition to the border between public and private life. In the antebellum years, republican motherhood became inflated into what one writer called the "empire of the mother." The maternal role of socializing citizens was codified into an exacting profession, accorded its own literary channel of communication in women's magazines, and touted as an extensive sphere of female influence. By popularizing the notion of a separate female sphere of discourse and social practice, the antebellum cult of domesticity distanced vital civic concerns, as well as issues of specific interest to women, from the world of open public debate.[14]

Antebellum middle-class privacy was more than the residue of the public; it expanded and engendered a realm that bourgeois political theory regarded as the uncontaminated wellspring of civic virtue. The centrifugal force that an expanded private domain exerted on the public sphere was powerful enough by midcentury to generate platitudinous formulations of the relation between the public and private, to wit, the assertion that private virtue is the fountainhead of public order. One newspaper editor put it this way: the family is "the foundation of public morality and intelligence." Another wrote, "If all is right in the private domain, we need not be concerned for the public." Yet another editor cast the symbiotic relationship between public and private in liberal economistic terms by defining the public as an "aggregation of our personal obligations." As the ideal of the public good dissolved into these popular platitudes, the middle-class residents of the city were observed retreating from public spaces, vacating the streets, squares, and public halls for their homes and offices.[15]

The democratic public space of antebellum America was situated in a complicated and shifting civic geography. Even as the open spaces of the city were populated by a more diverse and active constituency, an equally robust, private sphere grew up and exerted a gravitational pull away from the public. The force of that pull stemmed not just from the splintering of the public into specialized interest groups but also grew up along an axis of gender. It was women—excluded, silenced, or shouted down in the public, democratic, and male-dominated spaces—who carved out another space in which to invest psychic, social, and political energies. If social life was divided between male and female, public and private, the history enacted on each side of that shifting border was deeply politicized and intricately interrelated. Indeed, as early as the midpoint of the last century the elaboration of private space had begun to eat away at the commonweal.

4 Civil War and the Modern State

This pattern of public life had been set in place at a time when the American state was relatively weak and functioned in the unobtrusive ways of the courts and local governments. All this was to change in the 1860s, as signified by the Civil War, which recast civil society into two militarized sections. During the war the municipality of New York witnessed the power of the state with especial force. Resistance to military conscription brought the Union Army into the streets firing on civilians and mounting howitzers on public buildings. In the Southern city of New Orleans the power of the state intruded into everyday life when the Union Army marched into the municipality and set up a government, which would endure for over a decade. The victorious Yankees legislated everything from public health to public assembly. The growing size of urban populations throughout the nation (New York surpassed the 1 million mark) necessitated the expansion of public services and the recourse to more bureaucratic methods of public administration. The city manuals of the late nineteenth century ran on for pages, listing the departments and commissions of municipal government along with their appointed, rather than elected, officers. Cities also increasingly lost local autonomy— a process typified by the creation of metropolitan police districts whose commissioners were selected by the governor rather than the mayor or city council.

The transformation of government procedures transpired within a shifting economic context. The expanding industrial sector was now the largest employer in most cities, and it was organized on a national scale of finance, production, and distribution. In the 1870s the railroads became the staging ground for the most tumultuous display of the new class configurations of industrial America. The rash of strikes by railroad workers in 1877 converted the public life of American cities into a violent clash between capital and labor. At this point Habermas's concept of welfare-state mass democracy begins to bear some resemblance to American historical development. The major interests, labor and capital, squared off with one another against a background of mass political parties, which, by the late nineteenth century, had perfected rituals of popular acclamation, had diluted the politics of substantive issues, and continued to generate a huge popular vote. The zenith of national electoral politics was not a convention of the public sphere but a "monster mass meeting" on the eve of the election.[16]

The monster mass meeting was but one linguistic marker of the new modes of convening the public under industrial capitalism. Calls to "Mass Union Meetings," "Monster Torchlight Parades," "Spontaneous Congregations of the Working Class," "People's Mass Meetings," "Public Political Demonstrations," and "Citizens' Mass Meetings" all evoked the rising scale and impersonality of mass politics. Behind these wide-open invitations to political rallies and the gargantuan size of outdoor meetings (with audiences of up to 50,000) stood more bureaucratic methods of convening the public. The biggest rallies were "Ratification Meetings," called to rubber-stamp the nominee chosen by committees or conventions. As befitting this less public, more bureaucratic style of politics, the term "committee" became ubiquitous in the language of politics. Californians were invited to assemble under the instructions of the "executive committee of the people" or the "popular nominating committee of one hundred."

Nonetheless, a crazy quilt of social groups continued to make their way around and through mass politics and into public prominence and public space. The parties were crosshatched by motley lines of class and ethnicity; merchants and workers alike paraded as the public; and alternate and selective groups mobilized around specific issues, pretending to represent the "sovereign will of the people." The demographic overlay of public space assumed a slightly different shape during and after the Civil War. Newspapers recorded how the lower classes commandeered a larger, more aggressive, and self-conscious place in open public spaces. Thompkins Square in New York became a congregating point for the unemployed and the trade unions, while the streets of the East Side were regularly filled with parades of striking workers. In San Francisco through the

1860s and 1870s the Workingmen's Party of California had a constant and vocal public presence, meeting thousands-strong outside of city hall, organizing major public processions, and taking up reams of newspaper headlines. In occupied New Orleans workers found public access to even the military government. For example, 5,000 marched to the headquarters of General Banks to oppose restrictions on the rights of the foreign-born among them. An estimated 200 colored citizens were counted in this particular crowd. Civil War and Reconstruction opened up the possibility that this marginalized, recently enslaved racial group could make political use of public space. Under the sponsorship of Radical Republicans, African-Americans of New Orleans swiftly and energetically claimed their right of public assembly. The *Lousianna Tribune,* a radical reconstruction paper, enjoined African-Americans to use the streets and squares as schools of citizenship and bask in public legitimacy by displaying their hard-won political status before their former masters. They responded by congregating in public meetings, conventions, and street parades.

These public assemblies only rarely galvanized the whole of the people. The largest public gatherings were called to display sectional solidarity during the heights of wartime patriotism. Yet even the great Union and Confederate rallies staged during the war and based on this lowest common denominator of civic loyalty soon lost their luster. The prolonged and bloody conflict led disgruntled New Yorkers to mount peace rallies, while the Union occupation of New Orleans drove rebels into a sullen retirement from public life. Only when radical reconstruction was about to end did the public life of white New Orleans rejuvenate. In 1874, claiming that "public opinion would no longer support military rule," the former rebels reclaimed the rights of public assembly, along with the constitutional privilege of bearing arms. Thousands of white men marched on military headquarters and temporarily took the reins of local government. As the Union army finally prepared to leave the city in January 1877, New Orleanians were called to a "Citizens Mass Meeting" at Lafayette Square, there to "represent the Sovereign will." An estimated 20,000 people assembled in response to this public appeal and stayed to celebrate the restoration of political authority to unregenerate Confederates. In this instance, like many before and after, the invocation of popular sovereignty poorly disguised the special, private, and racial interests at work; the public that gathered in Lafayette Square in 1877 was reinstalling white men to their customary position of dominance in civic life.[17]

Those social groups that dominated cultural and industrial production late in the nineteenth century seldom presented such a clear and public display of their power. Be it public ceremony or public meetings, parades or party rallies, the professional, financial, and industrial elites had retreated from public view after midcentury. This disappearance of the upper echelons of the public was registered by newspaper editors as the decline of public spirit among "the best men," who were said to have ceded the commonweal to corrupt professional politicians, city bosses, and their foreign-born henchmen. In the 1870s the "better class" became more visible in the public sphere, but on terms that diluted the former meaning of the concept. Organized for the purpose of reforming corrupt municipal government, these groups of businessmen directly challenged the political principle of openness and democracy and even called for restrictions on the franchise. While those who joined forces against the Tweed Ring in New York City called their movement a "glorious resurrection of public virtue," they aimed to reserve public office for the "wisest and best citizens." Significantly, municipal reformers often rejected citizenship as the ground for public participation, instead issuing invitations to public meeting only to "taxpayers", "property holders," the "most respectable citizens," or even "capitalists." The economic interest of the affluent but parsimonious taxpayer was now the measure of public virtue.[18] This vitiation of the notion of publicness was not necessarily a corruption of the bourgeois public sphere but rather a recognition of the social restrictions that had applied to this domain from the outset. The political formations of the late nineteenth century seemed only to reverse the spatial ordering, if not the power relations, of public life: the lower classes claimed open public places as the sites of political resistance, while their social superiors retreated into private recesses to exert power behind the scenes, in reform associations or bureaucratic channels.

On this reordered plane of late-nineteenth-century public life, women continued to locate and exploit the political possibilities for their sex. In many ways women's public presence remained veiled and distorted by the manipulation of gender symbolism dating from antebellum political culture, which was now used to garnish the increasingly stark racial and class partitions of the public. During the war women were an honored presence, and female symbols were prolifically displayed amid the pageantry of sectional solidarity. When white dominance was restored in the South, it was portrayed as an act of public purification, a defense of the honor of the ladies. Meanwhile, antiwar Democrats in the North raised cheers to white ladies. Both labor and capital draped their interests in female symbols. The parades of the Workingmen's Party of California mounted wives and daughters in carriages as testimony to the respectability of their membership, support of their demand for a family wage, and a countersymbol to Chinese immigration, which they pictured as a flood of bachelors and prostitutes. According to this gender logic, immigration from Asia robbed working-class women of jobs as domestic servants and bred Chinese prostitution, which was especially offensive to ladies. The upper-class opponents of the Tweed Ring in New York characterized the rapacious city politicians as simian featured Irishmen preying on a demure Miss Liberty. The stock of gender symbols had not been exhausted by the late nineteenth century and still provided ample images with which to drape the multifarious interests that competed with one another in the male-dominated political domain.

At the same time women could still be found congregating on their own turf and in convocations, which, like those of their menfolk, were enlarged to a massive scale. Mobilization for the Civil War brought women into service provisioning Union troops. The press labeled meetings called to recruit women's sewing skills and culinary abilities as part of the war effort "mass meetings of the ladies" and "another mass ladies' movement." The national organization that coordinated these efforts, the Sanitary Commission, was a well-oiled machine,

producing, collecting, and distributing vital war supplies. Ex-
cused by the exigency of wartime and disguised as feminine
charity, these efforts demonstrated that women could be highly
effective administrators of public services.[19]

The unobtrusive but critically important public work of the
Sanitary Commission was but one example of women's increasing assumption of public functions—a practice that began well
before the war and flourished thereafter. Even in the days
when municipalities were private corporations with tiny bud-
gets, women had taken on themselves the responsibility of
caring for dependent and impoverished classes. First founding
orphan asylums and societies to care for widows, then organizing a variety of relief and charitable associations, and ultimately
creating institutions that provided education, vocational training, and moral guidance to the poor, women volunteers constructed a private system of public welfare. This female sector
of the urban political economy generally abided by laissez-faire
principles and financed their benevolent operations through
the proceeds of bazaars and bake sales. At the same time,
female charities were less reluctant than most male politicians
to seek state funding for social welfare. From early in the
century and with increasing persistance and success after the
Civil War, women went directly to the city council and to state
legislatures, soliciting appropriations for these projects. Civic
leaders and newspaper editors chivalrously acknowledged the
beneficent public consequences of women's charitable work. As
one San Francisco editor put it, women's unremunerated labors
revealed that beneath the masculine mind of the city there beat
a "mother's heart."

Beyond this flimsy scrim of privacy, women met a public
need, saved public funds, and behaved as shrewd politicians.
Their parlors and churches were the perfume-filled backrooms
of gender politics where women set policy about the practice
of social welfare without being subject to public scrutiny. Their
method of ministering to the needy was never subjected to
open discussion and as a consequence flowed through class and
ethnic hierarchies as a condescending, restrictive, and niggardly distribution of alms and advice. Rather than operating
in a spirit of open, public largesse, female charities were a

closed welfare system extending only from middle-class, usually Protestant matrons to those they deemed the "worthy
poor." Like the welfare state of the twentieth century, this
extensive sphere of female municipal service was bureaucrati-
cally organized, lobbied to garner state funds for its selective
purposes, and carved out a sphere of hierarchical relations
with a dependent class. Once again, behind a veil of privacy
and femininity, women navigated a political history deeply imbricated in the transformation of the public sphere.[20]

Although women's charitable and reform associations were
especially solicitous about the welfare of their own sex, their
efforts were as much an outgrowth of the class position they
shared with their husbands as an extension of their gender
roles. Before 1880, moreover, their activities seldom generated
a challenge to sexual inequality itself. Other, smaller bands of
women activists did position themselves in or near public spaces
where their own gender interests and identity became more
visible. One such strategic location was an early confrontation
with a particularly aggressive arm of the welfare state bureaucracy, the board of public health. After the Civil War, members
of the medical profession flexed their political muscles to create
public health agencies at the municipal, state, and national
levels. One of their earliest routes toward public power was by
way of gender politics through the regulation of prostitution.
In the 1860s and 1870s, public health officials across the country hoped to stem the growth of venereal disease by subjecting
prostitutes to compulsory medical examinations and hospitali-
zation.[21]

This offensive of the bureaucratic state was promptly
squelched by a group of women who entered the public sector
to defend these least reputable members of their sex. The
female politicians who opposed the regulation of prostitution
in New York and San Francisco used every political force they
could muster to resist this legislation, which, as they saw it,
legitimated the traffic in women, institutionalized the double
standard, and constituted state intrusion into the private lives
of the second sex. The techniques they deployed were various,
ingenious, and indicative of the many ways in which some
intrepid women found access to the public affairs of industrial

capitalism. Occasionally they held public meetings calculated to influence public opinion on the subject. At other times they directly petitioned the state legislature and appeared at city council meetings, arguing their position. In other circumstances they choose to use the private techniques of lobbying legislatures and capitalizing on their personal contacts among public officials. They even opened an office in Washington to monitor developments in the nation's capital. Nor were these wily politicians above deploying the established codes of gender politics to their own ends. They alternately used the threat of publicity and the mantle of female privacy to affect public opinion. The most notable leader of the campaign against prostitution regulation, Susan B. Anthony, reputedly blackmailed a New York official by threatening to open the whole unseemly question of sexuality to public scrutiny, should New York legislators permit this practice. In keeping with the Victorian moral code, female sex reformers of the 1870s used the stereotype of pure womanhood as a point of personal privilege in the matter of prostitution legislation. In the 1870s, even as public politics began to corrode into state bureaucracy, the private sex found an arsenal of weapons and an array of avenues through which to influence public policy.[22]

5 Feminism in the Public Sphere

Such public access put women in a position to ponder their own political identity and to formulate the claims of their sex on the public good. In political skirmishes like the campaign against prostitution legislation, some women even forged an ad hoc gender identity that bridged class divisions. Still, the politics of prostitution, like female moral reform, was but one rather prickly way to generate gender identity. It placed the woman citizen in a defensive position and identified her by her sexual and reproductive biology. To contemporary feminists, this is an invitation to essentialism and a narrow base on which to mount gender politics. Fortunately, at the time of the anti-prostitution campaign, women were also assembling in the public sphere on an altogether broader and more radical principle, that of women's rights. The women's rights conventions first convened in 1848 and meeting irregularly through the next decade did not cohere as a national and sustained organization until the Civil War. The National Loyal Women's League and subsequently the Equal Rights Association, both headquartered in New York and presided over by Elizabeth Cady Stanton, were the crucible of an independent women's movement that would appropriate the ideal of the public sphere for the second sex.

The Loyal Women's League was founded as an appendage of the antislavery movement with the specific goal of pushing the Lincoln administration toward emancipating the slaves. Its postwar, postemancipation sequel, the Equal Rights Association, championed the civil and political liberties of African-Americans. At the very first meeting of the LWL, however, Stanton and her partner in feminism Susan B. Anthony placed women's public interest on the same agenda, forcing through a resolution in favor of women's suffrage. In a now familiar story, the alliance between African-Americans and women was broken when "the negro first" policy of Radical Republicans secured suffrage and the privileges of citizenship for African-American men and simultaneously wrote a gender restriction into the Constitution. Stanton and Anthony promptly founded a national association for the single and explicit purpose of securing the rights of women. Stanton, Anthony, and their colleagues across the country decided forthwith to form a women's suffrage association and to build their politics on the solid, independent base of their own gender position. As this autonomous public, the women's rights movement proceeded to identify a broad agenda of gender issues for black and white women, not just suffrage but also marriage reform, equal pay, sexual freedom, and reproductive rights.[23]

For veteran politicians like Stanton, the time had come to purge the public sphere of gender distinctions. She turned to the Republican tradition, "the birth right of the revolution," and "the rights of man" to legitimate women's direct assault on the public sphere. But Stanton had learned through more than thirty years experience in every sector of politics open to her sex that to win rights for those who occupied the social position of women required the explicit acknowledgment of gender difference. Only by taking up a political position explicitly as feminists, rather than trusting in formal commitments to abstract principles of public discourse, could women escape from the obfuscation, occlusion, and manipulation that had hitherto characterized their place in American public life. From this position Stanton slightly but critically revised the concept of the public handed down by her forefathers. Her goal was that "government may be republican in fact as well as form; a government by the people, and the whole people; for the people and the whole people." To Stanton, the whole was made up of separate parts, especially excluded populations like African-Americans and women. Stanton was still a lonely voice in the American public, still likely to be ridiculed in the public press, and scarcely heard in the citadels of power. But at a time when public ideology and deep-rooted social structures sentenced women to privacy, she had taken a critical step toward the longest yet incomplete revolution.[24]

Even at a time when the public was supposedly in decline and as avenues to power seemed to narrow, women like Stanton laid claim to a public space for their sex. Late in the nineteenth century, in the face of a more powerful state apparatus and amid the cacophony of mass politics, women had found multiple points of access to the public. They won state funds for their private welfare schemes, lobbied for their sex-specific interests, and prohibited state bureaucracies from trampling on the liberties of their sex. By occupying these scattered public places, nineteenth-century women worked out their own political identities, opened up the public to a vast new constituency, and enlarged the range of issues that weighed into the "general interest."

These peregrinations through gender politics are but one illustration of the transformation of American public life that progressed outside of the bourgeois public sphere during the nineteenth century. Much of this critical history was located in democratic public spaces, at proliferating points of access to political discussion where established authority could be challenged. Whether the occupants of these dispersed public spaces were working men, immigrants, African-Americans, or women, each fought their way into the public from a distinctive position in civil society, usually a place of political marginality and social injustice. Like the bourgeoisie before them, these social groups gave definition to their own particular stakes in the public interest as they expanded the domain of the public. The imperfect public they constituted was grounded in a historical construction and political articulation of diverse, malleable, and separate identities and interests. In a complex and far from egalitarian society like the nineteenth-century United States, this method of broadening access to public space proved to be the vehicle for democratizing public discourse and public policy.

Women's politics is a powerful example of this democratizing process and a critical index of publicness. Gender restrictions patently contradicted public ideology and had built exclusion into the very foundation of the public sphere. Denied public, formal, and direct legitimacy, gender issues found their way into politics in corrupted forms, like the cloying feminine symbols used in electoral campaigns or the periodic, partisan-inspired crackdowns on prostitution. Denied admission to the public sphere directly and in their own right, women found circuitous routes to public influence. The ways women maneuvered around the gender restrictions of the public are stocked with meaning for those who cherish the public. As sex reformers, for example, women exposed the fictions of privacy on which the segregation of gender and politics was supposedly based, while female-run charities built up a private system of meeting public needs that presaged the welfare state and some of its more antidemocratic features. Before 1880 it was only a small group of women's rights advocates who saw through all the obfuscations and contradictions of this largely clandestine gender politics and made their claim for full citizenship in the public sphere. Yet the tenacious efforts of women to subvert these restrictions and to be heard in public testify to the power of public ideals, that persistent impulse to have a voice in some space open and accessible to all where they could be counted in the general interest.

Each of the many ways whereby nineteenth-century women became political tells us something important about that privileged space called the public sphere. I will suggest just a few implications we might draw from the experience of our fore-mothers. First, the public as read through women's history spotlights the simple colloquial meaning of "public," that of open access to the political sphere. The women's politics of the last century warns against a spatial or conceptual closure that constrains the ideal of the public to a bounded sphere with a priori rules about appropriate behavior therein. Feminists and female citizens played for high stakes in a real world of politics and would find far more comfort in a plural and decentered concept of the public.

Second, women's assiduous efforts to win and practice the right of public access is an example of the practical ways in which the public ideal has maintained its resilience over time, that is, through a progressive incorporation of once-marginalized groups into the public sphere. As long as the distributive issues of justice remain unachieved civic goals, this proliferation of publics is a particularly significant measure of the public well-being. Furthermore, as Andrew Arato and Jean Cohen have pointed out, demands for public access by once marginalized groups or insurgent social movements serve over time to accumulate and expand the rights of all citizens.[25]

Third, the history of women in and on the way to the public sphere suggests that the notions of interest and identity need not be antithetical to the public good. From the vantage point of women's history, the identification of a political interest of one's own was not a fall from public virtue but a step toward empowerment. Because the second sex, like many marginalized populations, was socially dependent on their politically dominant superiors, their empowerment necessitated the construction of a separate identity and the assertion of self-interest. In practice, inclusive representation, open confrontation, and full articulation of social and historical differences are as essential to the public as is a standard of rational and disinterested discourse.

Finally, the history of women in public challenges us to listen carefully and respectfully for the voices of those who have long been banished from the formal public sphere and polite public discourse. Those most remote from public authorities and governmental institutions and least versed in their language sometimes resort to shrill tones, civil disobedience, and even violent acts in order to make themselves heard. Therefore, my chronicle would not be complete without reference to those women least likely to find a voice in the formal public sphere and those most likely, therefore, to express their interests in loud, coarse, and, yes, abrasive ways. These women citizens are represented by the participants in the New York Draft Riots of 1863. The women rioters, mostly poor Irish-Americans, were found looting businesses, physically assaulting policemen, helping to set the Colored Orphan Assylum afire, and committing ugly violent acts on the corpses of their adversaries. There was no civility, virtue, or logic in their political acts, yet their grievances against a draft policy that exacted an excessive cost of war from their class and sex were both just and reasoned, if tragically misdirected. However we draw the normative or procedural boundaries of the public sphere, they must be permeable to even distorted voices of people like these, many of whom still remain outside its reach.

These stray morals of my story might be drawn together in a simple public sentiment. Because everyday politics inevitably falls short of standards of perfect rational discourse, a chimera even in the heyday of the bourgeois public sphere, the goal of publicness might best be allowed to navigate through wider and wilder territory. That is, public life can be cultivated in many democratic spaces where obstinate differences in power, material status, and hence interest can find expression. The proliferation of democratic publics that posed a major counterforce to the escalating dominance of the state and capitalism in the nineteenth-century United States is carried forward in our own time by feminist movements. The movement of women into the public is a quantum leap in our public life; it both expands membership in the public and articulates vital aspects of the general interest that have hitherto been buried in gender restrictions and disguised as privacy. In the late twentieth century, women's historically problematic relationship to the public has become transformed into a public asset, both a practical and theoretical boon to the utopian aspirations that Jürgen Habermas set before us twenty-five years ago.

Notes

1. Michelle Zimbalist Rosaldo, "Women, Culture, and Society: A Theoretical Overview," in Rosaldo and Louise Lamphere, eds., *Women Culture and Society* (Stanford, 1974) pp. 17–42.

2. For recent examples, see Carole Pateman, *The Sexual Contract* (Stanford, 1988); Susan Moller Okin, *Justice, Gender, and the Family* (New York, 1989); Nancy Fraser, *Unruly Practices* (Minneapolis, 1989).

3. Joan B. Landes, *Women and the Public Sphere in the Age of the French Revolution* (Ithaca, 1988); Anna Yeatman "Gender and the Differentiation of Social Life into Public and Domestic Domains" *Social Analysis: Journal of Cultural and Social Practices* 15 (1984): 32–49; Lenore Davidoff and Catherine Hall, *Family Fortunes* (Chicago, 1987), chapter 10.

4. See, for example, Nancy Fraser, "What's Critical about Critical Theory? The Case of Habermas and Gender," *New German Critique*, 1985, pp. 97–133; Iris Marion Young, "Impartiality and the Civic Public: Some Implications of Feminist Critiques of Moral and Political Theory," in *Feminism as Critique*, ed. Seyla Benhabib and Drucilla Cornell (Minneapolis, 1987); Carole Pateman, *The Sexual Contract*.

5. Stephen Skowronek, *Building a New American State* (Cambridge, 1982).

6. See Mary P. Ryan *Women in Public: Between Banners and Ballots* (Baltimore, 1990); Hendrik Hartog, *Public Property and Private Power: The Corporation of the City of New York in American Law, 1730–1870* (Chapel Hill, 1983); Jon C. Teaborg, *The Municipal Revolution in American: Origins of Urban Government, 1650–1825* (Chicago, 1975).

7. Hanna Fenichel Pitkin, *Fortune Is a Woman: Gender and Politics in the Thought of Niccolo Machiavelli* (Berkeley, 1984); Ruth Bloch, "Gender and the Meaning of Virtue in Revolutionary America," *Signs* 13, no. 1 (August 1987): 37–58.

8. For examples of public meetings, see *New York Evening Post*, July 2, 1827, March 28, April 5, 1834; *New Orleans Daily Picayune*, November 22, 27, 1837; *Daily Alta California*, February 15, 1849.

9. R. A. Burchell, *The San Francisco Irish, 1848–1880* (Berkeley, 1980) 117–132; *Daily Alta California*, May 24, 1855.

10. Celia Morris Eckhardt, *Fanny Wright, Rebel in America* (Cambridge, 1984), pp. 258–267; Leonard Richards, *Gentlemen of Property and Standing* (New York, 1970) pp. 110–135; *New York Tribune*, November 11, 1857.

11. Mary P. Ryan, "The American Parade: Representations of the Nineteenth Century Social Order, in *The New Cultural History*, ed. Lynn Hunt (Berkeley, 1988), pp. 131–153.

12. Richard Tansey, "Prostitution and Politics in Antebellum New Orleans," *Southern Studies* 18 (1979): 449–479; James F. Richardson, "Fernando Wood and the New York Police Force, 1855–57," *New York History* 1 (1965): 5–54; Jacqueline Baker Barnhart, *The Fair but Frail: Prostitution in San Francisco, 1849–1900* (Reno, 1986).

13. Carroll Smith-Rosenberg, *Disorderly Conduct: Visions of Gender in Victorian America* (New York, 1985); Barbara Meil Hobson, *Uneasy Virtue: The Politics of Prostitution and the American Reform Tradition* (New York, 1987).

14. Anne Douglas, *The Feminization of American Culture* (New York, 1979); Gillian Brown, *Domestic Individualism* (Berkeley, 1991); Mary P. Ryan, *The Empire of the Mother* (New York, 1981).

15. *New York Tribune*, December 25, 1844; Edward Crapsey, *The Netherside of New York* (Montclair, New Jersey, 1969, reprint of 1872 edition); Preface, pp. 9, 120; Rev. E. H. Chapin, *Humanity in the City* (New York, 1854) pp. 11–45.

16. Michael McGerr, *The Decline of Popular Politics* (New York, 1986).

17. *New Orleans Picayune*, April 6, 1877.

18. *New York Herald*, October 29, 1875; Crapsey, *The Netherside of New York*; *New Orleans Picayune*, March 1877; *San Francisco Examiner*, October 21, 1875.

19. *New York Herald*, April 30, 1861; *New York Times*, May 1, 1861.

20. Suzanne Lebsock, *The Free Women of Petersberg: Status and Culture in a Southern Town, 1784–1860* (New York, 1984), chapter 7; Nancy Hewitt, *Women Activism and Social Change: Rochester, 1822–1872* (Ithaca, New York, 1984); Mary Ryan, *Cradle of the Middle Class: The Family in Oneida County, New York, 1790–1860* (Cambridge, 1981), pp. 210–218; Michael Katz, *The Undeserving Poor: From the War on Poverty to the War on Welfare* (New York, 1989); Paula Baker, "The Domestication of Politics: Women and American Political Society, 1780–1920," *American Historical Review* 89 (1984): 620–647.

21. John Duffy, *A History of Public Health in New York City, 1625–1866*, (New York, 1968); David Pivar, *Purity Crusade: Sexual Morality and Social Control, 1868–1900* (Westport, Connecticut, 1873).

22. See Mary P. Ryan, *Women in Public: Between Banners and Ballots, 1825–1880* (Baltimore, 1990), pp. 122–127.

23. Ellen Carol DuBois *Feminism and Suffrage: The Emergence of an Independent Women's Movement in America, 1848–1869* (Ithaca, 1978).

24. Stanton, quoted in Nanette Paul, *The Great Woman Statesman* (New York, 1925), pp. 63–64.

25. Andrew Arato and Jean Cohen, "Civil Society and Social Theory," *Thesis Eleven*, no. 21 (1988): 40–64.

12

Nations, Publics, and Political Cultures: Placing Habermas in the Nineteenth Century

Geoff Eley

By "the public sphere" we mean first of all a realm of our social life in which something approaching public opinion can be formed. Access is guaranteed to all citizens. A portion of the public sphere comes into being in every conversation in which private individuals assemble to form a public body. They then behave neither like business or professional people transacting private affairs, nor like members of a constitutional order subject to the legal constraints of a state bureaucracy. Citizens behave as a public body when they confer in an unrestricted fashion—that is, with the guarantee of freedom of assembly and association and the freedom to express and publish their opinions—about matters of general interest. In a large public body this kind of communication requires specific means for transmitting information and influencing those who receive it. Today newspapers and magazines, radio and TV are the media of the public sphere. We speak of the political public sphere in contrast, for instance, to the literary one, when public discussion deals with objects connected to the activity of the state. Although state activity is so to speak the executor, it is not a part of it. . . . Only when the exercise of political control is effectively subordinated to the democratic demand that information be accessible to the public, does the political public sphere win an institutionalized influence over the government through the instrument of law-making bodies.[1]

In this summary statement Habermas reveals perhaps better than in the book itself how far his conception of the public sphere amounts to an ideal of critical liberalism that remains historically unattained. History provides only distorted realizations, both at the inception of the public sphere (when the participant public was effectively limited to the bourgeoisie) and with the later transformations (which removed this "bourgeois ideal" of informed and rational communication still further from any general or universal implementation). *Strukturwandel der Öffentlichkeit* rests on an immanent critique, in which Habermas confronts the liberal ideal of the reasoning public with the reality of its own particularism and long-term disempowerment. From a vantage point in the late 1950s the main direction of Habermas's perspective was, not surprisingly, pessimistic: "etching an unforgettable portrait of a degraded public life, in which the substance of liberal democracy is voided in a combination of plebiscitary manipulation and privatized apathy, as any collectivity of citizenry disintegrates."[2] But the book was not just a story of decay. It remains a careful exploration of a particular historical moment at which certain possibilities for human emancipation were unlocked, possibilities that for Habermas were ordered around the "central idea of communicatively generated rationality," which then became the leitmotif of his own life's work.[3]

In a nutshell, the public sphere means "a sphere which mediates between society and state, in which the public organizes itself as the bearer of public opinion." Historically, its growth occurred in the later eighteenth century with the widening of political participation and the crystallizing of citizenship ideals. It eventuated from the struggle against absolutism (or in the British case, from the struggle for a strengthening of constitutional monarchy) and aimed at transforming arbitrary authority into rational authority subject to the scrutiny of a citizenry organized into a public body under the law. It was identified most obviously with the demand for representative government and a liberal constitution and more broadly with the basic civil freedoms before the law (speech, press, assembly, association, no arrest without trial, and so on). But Habermas was less interested in this more familiar process of overt political change. More fundamentally, the public sphere presumed the prior transformation of social relations, their condensation into new institutional arrangements, and the generation of new social, cultural, and political discourse around this changing environment. Conscious and programmatic *political* impulses emerged most strongly where such underlying processes were reshaping the overall context of social communication. The public sphere presupposed this larger accumulation of socio-cultural change. It was linked to the growth of urban culture—metropolitan and provincial—as the novel arena of a locally organized public life (meeting houses, concert halls, theaters, opera houses, lecture halls, museums), to a new infrastructure of social communication (the press, publishing companies, and other literary media; the rise of a reading public via reading and language societies; subscription publishing and lending libraries; improved transportation; and adapted centers of sociability like coffeehouses, taverns, and clubs), and to a new universe of voluntary association.

In other words, the public sphere derives only partly from the conscious demands of reformers and their articulation into government. Indeed, the latter were as much an effect of its emergence as a cause. Socially, the public sphere was the manifest consequence of a much deeper and long-term process of societal transformation that Habermas locates between the late Middle Ages and the eighteenth century as a trade-driven transition from feudalism to capitalism in which the capital accumulation resulting from long-distance commerce plays the key role and for which the mercantilist policies of the later seventeenth and eighteenth centuries were the midwife. The category of the public was the unintended consequence of long-run socioeconomic change eventually precipitated by the aspirations of a successful and self-conscious bourgeoisie whose economic functions and social standing implied a cumulative agenda of desirable innovation. Habermas postulates a causal homology of culture and economics in this sense, growing from "the *traffic in commodities and news* created by early capitalist long-distance trade" (p. 15). On the one hand, commercialization undermined the old basis of the household economy, reoriented productive activity "toward a commodity market that had expanded under public direction and supervision," and reconstituted state/society relations on the basis of a new distinction between the private and the public. On the other hand, the flow of international news attendant on the growth of trading networks generated a new category of public knowledge and information, particularly in the context of the seventeenth-century wars and intensified competition among "nations" in the mercantilist sense, which lead to a new medium of formal exchange and the invention of the press. This model of change, in which both new cultural possibilities and new political forms appear as the excrescence of an accumulating structural transformation, might be applied to a range of phenomena normally associated with industrialization or the developmental process. Thus in very general terms, the nineteenth-century growth of local government owed much to improvised grappling with the problems of an urbanizing society (poverty, policing, amenities like lighting and sewage, commercial licensing, revenue creation, and so on), to the extent of the local state being actually *constituted* by the practical associational initiatives of a new citizenry in the making, but as the unintended, rolling effect of structurally invited interventions, as opposed to the strategic result of a coherent design.

Ultimately, though, Habermas is less interested in the realized political dimension of the public sphere, that is, the particular political histories of the late eighteenth and earlier nineteenth centuries, than in abstracting a strong ideal against which later forms of the public sphere can be set. His own vantage point as the legatee of the Frankfurt School, who resumed their critique of mass culture at the height of the Christian Democratic state and the postwar boom and at a low ebb of socialist and democratic prospects, is crucial to understanding the book's motivating problematic. Habermas affirmed the critique of the present (the consciousness industry, the commodification of culture, the manipulation and manipulability of the masses), while he specifically retrieved the past (the Enlightenment as the founding moment of modernity). In contrast with Horkheimer and Adorno, he upheld the Enlightenment's progressive tradition. Thus his model of the public sphere has an avowedly double function: as Hohendahl says, "It provides a paradigm for analyzing historical change, while also serving as a normative category for political critique."[4] Arguably, it is the latter that really drives the analysis. Moreover, while the public-sphere argument is clearly crucial to politics in the full democratic sense (as the enlargement of human emancipation), its main thrust is anterior to parliamentary or institutional politics. For Habermas, the parliamentary stands of a Charles James Fox were less important than the larger context of rational and unrestricted discourse from which they had grown and which they could presuppose. The faculty of publicness begins with reading, thought, and discussion, with reasonable exchange among equals, and it is this ideal that really focuses Habermas's interest. It resided in the act of discussion and the process of exchange: "The truly free market is that of cultural discourse itself, within, of course, certain normative regulations. . . . What is said derives its legitimacy neither from itself as message nor from the social title of the utterer, but from its conformity as a statement with a certain paradigm of reason inscribed in the very event of saying."[5]

It is perhaps unclear how far Habermas believes his ideal of rational communication, with its concomitant of free and equal participation, to have been actually realized in the classical liberal model of *Öffentlichkeit*. Sometimes he acknowledges the class and property-bound basis of participation, but not to the extent of compromising his basic historical claim. However, the model also postulates a "structural transformation of the public sphere," and as suggested above, the narrowing of the ideal's possibilities over the longer run forms the main starting point of the book. Particularly from the last third of the nineteenth century, the growing contradictions of a capitalist society—the passage of competitive capitalism into monopoly or organized capitalism, the regulation of social conflicts by the state, and the fragmentation of the rational public into an arena of competing interests—serve to erode the independence of public opinion and to undermine the legitimacy of its institutions. In the cultural sphere proper, from the arts to the press and the mass entertainment industry, the processes of commercialization and rationalization have increasingly targeted the individual consumer, while eliminating the mediating contexts of reception and rational discussion, particularly in the new age of electronic mass media. In this way the classic basis of the public sphere—a clear distinction between public good and private interest, the principled demarcation of state and society, and the constitutive role of a participant citizenry defining public policy and its parameters through reasoned exchange and free of domination—disappears. The relations between state and society are reordered to the advantage of the former and to the detriment of a free political life.

Now the strengths and weaknesses of Habermas's work on the public sphere have been much discussed (though mainly in the German-speaking world rather than the English-speaking one, it should be said), not least in the papers and sessions of the present conference that precede my own.[6] A certain amount of overlap is inevitable, and I certainly would not want to discuss the historical dimensions of the argument in isolation from its theoretical value. But I want to confine myself to a series of comments that confront Habermas's work with a corpus of intervening historical writing (not all of it by historians) that sometimes confirms, sometimes extends, and sometimes undermines his argument. These concern (1) a wide variety of literatures that confirm the usefulness of the core concept of the public sphere, (2) the question of gender and the implications of women's history and feminist theory, (3) the state and politics in the strict sense, and (4) the problem of popular culture.

1 The Findings of Social History

The value of Habermas's perspective has been fundamentally borne out by recent social history in a variety of fields. On rereading the book (after originally discovering it in the early 1970s and then being systematically engaged with it in the later part of that decade) I found it striking to see how securely and imaginatively the argument is historically grounded, given the thinness of the literature available at the time. In this respect, I am struck by the affinity with the work of Raymond Williams, on whose argument in *Culture and Society, 1780–1950* (London, 1958) Habermas draws extensively in the early part of the book. The form of the argumentation is very similar to that of Williams, e.g., the whole introductory discussion culminating in the treatment of the shift in the meanings of the terms for "public" in English, German, and French between the late seventeenth and late eighteenth centuries (pp. 1–26). The very method of moving from the "world of letters" to the structure of society is characteristic of Williams's project in his early work. The later stage of Habermas's argument about the public sphere's transformation and degeneration (e.g., chaps. 18 and 20) anticipates the broad historical argument of *The Long Revolution* (London, 1961) and *Communications* (Harmondsworth, 1962), in which Williams developed his ideas about the long-term decline in the forms and degree of popular access and control in the area of culture. On the other hand, Williams's subsequent work on mass media has always maintained a strong affirmative stance on the democratic potentials of new communications technologies (see especially his *Television: Technology and Cultural Form* [London, 1974], or the chapter "Culture and Technology" in *The Year 2000* [New York, 1983], pp. 128–152). His view of film, radio, TV, popular fiction, popular music, and so on is far removed from the Frankfurt School's critique of mass culture and popular taste via the notion of commodity fetishism, a critique that it is unclear whether, and how far, Habermas himself would share. Incidentally, rather remarkably there is no entry for "public" in Williams's *Keywords: A Vocabulary of Culture and Society* (London, 1976; revised and expanded ed., 1983).[7]

Moving from Habermas's general approach and mode of argument to areas of research that fall concretely or empirically within the framework of the public sphere, I wish to mention a number of examples, which certainly don't exhaust the contexts in which Habermas's idea could be embodied but which are those most familiar to me. These are as follows:

• A large amount of eighteenth-century British social history, mainly associated with the influence of J. H. Plumb but also including a range of urban history, that effectively fills in the framework Habermas proposed without (so far as I know) being explicitly aware of it.[8]

• A similar literature on popular liberalism in Britain, concentrated in the period of William Ewart Gladstone between the 1860s and 1890s but with some anticipation earlier in the nineteenth century in the politics and moral campaigning of provincial religious Dissent.[9]

• A less plentiful literature on the social context of liberalism in Germany, running from the social history of the Enlightenment to the period of unification in the 1860s.[10]

• A disparate literature on political socialization and political mobilization in peasant societies, partly in social history, partly in sociology, and to a lesser extent in anthropology. The breaking down of parochial identities and the entry of rural societies into national political cultures, or the nationalization of the peasantry, as it might be called, is in one dimension the creation of local public spheres and their articulation with a national cultural and political arena. The literature on rural politics and peasant mobilization in nineteenth-century France is especially interesting from this point of view.[11]

• An equally disparate literature in the sociology of communications, focused on the history of the press and other media, the rise of a reading public, popular literacy, and mass communications. As already mentioned above, the work of Raymond Williams is especially central here, together with a considerable body of work in British cultural studies, much of it filtered through the British reception of Antonio Gramsci. But another fundamental point of departure is the classic work of Karl Deutsch, *Nationalism and Social Communication: An Inquiry into the Foundations of Nationality* (Cambridge, Mass., 1966; orig. ed., 1954), which has been most imaginatively taken up by the Czech historian Miroslav Hroch for a systematic analysis of the emergence of nationalities in the nineteenth century. In practice, in large parts of southern and eastern Europe in the later nineteenth century (and in the extra-European colonial world in the twentieth century) the emergence of nationality (that is, the growth of a public for nationalist discourse) was simultaneously the emergence of a public sphere. This codetermination makes a large body of literature on nationalism relevant to the historical discussion of Habermas's idea.[12]

What all of these literatures have in common is a focus on voluntary association and associational life as the main medium for the definition of public commitments. If we take seriously one of the above arguments about the conditions of existence for the public sphere—that it presumed the prior transformation of social relations and took clearest shape where the overall context of social communication was being institutionally reformed—there are good grounds for taking voluntary association as a main indicator of social progress in Habermas's sense. In fact, Habermas treats this subject himself to some extent by noting the importance of reading and literary societies to the new public aspirations. But the confluence of these older eighteenth-century associations (reading societies, patriotic clubs, political-discussion circles, freemasonry, and other secret societies) with more specific political ambitions during the era of the French Revolution and with the desire for social prestige on the part of the emergent bourgeoisie also produced a more visible push for social leadership and domination. Thus throughout Germany in the early decades of the nineteenth century the urban and small-town bourgeoisie crystallized their nascent claims to social primacy by forming themselves into an exclusive social club, usually called something like Harmony, Concordia, Ressource, or Union. A club of this kind was the matrix for the formation of a local elite. It acquired its own buildings, recruited only the most prestigious pillars of local society (who might number some thirty businessman, merchants, lawyers, doctors, and civil servants in a local population of some 6,000 at the start of the century), admitted new members only by careful election, offered a wide range of social facilities (including a reading room), and organized balls, concerts, banquets, and lectures. It was the obvious center of political discussion and generated a variety of philanthropic, charitable, and recreational activities in the community at large. Thus in Heilbronn in southwest Germany, the Harmony had its own building, with club rooms, reading rooms, library, and a surrounding park called the Shareholders' Garden. It was the center of a fine web of informally organized activity radiating into the local social scene. Indeed, the visible performance of civic duties was vital to a notable's moral authority in the town, whether by sitting in charitable or philanthropic committees, improving public amenities, patronizing the arts, promoting education, organizing public festivals, or commemorating great events.[13]

Such associational initiatives were fundamental to the formation of a bourgeois civil society (*bürgerliche Gesellschaft*) in
nineteenth-century Germany in ways that are intimated and
assumed in Habermas's text, but which perhaps lack the necessary concrete elaboration for the nineteenth century. Put
simply, voluntary association was in principle the logical form
of bourgeois emancipation and bourgeois self-affirmation. This
was true in three strong ways. First, the ideal and practice of
association were explicitly hostile, by organization and intent,
to older principles of corporate organization, which ascribed
social place by hereditary and legal estate. By contrast, the new
principle of association offered an alternative means of expressing opinion and forming taste, which defined an independent *public* space beyond the legal prescriptions of status
and behavior of the monarchical and/or absolutist state. It is
central to Habermas's conception of the public sphere in this
sense. Second, sociologically, associationism reflected the growing strength and density of the social, personal, and family ties
among the educated and propertied bourgeoisie (*Bildung und
Besitz*). It described a public arena where the dominance of the
bourgeoisie would naturally run. It was the constitutive organizational form of a new force for cultural and political change,
namely, the natural social power and self-consciously civilized
values of a bourgeoisie starting to see itself as a general or
universal class. Third, voluntary association was the primary
context of expression for bourgeois aspirations to the general
leadership of nineteenth-century society. It provided the theatrical scaffolding for the nineteenth-century bourgeois drama.
In this context the underlying principles of bourgeois life—
economic, social, moral—were publicly acted out and consciously institutionalized into a model for the other classes,
particularly the petty bourgeoisie and the working class, who
became the objects of philanthropic support and cultural edi-
fication.[14]

The treatment of this theme in nineteenth-century German
historiography is rather truncated, mainly because the liberal
ideal of emancipation (to which the arguments from voluntary
association and the public sphere are hitched) is usually
thought to have been decisively blocked by the 1860s and

1870s: if liberalism in Bismarckian and Wilhelmine Germany was such a broken reed, historians see little point in studying the emancipatory purposes of local associational life. If the main story was of decline and degeneration of liberalism and the public sphere, then the value of looking at the associational arena tends to fall.[15] We can find stronger coverage of such matters, therefore, in a national historiography where the unity of the bourgeoisie's social progress and liberal political success have remained intact in historians' understanding, namely that of Britain.

For many years J. H. Plumb's *Growth of Political Stability in England, 1675–1725* (London, 1967) was one of the few texts keeping open a broader and more developed approach to eighteenth-century British politics, as opposed to the narrow interest-based conception of high politics that had come to dominate the field in general. In the intervening two decades Plumb himself published a series of essays that carried this farther and explored the cultural changes that allowed something like a free political life to begin to take shape. Though the shadow of a theory barely darkens his pages, Plumb's contributions fall interestingly within the framework Habermas lays out, concerning things like the growth of a reading public, the commercialization of leisure, expanding educational provision, the transition from private to public entertainment, and the general spread of such trends from the capital to the provinces. In effect, this amounted to the gradual coherence of a self-conscious middle-class public, which wore its provincialism less as an embarrassment than as an expression of buoyant creativity.[16]

Moreover, Plumb has inspired a wider body of work, of which John Brewer's study of politics in the 1760s is a splendid example. While Brewer tackles the structure of politics in general, his most important chapters concern the impact of extra-parliamentary activity on the parliamentary arena. His chapter on the press covers the entire institutional fabric of public debate in the 1760s, including the nature of literacy, media of publication (newspapers, periodicals, pamphlets, squibs, handbills, songs), the complexities of literary production (as in the seasonality and varied media of circulation), the discrepancies between circulation and actual readership, the role of "bridging" ("the transmission of printed information in traditional oral forms," as in ballads), the social universe of coffeehouse and club, and the spread of postal and turnpike communications. He adds an analysis of the ritual and symbolic content of crowd behavior during the Wilkesite manifestations that deepens George Rudé's classic treatment and tells us much about the nascent forms of a new popular politics. When combined with the substantive treatments of midcentury radicalism and its transformations (particularly via the impact of the American radicals), these discussions present "an alternative structure of politics," which in the conjunctures of the 1780s and 1790s had major democratic and oppositional implications. How far the "alternative structure" coincided, organizationally, sociologically, and ideologically, with the emergence of the public sphere described by Habermas is a moot question (which I will return to in section 4 below). But for present purposes, I simply note the detailed embodiment of a novel notion of the public.[17]

John Money's study of the West Midlands, likewise influenced by Plumb, makes a related contribution. Money is concerned with the transition from a rural to a mainly urban-industrial society and with the cultural adaptations that managed to contain much of the potential for social conflict in the new manufacturing center of Birmingham. He suggests that Birmingham's social, economic, and political integration within the wider county community of Warwick was strengthened rather than fractured by the experience of urban growth, and between the 1760s and 1790s this cultural resilience allowed a new sense of regional identity to form. This claim is explored through careful analyses of the local notables—Birmingham merchants and manufacturers—who both kept their links with the county landowners via projects like the Birmingham General Hospital and societies like the Bean Club and the masonic lodges and defined a separate identity vis-à-vis London and the other regions. Naturally, the process of regional development was not without tensions, and Money devotes much space to the unfolding of religious and other ideological disagreements, and to the emergence of a more popular radicalism.

But in the end neither the hostilities of Anglicanism and Dissent nor the pressure for reform nor the promise of Jacobinism were strong enough to tear the fabric of regional community.[18]

More than anything else, Money's book is a study of regional political culture. With Brewer, he shares an intimate knowledge of the structure of public discourse in the chosen period—not just the press but also the public spectacle of music and the stage, the associational milieu of "taverns, coffee houses and clubs," and the literary world of "printing, publishing and popular instruction"—what Money calls "the means of communication and the creation of opinion." It becomes clear from this kind of analysis that the origins of an independent political life, i.e., a public sphere in Habermas's sense, must be sought in this wider domain of cultural activity, from which a self-confident middle class began to emerge. The foundations were laid before Brewer's and Money's period between the 1680s and 1760s in what has been called an "English urban renaissance," when the growth of towns; new patterns of personal consumption; expanding demand for services, professions, and luxury trades; and the commercialization of leisure all combined to stimulate a new culture of organized recreation, public display, improved amenities, and urban aesthetics.[19] But the political consequences of this process could flourish only in the later part of the eighteenth century with the commercialization that produced "the birth of a consumer society" and the growing differentiation and self-consciousness of "the middling sort or bourgeoisie" (the "men of moveable property, members of professions, tradesmen and shopkeepers," who comprised some "million of the nation's nearly seven million" inhabitants and who strove for independent space between the "client economy" of the aristocracy and the real dependence of the laboring poor).[20]

Money shows how this flourishing could happen in very practical ways. First, the extension of formal culture to the provinces presupposed public places in which performances and concerts could be held. Hence the phenomenon of the assembly room built by private subscription, where the social elite could meet for balls, music, lectures, and theater, what Plumb calls a "transitional stage between private and fully public entertainment."[21] Such assemblies were sustained by associational action, which in Birmingham extended from the freemasons and other secret circles to an elite formation like the Bean Club or equally exclusive intellectual groups like the Lunar Society and reading societies. From this crystallized a wider sense of cultural and political identity, of which the building of the Birmingham General Hospital between 1765 and 1779 by private subscription was the archetypal case. The hospital's triennial music festivals established themselves as major occasions for the gathering of the West Midlands' leading families and played a key part in attracting patronage and realizing the town's cultural ambitions.[22] Second, new networks of communication seem especially important not just because the press and a reading public ease the exchange of information and ideas but in the larger sense of providing a new institutional context for political action. Money stresses the canal building of the last third of the century, which had an enormous effect in solidifying the new regional and eventually national identities. The floating of a canal scheme entailed an entire repertoire of political initiatives (the creation of new regional political networks, deliberate cultivation of public opinion, participation within the national parliamentary institutions, widespread lobbying of the affected private and public interests), which eventually culminated in the call for a more rational public authority to expedite the whole unwieldy process. This last was key, for to avoid the duplication of projects and an anarchy of particularistic interests, there developed an urgent need to rationalize the activity, and this was increasingly done by reference to some larger "national interest." As Money says, such conflicts became best handled by an appeal to Parliament "as mediator between the public interest on the one hand and private property and enterprise on the other."[23] In the related area of road building, such resolution was achieved by inventing the institution of the turnpike trust. As a third case I cite the abortive General Chamber of Manufacturers of Great Britain, formed between 1785 and 1787 as a shortlived response to some of the government's fiscal measures. Though indifferently successful outside the West Midlands and Manchester, this further solidified regional networks and simultaneously oriented them toward national institutions, both existing (Parliament) and notional (a national market).

Illustrative analysis of this kind that puts Habermas's idea to work can be easily duplicated because the formation of political culture in this sense has been a fundamental dimension of the capitalist developmental process (except, one should immediately say, where capitalism has been imposed from above or without by authoritarian vanguards in situations of extreme societal "backwardness"). But how are we to judge Habermas's idea in the light of capitalism? The basic point is clear enough, namely, the relationship of the new liberal values of the later eighteenth and early nineteenth centuries to definite developmental processes of class formation and social growth (the transition from feudalism to capitalism, as Habermas describes it, with the concomitant rise of the bourgeoisie). For Brewer, no less than for Habermas, a particular ideological structure or cultural formation (liberalism, the ideal of emancipation grounded in rational communication, the Enlightenment discourse of freedom) is the complex effect of a socioeconomic developmental process (the transition from feudalism to capitalism, the rise of capitalism, commercialization, the birth of a consumer society) mediated via the novel institutional structures of the public sphere.[24] At one level Habermas shows how the genesis of the liberal tradition can be grounded in a particular social history, and analyses such as Brewer's or Money's are an excellent concretizing of that project.

On the other hand, what are the problems? Basically, Habermas confines his discussion too much to the bourgeoisie. In his preface Habermas does specifically limit himself to "the *liberal* model of the bourgeois public sphere" (p. xviii) on the grounds of its dominance, distinguishing it from both "the plebeian public sphere" associated with the Jacobin phase of the French Revolution, which later manifested itself in Chartism and the anarchist strains of the continental labor movement, and "the plebiscitary-acclamatory form of regimented public sphere characterizing dictatorships in highly developed industrial societies" (by which he presumably means fascism). The reference to these alternative forms is too cryptic to allow any sensible speculation about what Habermas means in detail, but he does describe the plebeian version as being "suppressed in the historical process" and in any case "oriented toward the intentions of the bourgeois public sphere" (and therefore a dependent variant). I will be returning to this point again below. But here I want to stress the *variable* origins of *Öffentlichkeit*. The virtue of publicness could materialize other than by the intellectual transactions of a polite and literate bourgeois milieu. Despite the best efforts of the latter precisely to appropriate such a function to itself and to establish exclusive claims on the practice of reason, "private people putting reason to use" (p. xviii) could also be found elsewhere. In this respect I want to make three important points:

1. The liberal disideratum of reasoned exchange also became available for nonbourgeois, subaltern groups, whether the radical intelligentsia of Jacobinism and its successors or wide sections of social classes like the peasantry or the working class. In both literary terms (the production and circulation/diffusion of ideas) and political terms (the adoption of constitutions and liberties under the law) the global ideological climate encouraged peasant and working-class voices to strive for the same emancipatory language. That is, the positive values of the liberal public sphere quickly acquired broader democratic resonance, with the resulting emergence of impressive popular movements, each with its own distinctive movement cultures (i.e., form of public sphere). It's open to question how far these were simply derivative of the liberal model (as Habermas argues) and how far they possessed their own dynamics of emergence and peculiar forms of internal life. There is enough evidence from the literature on Owenism, Chartism, and British popular politics and on the forms of political sociability in the French countryside to take this argument seriously.[25] Some recent writing, it is true, has stressed the confinement of Chartism in an inherited political framework and its indebtedness to a given language of political opposition.[26] But we can see such a movement as in one sense "a child of the eighteenth century" (p. xviii), and therefore bound by a dominant model,

and at the same time acknowledge its historical specificity and autonomous forms of expression. In particular, Habermas's oppositions of "educated/uneducated" and "literate/illiterate" simply don't work, because (as we shall see) the liberal public sphere was faced at the very moment of its appearance by not only a "plebeian" public that was disabled and easily suppressed but also a radical one that was combative *and* highly literate.

2. Because of the international impact of the French Revolution, the liberal political ideal encapsulated by the concept of the public sphere was made available in many parts of Europe way ahead of the long-run social transformations, which in western Europe form the starting point of Habermas's argument. All over east-central and southern Europe, and frequently representing little more than themselves, small groups of intellectuals responded to the French Revolution and its legacy by lodging their own claims to nationhood. The French experience bequeathed a political vocabulary in which such new aspirations could be engaged, a structured ideological discourse of rights and self-government into which such emergent intelligentsias might naturally insert themselves. The encounter with revolutionary France induced conscious reflection not only on the circumstances of political dependence in which such societies invariably found themselves but also on the associated handicaps of socioeconomic backwardness. Indeed, the radical departures of the French Revolution not only gave sympathetic intellectuals in more "backward" societies a new political language for articulating their own aspirations, it also allowed them to conceptualize their situations as "backward" to begin with. It interpellated them in that sense via the new forms of nationalist political address. Armed with the new political consciousness, they then set about constituting a national public sphere in all the ways discussed above—from literary societies, subscription networks, the press, and a national reading public, to the gymnastic and sharpshooter clubs, and the popular reading rooms that carried the activity into the countryside—but with the crucial differences: it was stimulated from the outside rather than being the spontaneous outgrowth of indigenous social development, in response to

backwardness rather than progress, and it was consciously expansive rather than narrowly restrictive, oriented toward proselytizing among the people rather than closing ranks against them.[27]

3. It is important to acknowledge the existence of *competing* publics not just later in the nineteenth century, when Habermas sees a fragmentation of the classical liberal model of *Öffentlichkeit,* but at every stage in the history of the public sphere and, indeed, from the very beginning. I've argued immediately above in (1) and (2) that emancipatory activity meeting Habermas's criteria could originate in ways that seem not to be encompassed in his classical model (in popular peasant and working-class movements and in nationalist activity). His conception is needlessly restrictive in other ways too. He *both* idealizes its bourgeois character (by neglecting the ways in which its elitism blocked and consciously repressed possibilities of broader participation/emancipation) *and* ignores alternative sources of an emancipatory impulse in popular radical traditions (such as the dissenting traditions studied by Edward Thompson and Christopher Hill).[28] By subsuming all possibilities into his "liberal model of the bourgeois public sphere," Habermas misses this diversity. More to the point, he misses the extent to which the public sphere was always constituted by conflict. The emergence of a bourgeois public was never defined solely by the struggle against absolutism and traditional authority. Also, it necessarily addressed the problem of popular containment as well. The classic model was already being subverted at the point of its formation, as the actions of subordinate classes threatened to redefine the meaning and extent of the "citizenry." And who is to say that the discourse of the London Corresponding Society was any less rational than that of, say, the Birmingham Lunar Society (let alone the Birmingham Bean Club)? Consequently, the public sphere makes more sense as the structured setting where cultural and ideological contest or negotiation among a variety of publics takes place, rather than as the spontaneous and class-specific achievement of the bourgeoisie in some sufficient sense. I will return to this point again below.

2 Gender and the Public Sphere

So far I have considered Habermas's idea mainly in its own terms, by elaborating on what I take to be his conception of bourgeois culture and seeing how the latter might be concretized by using bodies of recent work in social history. And I have begun to indicate some of the ways in which his limitation of the public-sphere model to the bourgeoisie becomes problematic in this light. In fact, Habermas's idea works best as the organizing category of a specifically liberal view of the transition to the modern world and of the ideal bases on which political and intellectual life should be conducted. But his model of how reason in this sense is attained—a "subjectivity originating in the interiority of the conjugal family" (p. 51), becoming conscious first of itself and then of a wider domain of communicative human relations, traveling into a larger associational arena (book clubs, reading societies, salons) of literary-intellectual exchange and rational-critical debate, and then replicating itself in a political public sphere of property owners—is an extremely idealized abstraction from the political cultures that actually took shape at the end of the eighteenth and start of the nineteenth centuries. At one level this is a familiar historian's complaint that "reality" was more complicated than that (and too complicated for *any* theory to be adequate, it is often implied), and indeed, the kind of associational initiatives discussed above were certainly subject to a messier set of particular causalities than Habermas appears to allow, at least for the purposes of his immediate theorization. But this is not just a matter of "the facts" and getting them straight. The formation of Birmingham's later-eighteenth-century associational networks, the creation of an elite club in early-nineteenth-century German small towns, and the creation of literary societies in mid-nineteenth-century Bohemia all involved questions of *interest, prestige,* and *power,* as well as those of rational communication. The public sphere in its classical liberal/bourgeois guise was partial and narrowly based in that sense, and was constituted from a field of conflict, contested meanings, and exclusion.

The most consistent of these exclusions—preceding and out-lasting, for instance, the calling into question of the public sphere's boundaries according to class—is based on gender. Nancy Fraser has done an excellent job of facing Habermas's basic categories of social analysis—the systematically integrated domains of the economy and state and the socially integrated domains of the lifeworld (namely, the public sphere of citizenship and the private sphere of the family), where each constitutes a distinct action context (of functionally driven transactions secured via the media of money and power and of value-driven interactions focused on intersubjective consensus), corresponding to processes of material and symbolic reproduction respectively—with the "gender subtext" that runs continuously through these separations. As she says, in Habermas's theory the economic and state systems are simultaneously "disengaged or detached from the lifeworld" and then "related to and embedded in it." The systems have to be situated "*within* the lifeworld* . . . in a context of everyday meanings and norms," and for this purpose the lifeworld "gets differentiated into two spheres that provide appropriate complementary environments for the two systems": "the 'private sphere' or modern, restricted, nuclear family . . . linked to the (official) economic system" via the medium of monetary exchange, and "the 'public sphere' or space of political participation, debate, and opinion formation . . . linked to the state-administrative system" via the exchange medium of power. To cut a long and extremely careful critique short, Fraser concludes that the addition of the gender perspective cuts through the structure of distinctions Habermas maintains:

Once the gender-blindness of Habermas's model is overcome, however, all these connections come into view. It then becomes clear that feminine and masculine gender identity run like pink and blue threads through the areas of paid work, state administration and citizenship as well as through the domain of familial and sexual relations. This is to say that gender identity is lived out in all arenas of life. It is one (if not the) "medium of exchange" among all of them, a basic element of the social glue that binds them to one another.[29]

I want to take this basic feminist critique as given and confine myself to a few general observations about the directions of some recent historical work. First, an accumulating tradition of feminist critique has shown how modern political thought is highly gendered in its basic structures, particularly in the context of the Enlightenment and the French Revolution, when the key elements of liberal and democratic discourse were originally formed. Thus the constitutive moment of modern political understanding was itself constituted by newly conceived or rearranged assumptions about woman and man: this was not only registered in the practical achievements of constitutions, legal codes, and political mobilization and their forms of justification; it also ordered the higher philosophical discourse around the universals of reason, law, and nature, grounding it in an ideologically constructed system of differences in gender. The elaboration of this system was complex and need not concern us in detail here. Though I would not question the continuity of women's oppression in earlier periods and societies, there is a strong case for seeing the form of women's exclusion from political participation and civil rights as the historically specific consequence of processes that worked themselves out in the context of the French Revolution. The new category of the "public man" and his "virtue" was constructed via a series of oppositions to "femininity," which both mobilized older conceptions of domesticity and women's place and rationalized them into a formal claim concerning women's "nature." At the most fundamental level, particular constructions of "womanness" defined the quality of being a "man", so that the *natural* identification of sexuality and desire with the feminine allowed the *social* and *political* construction of masculinity. In the rhetoric of the 1780s and 1790s, reason was conventionally counterposed to "femininity, if by the latter we mean (as contemporaries did) pleasure, play, eroticism, artifice, style, politesse, refined facades, and particularity."[30] Given this mannered frivolity, women were to be silenced to allow masculine speech, in the language of reason, full rein.

Thus the absence of women from the political realm "has not been a chance occurrence, nor merely a symptom of the regrettable persistence of archaic patriarchies," but a specific product of the French Revolutionary era. In addition to the other radical departures of that time, modern politics was also constituted "*as* a relation of gender."[31] Moreover, the very breakthrough to new systems of constitutional legality—in which social relations were reordered by conceptions of right, citizenship, and property and by new definitions of the public and the private—necessarily forced the issue of woman's place, because the codification of participation allowed, indeed required, conceptions of gender difference to be brought into play. As Landes says, this occurred via "a specific, highly gendered bourgeois male discourse that depended on women's domesticity and the silencing of 'public' women, of the aristocratic and popular classes," and "the collapse of the older patriarchy gave way to a more pervasive *gendering* of the public sphere."[32] This obviously has major implications for Habermas's argument. Habermas is certainly not unaware of the exclusion of women from the nineteenth-century polities and of the patriarchal nature of the eighteenth- and nineteenth-century family (see, e.g., pp. 43–56, 132). But these matters are assimilated to his general notion of the widening discrepancy between ideal and reality in the nineteenth-century history of the public sphere, and the major ambiguity at the center of Habermas's thinking (the abstraction of an ideal of communicative rationality from historical appearances that were always already imperfect in its terms) lessens the force of the recognition. In fact, the critique of women's subordination can proceed at two levels. On the one hand, there is the synthetic attack on patriarchy as a continuous figure in European political thought from Hobbes through Locke to the Enlightenment and beyond. Women are essentially confined within the household. "Within this sphere, women's functions of child-bearing, child-rearing and maintaining the household are deemed to correspond to their unreason, disorderliness and 'closeness' to nature. Women and the domestic sphere are viewed as inferior to the male-dominated 'public' world of civil society and its culture, property, social power, reason and freedom."[33] But on the other hand, the beauty of Landes's analysis is to have shown how this pattern of subordination was reformulated and recharged in the midst of the major political cataclysm, the

French Revolution, through which the ideal of human emancipation was otherwise radically enlarged. In other words, Habermas's model of rational communication was not just vitiated by persisting patriarchal structures of an older sort; the very inception of the public sphere was itself shaped by a new exclusionary ideology directed at women. As Carol Pateman puts it, "In a world presented as conventional, contractual and universal, women's civil position is ascriptive, defined by the natural particularity of being women; patriarchal subordination is socially and legally upheld throughout civil life, in production and citizenship as well as in the family. Thus to explore the subjection of women is also to explore the fraternity of men."[34]

Second, the story of associational activity may also be retold in gendered terms, i.e., by highlighting the exclusionary treatment of women not just as an additive retrieval of a previously neglected aspect but as an insight that fundamentally reconstructs our sense of the whole. Again, simply invoking traditional patriarchal structures to explain the exclusion of women from politics is perhaps too easy. As Catherine Hall says, middle-class *men* had not been involved in the English political process before the late eighteenth and early nineteenth centuries, and given the general radicalism of the road that led to 1832, the marginalization of middle-class women from this process, i.e., why the attack on traditional values stopped short of patriarchy, needs some specific explanation.[35] In supplying the latter, Davidoff and Hall have stressed *both* the constitutive importance of gender (i.e., the historically specific structuring of sexual difference) in the ordering of the middle-class social world (via particular structures of family and domesticity, and particular styles of consumption) *and* the reciprocal interactions between this private sphere and the public sphere of associational life and politics, in which the latter both reflected and actively reproduced the gendered distinctions of class identity generated between home and work.[36] At a time of enormous socioeconomic and political disorder (from the 1790s to the 1840s) "middle-class farmers, manufacturers, merchants and professionals . . . , critical of many aspects of aristocratic privilege and power, sought to translate their increasing economic

weight into a moral and cultural authority . . . not only within
their own communities and boundaries, but in relation to other
classes," and they did so via the same associational trajectory
(from informal family/friendship/religious/business networks,
through clubs and coffeehouses, to public voluntary associations of a philanthropic-cum-charitable, scientific/cultural/ed-
ucational, business/professional/property-related, and political-
campaigning kind), which I have argued carried Habermas's
public sphere concretely into existence. But—and this is the
point to note here—this activity strictly demarcated the roles
of men and women via a mobile repertoire of ideologies and
practices, which consistently assigned women to a nonpolitical
private sphere, "having at most a supportive role to play in the
rapidly expanding political world of their fathers, husbands
and brothers."[37] Davidoff and Hall present this gendering of
the public sphere in a remarkable richness of detail. It is salutary to substitute their summary description for the characterization of the associational context of the public sphere
unfolded above:

Middle-class men's claims for new forms of manliness found one of
their most powerful expressions in formal associations. The informal,
convivial culture of eighteenth-century merchants, traders and farmers was gradually superseded by the age of societies. Men organized
themselves in myriad ways, promoting their economic interests, providing soup kitchens for the poor, cultivating the arts, reaching into
populated urban areas and rural outposts. This network of association redefined civil society, creating new arenas of social power and
constructing a formidable base for middle-class men. Their societies
provided opportunities for the public demonstration of middle-class
weight and responsibility; the newspaper reports of their events, the
public rituals and ceremonials designed for their occasions, the new
forms of public architecture linked to their causes. The experience
of such associations increased the confidence of middle-class men and
contributed to their claims for political power, as heads of households,
representing their wives, children, servants and other dependents.
This public world was consistently organized in gendered ways and
had little space for women. Indeed, middle-class women in the second
half of the nineteenth century focused many of their efforts on
attempting to conquer the bastions of this public world, a world which
had been created by the fathers and grandfathers.[38]

Third, this separation of spheres—between the masculine realm of public activity and the feminine realm of the home, which certainly didn't preclude (and was finely articulated with) relations of interconnectedness between business/occupation and household, and engendered a particular conception of the public and the private for the emergent nineteenth-century middle class[39]—was replicated in the situation of the working class. In most of the early democratic movements of the late-eighteenth and early-nineteenth centuries, with the significant exception of the followers of Owen, Fourier, and some other utopian socialists, popular sovereignty was basically a male preserve. Chartism in Britain, as the strongest and most impressive of these movements, is a good example, because the famous Six Points for the democratization of the constitution drawn up in 1837–1838 expressly excluded votes for women. While individual Chartists raised the issue intermittently thereafter, the enduring consensus (shared by the movement's women no less than the men) was that female suffrage deserved a low priority. This was even clearer elsewhere in movements of peasants, shopkeepers, and artisans, where democratic aspirations were practically linked to the economics of small-scale household production and to a sexual division of labor in which women had a significant but subordinate place. By the end of the nineteenth century European socialist parties had certainly put women's political rights into their programs. But it's worth recalling how little female suffrage had actually progressed before 1914, with women enjoying the vote only in parts of the North American West and just four of today's parliamentary states—New Zealand (1893), Australia (1903), Finland (1906), and Norway (1913)—interestingly, all of them frontier states in one way or another.

The reasons for such entrenched discrimination were naturally complex but ultimately had to do with ideas about the "naturalness" of woman's place and the proper social ordering of sexual difference. Women had no autonomous political standing in the prevailing theories of government and representation. As Sally Alexander says, "The legal, economic and political subject in radical popular speech reaching back to the seventeenth-century Levellers, was the propertied individual, and the propertied individual was always masculine—whether head of household, skilled tradesman or artisan whose property was his labor." Inscribed in the political language of radical democracy were definite notions of masculinity and femininity organized around a clear distinction between the *public world* and a *domestic-cum-communal sphere*, where patriarchal "notions of labor, property and kin" structured and limited "women's access to knowledge, skill and independent political subjectivity." Women were highly active in Chartism and other radical agitations of the early nineteenth century. But when they spoke, they did so within the walls of the embattled popular community itself. It fell to men to speak to the outside world "in the first person for the community as a whole." *Public* discourse in the full sense, involving the whole field of popular socioeconomic discontents, campaigns for civil freedoms, struggles over the law, and the demand for the vote, was closed to women. It was conducted as "a dialogue of negotiation between the men of the communities and the ruling class—'capitalists and lawgivers.'"[40]

For the various groups of radical working men—"the small master craftsmen, the displaced domestic worker, the artisan and mechanic, the skilled factory operatives," who provided the backbone of Chartism and the related movements—the integrity of the household was constitutive for political identity, and whatever complementarities and reciprocities there may have been between men and women in the household division of labor, as a system of domestic authority the family was centered on masculine privilege. Thus in voicing their anger against the advance of capitalist industry, which undermined their skills and pulled their wives and children into the factory, radical artisans were also defending their own sexual and economic regime in the family. In their minds "their status as fathers and heads of families was indelibly associated with their independence through 'honorable' labor and property in skill, which identification with a trade gave them." Women, by contrast, had no access to such independence. In their own right they were excluded from most trades and could practice a craft only by virtue of their male kin. Usually, they "assisted" the latter. Her "skill" was in the household, her "property in the virtue of her person." But "separated from the home, her family and domestic occupations, or outside the bonds of matrimony, a woman was assured of neither." Logically enough, a woman's political identity was subsumed in that of the man, and it was no accident that the rare proponents of female suffrage among the Chartists also limited their advocacy to "spinsters and widows," because wives and husbands were simply deemed to be one.[41]

This thinking was easily adapted to the changed circumstances of industrialization. The manner of the adjustment was already signaled by the calls for "protective" laws that became especially clamorous in the 1830s and 1840s. Demanding the protection of women and children against the degrading and brutalizing effects of work in the new mills, they also reflected the desire for an idealized notion of family, hearth, and home, where benign patriarchy and healthy parental authority ordered the household economy by the "natural differences and capacities" of women and men. When wives and children were forced into the factory by the unemployment or depressed earning power of the husband-father, this natural order was upset. To this dissolution of moral roles—the "unsexing of the man," in Engels' phrase—were then added the effects of women's cheap labor, whose increasing utilization by the new capitalists spelled a loss of jobs, status, and skill for the skilled man. Whatever the real basis of these fears, this fusion of economic and ideological anxieties—resistance to the capitalist reorganization of industry and the desire to quarantine the family's moral regime—proved a potent combination for those categories of skilled workers strong enough actually to secure a strong bargaining position for themselves.[42] In the new prosperity and greater political stability in British society after 1850 such groups of workers were able to come into their own.

The result was a recharged domestic ideology of masculine privilege, whose realistic attainment was now confined to those groups of skilled workingmen able to support a wife and children on the strength of their own earning power alone. The nature of the labor market for most men—involving the irregularity, casualness, and seasonality of most unskilled and much skilled employment, with the connected difficulties of low, irregular wages and weak organization—ensured that male earnings had to be supplemented by whatever income the wife and the rest of the family could produce, usually in casual, sweated, or home-based employment or in the locally based informal economy. Measured by the rest of the working class, therefore, the position of the skilled craftsman able to keep his wife in domesticated nonemployment was becoming an extremely privileged one—not just in relation to women but in relation to the mass of unskilled males too. Trade unionism before the 1890s was virtually predicated on this system of exclusion, and the new ideal of the "family wage" was a principal mechanism separating the small elite of trade unionized craftsmen from the mass of ordinary workers. But not only did it strengthen the material advantages enjoyed by the craft elite. It also postulated a normative definition of women's employment as something exceptional and undesirable and delivered ideological justifications for "keeping women in their place," or at least for not according their interests the same priority as male workers' in trade union terms, that proved persuasive far outside the ranks of the labor aristocrats themselves and became a pervasive feature of working-class attitudes towards women's political status. Thus it was a paradox of socialist politics before 1914 that parties which were in many ways the staunchest advocates of women's rights in the political arena had also originated in the activism of skilled workers who practiced the worst systems of craft exclusiveness against women—both in immediate terms and in terms of the larger social discrimination/subordination they implied. As we know from the scholarship of the last two decades, the socialist tradition's official supportiveness for women's rights usually concealed a practical indifference to giving them genuine priority in the movement's agitation. More basically, such political neglect was linked to attitudes and practices deeply embedded in the material conditions of working-class everyday life, at work, in the neighborhood, and at home. Behind the labor movement's neglect of women's issues were historically transmitted patterns of masculinist behavior and belief, which trade unionists and left-wing politicians were consistently unwilling to challenge.[43]

I can best express the relevance of this to the discussion of the public sphere by considering the relationship of the private and the public. The specification of a public sphere necessarily implies the existence of another sphere that's private, and in contrast with what Habermas sometimes implies, as Fraser has argued, the boundaries between these two domains are not fast but permeable. The discussion here is also complicated by the recent revival of theorizing around "civil society": as John Keane reminds us, in the eighteenth and nineteenth centuries the state/civil society couplet was operated by political theorists in a rich variety of ways; I might add that such diversity is compounded by the difficulties of distinguishing the autonomies of the private realm in these traditions (e.g., where does the economic belong in this three-way schema of state, civil society, and private sphere; how far is morality the vector of an interventionism that transcends all three; how do we deal with subjectivity?). And it is by no means clear how Habermas's theory of the public sphere fits with this older tradition of thought.[44] But allowing for this diversity of meanings, it may be useful to remind ourselves in a simplified way of the varying definition the public realm may be given. Is this a purely "political" matter in the narrower sense of government and public administration, for instance, or should the legitimate reach of political intervention extend to other more "private" spheres like the economy, recreation, the family, sexuality, and interpersonal relations? Broadly speaking, there have been probably three main answers within the classical left-wing tradition:

• A *pure democratic* one, stressing the political rights of democracy and based in a clear separation of the public from the private sphere, in which the constitution guarantees strong rights of autonomy to the latter through civil freedoms, freedom of conscience and religion, property rights, rights of privacy, and so on

• A *socialist* one, in which the public sphere of democracy becomes extended to the economy through nationalization, the growth of the public sector, trade unionism, the welfare state and other forms of socialized public provision in the areas of health care, social insurance, education, recreation, and so on

• A *utopian* one, in which democracy becomes radically extended to social relations as a whole, including large areas of
personal life, domestic living arrangements, and child raising,
usually in the form of some kind of communitarianism

In the period since 1968 we may add a fourth version of this
relationship between the public and the private, which subjects
each of the above to searching critique, and that is the *feminist*
one. Aside from facing the earlier versions with the need to
address the interests/aspirations of women as well as men, the
feminist version brings the principle of democracy to the center
of the private sphere in a qualitatively different way. It systematically politicizes the personal dimension of social relations in
a way that transforms the public/private distinction in terms of
family, sexuality, self, and subjectivity. Obviously, contemporary feminism is not without its antecedents. Thus the utopian
socialists of the 1830s and 1840s had politicized the personal
sphere in ways that seem strikingly radical when set against
the staider preoccupations of the later nineteenth-century socialist tradition. Strong notions of women's reproductive rights
and liberated sexuality could also be found on the margins of
the left between the 1880s and 1914, and more extensively in
the cultural radicalism of 1917–1923. But it is only really in
the last third of the twentieth century that the gendered characteristics of the classical public sphere have been properly
opened to critique—by elaborating theories of sexuality and
subjectivity, identifying ideologies of motherhood, confronting
the sexual division of labor in households, and developing a
critique of the family as such. As Pateman says:

The meaning of "civil society" . . . has been constructed through the
exclusion of women and all that we symbolize. To create a properly
democratic society, which includes women as full citizens, it is necessary to deconstruct and reassemble our understanding of the body
politic. This task extends from the dismantling of the patriarchal
separation of private and public, to a transformation of our individ-
uality and sexual identities as feminine and masculine beings. These
identities now stand opposed, part of the multifaceted expression of
the patriarchal dichotomy between reason and desire. The most profound and complex problem for political theory and practice is how
the two bodies of humankind and feminine and masculine individ-

uality can be fully incorporated into political life. How can the present of patriarchal domination, opposition and duality be transformed into a future of autonomous, democratic differentiation?[45]

3 State Formation and the Public Sphere

Despite the empirical and imaginative richness of Habermas's account of the formation of (west) European political culture in the eighteenth and early nineteenth centuries, there is little discussion of the state per se or of specific political histories, at least in the senses we've become familiar with during the last two decades, whether via the state-theoretical literatures generated/provoked by Marxists in the 1970s or in the more heterogeneous work on state formation, which was already under way when Habermas conceived his book in the 1950s and early 1960s (most obviously associated with the influence of the Committee on Comparative Politics of the U.S. Social Science Research Council set up in 1954). At the same time, although this omission is significant (in that it has a necessary bearing on how the overall problematic of modern political development is constructed/implied in Habermas's text), Habermas's purpose was different and legitimately specific, concerned, as we have seen, with the "free space" of society rather than a state-centered approach to public authority or political development. He also has lots to say with relevance to the latter, particularly in his extensive and very interesting discussions of the law. Moreover, if we consider the major contributions to the historical discussion of comparative political development produced since the late 1960s (most of them by nonhistorians in the professional sense, incidentally), they have remarkably little to say to the questions of the public sphere and political culture formation raised by Habermas. These works include the writings of Barrington Moore, Jr., and Charles Tilly, both of whom pioneered the turn by U.S. sociology to history in this area; Immanuel Wallerstein's studies of the "modern world-system," Perry Anderson's of absolutism, and Theda Skocpol's of "states and social revolutions"; and the more recent and differently accented projects of Anthony Giddens and Michael Mann. Wallerstein is only secondarily concerned with political, as opposed to economic, history; Anderson deals with state and society relations, but for an earlier period and at a level of generality that makes it hard to engage with Habermas's questions (the latter will in any case be more pertinent to the next installment of Anderson's project, namely, the comparative analysis of bourgeois revolutions); Skocpol focuses rather stolidly on the state in the narrower sense, as a central nexus of government institutions. Tilly's work on collective action and state formation brings us closer to political culture but deals with "the extractive and repressive activities of states" rather than the cultural and ideological ones. Barrington Moore poses the problem of comparative political development through the gross interactions of social forces ("lord and peasant in the making of the modern world") and has little directly to say about the structure of states, the shaping of a public sphere, or the contribution of urban classes. Neither Mann nor Giddens have anything to say about the public sphere in the sense discussed here; the former's forthcoming second volume may well treat this theme directly, but the latter's discussion of "Class, Sovereignty and Citizenship" is bizarrely perfunctory and deals with the subject under an entirely "administrative" perspective.[46] Each of these otherwise extremely interesting works pays little attention to political culture, to the wider impact of the state in society and the modalities of popular consent and opposition, or to the social processes from which political activity ultimately derived. From this point of view, Habermas's translation of the discussion onto a sociocultural terrain, particularly for its time, represents a welcome shift of perspective and might well have found greater resonance in the literature on state formation than it has.

As a view of political development, though, Habermas's framework has a number of drawbacks, some of which have already been mentioned. For one thing, by using a model of communicative rationality to mark the rise of liberalism and the constitutionalizing of arbitrary authority and by stressing the transition to a more interventionist state under advanced capitalism, he strongly implies a *weak* state during the classical public sphere's period of initial formation. But it is unclear how the boundaries between state and society are to be drawn from Habermas's analysis of this period. Was the liberal state really so uninterested in regulating the private sphere or so noninterventionist in the resolution of social and political conflict? Habermas is very good on the legal reforms necessary to promote and ratify the changing bases of property, and as Karl Polanyi always insisted, the road to laissez-faire was paved in state intervention. The same was true of sociocultural and political, no less than of economic freedoms: to deregulate society and confirm a protected space for the public, an entire regulative program was required.[47] Second, and in a similar vein, Habermas's argument idealizes the element of rational discourse in the formation of the public sphere and neglects the extent to which its institutions were founded on sectionalism, exclusiveness, and repression. In eighteenth-century Britain, parliamentary liberty and the rule of law were inseparable from the attack on customary right, popular liberties, and nascent radical democracy, as Edward Thompson's work has so eloquently reminded us.[48] As I suggested above, the participants in the bourgeois public always faced two ways in this sense: forward in confrontation with the old aristocratic and royal authorities, but also backward against the popular/plebeian elements already in pursuit. We can't grasp the ambiguities of the liberal departure—the consolidation of the classical public sphere in the period, say, between 1760 and 1850—without acknowledging the fragility of the liberal commitments and the element of contestation in this sense. It is only by extending Habermas's idea in this direction—toward the *wider* public domain, where authority is not only constituted as rational and legitimate but its terms may also be contested and modified (and occasionally overthrown) by society's subaltern groups—that we can accommodate the complexity.

For this purpose, I want to suggest, an additional concept may be introduced, namely, Antonio Gramsci's idea of "hegemony." Some basic awareness of this is now fairly extensive, but while there is now no shortage of careful critical exegesis around Gramsci's own intentions, the wider usage can be ill informed and glib, and it is important to clarify the purposes the idea is meant to serve. It is worth beginning with Gwyn A. Williams's useful definition, which was also the form in which most of us first encountered the concept before the more extensive translation and discussion of Gramsci's thought in the 1970s: hegemony signifies "an order in which a certain way of life and thought is dominant, in which one concept of reality is diffused throughout society in all its institutional and private manifestations, informing with its spirit all taste, morality, customs, religious and political principles, and all social relations, particularly in their intellectual and moral connotation."[49]

Now this is fine as far as it goes, but it can also license a number of misconceptions, so several points need to be made in elaboration. First, hegemony should not be used interchangeably with "ideology" or "ideological domination" *tout court* in a perspective stressing the "manipulations" or "social control" deliberately exercised by a ruling class. As Raymond Williams says in the course of a brilliant exposition: hegemony comprises "not only the conscious system of ideas and beliefs [i.e., 'ideology' in a commonly accepted sense] but the whole lived social process as practically organized by specific dominant meanings and values," "a sense of reality for most people in the society, a sense of absolute because experienced reality beyond which it is very difficult for most members of the society to move, in most areas of their lives." Hegemony should be seen

as in effect a saturation of the whole process of living—not only of political or economic activity, nor only of manifest social activity, but of the whole substance of lived identities and relationships, to such a depth that the pressures and limits of what can ultimately be seen as a specific economic, political and cultural system seem to most of us the pressures and limits of simple experience and common sense. Hegemony is then not only the articulate upper level of "ideology," nor are its forms of control only those ordinarily seen as "manipulation" or "indoctrination." It is the whole body of practices and expectations, over the whole of living: our senses and assignments of energy, or shaping perceptions of ourselves and our world.[50]

This sense of completeness and externally structured experience, of "the wholeness of the process" by which a given social order holds together and acquires its legitimacy, is the most obvious feature of Gramsci's idea.[51]

Second, however, Gramsci's idea of hegemony was not a "totalitarian" concept (contrary to some of the older commentaries of the 1950s and 1960s, such as H. Stuart Hughes, *Consciousness and Society* [New York, 1958], pp. 96–104). In fact, he used it carefully to distinguish elements of pluralism and competition, of persuasion and consent, from the more repressive and coercive forms of rule and the conventional process of governing in the administrative sense. Though he takes careful note of direct interventions by the state against society to suppress opposition, to contain dissent, and to manipulate educational, religious, and other ideological apparatuses for the production of popular compliance, therefore, Gramsci expressly links hegemony to a domain of public life (which he calls "civil society," but which might also be called the "public sphere") that is relatively independent of such controls and hence makes its achievement a far more contingent process. To establish its supremacy, in Gramsci's view, a dominant class must not only *impose* its rule via the state, it must also demonstrate its claims to "intellectual and moral leadership," and this requires the arts of persuasion, a continuous labor of creative ideological intervention. The capacity "to articulate different visions of the world in such a way that their potential antagonism is neutralized," rather than simply suppressing those visions beneath "a uniform conception of the world," is the essence of hegemony in Gramsci's sense.[52] But by the same virtue, hegemony is also susceptible to change and negotiation not just because it involves the pursuit of consent under conditions of pluralism (however limited) but also because this process nonetheless operates through social relations of dominance and subordination structured by class inequality and therefore involves contradictory and opposing interests.

Third, therefore, hegemony is characterized by uncertainty, impermanence, and contradiction. As I put it with Keith Nield on an earlier occasion, hegemony "is not a fixed and immutable *condition,* more or less permanent until totally displaced by determined revolutionary action, but is an institutionally negotiable *process* in which the social and political forces of contest, breakdown and transformation are constantly in play."[53] In this sense, hegemony is always in the process of construction, because bringing the process to closure would entail either a utopia of social harmony or the replacement of hegemonic by coercive rule. Hegemony is always open to modification, and under specific circumstances may be more radically transformed or even (though not very often) break down altogether. Thus civil society provides opportunities for *contesting* as well as *securing* the legitimacy of the system. More than anything else, then, hegemony has "to be won, secured, constantly defended." It requires "a struggle to win over the dominated classes in which any 'resolution' involves both *limits* (compromises) and *systematic contradictions*."[54] The dominance of a given social group has to be continually renegotiated in accordance with the fluctuating economic, cultural, and political strengths of the subordinate classes.

Gramsci's distinction between "hegemonic" and "coercive" forms of rule is also operated historically. That is, developed capitalist polities whose legitimacy rests on a fairly stable "equilibrium of hegemonic and coercive institutions" are directly contrasted with an older type of state that lacks this vital reciprocity with civil society:

In the ancient and medieval state alike, centralization, whether political-territorial or social . . . , was minimal. The state was, in a certain sense, a mechanical bloc of social groups. . . . The modern state substitutes for the mechanical bloc of social groups their subordination to the active hegemony of the directive and dominant group, hence abolishes certain autonomies, which nevertheless are reborn in other forms, as parties, trade unions, cultural associations.[55]

The passage from one type of state to another presupposes processes of social change that allow new political ambitions to be crystallized. For Gramsci, the latter consist of three moments: the growth of corporate solidarities, their organization into a larger class collectivity, and their translation onto the highest political plane of "universal" interest. With the development of the last of these aspirations, the process of hegemonic construction may be said to have begun, along with the growth of a new "national-popular" dimension to public life and a new claim to "intellectual and moral leadership" in the society as a whole. It is in the context of such a history that the institutional landscape of civil society gradually takes shape. In a now famous and much-quoted passage, Gramsci hinted at the comparative possibilities of this approach:

> In Russia the state was everything, civil society was primordial and gelatinous; in the West there was a proper relation between state and civil society, and when the state trembled a sturdy structure of civil society was at once revealed. The state was only an outer ditch, behind which there stood a powerful system of fortresses and earthworks.[56]

For Gramsci, this contrast was specifically a way of explaining the success of the Bolsheviks in the Russian Revolution, which simultaneously illustrated the fundamentally different strategy required of the left in Western Europe, where the greater complexity of the social fabric, the liberal traditions of citizenship and constitutionalism, and the functioning pluralism of the political system meant that power was diffused more intangibly through a wide variety of nonofficial practices and organizations, as opposed to being physically embodied in a central core of state institutions in the capital city: if in Russia the backwardness of civil society left the state an isolated citadel, which could then be stormed, in the West the structures of existing society were far more complex, requiring a long-term war of position on the part of a revolutionary opposition, and not the insurrectionary war of movement. For our purposes, nineteenth-century Russia provides an excellent counterexample for the growth of the public sphere. It displayed the absence of all those processes—particularly the emancipatory impulse of free associational initiative, which under Tsarism was precluded by a combination of social backwardness and repressive state authority—that Habermas's concept of *Öffentlichkeit* presupposed.

4 Popular Culture and the Public Sphere

Of course, for Gramsci civil society was not quite the neutral context for the emergence of rational political discourse in the ideal and abstract sense intended by Habermas. As I have argued, it was an arena of contested meanings, in which different and opposing publics maneuvered for space and from which certain "publics" (women, subordinate nationalities, popular classes like the urban poor, the working class, and the peasantry) may have been excluded altogether. Moreover, this element of contest was not just a matter of coexistence, in which such alternative publics participated in a tolerant pluralism of tendencies and groupings. Such competition also occurred in class-divided societies structured by inequality. Consequently, questions of domination and subordination—power, in its economic, social, cultural, and political dimensions—were also involved. That being so, hegemony—as the harnessing of public life to the interests of one particular group, i.e., a social bloc ordered around the dominant classes—had to be systematically worked at, whether consciously and programmatically (as in the early stages of such a process of hegemonic construction) or increasingly as the "natural" and unreflected administration or reproduction of a given way of doing things. *Intellectuals* in Gramsci's schema—as a broadened social category including journalists, party officials, teachers, priests, lawyers, technicians, and other professionals, as well as writers, professors, and intellectuals in the narrower conventional sense—were the functionaries of this process.

I want to explore this element of conflict—the fractured and contested character of the public sphere—by looking again at the latter's constitutive moment as Habermas presents it in the later-eighteenth century in Britain, and I want to do so by drawing on the extremely interesting work of Günther Lottes, who (by contrast with most of the Anglo-American work on the subject) is familiar with Habermas's framework and, indeed, uses it to develop his argument.[57] Lottes's book is a reworking of a key part of Edward Thompson's *Making of the English Working Class* and revolves around a careful analysis of the emergence of a radical intelligentsia and its relationship to a plebeian public in later-eighteenth-century England, conducted in two stages. During the first, in the 1770s and 1780s, radical intellectuals postulated a regeneration of the constitution through popular education and parliamentary reform. The corruption and besetting factionalism of the governing system were to be challenged by an extraparliamentary campaign of public enlightenment. At this stage, Lottes argues, the links between intelligentsia and public were external rather than organic, asserted at the level of principle and propaganda, but not yet consummated through new forms of communication or structures of popular participation. Moreover, this earlier intelligentsia was recruited from the upper reaches of society, from three overlapping groups of notables (*Honoratioren*): landowners, merchants, and other prosperous businessmen, whose intellectual pursuits presumed (though not complacently) the material security of their social position; representatives of the academic professions, mainly lawyers and Nonconformist clergy; and the literati and writers in the narrower sense, newly constituted as a separate profession by the emergent literary marketplace. Their activity was loosely structured around London's coffeehouse society, in the discussion circles and debating clubs typified by the Robin Hood Society, the Speculative Society, or the Debating Society in Coachmakers' Hall. If anything, the provincial counterparts were more ramified and vital, certainly in the major centers of Manchester and Birmingham. At the political apex was the Society for Constitutional Information founded in 1780, which remained the principal forum of the radical intelligentsia until the launching of the London Corresponding Society (LCS) in 1792. Thus far, it may be thought, Lottes's account fits very nicely into Habermas's framework and adds further to the illustrative materials provided by Brewer, Money, and others discussed earlier. But the subsequent unfolding of his argument is more subversive.

At one level, the reform movement of the 1780s, which was expressly committed to the creation of an extraparliamentary public, broke the existing frame of legitimate politics. By seeking to educate the general populace into citizenship, the pre-Jacobin radicals raised the issue of universal manhood suffrage and broke "with the previously uncontested dogma of political theory that property alone justified a claim to political participation."[58] Yet at the same time, the Society for Constitutional Information made no attempt at direct popular mobilization. This the open agitation of the masses within a new practice of participatory democracy occurred only with the *second* of Lottes's two stages, that of the English Jacobinism proper. As the organizing instance of the new activity, the LCS then had two distinguishing features. By comparison with the earlier radicals its leadership was drawn more broadly from the less prestigious and established circles of the intelligentsia: not only recognized intellectuals like the merchant son Maurice Margarot, the Unitarian minister Jeremiah Joyce, or the lawyers Felix Vaughan, John Frost, and John Martin, but also "not yet arrived or declassed marginal existences of the London literary-publicist scene" like John Gale Jones, Joseph Gerrald, William Hodgson, the Binns brothers (John and Benjamin), and John Thelwall ("the prototype of the literatus from a modest background who tried vainly for years to find a foothold in the London artistic and literary scene"), the numerous small publishers and book dealers, and the "first representatives of an artisan intelligentsia" like the shoemaker Thomas Hardy, the silversmith John Baxter, the hatter Richard Hodgson, and the tailor Francis Place.[59] Then, second, this new Jacobin intelligentsia set out deliberately to mobilize the masses by carrying the work of political education into the turbulent reaches of the plebeian culture itself.

Thus the key to the LCS's originality was its relationship to the ebullient but essentially prepolitical culture of the urban masses, what Lottes calls "the socio-cultural and institutional context of the politicization of the petty and sub-bourgeois strata."[60] In adopting the democratic principle of "members unlimited," the LCS committed itself not only to a program of popular participation but also to a "confrontation with the traditional plebeian culture," of which it was certainly no uncritical admirer. As Lottes says, "The Jacobin ideal of the independent, well-informed and disciplined citizen arriving at decisions via enlightened and free discussion stood in crass contradiction with the forms of communication and political action characteristic of the plebeian culture."[61] In other words, riot, revelry, and rough music were to be replaced by the political modalities of the pamphlet, committee room, resolution, and petition, supplemented where necessary by the disciplined democracy of an orderly open-air demonstration. The most valuable parts of Lottes's account are those exploring the practicalities of this departure—in the meticulous constitutionalism of the LCS, in the creation of an atmosphere for rational political discussion, in the radicals' critique of the "mob," and in the details of their "enlightenment praxis." A new "plebeian public sphere" (*plebejische Öffentlichkeit*) emerged from these endeavors, nourished on the intense political didacticism of the LCS sections, a rich diet of pamphlets, tracts, and political magazines, and the theatrical pedagogy of Thelwall's Political Lectures. Unlike the radicals of the 1780s, the Jacobins entered into a *direct* relationship with their putative public, and unlike conventional parliamentarians, they did so in a nonmanipulative and nondemagogic way.

This was the real significance of the popular radicalism of the 1790s in Britain. It was more than a mere stage in the long-term movement toward parliamentary reform between the 1760s and 1832 and more than a mere epiphenomenon of the deeper trend toward extraparliamentary "association." It was also more than the founding moment of the nineteenth-century labor movement (which was how it was mainly presented in the older labor history and allied accounts). It was a specific attempt—defined by the global context of the "Atlantic Revolution," the national dynamics of the movement for parliamentary reform, the complex sociology of the English intelligentsia, and the political economy of the London and provincial handicrafts—to educate the masses into citizenship. It should be viewed as "partly the achievement and partly the continuing expression of a comprehensive effort at enlightenment and education, aimed at bringing the urban stratum of small tradesmen and artisans to the point where they could articulate their social and political discontent no longer in the pre-political protest rituals of the traditional plebeian culture, but instead in a political movement with firm organization, a middle and long-term strategy, and a theoretically grounded program."[62] As such, it was as much the "end product of the bourgeois enlightenment of the eighteenth century" as it was the herald of the nineteenth-century working-class movement. As Albert Goodwin, another historian of the English Jacobinism, puts it, the tradesmen, shopkeepers, and mechanics addressed by the LCS were to be educated into political knowledge not just to ensure "their more effective participation in politics," but "to rid society of the turbulence and disorder which was then often inseparable from the ventilation of popular grievances."[63]

At the same time, there were definite limits to the English Jacobin's possible achievement. For one thing, the advanced democracy of the LCS *presumed* the very maturity and sophistication it was meant to *create*. The goals of political pedagogy were hard to reconcile with the competing demands of effective organization, creative leadership, and maximum participation of the members—what Lottes calls "the triangular tension of organizational effectiveness, fundamental democratic consciousness at the grass roots, and educational mission"—particularly when government repression was stepped up after 1793.[64] Moreover, tactically it was hard to confront the "backwardness" of the popular culture too intransigently without beginning to compromise the resonance of the radical propaganda and undermining the movement's basic democratic legitimacy. The Jacobins were also confined in a different direction by the tenacity of the dominant eighteenth-century oppositionist ideology, a potent combination of "Country" ideology and natural rights thinking that stressed the degeneration of an originally healthy constitution and raised serious obstacles to the adoption of Tom Paine's more radical break with the English constitutional tradition. In this respect, the Jacobin radicals remained dependent on the intellectual legacy of the 1780s, and most of their distinctive achievements (e.g., Thelwall's social theory as opposed to his political theory) were well within the limits of this earlier tradition.[65]

Lottes's account nicely brings together the points I've been trying to make (although it should be said straight away that his discussion remains as gender blind as Habermas's own). On the one hand, the actual pursuit of communicative rationality via the modalities of the public sphere at the end of the eighteenth century reveals a far richer social history than Habermas's conception of a specifically bourgeois emancipation allows; on the other hand, Habermas's concentration on *Öffentlichkeit* as a specifically *bourgeois* category subsumes forms of popular democratic mobilization that were always already present as contending and subversive alternatives to the classical liberal organization of civil society in which Habermas's ideal of the public sphere is confined. From a vantage point in 1989, when the French Revolution is being divested of its radical democratic and popular progressive content and discussion of the latter returned to certain Cold War simplicities of the 1950s (as "the origins of totalitarian democracy"), apparently without serious dispute, it is no unimportant matter to point to the foreshortening of Habermas's conception in this respect. (Of course, this is *not* to convict Jürgen Habermas himself of the same ideological syndrome but merely to identify a difficulty that needs clarification.) My four headings of discussion—the findings of current social history, the problem of gender, processes of state formation, and the question of popular politics—are not the only ones under which Habermas's work could be historically considered. A more extensive discussion of nineteenth-century nationalist movements or the literature on communications or the question of popular/mass culture in the Frankfurt School's notation would all have been interesting candidates for inclusion. More fundamentally, perhaps, the "linguistic turn" and the "new cultural history" could also be used to cast Habermas's work in an interesting critical light, as Habermas's own recent engagement with the legacy of Foucault has already made clear. In particular, the claim to *rational* discourse, certainly in the social and gendered exclusiveness desired by the late-eighteenth-century bourgeoisie, was simultaneously a claim to *power* in Foucault's sense, and given the extent of Foucault's influence during the last decade, a whole other discussion might have been developed around this insight. To repeat, none of this diminishes the value and interest of Habermas's original intervention, particularly given its timing three decades ago. My purpose has not been to dismiss the latter but to indicate some of the ways in which it needs to be clarified and extended.

Notes

1. Jürgen Habermas, "The Public Sphere," *New German Critique* 3 (1974): 49. Habermas originally developed his argument in *Strukturwandel der Öffentlichkeit* (Neuwied,

1962). The page references in parentheses in my text are to *The Structural Transformation of the Public Sphere.*

2. Perry Anderson and Peter Dews, in their interview with Habermas, "A Philosophico-political Profile," in Peter Dews, ed., *Autonomy and Solidarity: Interviews with Jürgen Habermas* (London, 1986), p. 178.

3. Rick Roderick, *Habermas and the Foundations of Critical Theory* (New York, 1986), p. 43.

4. Peter U. Hohendahl, "Critical Theory, Public Sphere, and Culture: Jürgen Habermas and His Critics," *New German Critique* 16 (1979): 92.

5. Terry Eagleton, *The Function of Criticism: From "The Spectator" to Post-structuralism* (London, 1984), p. 15.

6. Given the close attention to Habermas's work in the 1970s and 1980s, it is interesting that this, his first major work, which established both his reputation and enduring theoretical interests, has only now received its translation, and indeed, the general ignorance and neglect of its significance in the English-speaking world is rather remarkable. Peter Hohendahl is an exception in this respect. Aside from the commentary cited in note 4 above, he also introduced Habermas's work in *New German Critique* 3 (1974): 45–48, and applied it in "Prolegomena to a History of Literary Criticism," *New German Critique* 11 (1977): 151–163. See also his *Literatur and Öffentlichkeit* (Munich, 1974) and *The Institution of Criticism* (Ithaca, 1982). Discussion of *Öffentlichkeit* is strikingly absent from the main English language commentaries on Habermas's work: Thomas McCarthy, *The Critical Theory of Jürgen Habermas* (Cambridge, Mass., 1978); David Held, *Introduction to Critical Theory* (Berkeley, 1980); Rick Roderick, *Habermas and the Foundations of Critical Theory*; Anthony Giddens, "Jürgen Habermas," in Quentin Skinner, ed., *The Return of Grand Theory in the Human Sciences* (Cambridge, 1985), pp. 121–139; John B. Thompson and David Held, eds., *Habermas: Critical Debates* (Cambridge, Mass., 1982). This is perhaps most striking of all in John Keane, *Public Life and Late Capitalism: Toward a Socialist Theory of Democracy* (Cambridge, 1984), a work avowedly inspired by a reading of Habermas but remarkably manages not to discuss directly or at any length the intellectual context and historical validity of *Öffentlichkeit* itself. The same is true of Keane's two recent volumes on the current discourse of civil society, which fail to pose the relevance of Habermas's pioneering analysis to the terms of that discussion. See John Keane, *Democracy and Civil Society* (London, 1988), and Keane, ed., *Civil Society and the State: New European Perspectives* (London, 1988). In this respect, Joan B. Landes, *Women and the Public Sphere in the Age of the French Revolution* (Ithaca, 1988) is an equally striking exception. See also Richard Sennett, *The Fall of Public Man: On the Social Psychology of Capitalism* (New York, 1976).

7. There is an entry for "Private," but even this doesn't deal with the public/private distinction. See Raymond Williams, *Keywords: A Vocabulary of Culture and Society,* revised ed. (New York, 1983), pp. 242–243. For a similar but immensely more grandiose project, with its place in a very different national intellectual tradition, see Otto Brunner, Werner Conze, and Reinhart Koselleck, eds., *Geschichtliche Grundbegriffe,* 5 vols. (Stuttgart, 1972–1989), and for a succinct introduction to this project, see Keith Tribe, "The *Geschichtliche Grundbegriffe* Project: From History of Ideas to Conceptual History," *Comparative Studies in Society and History* 31 (1989): 180–184.

8. See the following: J. H. Plumb, "The Public, Literature, and the Arts in the Eighteenth Century," in Michael R. Marrus, ed., *The Emergence of Leisure* (New York, 1974), pp. 11–37; Plumb, *The Commercializatin of Leisure* (Reading, 1973); Plumb, "The New World of Childhood in Eighteenth-Century England," *Past and Present* 67 (1975):

64–95; Neil McKendrick, John Brewer, and J. H. Plumb, *The Birth of a Consumer Society: The Commercialization of Eighteenth-Century England* (Bloomington, 1982); P. J. Corfield, *The Impact of English Towns, 1700–1800* (Oxford, 1982); Peter Clark and Paul Slack, eds., *Crisis and Order in English Towns, 1500–1700* (London, 1972); Peter Clark, ed., *Country Towns in Pre-industrial England* (Leicester, 1981); Peter Borsay, "The English Urban Renaissance: The Development of Provincial Urban Culture, c. 1680–c. 1760," *Social History* 5 (1977): 581–603; Borsay, "Culture, Status, and the English Urban Landscape," *History* 67 (1982): 1–12; Borsay, "The Rise of the Promenade: The Social and Cultural Use of Space in the English Provincial Town, c. 1660–1800," *British Journal of Eighteenth-Century Studies* 9 (1986): 125–40; Angus McInnes, "The Emergence of a Leisure Town: Shrewsbury 1660–1760," *Past and Present* 120 (1988): 53–87; John Brewer, *Party Ideology and Popular Politics at the Accession of George III* (Cambridge, 1976); Brewer, "English Radicalism in the Age of George III," in J. G. A. Pocock, ed., *Three British Revolutions: 1641, 1688, 1776* (Princeton, 1980), pp. 265–288; Linda Colley, *In Defiance of Oligarchy: The Tory Party, 1714–1760* (Cambridge, 1982); Colley, "Whose Nation? Class and National Consciousness in Britain, 1750–1830," *Past and Present* 113 (1986): 97–117; John Money, *Experience and Identity: Birmingham and the West Midlands, 1760–1800* (Montreal, 1977); Nicholas Rogers, "The Urban Opposition to Whig Oligarchy, 1720–60," in Margaret Jacob and James Jacob, eds., *The Origins of Anglo-American Radicalism* (London, 1984), pp. 132–148.

9. The classic account is John Vincent, *The Formation of the British Liberal Party 1857–68* (Harmondsworth, 1972). Patricia Hollis, ed., *Pressure from Without* (London, 1974) is a good introduction to the associational world of British liberalism at midcentury, while Eileen Yeo and Stephen Yeo, eds., *Popular Culture and Class Conflict, 1590–1914* (Brighton, 1981) opens a window on its relationship to popular culture. See also the essays "Animals and the State," "Religion and Recreation," "Traditions of Respectability," and "Philanthropy and the Victorians," in Brian Harrison, *Peaceable Kingdom: Stability and Change in Modern Britain* (Oxford, 1982), pp. 82–259, which (despite the book's overall complacency) remain fundamental to this subject. A sense of the earlier-nineteenth-century ambience can be had from two collections of the antislavery movement, Christine Bolt and Seymour Drescher, eds., *Anti-slavery, Religion, and Reform: Essays in Memory of Roger Anstey* (Folkestone, 1980), and David Eltis and James Walvin, eds., *The Abolition of the Atlantic Slave Trade: Origins and Effects in Europe, Africa, and the Americas* (Madison, 1981). Monographs on particular associations and places are legion. Stephen Yeo's *Religion and Voluntary Associations in Crisis* (London, 1976), on Reading, is the most unruly but also the most interesting. For an excellent view of the whole Gladstonian show in motion, see Paul McHugh, *Prostitution and Victorian Social Reform* (London, 1980).

10. The best introduction to the social context of the Enlightenment is via the work of Franklin Kopitzsch: "Die Aufklärung in Deutschland: Zu ihren Leistungen, Grenzen und Wirkungen," *Archiv für Sozialgeschichte* 23 (1983): 1–21 (which contains an excellent guide to the wider bibliography); *Grundzüge einer Sozialgeschichte der Aufklärung in Hamburg und Altona,* 2 vols. (Hamburg, 1982); Kopitzsch, ed., *Aufklärung, Absolutismus und Bürgertum in Deutschland: Zwölf Aufsätze* (Munich, 1976). More generally, see Otto Dann, "Die Anfänge politischer Vereinsbildung in Deutschland," in Ulrich Engelhardt, Volker Sellin and Horst Stuke, eds., *Soziale Bewegung und politische Verfassung: Beiträge zur Geschichte der modernen Welt* (Stuttgart, 1976), pp. 197–232; Dann, ed., *Lesegesellschaften und bürgerliche Emanzipation: Ein europäischer Vergleich* (Munich, 1981); Rolf Engelsing, *Analphabetentum und Lektüre: Zur Sozialgeschichte des lesens in Deutschland zwischen feudaler und industrieller Gesellschaft* (Stuttgart, 1973); Engelsing, *Der Bürger als Leser: Lesergeschichte in Deutschland, 1500–1800* (Stuttgart, 1974); Thomas Nipperdey, "Verein als soziale Struktur in Deutschland im späten 18. und frühen 19. Jahrhundert," in *Gesellschaft, Kultur, Theorie* (Göttingen, 1976), pp. 174–205; Dieter Düding, *Organisierter gesellschaftlicher Nationalismus in Deutschland (1808–1847): Bedeutung und*

Funktion der Turner- und Sängervereine für die deutsche National-bewegung (Munich, 1984); Gert Zang, ed., *Provinzialisierung einer Region: Regionale Unterentwicklung und liberale Politik in der Stadt und im Kreis Konstanz im 19. Jahrhundert, Untersuchungen zur Entstehung der bürgerlichen Gesellschaft in der Provinz* (Frankfurt, 1978); Geoff Eley, *Reshaping the German Right: Radical Nationalism and Political Change after Bismarck* (London and New Haven, 1980); Rudy Koshar, *Social Life, Local Politics, and Nazism: Marburg, 1880–1935* (Chapel Hill, 1986), esp. pp. 91–125.

11. The *Journal of Peasant Studies* is the best general guide to this literature, but for access to the discussion of a particular region, see Grant Evans, "Sources of Peasant Consciousness in South-east Asia: A Survey," *Social History* 12 (1987): 193–211. For the French literature, see Peter McPhee, "Recent Writing on Rural Society and Politics in France, 1789–1900," *Comparative Studies in Society and History* 30 (1988): 750–752; Edward Berenson, "Politics and the French Peasantry: The Debate Continues," *Social History* 12 (1987): 213–229; Ted W. Margadant, "Tradition and Modernity in Rural France during the Nineteenth Century," *Journal of Modern History* 56 (1984): 667–697.

12. See Miroslav Hroch, *Social Preconditions of National Revival in Europe: A Comparative Analysis of the Social Composition of Patriotic Groups among the Smaller European Nations* (Cambridge, 1985), a combined and revised edition of two earlier books in German (1968) and Czech (1971) that enjoyed some subterranean influence in the English-speaking world by the later 1970s, mainly through the occasional writings on nationalism of Eric Hobsbawm. See also Tom Nairn, *The Break-up of Britain: Crisis and Neo-nationalism* (London, 1977, revised ed. 1981). For an introduction to cultural studies, see Richard Johnson, "What Is Cultural Studies Anyway?" *Social Text* 10 (1986/1987): 38–80; Stuart Hall, "Cultural Studies and the Center: Some Problematics and Problems," in Hall et al., eds., *Culture, Media, Language* (London, 1980), pp. 25–48. For relevant work in communications, see James Curran, Michael Gurevitch, and Janet Woollacott, eds., *Mass Communication and Society* (London, 1977); George Boyce, James Curran, and Pauline Wingate, eds., *Newspaper History from the Seventeenth Century to the Present Day* (London, 1978); Harry Christian, ed., *The Sociology of Journalism and the Press,* Sociological Review Monograph 29 (Keele, 1980); Michael Gurevitch, Tony Bennett, James Curran, and Janet Woollacott, eds., *Culture, Society, and the Media* (London, 1982). For Raymond Williams, see esp. *Marxism and Literature* (Oxford, 1977), and *Culture* (London, 1981). For Gramsci, see Geoff Eley, "Reading Gramsci in English: Observations on the Reception of Antonio Gramsci in the English-Speaking World, 1957–82," *European History Quarterly* 14 (1984): 441–477. Work on Eastern Europe may be approached through Gale Stokes, "The Social Origins of East European Politics," *East European Politics and Societies* 1 (1987): 30–74, and Stokes, ed., *Nationalism in the Balkans: An Annotated Bibliography* (New York, 1984). For other regions, see Tom Garvin, "The Anatomy of a Nationalist Revolution: Ireland, 1858–1928," *Comparative Studies in Society and History* 28 (1986): 468–501; Samuel Clark and James S. Donnelly, eds., *Irish Peasants: Violence and Political Unrest, 1780–1914* (Madison, 1983); Rosalind Mitchison, ed., *The Roots of Nationalism: Studies in Northern Europe* (Edinburgh, 1980).

13. See Eley, *Reshaping the German Right,* pp. 32 ff., 150 ff. The Heilbronn example comes from Theodor Heuss, *Preludes to Life: Early Memoirs* (London, 1955), pp. 34 f. Otherwise, see the basic literature cited in note 10 above, esp. Dann, "Anfänge politischer Vereinsbildung," and Nipperdey, "Verein als soziale Struktur."

14. The best analyses are by David Blackbourn, "The Discreet Charm of the Bourgeoisie: Reappraising German History in the Nineteenth Century," in Blackbourn and Geoff Eley, *The Peculiarities of German History: Bourgeois Society and Politics in Nineteenth-Century Germany* (Oxford, 1984), pp. 159–192; and "Politics as Theatre: Metaphors of the Stage in German History, 1848–1933," in Blackbourn, *Populists and Patricians: Essays in Modern Germany History* (London, 1987), pp. 246–264. In its cultural dimen-

sions, Blackbourn's is *the* classic Habermasian analysis. See also H. Barmeyer, "Zum Wandel des Verhältnißes vom Staat und Gesellschaft: Die soziale Funktion von historischen Vereinen und Denkmalsbewegung in der Zeit liberaler bürgerlicher Öffentlichkeit," *Westfälische Forschungen* 29 (1978–1979): 125.

15. *Peculiarities of German History*, by Blackbourn and Eley, was written to contest this tradition of explanation. In the second half of the 1980s Jürgen Kocka began to revisit the latter in cultural terms, while leaving the political argument about the weakness of liberalism intact. There has also been remarkably little attention to *Vereine*/voluntary associations under the auspices of Kocka's project. See the following: Kocka, ed., *Bürger und Bürgerlichkeit im 19. Jahrhundert* (Göttingen, 1987); Kocka, ed., *Arbeiter und Bürger im 19. Jahrhundert: Variante ihres Verhältnisses im europäischen Vergleich* (Munich, 1986); Kocka, ed., *Bürgertum im 19. Jahrhundert: Deutschland im europäischen Vergleich*, 3 vols. (Munich, 1988); Ute Frevert, ed., *Bürgerinnen und Bürger: Geschlechterverhältnisse im 19. Jahrhundert* (Göttingen, 1988); Dieter Langewiesche, ed., *Liberalismus im 19. Jahrhundert: Deutschland im europäischen Vergleich* (Göttingen, 1988); Hannes Siegrist, ed., *Bürgerliche Berufe: Beiträge zur Sozialgeschichte der Professionen, freien Berufe und Akademiker im internationalen Vergleich* (Göttingen, 1988). With the exception of the second of these titles (which issued from a conference organized by Kocka at the *Historische Kolleg* in Munich in June 1984), this activity focused on a year-long research project at the Center of Inter-disciplinary Research at Bielefeld University in 1986–1987. In addition, twelve meetings of the *Arbeitskreis für moderne Sozialgeschichte* under the direction of Werner Conze were devoted to the theme of *Bildungsbürgertum* during 1980–1987. See Conze and Kocka, eds., *Bildungsbürgertum im 19. Jahrhundert* (Stuttgart, 1985). Three further volumes from these meetings were planned.

16. See the works by Plumb cited in note 8 above.

17. See Brewer, *Party Ideology and Popular Politics,* and "Commercialization and Politics," in McKendrick, Brewer, and Plumb, *Birth of a Consumer Society*, pp. 197–262.

18. See Money, *Experience and Identity.*

19. See the works by Borsay cited in note 8 above.

20. Brewer, "Commercialization and Politics," p. 197.

21. Plumb, "The Public, Literature, and the Arts," p. 32.

22. Here see Borsay, "English Urban Renaissance," pp. 590–593, for the growth of towns as a new type of social center. He picks out four main instances: health resorts (Bath, Tunbridge, Scarborough, Buxton, Harrogate, Cheltenham), county towns and other administrative centers (diocesan centers like Lichfield or other legal centers like Preston, Lancashire, for the Duchy Courts), "travel towns" such as Stamford, and new industrial towns (Birmingham, Manchester, Liverpool, and Bristol). For a dissenting view, see McInnes, "Emergence of a Leisure Town," which adds to Borsay's picture rather than supplanting it.

23. Money, *Experience and Identity*, p. 29.

24. However, Habermas is silent on the grand question of causality, i.e., the specific causal mechanisms/relationships between, on the one hand, the longer-term processes of social development and, on the other hand, the emergence of specific ideologies, traditions of thought, and cultural patterns, or between each of these and specific political events (whether on the global scale of the French Revolution or the smaller scale of local political conflicts). The question of the bourgeoisie's collective agency is

not faced. For my own attempt to pose this question (if hardly to answer it), see Geoff Eley, "In Search of the Bourgeois Revolution: The Particularities of German History," *Political Power and Social Theory* 7 (1988): 105–133.

25. I have made this argument for Britain in Geoff Eley, "Rethinking the Political: Social History and Political Culture in Eighteenth- and Nineteenth-Century Britain," *Archiv für Sozialgeschichte* 21 (1981), esp. pp. 438–57, and in a reworked form in "Edward Thompson, Social History, and Political Culture: The Making of a Working-Class Public, 1780–1850," in Harvey J. Kaye and Keith McClelland, eds., *E. P. Thompson: Critical Debates* (Cambridge, 1990), pp. 12–49. Some of the most suggestive contributions to this theme have been by Eileen Yeo: "Robert Owen and Radical Culture," in Sidney Pollard and John Salt, eds., *Robert Owen: Prophet of the Poor* (London, 1971), pp. 104 ff.; "Christianity in Chartist Struggle, 1838–1842," *Past and Present* 91 (1981): 99–139, and "Some Practices and Problems of Chartist Democracy," in James Epstein and Dorothy Thompson, eds., *The Chartist Experience: Studies in Working-Class Radicalism and Culture, 1830–1860* (London, 1982), pp. 345–380. See also James Epstein, "Some Organizational and Cultural Aspects of the Chartist Movement in Nottingham," in *The Chartist Experience*, pp. 221–268; and Barbara Taylor, *Eve and the New Jerusalem: Socialism and Feminism in the Nineteenth Century* (New York, 1983). For the wider literature on the political sociability of the French peasantry, see the essays by Agulhon, McPhee, Berenson, and Margadant cited in note 11 above. In particular, see Maurice Agulhon, *The Republic in the Village: The People of the Var from the French Revolution to the Second Republic* (Cambridge, 1982); Edward Berenson, *Populist Religion and Left-Wing Politics in France, 1832–52* (Princeton, 1984); and Peter McPhee, "On Rural Politics in Nineteenth-Century France: The Example of Rodès, 1789–1851," *Comparative Studies in Society and History* 23 (1981): 248–277.

26. Gareth Stedman Jones, "Rethinking Chartism," in Stedman Jones, *Languages of Class: Studies in English Working-Class History, 1832–1982* (Cambridge, 1983), pp. 90–178.

27. See Goeff Eley, "Nationalism and Social History," *Social History* 6 (1981): 83–107, and Eley, "Remapping the Nation: War, Revolutionary Upheaval, and State Formation in Eastern Europe, 1914–1923," in Peter J. Potichnyj and Howard Aster, eds., *Ukrainian-Jewish Relations in Historical Perspective* (Edmonton, 1988), pp. 220–230.

28. The classic sources, of course, are Edward Thompson, *The Making of the English Working Class* (London, 1963), pp. 17–185, and Christopher Hill, *The World Turned Upside Down* (London, 1972). Also see the more recent following works by Hill: *The Experience of Defeat: Milton and Some Contemporaries* (London, 1984); *Turbulent, Seditious, and Factious People: John Bunyan and His Church* (Oxford, 1988); "Why Bother about the Muggletonians?" in Hill, Barry Reay, and William Lamont, *The World of the Muggletonians* (London, 1983), pp. 6–22. See also Lamont, "The Mugglestonians, 1652–1979: A 'Vertical Approach,'" *Past and Present* 99 (1983): 22–40, and the subsequent debate between Hill and Lamont, *Past and Present* 104 (1984): 153–163. For some general commentary, see Barry Reay, "The World Turned Upside Down: A Retrospect," in Geoff Eley and William Hunt, eds., *Reviving the English Revolution: Reflections and Elaborations on the Work of Christopher Hill* (London, 1988), pp. 53–71.

29. Nancy Fraser, "What's Critical about Critical Theory? The Cae of Habermas and Gender," in Seyla Benhabib and Drucilla Cornell, eds., *Feminism as Critique* (Minneapolis, 1987), pp. 31–55. The quotations are from pp. 41, 45.

30. Landes, *Women and the Public Sphere*, p. 46. Landes explains this opposition to a great extent by a counterreaction against the public role of aristocratic women in the salons of the ancien regime, which then generalized its hostility to the "unnatural"

prominence of women in public life and made femininity a general repository for vices that republican virtue would overcome.

31. Landes, *Women and the Public Sphere,* p. 204.

32. Landes, *Women and the Public Sphere,* p. 2.

33. John Keane, Introduction, in Keane, ed., *Civil Society and the State,* p. 21.

34. Carole Pateman, "The Fraternal Social Contract," in Keane, ed., *Civil Society and the State,* p. 121. See also Pateman, *The Sexual Contract* (Cambridge, 1988); Landes, *Women and the Public Sphere;* Jean Bethke Elshtain, *Public Man, Private Woman: Women in Social and Political Thought* (Princeton, 1981); Ellen Kennedy and Susan Mendus, eds., *Women in Western Political Philosophy: Kant to Nietzsche* (New York, 1987); and the brilliant discussions scattered through Dorinda Outram, *The Body and the French Revolution: Sex, Class, and Political Culture* (London and New Haven, 1989). For a dissentient view, see Sylvana Tomaselli, "The Enlightenment Debate on Women," *History Workshop Journal* 20 (1985): 101–124.

35. Catherine Hall, "Private Persons versus Public Someones: Class, Gender, and Politics in England, 1780–1850," in Carolyn Steedman, Cathy Urwin, and Valerie Walkerdine, eds., *Language, Gender, and Childhood* (London, 1985), p. 11.

36. The approach is much more nuanced than can be described here. See in particular the definition of consumption (heavily influenced by the current discourse of the British intellectual left) as a way of integrating the "private" sphere of "the family and women's labour" into a Marxist discussion of production and social reproduction:

And yet, the creation of the private sphere has been central to the elaboration of consumer demand, so essential to the expansion and accumulation process which characterizes modern societies. The recent work which has analyzed consumption as a process of "cultural production," looks not only at its role in reproduction but also at the creation of need and the ways in which particular desires and pleasures come to define social identities and to be represented as cultural products. This approach has necessarily emphasized the gender dimension. Furthermore, consumption is instrumental in forming and maintaining status, the "relational" element of class, the continual claim and counter-claim to recognition and legitimation. Gender classification is always an important element in the positioning of groups and individuals and the competition for resources which takes place at every level of society. Women, in their association with consumption, are often seen as creators as well as the bearers of status.

See Leonore Davidoff and Catherine Hall, *Family Fortunes: Men and Women of the English Middle Class, 1780–1850* (London, 1987), p. 29 f.

37. Hall, "Private Persons versus Public Someones," p. 11.

38. Davidoff and Hall, *Family Fortunes,* p. 416.

39. Davidoff and Hall are excellent on the complex imbrication of family and economics in the late-eighteenth/early-nineteenth-century English middle class. See *Family Fortunes,* pp. 195–315.

40. Sally Alexander, "Women, Class, and Sexual Differences in the 1830s and 1840s: Some Reflections on the Writing of a Feminist History," *History Workshop Journal* 17 (1984): 136, 137, 139. The quotations that follow have the same source.

Geoff Eley

41. See Dorothy Thompson, *The Chartists: Popular Politics in the Industrial Revolution* (New York, 1984), p. 125, which cites pamphlets by the Manchester Chartist Reginald John Richardson and the London Chartist John Watkins to this effect.

42. Alexander is very good on this. Capitalist transformation of the work process and the concomitant dissolution of existing family controls reflected "the two themes which spurred all visions of a new social order" in the first half of the nineteenth century in Britain, namely, the idea that "labour, as the producer of wealth and knowledge, should receive its just reward" and the belief that "kinship was the natural and proper relation of morality, authority and law." See "Women, Class, and Sexual Differences," p. 138. Engels' phrase is taken from *The Conditions of the Working Class in 1844,* in Karl Marx and Friedrich Engels, *On Britain* (Moscow, 1962), p. 179.

43. There is a useful discussion of this point in Richard J. Evans, "Politics and the Family: Social Democracy and the Working-Class Family in Theory and Practice before 1914," in Evans and W. R. Lee, eds., *The German Family: Essays on the Social History of the Family in Nineteenth- and Twentieth-Century Germany* (London, 1981), pp. 256–288.

44. See Keane, "Remembering the Dead: Civil Society and the State from Hobbes to Marx and Beyond," in *Democracy and Civil Society,* esp. pp. 35 f.

45. Pateman, "The Fraternal Social Contract," p. 123.

46. See Immanuel Wallerstein, *The Modern World System,* vol. 1, *Capitalist Agriculture and the Origins of the European World-Economy in the Sixteenth Century* (New York, 1974), vol. 2, *Mercantilism and the Consolidation of the European World-Economy, 1600–1750* (New York, 1980), and vol. 3, *The Second Era of Great Expansion of the Capitalist World-Economy, 1730–1840s* (San Diego, 1989); Perry Anderson, *Lineages of the Absolutist State* (London, 1974); Charles Tilly, ed., *The Formation of National States in Western Europe* (Princeton, 1975); Theda Skocpol, *States and Social Revolutions: A Comparative Analysis of France, Russia, and China* (Cambridge, 1979); Barrington Moore, Jr., *Social Origins of Dictatorship and Democracy* (Boston, 1966); Michael Mann, *The Sources of Social Power,* vol. 1, *A History of Power from the Beginning to A.D. 1760* (Cambridge, 1986); Anthony Giddens, *The Nation-State and Violence,* vol. 2 of *A Contemporary Critique of Historical Materialism* (Berkeley, 1987), pp. 198–221.

47. See Karl Polanyi, *The Great Transformation: The Political and Economic Origins of Our Time* (Boston, 1944), esp. pp. 139 ff.; and Fred Block and Margaret R. Somers, "Beyond the Economistic Fallacy: The Holistic Social Science of Karl Polanyi," in Theda Skocpol, ed., *Vision and Method in Historical Sociology* (Cambridge, 1984), esp. pp. 52–62. The paraphrase of Polanyi is really Peggy Somers's.

48. See esp. the following works of Edward Thompson: "The Moral Economy of the English Crowd in the Eighteenth Century," *Past and Present* 50 (1971): 76–131; "Patrician Society, Plebeian Culture," *Journal of Social History* 7 (1973–1974): 382–405; *Whigs and Hunters: The Origin of the Black Act* (Harmondsworth, 1975); "Eighteenth-Century English Society: Class Struggle without Class?" *Social History* 3 (1978): 133–166. I have commented on this aspect of Thompson's work in "Rethinking the Political," pp. 432 ff.

49. Gwyn A. Williams, "The Concept of 'Egemonia' in the Thought of Antonio Gramsci: Some Notes in Interpretation," *Journal of the History of Ideas* 21 (1960): 587.

50. Williams, *Marxism and Literature,* p. 109f.

51. Williams, *Marxism and Literature,* p. 108.

52. Ernesto Laclau, *Politics and Ideology in Marxist Theory* (London, 1977), p. 161.

53. Geoff Eley and Keith Nield, "Why Does Social History Ignore Politics?" *Social History* 5 (1980): 269.

54. Stuart Hall, Bob Lumley, and Gregor McLennan, "Politics and Ideology: Gramsci," in *On Ideology*, Working Papers in Cultural Studies, 10 (Birmingham, 1977), p. 68.

55. Antonio Gramsci, *Selections from the Prison Notebooks* (London, 1971), p. 54. The earlier quoted phrase, "equilibrium . . . ," comes from Eric J. Hobsbawm, "The Great Gramsci," *New York Review of Books* 21, no. 5 (April 1974): 42.

56. Gramsci, *Selections from the Prison Notebooks*, p. 238.

57. Günther Lottes, *Politische Aufklärung und plebejisches Publikum: Zur Theorie und Praxis des englischen Radikalismus im späten 18. Jahrhundert* (Munich, 1979).

58. Lottes, *Politische Aufklärung*, p. 14.

59. Lottes, *Politische Aufklärung*, p. 223ff.

60. Lottes, *Politische Aufklärung*, p. 109.

61. Lottes, *Politische Aufklärung*, p. 337.

62. Lottes, *Politische Aufklärung*, p. 14.

63. Albert Goodwin, *The Friends of Liberty* (London, 1979), p. 157.

64. Lottes, *Politische Aufklärung*, p. 337.

65. Lottes, *Politische Aufklärung*, pp. 263–334.

13

The Pragmatic Ends of
Popular Politics

Harry C. Boyte

A persistent strain through contemporary social and political theory is the sharp division between what Jürgen Habermas has called "lifeworld" and "system." We experience this division as the difference between the terrain of the immediate, familiar, everyday, and close to home, on the one hand, and the large institutions and systems that tower over us, like granite mountains of the social landscape, with a seemingly immutable logic and force of their own.

Richard Flacks has rendered this distinction with special force for the activist generation that came of political age in the 1960s in his discussion of the difference between "making history" and "making life." The poignant memories of those moments when it seemed that ordinary people were participating on the stage of public affairs, "making history," through their impact on large systems and institutions gave way in the 1970s and 1980s to a far more circumscribed, privatized orbit of the everyday and the immediate, "making life." By the Reagan years, the actors and institutions of public history making, the system world, seemed like an uncomfortably distant spectacle.[1]

The pattern of division between lifeworld and system world, the people and the establishment, was anticipated by the way Jürgen Habermas conceived public life a generation ago, even as he recalled the historical period of the eighteenth and nineteenth centuries when a public sphere was more widely accessible. The English translation of his magisterial work in this vein, *Structural Transformation of the Public Sphere*, provides an occasion for reflection on the prospects of the public in the 1990s.

Habermas reminds us of a public world where citizens "confer in an unrestricted fashion about matters of general interest," which has been radically eclipsed in the contemporary political environment of television sound bites, interest group maneuvering, technocratic manipulation, and image advertising.

Social historians such as Mary Ryan and Geoff Eley, expressing the postmodernist sensibilities of scholarship informed by the sixties' social ferment, both build upon and challenge Habermas's account. In particular, they draw attention to the ways in which public involvements—and the very idea of the public sphere itself—have always been tied to questions of gender, power, interest, and justice. In their criticisms Ryan and Eley compellingly sketch an understanding of public different from the practices of rational debate and discourse of the bourgeois public sphere. In their historical treatments a second, *insurgent* construction of the public realm as unrealized ideal emerges when groups marginalized or formally excluded from the bourgeois public sphere—women, racial and cultural minorities, lower classes—challenge its logic, locations, patterns of discourse, and constructions of the public good. Eley and Ryan thus add a critical dimension: the insurgent sense of public that recalls the turbulent, contested, and value-laden quality of public life.

Yet in both cases the middle ground of pragmatic motive and action found within civil society disappears. Both Habermas and his critics on the postmodernist left accept a view of citizens as, in a sense, permanent outsiders, detached from the actual practices of decision making and action involved in solving the problems of social reproduction. Put differently, in both the understanding of deliberative public advanced by Habermas and the view of insurgent, protesting publics proposed by Ryan and Eley, citizens remain in the role of spectators, whether reflective and judicious, or aggrieved and enraged.

As Vaclav Havel has recently reminded us, even in settings of sharp inequality, injustice, and political corruption, the entire people, self-consciously or not, participates to some degree in the maintenance and reproduction of social life at every level. Attention to such agency, and the skills, capacities, conceptual themes, and moral responsibility involved in popular participation in political life, opens up a series of other crucial questions for historical and theoretical investigation, such as the senses in which ordinary people feel themselves to be creators and subjects of history, not simply spectators and objects. Moreover, this midground understanding of public as creator and public problem solver also provides a key to democratic political renewal.[2]

1

A number of elements formed the background for the emergence of the bourgeois public sphere that Habermas details. Long-term trends toward long-distance trade and commercialization undermined the household economy and created pressures toward a commodity market that reworked political relations and also created new "public knowledge" across communal and even national boundaries. A politicized and self-conscious language of public and public opinion was closely connected, moreover, to the development of a vibrant urban culture that formed a spatial environment for the public sphere: lecture halls, museums, public parks, theaters, meeting houses, opera houses, coffee shops, and the like. Associated with such changes was an emergent infrastructure of new social information created through institutions like the press, publishing houses, lending libraries, and literary societies.

Finally, the explosion of voluntary associations in the eighteenth and nineteenth century created a social setting in which a sense of a disparate, far-ranging, but self-conscious "public" could take shape. Habermas drew particular attention to politicized associations of debate and discussion, such as the new reading and literary societies and their associated institutional networks like the press, publishing houses, libraries, clubs, and coffeehouses. These formed a context in which older hierarchical principles of deference and ascribed social status gave way to public principles of rational discourse, and emergent professional and business groups could nourish and assert their claims to a more general social and political leadership. By the close of the eighteenth century or the beginning of the nineteenth, depending on the nation, a public sphere "was casting itself loose as a forum in which the private people, come together to form a public, readied themselves to compel public authority to legimate itself before public opinion. The *publicum* developed into the public, the *subjectum* into the reasoning subject, the receiver of regulations from above into the ruling authorities' adversary."[3]

By the last decades of the nineteenth century, Habermas argues, this public sphere had begun to atrophy radically. The growing replacement of a competitive capitalist economy with a monopolized economy dominated by large industrial and financial interests undermined the power and authority of the commercial and professional middle classes. The state itself increasingly took on the role of social regulator of conflicts, and the public began to break apart into a myriad of special interests. Meanwhile, in cultural systems of all kinds, from the arts to entertainment industry to the communications media, developments in the late nineteenth century and throughout the twentieth have eroded voluntary, interactive, and associational environments, recreating "the public" as a passive mass of individualized consumers.

Geoff Eley describes this process well to make the point that many historical critics of Habermas miss the importance of his argument. Habermas's concept of public sphere has a double function. In the first instance, while it involves historical description, whatever its particular flaws (for instance, critics have pointed to his exaggerated emphasis on the role of marketplace forces and his underestimation of the role of religion and science in the rise of a bourgeois public), his account is meant in a sense to prompt historical investigation. This it has certainly achieved.

In the second instance, Habermas's motives were not simply scholarly but also political. *Structural Transformation* sought to create a normative ideal of procedural radicalism in the service of democratic political critique. According to Habermas, by the middle nineteenth century a self-conscious quality and dynamic of "publicness" and public opinion as judgment had emerged with its own implicit and democratic ideals of communicative interaction. Habermas has been able to use this ideal of unrestricted communication subsequently in a variety of ways.[4]

2

Habermas's political motives have strong contemporary implications. But his politics in *Structural Transformation* also throws into relief major weaknesses in his account of the public sphere, especially its tendency to separate public discourse from questions of power and interest.

Geoff Eley and Mary Ryan focus on such problems. Both argue that Habermas's construction of the public sphere fails to problematize the highly gendered and class-defined division between bourgeois public (the arena of middle-class males) and private (the household, where women "belong"). In fact, they argue, Habermas's public sphere took shape in part through the explicit prohibition of women and in opposition not only to traditional elites but to popular groups. The understandings of "reason," "rationality," and "public good" associated with the processes Habermas describes were defined through a series of exclusions, as well as norms of inclusive discourse.

A more dynamic understanding of the public arena historically comes from looking at it as a series of diverse publics, created through a turbulent, provisional, and open-ended process of struggle, change, and challenge. Mary Ryan artfully depicts the decentered publics of street corner and outdoor society—far removed from the reading rooms and clubs of polite society—to make the point. Similarly, as she describes, political judgment and citizenship, far from abstract and universalist categories, are always infused with interests and points of view. Public judgment is not the search for objective "truth" in pursuit of the "public good," which Habermas often suggests is the aim of a process of public discussion. In actual living politics, judgment and public engagements are dependent on *context* and perspective, always suffused with power relations.

But this context-dependent, provisional, open-ended quality of public involvement and public judgments is further dramatized by attention to a second significant weakness in Habermas's account, which Eley and Ryan share. Simply put, they all separate the process of public talk from recognition of the roles citizens and those who would be full citizens play in directly acting with responsibility for the problems of society. In making such separation, Habermas and his political critics alike create a fateful division between different sorts of judgment making.

For the Greeks, public judgment was conveyed by the concept of *phronesis*, or practical wisdom. Practical wisdom involved the insight and practical theory accumulated through action around common issues in the space of public life. For Habermas, the public sphere in the modern world is different from that of the Greeks. "The theme of the modern (in contrast to the ancient) public sphere shifted from the properly political tasks of a citizenry acting in common (i.e., administration of law as regards internal affairs and military survival as regards external affairs) to the more properly civic tasks of a society engaged in critical public debate."[5]

When common action is separated from public debate, the processes through which citizens learn crucial dimensions of public life are lost because reflective reason is separated from experience of the consequences of action. What is left is "objective" and critical knowledge, on the one hand, especially as logic and analytic thinking. Education in our schools privileges this sort of knowledge. On the other hand, what is stressed is subjective, intuitive, and emotional knowledge, of the sort found in artistic endeavors and "personalized politics." But the sharpness of these divisions between ways of knowing and their separateness from political capacity have grave political consequences.

A conceptual severance of debate from responsible action corresponds in formal ways to political experience in modern republics, where political representatives make the formal decisions about public affairs and political authority is delegated, not practiced directly by the citizenry as a whole (conservatives regularly invoke "citizen responsibility" but tend to ignore the structural and institutional relations that strip citizens of power and authority). But an excessive formalism also plagues Habermas's construction. Even the deliberative voluntary activities, which Habermas describes in parks, coffeehouses, discussion groups, literary societies, and the like, involved direct popular authority and responsibility for maintenance. Moreover, the wider array of voluntary activities suggested by social historians like Eley and Ryan (dramatized especially in the American case) makes impossible any simple distinction between "acting in common" and "public debate."

Inattention to the action dimension of judgment means the citizen is inevitably a spectator. In contrast, the full range of practical action highlights the largely pragmatic, problem-solving motives that often move people in the public sphere, in both formal and informal contexts. American history has moments of formal direct democracy, such as the New England town meeting. But the traditions of practical public problem solving were mainly embodied in multiple voluntary traditions, which so transfixed Alexis de Tocqueville's observations of the American social landscape of the 1830s. These in turn had roots in the European experiences of most immigrants.[6]

The voluntary activities which both Eley and Ryan describe had dimensions of publicness that their accounts neglect. Eley's argument ends with the invocation of a Gramscian contest between historical blocs, which inexorably dissolves the possibility of pragmatic common ground in a process of class struggle. Writing about the American case, Ryan consigns women's problem solving to the "social sphere," whose teleological premise is constructed, a posteriori, as a "camouflaged pilot project for the welfare state."

Attention to the actual experience of problem solving by women's groups, for example, highlights a much more complex pattern of creation, communal sustenance, and practical action than Ryan's dismissive rendering of such activities as a "condescending, restrictive and niggardly distribution of alms and advice to those who met [women reformers'] middle class, usually Protestant standards of the 'worthy poor.'"

Through welfare organizations and other associational activities—educational institutions, religious groups, moral reform organizations of all kinds—women learned a series of public skills, capacities, and sensibilities like the exercise of power, judgment tied to action, listening, bargaining, negotiation, and practices of accountability. The Women's Christian Temperance Union of the late nineteenth century, for instance, combined decades of voluntary problem-solving effort and moral reform agitation in its slogan "Do Everything." Historian Ruth Bordin conveyed the scale of such efforts. By 1889 WCTU activities in Chicago included "two day nurseries, two Sunday Schools, an industrial school, a mission that sheltered four thousand homeless or destitute women in a twelve months period, a free medical dispensary that treated over 1600 patients a year, a lodging house for men that had to date provided temporary housing for over fifty thousand men, and a low-cost restaurant."[7]

Actual experiences of power-wielding and problem-solving lent nineteenth-century social movements an idiomatic style that unmistakably combined three elements of public: public as deliberator and public as insurgent force were wedded to an understanding of public as responsible and powerful actor. As Frances Willard, the WCTU's guiding force, put it, the temperance crusade gave women a transformed sense of their own agency, whether or not they understood themselves to be in political opposition:

Perhaps the most significant outcome of this movement was the knowledge of their own power gained by the conservative women of the Churches. They had never even seen a "woman's rights' convention," and had been held aloof from the "suffragists" by fears as to their orthodoxy; but now there were women prominent in all Church cares and duties eager to clasp hands for a more aggressive work than such women had ever before dreamed of undertaking.[8]

In parallel fashion, the African-American movement for justice was a freedom movement that expressed a sense of responsibility for the whole, while it also represented a clear challenge to the racial status quo. "The great problem to be solved by the American people is this," wrote the black poet Frances Harper in 1875, "whether there is strength enough in democracy, virtue enough in our civilization and power enough in our religion to deal justly with four millions of people lately translated from the old oligarchy of slavery to the new commonwealth of freedom." America's political culture in the latter decades of the nineteenth century still held for newly freed African-Americans sufficient political vibrancy to generate a vision of the "commonwealth of freedom."

Similarly, the message of Eugene V. Debs, central leader of American labor and radical movements in the late nineteenth and early twentieth centuries, was a plea to retrieve older understandings of public life as the realm of civic action. Debs described his ultimate goal—what he called "the crowning glory of our civilization"—as "the co-operative commonwealth." Though he had certain programmatic ideas in mind, issues were more the occasion than the content. The cooperative commonwealth in Debs's imagination was primarily a call to action. Only through self-organization could workers begin to redress the radically unequal power relationships he saw emerging in the new industrial era, relationships that threatened to make republican government and active citizenship simply empty phrases. "Liberty, be it known, is for those only who dare to strike the blow to secure and retain the priceless boon," he thundered. "To the unified hosts of American workmen fate has committed the charge of rescuing American liberties from the grasp of the vandal horde that have placed them in peril, by seizing the ballot and wielding it to re-gain the priceless heritage and to preserve and transmit it, without scar or blemish to the generations yet to come."9

In 1895 Debs spoke for an ideal of public freedom grounded in cooperative action by equal citizens who were ready and able to assume responsibility for public affairs, not simply protest injustice. Yet in a world of large-scale industry, big government, continentwide transportation and communications systems, and expert control over everything from schooling to child reading to health care, the idea of freedom as the exercise of power by ordinary citizens proved far more difficult to keep alive. Citizens came to assume, almost as a matter of course, their powerlessness and structural irresponsibility.

A hundred years ago citizens learned practical arts of public life like negotiation, accountability, granting of public recognition, exercise of power and authority from a continuing practice of community action in voluntary and informal community institutions. The public world, either formally construed as politics or informally experienced as the civic sphere, was not seen as radically separated from everyday life. In turn, the erosion of this dimension of pragmatic public action radically weakened the daily experiences of popular agency and public capacities.

Against this background the left made a Faustian bargain. Socialists and welfare-state liberals alike said in effect that if democracy understood as popular power is impossible in the modern world, they will settle for a more equal distribution of resources and incomes instead, to be accomplished primarily through the state. This theme, expressed as the singular focus on questions of justice (both distributive and prodedural) on the liberal left, was also given institutional foundations in the growing bureaucracies and large scale organizations of reform in the twentieth century: enormous unions, political parties, professional associations, and so forth. All of these progressively detached popular participation and agency from politics. As a consequence, justice, not power, has formed the main axis of political debate in welfare-state politics.

Such historical experience strongly colored Habermas's account in *Structural Transformation*. It also shaped the language and categories of the new left and subsequent social historians. But whatever phenomenological plausibility there is to a one- or two-dimensional construction of the public sphere, there is also considerable political cost.

The very division between lifeworld and system world, making life and making history, as obvious and natural as it first appears, obscures the actual living agency of ordinary people along the borders between the everyday and the systemic, the fashion in which power never operates simply in a monochromatic and unidirectional fashion but always is a complex, interactive ensemble of relationships.

Without attention to the actual experiences that produce *phronesis,* or the practical wisdom and "common sense" developed through communal reflection on action over time, political thought ineluctably tends toward the sort of "ideological" and dogmatic quality of public opinion described by Keith Baker in his account of the rise of the concept in eighteenth-century France. In modern political practice an excessively sharp distinction and contrast between the institutional world and the lived experience of "the people" lends itself to a romanticized and Manichean politics, where forces of light battle forces of evil and power is understood in primarily moral categories.

Such a pattern characterized the protest politics of the 1960s and turned the crusade between Free World and Iron Curtain into its moral obverse, a battle between flower children and "Amerikkka." Subsequently, such an understanding of issue conflicts has come to characterize virtually every popular dispute on both left and right, from prayer in the schools to abortion, garbage incinerators to AIDS. Despite the participatory flavor of the new social movements and other forms of grass roots activism, the result has been a restriction of any possibility for a genuine public sphere ever since. Seeing controversies as the clash between innocents and moral monsters severely constricts the possibilities of genuine engagement with one's opponents.

What gets lost in an inflamed and excessively ideological politics is the moral ambiguity and open-ended, provisional quality involved in the pragmatic tasks of the public world, where the search is not for "truth" or final vindication but rather appropriateness, fit, agreement, adjudication, and provisional, if sound, resolution of pressing concerns. In a problem-solving public, there are few saints or sinners. Rather there is an interplay among a variety of interests, values, and ways of looking at experience. Knowledge is not simply divided between categories like objective and analytic, or subjective and emotional. In a public sphere of actors as well as talkers or protestors, no one is simply a victim or an innocent. Power is not seen as one-directional or radically moralized. Questions of justice and social transformation enter more or less directly and explicitly, but however they appear, everyone bears a measure of responsibility for the solutions to the problems of the public that have been pragmatically identified.

Today, the starting point for a renewal of public judgment and public life are experiences of politics that retrieve memories of public action and cultivate once again the arts of public problem solving.

As society became more managerially ordered in the twentieth century, every organizational setting has tended to lose its public dimensions as goals shifted from civic problem solving to institutional resource allocation or service provision for clients by means of technical, economic, and therapeutic languages that privatize every interaction and hide power relations.

A shift from economic, technical, or therapeutic language means a reconstruction of the concept of public life as a realm where ordinary people reclaim authority and develop the skills for important problem solving. A conceptual framework that shows both the distinctions and the connections between public and private life proves a valuable resource for developing the skills of effective work with others beyond one's private life and community. In a fashion analogous to the legal distinction between substantive and procedural issues, this framework recognizes that personal concerns are relevant to public affairs, but how one acts on them needs to vary with different settings. Public life is a realm of difference, public work, accountability, respect and recognition, negotiation and bargaining; private life is an arena of intimacy, spontaneity, similarity, and loyalty. There is nothing completely "either-or" about such distinctions—private life always has public dimensions; public life has personal elements; and there is an overlapping realm in between that can be seen as the community setting, where it takes thought to distinguish what is appropriate.

The public realm is thus differently understood than in classical republican theory, where virtuous citizens put aside their particular interests and pursue the common good. In contemporary citizen groups that revive a conception of the public world, public life is first of all a place for difference. In private life we associate with people who share similar outlooks and values. In public life we meet people from backgrounds unlike our own. The first principle should not be that we're all the same—an assumption privileging dominant cultural groups—

but rather that we are dissimilar. This leads to a recognition of the moral ambiguity of politics, the awareness that we cannot expect simply to impose our values.

Citizen politics with this approach focus on capacities and political arts that one can develop, like the practice of judgment, the exercise of power, the skills of listening. Its conceptualization as a craft, like the craft one cultivates in music, means that people learn to control personal vulnerabilities and concentrate on public arts.

Ed Chambers, who is director of the network of the largest local citizen groups in America, the Industrial Areas Foundation, based largely in poor, minority, and working-class communities, describes their growing understanding of the centrality of political *development* as the single most important shift from the classic community-organizing tradition. Similarly, Ernesto Cortes, first organizer of Communities Organized for Public Service (COPS), a group in the barrios of San Antonio that has served as the model for much citizen action over two decades, called the organization a "university of public life, where people learn the arts of public discourse and public action." Extensive training, reflection on experience, and vigorous intellectual discussion are all central. "We began to see every action as an opportunity for eduction and training," described Maribeth Larkin, an organizer with the United Neighborhoods Organization of the IAF in Los Angeles. Such a development changes the definition of popular involvement from supplication or service to public action. Citizens become "co-creators of history," in the phrasing of Gerald Taylor, main architect of the Baltimore Commonwealth, a massive program to rebuild the Baltimore Public Schools that came from mainly black churches and community groups but involved a wide array of political and business interests as well. Taylor described blacks' involvement in the Baltimore Commonwealth and other efforts as entailing the shift from protest to participation in governance. "The first struggle for the black community, coming out of segregated history, is the fight to be recognized. When you've been out of power so long, there's a tendency not to want to be responsible or to be held accountable. But to participate—to develop a sense that you are creating history—one must move into power." "Moving into power" in Taylor's terms meant being prepared to "negotiate, compromise, understand that others have power and ways of viewing the world different than your own."[10]

The lessons of such contemporary citizen activism are still scattered and dispersed. But they point toward a political education for action in public sphere based more on the reworking of existing, mainstream settings and institutions than on the creation of counterinstitutions on the one hand or protest groups and new social movements on the other.

Renewal of the deliberative citizenry of Habermas is critical today in an environment of trivialized politics and profoundly corrupted public discourse. Protesting publics of the sort that Eley and Ryan invoke will remain prods to social change in the direction of greater justice and equality. But the development of a widespread sensibility and experience of citizen agency and authority, with the responsibilities and capacities those entail, is the key to any significant democratization of the everyday, large-scale, direct, and indirect relationships of the modern world. For this to occur, we need a different sort of political eduction, one especially attentive to the pragmatic foundations for a sustainable public sphere.[11]

Notes

1. This chapter benefits from the comments of Sara M. Evans and Peg Michels and from the close reading and commentary of Kathryn Stoff-Hogg.

Jürgen Habermas, *The Theory of Communicative Action* (Boston: Beacon, 1981), vol. 1 and 2; Richard Flacks, *Making History vs. Making Life* (Columbia, 1988). See Craig Calhoun, "Imagined Communities, Indirect Relationships, and Postmodernism," Conference on Social Theory and Emerging Issues, Chicago, April 5–8, 1989, for a critique of this distinction, and Sara M. Evans and Harry C. Boyte, *Free Spaces: The Sources of Democratic Change in America* (Chicago: University of Chicago Press, 1992).

2. Vaclav Havel, *Living in Truth* (Boston: Faber and Faber, 1990).

3. *Structural Transformation*, pp. 25–26.

4. One of the most interesting features of Eley's paper is his description of the radical disappearance of an engagment with themes of "public" over the past twenty years in most social history and social theory, even among those (such as Raymond Williams) once closest to Habermas's concerns. But these themes have vividly remained central

to Habermas's work. See, for instance, Richard Bernstein, *Beyond Objectivism and Relativism* (Philadelphia: University of Pennsylvania Press, 1985).

5. *Structural Transformation*, p. 52.

6. For instance, in English history deliberation by villagers about the exercise of the rights and upkeep of common lands, footpaths, food lands, and fishing areas, as well as maintenance of common buildings like the village church, gave to middle-level peasantry a constant, daily schooling in rough democracy.

Americans' original dream of communal equality sustained by an independent citizenry was nourished by wave after wave of other ethnic groups as well, who dreamed of recreating communities of self-sufficient, self-governing freeholders. Such aspirations fit common patterns in the European homelands immigrants came from. Typically, they were "middle peasants," whose families had worked mainly for themselves, handing over only a small portion of their produce to the nobility. They had considerable experience in a range of cooperative activities. Their land, by custom and sometimes by law, was handed down over generations. And with others of similar rank, the bulk of male adults in many villages, they had had considerable practice in self-government concerning day to day affairs. Women, though their participation was restricted, also shared in many communal deliberations.

The popular republicanism that emerged out of such traditions conveyed values such as hard work, rough equality, frugality, self-government, independence. Values and aspirations were similar, moreover, among immigrants from urban areas, who often retained older rural traditions and sustained communal participation through an array of craft, fraternal, sororal, and other associations. Such practices of daily problem solving found elaborations and expressions in the American context in practices from quilting bees to barn raisings, mutual-aid societies to voluntary fire departments. See Edward Miller and John Hatcher, *Medieval England: Rural Society and Economic Change, 1086–1348* (London: Longman, 1978), pp. 105–106. On these popular republican traditions and their antecedents, see Gary B. Nash, *The Urban Crucible: The Northern Seaports and the Origins of the American Revolution* (Cambridge: Harvard University Press, 1976); Rowland Bertoff, "Peasant and Artisan, Puritans and Republicans," *Journal of American History* 69 (1982): 579–598; John Bodnar, *The Transplanted: A History of Immigrants in Urban America* (Bloomington: Indiana University Press, 1985).

7. Ruth Bordin, *Woman and Temperance: The Quest for Power and Liberty, 1873–1900* (Philadelphia: Temple University Press, 1980), p. 98.

8. Quoted from Barbara Epstein, *The Politics of Domesticity: Women Evangelism and Temperance in Nineteenth Century America* (Middletown: Wesleyan University Press, 1981), p. 100.

9. For a look at the ways in which feminist movements throughout American history have drawn upon, challenged, and transformed dominant conceptions of public, see Sara M. Evans, *Born for Liberty: A History of Women in America* (New York: Free Press, 1989). Harper, quoted in Philip Foner, *The Voice of Black America* (New York: Simon and Schuster, 1972), p. 43; Debs, from Eugene V. Debs, *Debs: His Life, Writings, and Speeches* (Girard, Kans.: Appeal to Reason, 1908, 1st ed.), p. 14.

Part of the appeal of Martin Luther King, Jr., was his ability to retrieve older and more active understandings of citizen agency through his view of the civil rights movement as combining protest and assumption of responsibility. The problem with the movement—a tension endemic to any movement that is fundamentally a moral and political critique of the existing order—was that it had few ways of educating for the ongoing exercise of citizen power and the assumption of citizen authority in public affairs.

For a fascinating discussion of the ways in which questions of power are eclipsed and subordinated by questions of justice in political debate, in this case in feminist politics, see Sara M. Evans and Barbara Nelson, *Wage Justice: Comparable Worth and the Paradoxes of Technocratic Reform* (Chicago: University of Chicago Press, 1989).

The distinction of kinds of political language—justice language and power language—is described in my *Commonwealth: A Return to Citizen Politics* (New York: Free Press, 1989).

10. Interview with Ed Chambers, New York, Feb. 22, 1983; interview with Ernie Cortes, July 5, 1983; interview with Maribeth Larkin, May 17, 1977; interview with Gerald Taylor, Baltimore, November 12, 1987.

11. Walter Lippman's *Public Opinion* (1922) is the classic argument for the view that the public is an atomized mass and journalists' task is that of dispensing expert opinion. See, for instance, James Carey, "Journalists Just Leave: The Ethics of an Anomalous Profession," in Maile-Gene Sagen, ed., "Ethics and the Media," *Iowa Humanities Journal,* 1987. Alexis de Tocqueville, of course, is the paradigmatic observer of public life in the second sense; see also Robert Bellah et al. *Habits of the Heart* (Berkeley: University of California, 1986).

For a description of the development of a pragmatically grounded understanding of public, emerging out of some of the most successful and large citizen organizations in America, see my "Citizen Politics," *Dissent,* Fall 1990. For an extended description of some of the theoretical issues of this sort of organizing, see *Commonwealth*. Both works argue that classical republican categories and concepts are too idealized and hortatory to have much force in public renewal. A description of the implications for politics and civic education of this approach are developed in my "Democratic Re-engagement: Bringing Liberalism and Populism Together (*American Prospect*, no. 6 [Summer 1991], pp. 55–66).

III

Public Communication

14

The Media and the Public Sphere

Nicholas Garnham

We have had to wait over a quarter of a century for an English language edition of Habermas's *Structural Transformation of the Public Sphere.* Such a long time is a rigorous test of the work's continuing relevance.

Since its original appearance in German it has been subjected to vigorous criticism, and Habermas has himself pursued an intellectual path that has taken him far from the book's central concerns. Since I want to argue here for the continuing and indeed increased relevance of those concerns, it is best to get the criticisms out of the way first. While those criticisms are, in my view, broadly justified, they do not undermine the book's continuing claim to our attention as a fruitful starting point for work on urgent contemporary issues in the study of the mass media and democratic politics.

The criticisms have been these:

• That he neglects the importance of the contemporaneous development of a plebeian public sphere alongside and in opposition to the bourgeois public sphere, a sphere built upon different institutional forms, e.g., trade unions, and with different values, e.g., solidarity rather than competitive individualism.

• That he idealizes the bourgeois public sphere. Recent historical research, that of Robert Darnton for instance, has revealed the viciously competitive structure of the early print market controlled not by freely discoursing intellectuals in search of public enlightenment but by booty capitalists in search of a quick profit.

• That by excluding the household and the economy from the public sphere, he systematically suppressed the question of democratic accountability within both gender relations and relations of production.

• That his rationalist model of public discourse leaves him unable to theorize a pluralist public sphere and it leads him to neglect the continuing need for compromise between bitterly divisive and irreconcilable political positions. This in its turn leads him to lament the entry of political parties into the public sphere.

• That the last part of the book remains too dependent upon Adorno's model of the cultural industries with its elitist cultural tendencies, its exaggeration of the manipulative powers of the controllers of those industries, and its neglect of the possibilities of public-service models of state intervention within the informational sphere.

• That Habermas's model of communicative action, developed as the norm for public discourse, neglects, when faced by distorted communication, all those other forms of communicative action not directed toward consensus.

• That therefore he neglects both the rhetorical and playful aspects of communicative action, which leads to too sharp a distinction between information and entertainment and to a neglect of the link, in for instance Rousseau's notion of public festivals, between citizenship and theatricality. This last point is of particular importance in thinking about the role of the mass media in contemporary democracies.

These criticisms are all cogent and serve as a necessary basis for the development and refinement of Habermas's original approach. In my view, however, they do not detract from the continuing virtues of the central thrust of that approach.

Its first virtue is to focus upon the indissoluble link between the institutions and practices of mass public communication and the institutions and practices of democratic politics. Most study of the mass media is simply too media-centric. In recent years, research and debate has largely taken for granted the existing structure of both the media and politics, the one articulated around the relationship between a so-called free press and a state-regulated broadcasting system, the other around political parties and some form of representative parliamentary or congressional government.

The overwhelming focus of concern has been the problem of representation in the mediative sense of that word, that is, the question posed has been how well or badly do the various media reflect the existing balance of political forces and the existing political agenda, and with what effect upon political action, in particular, on voting patterns. Important as these questions are, they miss the central and most urgent question now raised by the developing relationship between the media and politics because they fail to start from the position that the institutions and processes of public communication are themselves a central and integral part of the political structure and process.

The second virtue of Habermas's approach is to focus on the necessary material resource base for any public sphere. Debate on the relationship between public communication and democracy is still dominated by the free press model. This model remains an essentially idealist transposition of the model of face-to-face communication to that of mediated communication. It occludes the problem raised by all forms of mediated communication, namely, how are the material resources necessary for that communication made available, and to whom?

Its third virtue is to escape from the simple dichotomy of free market versus state control that dominates so much thinking about media policy. Habermas, on the contrary, distinguishes the public sphere from both state and market and can thus pose the question of the threats to democracy and the public discourses upon which it depends coming both from the development of an oligopolistic capitalist market and from the development of the modern interventionist welfare state.

These virtues are perhaps of even greater relevance now than when the book originally appeared for two reasons. First, because the development of an increasingly integrated global market and centers of private economic power with global reach are steadily undermining the nation-state, and it is within the political structure of the nation-state that the question of citizenship and of the relationship between communication and politics has been traditionally posed. We are thus being forced to rethink this relationship and the nature of citizenship in the modern world. What new political institutions and new public sphere might be necessary for the democratic control of a global economy and polity? These questions have been given a new urgency by the development of a single European market and by the rapid breakup of the Soviet empire with its associated need to rebuild a civil society and public sphere from the ashes of Stalinism.

Second, because our inherited structures of public communication, those institutions within which we construct, distribute, and consume symbolic forms, are themselves undergoing a profound change. This change is characterized by a reinforcement of the market and the progressive destruction, at least in western Europe, of public service as the preferred mode for the allocation of cultural resources; by a focus on the TV set as the locus for an increasingly privatized, domestic mode of consumption; by the creation of a two-tier market divided between the information-rich (provided with high-cost specialized information and cultural services) and the information-poor (provided with increasingly homogenized entertainment services on a mass scale); by a shift from largely national to largely international markets in the informational and cultural spheres. Symptoms of this shift are the expansion of the new TV delivery services, such as video cassettes, cable, and direct-broadcasting satellites, under market control and on an international basis; the progressive deregulation and privatization of national telecommunication monopolies; the increased penetration of sponsorship into the financing of both sport and the arts; the move of education and research institutes, such as universities, toward the private sector under the pressure of public spending cuts; the growing tendency to make profitability the criteria for the provision of public information, whether via such government bodies as the U.S. Government Printing Office or the U.K. Stationary Office or increasingly via private agencies. All these are examples of a trend to what has been dubbed, usually by those in favor of these developments, the information society or information economy. The result of this trend will be to shift the balance in the cultural sector between the market and public service decisively in favor of the market and to shift the dominant definition of public information from that of a public good to that of a privately appropriable commodity.[1]

Responses to these problems are still largely posed within the terms of a debate that has traditionally understood the political function and effect of modes of public communication within the terms of the Hegelian state versus civil society dichotomy. The dominant theory within that debate has been the liberal theory of the free press, which has either simply assumed that the market will provide appropriate institutions and processes of public communication to support a democratic polity or, in its stronger form, argues that only the market can ensure the necessary freedom from state control and coercion. The critique of this position has been able to collect impressive evidence of the way in which market forces produce results, in terms of oligopoly control and the depoliticization of content, that are far from the liberal ideal of a free market place of ideas. But the strength of the hold that liberal theory still exercises can be judged by the inadequacy of proposals for press reform generated by the left and the weakness with which such proposals have been pursued. For the left itself remains trapped within a free-press model inherited from the nineteenth century. The hold of this model is also illustrated by the way in which no equally legitimated theory has been developed to handle the dominant form of public communication, broadcasting. The public service, state-regulated model, whether publicly or privately funded, has in effect always been seen not as a positive good but as an unfortunate necessity imposed by the technical limitations of frequency scarcity. Those on the left who are opposed to market forces in the press nonetheless have in general given no more than mealymouthed support to public-service broadcasting. They have concentrated their critique on the question of the coercive or hegemonic nature of state power. Seeing the public service form as either a smokescreen for such power or as occupied from within by commercial forces, they have concentrated on criticizing the inadequacy and repressive nature of the rules of balance and objectivity within which public service broadcasting is forced to operate. The left has, therefore, tended to fall back either on idealist formulations of free communications with no organizational substance or material support or on technical utopianism that sees the expansion of channels of communication as inherently desirable because pluralistic. Both positions are linked to some version, both political and artistic, of free expression, for example, in Britain, the long debate and campaign around the creation of channel 4, the touching faith in cable access, the support for "free" or "community" radio, and so on.[2]

In light of the inadequacy of these approaches I want to argue that Habermas's concept of the public sphere offers a sounder basis for the critical analysis of current developments both in the media and democratic politics and for the analysis and political action necessary to rebuild systems of both communication and representative democracy adequate to the contemporary world.

Let me now briefly outline the basic argument that I wish to make with regard to the relationship between the institutionalized practices of mass communication and democratic politics. First, I take it as axiomatic that some version of communicative action lies at the heart of both the theory and practice of democracy. The rights and duties of a citizen are in large part defined in terms of freedom of assembly and freedom to impart and receive information. Without such freedoms it would be impossible for citizens to possess the knowledge of the views of others necessary to reach agreements between themselves, whether consensual or majoritarian, as to either social means or ends; to possess knowledge of the actions of those to whom executive responsibilities are delegated so as to make them accountable; to possess knowledge of the external environment necessary to arrive at appropriate judgment of both personal and societal interests.

It then follows, I believe, that the key problem we face is the adaption of this basic theory, and of the ideological formations associated with it, to the conditions of large-scale societies in which both social and communicative relations are inevitably mediated through both time and space.

This mediation raises two distinct problems. First, so far as the media of communication themselves are concerned, both the initial theory and subsequent related ideologies were based upon face-to-face communication in a single physical space. Thus freedom of assembly guaranteed access to the channel of communication, while the natural human attributes of speech and gesture ensured universal, equal access to the means of communication. Once communication is mediated, these universal equalities can no longer be guaranteed. Even in a situation of face-to-face communication it was early recognized that unequal access to the learned manipulative skills of rhetoric could and did influence the outcome of democratic debate. But in a situation of mediated communication, access to both channel and means depends upon the mobilization of scarce material resources, the distribution of which is dependent upon the very structures of economic and political power that democratic processes of debate were intended to control.

Second, what also became mediated is the content of communication and the subject of debate, or to use Habermas's terminology, the experience of the lifeworld. This indeed is the core of the Marxist theory of ideology. The existence of ideology rests not upon the stupidity and manipulability of human agents, as some simplistic current media and cultural studies critics, in their claims for pluralist, postmodern freedoms and their disdainful dismissal of boring old class politics, would have it. On the contrary, it rests on the nontransparency of the lifeworld, a nontransparency that makes interpretation always both difficult and provisional and the possibility of error ever present. Our everyday social relations, our very individual social identities, are constructed in a complex process of mediations. We see ourselves as husbands, wives, lovers, fathers, mothers, friends, neighbors, workers, and consumers increasingly in terms of ways of seeing those identities that are constructed in and through mediated communication: soap operas, novels, films, songs, etc. And we often act out those roles using objects of consumption provided and in large part determined by the system of economic production and exchange.

Third, a mismatch has developed between our theories and practices of democratic politics and our theories and practices of communication. Politics has in part adapted to large-scale societies through structures of representation: political parties, elected representatives, and full-time bureaucratic state officials. This development has, of course, always been fought, as in some sense inauthentic, by the advocates of forms of direct democracy. A suspicion of representation as a form of alienation and thus the adoption of the goal of the supersession of politics and of the "withering away of the state" have occupied an important place in the Marxist tradition. This links, of course—and this is important for my discussion in relation to Habermas's intellectual project—to a romantic opposition to the processes of modernist rationalization. But in general, for better or worse, representative forms have been established. To make my position clear, it is for me axiomatic both that representative structures cannot be bypassed and that the processes of rationalization and alienation involved in the modernizing process are a liberating gain rather than any sort of loss of supposed preexisting authenticity. The arguments against direct democracy bear repetition if only because visions of direct democracy are used as an escape from the problems that the concept of the public sphere raises. As Bobbio has argued, direct democracy works best with simple either/or choices (e.g., whether or not to have nuclear power) but cannot deal with the multiple variables that are more typical of political decisions in a complex and pluralistic modern society. The sifting of options necessary for such decision making can only be done by representatives. Moreover, these representatives then require space for free thought; they cannot be mandated. A further powerful argument against forms of direct democracy is that they overpoliticize life and turn into tyrannies that leave little if any time for the leading of private, autonomous personal lives.

These problems were in a sense sidestepped in classic Enlightenment thought, for instance, in the writings of Tom Paine, because at that period the market was simply assumed to be a benign mediator between private individuals, an anonymous system within which no one ruled.

The operation of the media of communication, however, has never really confronted this problem of representation. Our thinking about communications still remains largely trapped within a paradigm of direct individual face-to-face communication. This takes three forms. First, it is argued that the media, through the market, are driven by the satisfaction of individual consumer choice. This individualistic rational-choice model of economic interaction has been widely criticized within economics for its unreality and, in particular, for neglecting the realities of unequally distributed economic power, for concentrating upon distribution at the expense of production, for being static and thus ahistorical, for neglecting externalities, and for making assumptions of perfect information that neglect the costs to the individual or group of information acquisition.

Second, mediated symbolic forms are seen either as the expression of a single author (we see this for instance in the left demonology of the press baron) or as the objective, and therefore unmediated, reflection of an external reality—the journalist is seen as the witness of an event, a stand-in therefore for the individual reader's or viewer's direct, unmediated experience. Here the problem is that the complex institutional processes of mediation are ignored and along with them the problem of the existence of media workers as a distinct socioeconomic group with its own interests.

Third, current technical developments in communication (based upon the convergence of computing and switched telecommunications) are legitimated in terms of a desirable move away from mass communication and back toward forms of interpersonal communication that are seen as inherently more desirable and liberating. A classic and symptomatic text in this regard is Ithiel de Sola Pool's *Technologies of Freedom* and its notion of constant electronic referenda.

Fourth, this last point underlines the fact that while the rights to free expression inherent in democratic theory have been continually stressed, what has been lost is any sense of the reciprocal duties inherent in a communicative space that is physically shared. I think two crucial duties follow from this.

First, there is the duty to listen to the views of others and to alternative versions of events. Second, participation in debate is closely linked to responsibility for the effects of the actions that result. A crucial effect of mediated communication in a context of mediated social relations is to favor irresponsible communication. In a sense, this is the idea covered by Habermas's notion of the appropriateness of a speech act, but it tends, I think, to be lost in the rationalist stress of Habermas's general theory. That is, it is not just that communicative action in the lifeworld is directed toward agreement, a questionable proposition. It is that the speaker cannot dissociate him- or herself from the possible effects of his or her discourse.

This question of responsibility brings us to perhaps the central question I wish to raise, namely that of universality. There are two different concepts of universality at stake. The first is procedural and refers to the minimum set of shared discourse rules that must constitute a public sphere. Here the question is whether the rationality claimed for discourse within the public sphere is universal in the sense that neither the normative nor the validity claims made are culturally specific, but the debate on both ends and means is potentially capable of producing consensus among all human beings. The second refers to the size and nature of the political entity of which we are citizens and with which, I want to argue, the public sphere must be coterminous. How widely are we to conceive of the writ of the consensus decisions arrived at among citizens in the public sphere? Are we to conceive of ourselves as citizens of the world or of a nation-state or of a community or of what? Finally, what is the relationship, and what could or should be the relationship, between the particularisms of the lifeworld and the generalized rationalizations of the systems world? My argument here leads me to argue against the politics of what Habermas, giving altogether too much, in my view, to the postmodernists, has called a pluralist decentered postmodern world and against the parallel validation of those developments in media technology and media markets that are moving us toward interpersonal systems of communication at the expense of mass communication and toward a highly segmented media market place made up of interest-specific market niches at the expense of more generalized media. In brief, I would want to argue against the pluralists that it is impossible to conceive of a viable democratic polity without at the same time conceiving of at least some common normative dimension. What the elements of that common normative dimension should be and what room it should leave for personal and group autonomy within it are, of course, at the center of this debate. To put it more strongly, I want to argue that at some level cultural relativism and a democratic polity are simply incompatible. If we wish to preserve the notion of cultural relativism, we must at the same time conceive of a universe of plural but mutually isolated polities. In my view, that is no longer a realistic option.

As regards the question of universality and cultural relativism, there are, I think, two issues. First, is discourse either actually or at least potentially universal; can all human beings, as a species characteristic, arrive at a common view as to both the nature and the truth of a proposition? Second, are there universal interests? For me, the answer to the second question determines the first. I would argue that historically both the economic and political aspects of system rationality have not only become global but are also understood as global by a growing proportion of the world's population, in part precisely because of the growth and spread of global systems of mediated communication. As recent events in China have shown, all political actors are now playing on a world stage and employing, in spite of the problems of linguistic and cultural translation, a world language of symbols. To claim the Enlightenment project, out of misplaced ethnocentric guilts, as exclusively (and detrimentally) Western, for instance, or to claim rationality as exclusively (and detrimentally) male seems to me to condescend to those of other cultures or subordinated social groups who are fighting our common struggle to understand and control the world in pursuit of human liberty. In Britain it has been interesting, for instance, to see how shallow the political and intellectual positions based on cultural relativism have looked in the light of the Salman Rushdie affair. But I would go further. If we accept that the economic system is indeed global in scope and at the same time crucially determining over large areas of social action, the Enlightenment project of democracy requires us to make a Pascalian bet on universal rationality. For without it the project is unrealizable, and we will remain in large part enslaved to a system outside our control.

This brings me back to the question of the desirability of a pluralist decentered politics. I should stress for an American audience that my general approach is placed firmly within a European political and intellectual context. In particular, it focuses upon the characteristically Western European institutional form of public service broadcasting and current threats to that form's survival.

It is also set, as Habermas himself sets his more recent work on the public sphere, against the background of a crisis in the welfare-state form and in the modes and institutions of social-democratic politics that created and sustained that form in Western Europe since 1945. This crisis has, of course, been deepened by recent developments in the Soviet Union and Eastern Europe into a more general critique of the socialist vision and the historical model of social progress that underpinned that vision, at both the intellectual and popular levels. In particular, problems of bureaucratic power have loomed larger for a significant majority of citizens than those of economic power, and this, allied to the experience of economic slowdown and the impact of global economic restructuring, has led to a revalidation of market mechanisms allied to the rise of forms of populist neoconservatism.

In short, the problems posed are, first, What might be the conditions for democracy in societies such as those of Western Europe; indeed, is democracy in the classic form thinkable at all outside the problematic of the Enlightenment? Second, what is the desirable or realizable relationship between the economic system and the political system and between, to use Habermas's terminology, lifeworld and systems world?

One of the left's characteristic responses to this situation, at least in Britain, has been, at the level of economic policy, to embrace consumerism, underpinned in production by theories of post-Fordist flexible specialization and of the service or information economy, and, at the level of politics, to argue for a version of the rainbow coalition, that is, for a neo-Gramscian, postmodernist politics based not on a working class party but on a shifting coalition of a range of those fragmented social-interest groups produced, it is argued, by the "decentered pluralism" (to use Habermas's description) of our new consumer society.

The mirror image of this position on the right is that of Hayek, who argues that so complex are the interactions within an economic system that the project of rational politics is doomed to founder and who thus advocates the dissolution of politics as such in favor of the universal pursuit of self-interest within a market.

But the fact remains that we should not exaggerate economic systematicity. While total control is clearly impossible, it is possible to envisage interventions that limit the randomly determining impact of the economic system. Indeed, political and corporate actors are every day making willed interventions in what they see as their calculated interest, and this system of interventions is underpinned by systems of information gathering, assessment, and communication. The problem is to open up both the actions and the related informational exchanges to processes of democratic accountability.

In short, the problem is to construct systems of democratic accountability integrated with media systems of matching scale that occupy the same social space as that over which economic or political decisions will impact. If the impact is universal, then both the political and media systems must be universal. In this sense, a series of autonomous public spheres is not sufficient. There must be a single public sphere, even if we might want to conceive of this single public sphere as made up of a series of subsidiary public spheres, each organized around its own political structure, media system, and set of norms and interests. Thus even if we accept that debate within the public sphere is riven with controversy and in many instances may be directed at agreeing to disagree rather than toward consensus, we are still faced with the unavoidable problem of translating debate into action. If, whether we like it or not, the problem faced has a general impact upon us all, then there can only be one rationally determined course of interventionist political action. This course of action either has to be agreed to consensually or has to be imposed, whether by a majority or a minority. If market forces are global in scope, any effective political response has to be global. The individual citizen or group cannot, except in very rare circumstances, simply opt out and refuse to play whatever game has been decided upon. The same applies equally strongly to issues of nuclear weapons or the environment.

In particular, we cannot ignore the continuing role of the nation-state as both an economic actor and as a "power container," in Giddens's phrase, as the structure at the political level within which democratic political action, allegiance, and identity is still largely organized. It is no accident, in my view, that such states are associated with a dominant linguistic group, and thus discourse space, and with national media systems. We are witnessing at present parallel developments that both undermine the powers of the nation-state, especially economically, and internationalize media, both its systems of distribution and its content. How, therefore, should we envisage the construction of a new international public sphere and parallel system of democratic political accountability?

In my view, our attitude to this pluralist political project is crucial to our discussion of the media and the public sphere, because those social groups identified as potential elements in this shifting coalition largely exist in terms of group identities created via the forms and institutions of mediated communication (magazines, radio stations, record labels) or via consumer-taste publics that themselves use, as their badges of identity, symbols created and circulated in the sphere of advertising.

The issues this raises for us are, I believe, twofold. First, are these group identities and the individual identities that subtend them the "authentic" expression of the lifeworld erupting into the systems world and using the products and systems of that world for their own plural purposes, or on the contrary, are they a determined symptom of that systems world? We are, in short, here presented with the old linguistic conundrum of the relation between *langue* and *parole*. While accepting the relative autonomy of the meaning-creating agent and the possibilities of cultural bricolage, they are at present much exaggerated by media and cultural analysts. We have to raise the question of how much room for maneuver agents actually have within a symbolic system within which both the power to create symbols and access to the channels of their circulation is heirarchically structured and intimately integrated into a system of economic production and exchange, which is itself heirarchically structured. There is a left cultural romanticism, increasingly prevalent in media and cultural studies, that sees all forms of grassroots cultural expression as "resistance," although resistance to what is not at all clear. The problem here is twofold. To accept them as resistance does not avoid the problem that both the forms and the potential success of resistance can be determined by the system being resisted. Second, it fails to take account of that element of misrecognition that Bourdieu, for instance, has in my view rightly identified as essential to the relatively smooth reproduction of a system of social relations by interacting intelligent agents. Here we confront a major problem with Habermas's approach to the problem via the theory of universal pragmatics. That is, his notion of communicative rationality does not allow for the possibility of the rational acceptance of misrecognition within the terms of the limited material resources and time boundedness of actions in the lifeworld. Nor does it allow for what I can only describe as the rational cynicism, identified, for instance, by Abercrombie and his colleagues in *The Dominant Ideology Thesis,* which recognizes very clearly the realities of domination but calculates that the risks of change are greater than those of the status quo.

This brings me to the problem of rationality in another form. My position on the public sphere and on public service broadcasting has been criticized on the grounds that I overvalue politics and a particular model of rationalist discourse at the expense of disregarding the modes and functions of most mediated communication, which is nonrationalist and is concerned with psychological and imaginative satisfactions that have little to do with politics. Such an approach, it is argued, tends to concentrate analysis on news, current affairs, and documentaries and on the model of the so-called quality press, while neglecting all forms of popular entertainment. There is a lot of truth in this criticism, or rather, it points to a real problem to which I have no satisfactory answer. This is the problem I have posed in terms of the relation between the lifeworld and the systems world and the role of the media in mediating between them. In short, it is part of the problem posed by Habermas in *The Structural Transformation of the Public Sphere,* a problem that was always part of the Frankfurt School problematic, namely the relation between psychology, politics, and economics. Habermas posed it originally in terms of the relation of the creation of a private sphere and private sentiments to the creation of the public sphere. I would certainly want to stress that I am not claiming that the properly political debates in the public sphere are only carried by forms of media content overtly labeled as being concerned with politics. On the contrary, what I shall call as shorthand the entertainment content of the media is clearly the primary tool we use to handle the relationship between the systems world and the lifeworld. It is on the basis of understandings drawn from those communicative experiences and of identities formed around them that we arrive at more overtly rational and political opinions and actions. The dynamics of this process and the relative weight within it of rationalized systems determinants and of the nonrationalized experiences of the lifeworld are a crucial and neglected area for media and cultural-studies research. If pursued, they may enable us to chart the limits of both politics and economics and at the same time to discover the media forms and structures most likely to foster the development of citizens, rather than mere consumers.

In conclusion, I want to raise the question, central to Habermas's project, of the validation of the Enlightenment project. Habermas has sought an ontological validation in universal pragmatics. This approach has been widely and, in my view, correctly criticized on linguistic grounds. But I do not believe that such a grounding is necessary. For me, the grounding can only be in history itself. That is, the evidence for the possibility of the Enlightenment project is that large numbers of human beings from different cultures have actually believed in it and fought to realize it. Only history will show whether the project is in fact realizable. The possibility of arriving at a rationally grounded consensus can only be demonstrated in practice by entering into a concrete and historically specific process of rational debate with other human beings on the assumption that the system world is at least partially subjectable to rational control, that it is in the ultimate interest of most human beings so to control it, that other human beings can be led both to a rational recognition of that interest within a common discourse space and to a consensual agreement as to the appropriate cooperative courses of action to follow. On the basis of those assumptions the task is to cooperate in building the political, economic, and communicational institutions conducive to that end. This will be no easy task. There is no guarantee of success. But in my view the only alternative is to accept the impossibility of liberation either in an irrational Hobbesian world dominated by war of all against all or in a totally rationalized world in which our actions are determined by a structure beyond our control. If that is the only truth, our own deliberations are reduced to the merest trivia.

In the face of postmodernist critiques of this whole tradition of thought and these critics' rejection of rationality in favor of a utopian and romantic pursuit of difference for its own sake, it is necessary to stress that the strand of the Enlightenment project, of which Habermas's work on the public sphere is a part, expresses a tragic, not a utopian, vision. It is a preromantic, classical vision that in constant awareness of human limitation recognizes the extreme fragility of human civilization and the need, but at the same time the difficulty, of sustaining the social bonds of mutual obligation upon which that civilization depends in the face of the manifold forces that threaten it, forces that are internal and psychological as well as external. It sets out to save a small portion of our existence from the rule of fate. Its rationalist and universalist vision must thus be distinguished from that other strand in the dialectic of the Enlightenment, that of scientific rationality and the hubris of human power that accompanied it. The model of the public sphere and of the democratic polity of which it is a part is thus that of the classical garden, a small tamed patch within a sea of untamed nature (fate) ever ready to take over if the attention of the gardeners slackens for an instant. Its ruling virtue is stoicism rather than the untrammeled pursuit of happiness.

Nicholas Garnham

Acknowledgment

In revising this paper for publication I have benefited immeasurably from the critical comments of my colleague John Keane.

Notes

1. For a fuller treatment of these problems, see my "Public Service versus the Market," *Screen* 24, no. 1 (1983).

2. For a fuller treatment of these problems and, in particular, of the relation between the concept of the public sphere and the tradition of public service broadcasting, see my "Media and the Public Sphere" in P. Golding et al., eds., *Communicating Politics* (Leicester: Leicester University Press, 1986).

15

The Mass Public and the Mass Subject

Michael Warner

The Egocrat coincides with himself, as society is supposed to coincide with itself. An impossible swallowing up of the body in the head begins to take place, as does an impossible swallowing up of the head in the body. The attraction of the whole is no longer dissociated from the attraction of the parts.

Claude Lefort, "The Image of the Body and Totalitarianism"[1]

During these assassination fantasies Tallis became increasingly obsessed with the pudenda of the Presidential contender mediated to him by a thousand television screens. The motion picture studies of Ronald Reagan created a scenario of the conceptual orgasm, a unique ontology of violence and disaster.

J. G. Ballard, "Why I Want to Fuck Ronald Reagan"[2]

As the subjects of publicity—its hearers, speakers, viewers, and doers—we have a different relation to ourselves, a different affect, from that which we have in other contexts. No matter what particularities of culture, race, and gender, or class we bring to bear on public discourse, the moment of apprehending something as public is one in which we imagine, if imperfectly, indifference to those particularities, to ourselves. We adopt the attitude of the public subject, marking to ourselves its nonidentity with ourselves. There are any number of ways to describe this moment of public subjectivity: as a universalizing transcendence, as ideological repression, as utopian wish, as schizocapitalist vertigo, or simply as a routine difference of register. No matter what its character for the individual subjects who come to public discourse, however, the rhetorical contexts of publicity in the modern Western nations must always mediate a self-relation different from that of personal life. This becomes a point of more than usual importance, I will suggest, in a period such as our own when so much political conflict revolves around identity and status categories.

Western political thought has not ignored the tendency of publicity to alter or refract the individual's character and status. It has been obsessed with that tendency. But it has frequently thought of publicity as distorting, corrupting, or, to use the more current version, alienating individuals. The republican notion of virtue, for example, was designed exactly to avoid any rupture of self-difference between ordinary life and publicity. The republican was to be the same as citizen and as man. He was to maintain continuity of value, judgment, and reputation from a domestic economy to affairs of a public nature. And lesser subjects—noncitizens such as women, children, and the poor—were equally to maintain continuity across both realms, as nonactors. From republicanism to populism, from Rousseau to Reagan, self-unity has been held to be a public value, and publicity has not been thought of as requiring individuals to have discontinuous perceptions of themselves. (Hegel, it is true, considered the state as a higher-order subjectivity unattainable in civil society. But because he considered the difference both normative and unbridgeable within the frame of the individual, a historical and political analysis of discontinuous self-relations did not follow.)

One reason why virtue was spoken about with such ardor in the seventeenth and eighteenth centuries was that the discursive conventions of the public sphere had already made virtuous self-unity archaic. In the bourgeois public sphere, talk of a citizen's virtue was already partly wishful. Once a public discourse had become specialized in the Western model, the subjective attitude adopted in public discourse became an inescapable but always unrecognized political force, governing what is publicly sayable—inescapable because only when images or texts can be understood as meaningful to a public rather than simply to oneself, or to specific others, can they be called public; unrecognized because this strategy of impersonal reference, in which one might say, "The text addresses me" *and*

"It addresses no one in particular," is a ground condition of intelligibility for public language. The "public" in this sense has no empirical existence and cannot be objectified. When we understand images and texts as public, we do not gesture to a statistically measurable series of others. We make a necessarily imaginary reference to the public *as opposed to* other individuals. Public opinion, for example, is understood as belonging to a public rather than to scattered individuals. (Opinion polls in this sense are a performative genre. They do not measure something that already exists as public opinion, but when they are reported as such, they *are* public opinion.) So also it is only meaningful to speak of public discourse where it is understood as the discourse of a public rather than as an expansive dialogue among separate persons.

The public sphere therefore presents problems of rhetorical analysis. Because the moment of special imaginary reference is always necessary, the publicity of the public sphere never reduces to information, discussion, will formation, or any of the other scenarios by which the public sphere represents itself. The mediating rhetorical dimension of a public context must be built into each individual's relation to it, as a meaningful reference point against which something could be grasped as information, discussion, will formation. To ask about the relation between democracy and the rhetorical forms of publicity, we would have to consider how the public dimension of discourse can come about differently in different contexts of mediation, from official to mass-cultural or subcultural. There is not simply "a" public discourse and a "we" who apprehend it. Strategies of public reference have different meanings for the individuals who suddenly find themselves incorporating the public subject, and the rhetorics that mediate publicity have undergone some important changes.

1 Utopias of Self-Abstraction

In the eighteenth century, as I have argued elsewhere, the imaginary reference point of the public was constructed through an understanding of print.[3] At least in the British American colonies, a style of thinking about print appeared in the culture of republicanism according to which it was possible to consume printed goods with an awareness that the same printed goods were being consumed by an indefinite number of others. This awareness came to be built into the meaning of the printed object, to the point that we now consider it simply definitional to speak of printing as "publication." In print, understood this way, one surrendered one's utterance to an audience that was by definition indefinite. Earlier writers might have responded with some anxiety to such mediation or might simply have thought of the speaker-audience relation in different terms. In the eighteenth century the consciousness of an abstract audience became a badge of distinction, a way of claiming a public disposition.

The transformation, I might emphasize, was a cultural rather than a technological one; it came about not just with more use of print but rather as the language of republicanism was extended to print contexts as a structuring metalanguage. It was in the culture of republicanism, with its categories of disinterested virtue and supervision, that a rhetoric of print consumption became authoritative, a way of understanding the publicness of publication. Here, for example, is how the *Spectator* in 1712 describes the advantage of being realized in the medium of print:

It is much more difficult to converse with the World in a real than a personated Character. That might pass for Humour, in the *Spectator,* which would look like Arrogance in a Writer who sets his Name to his Work. The Fictitious Person might contemn those who disapproved him, and extoll his own Performances, without giving Offence. He might assume a Mock-Authority; without being looked upon as vain and conceited. The Praises or Censures of himself fall only upon the Creature of his Imagination, and if any one finds fault with him, the Author may reply with the Philosopher of old, *Thou dost but beat the Case of* Anaxarchus.[4]

The Spectator's attitude of conversing with the world is public and disinterested. It elaborates republican assumptions about the citizen's exercise of virtue. But it could not come about without a value placed on the anonymity here associated with print. The Spectator's point about himself is that he is different from the person of Richard Steele. Just as the Spectator here secures a certain liberty in not calling himself Richard Steele, so it would take a certain liberty for us to call the author of this passage Richard Steele—all the more so since the pronoun reference begins to slip around the third sentence ("those who disapproved *him*"). The ambiguous relation between Spectator and writer, Steele says, liberates him. The Spectator is a prosthetic person for Steele, to borrow a term from Lauren Berlant—prosthetic in the sense that it does not reduce to or express the given body.[5] By making him no longer self-identical, it allows him the negativity of debate—not a pure negativity, not simply reason or criticism, but an identification with a disembodied public subject that he can imagine as parallel to his private person.

In a sense, however, that public subject does have a body, because the public, prosthetic body takes abuse for the private person. The last line of the passage refers to the fact that Anaxarchus was pommeled to death with iron pestles after offending a despotic ruler. In the ventriloquistic act of taking up his speech, therefore, Steele both imagines an intimate violation of his person and provides himself with a kind of prophylaxis against violation (to borrow another term from Berlant). Anaxarchus was not so lucky. Despite what Steele says, the privilege that he obtains over his body in this way does not in fact reduce to the simple body/soul distinction that Anaxarchus' speech invokes. It allows him to think of his public discourse as a routine form of self-abstraction quite unlike the ascetic self-integration of Anaxarchus. When Steele impersonates the philosopher and has the Spectator (or someone) say, "Thou dost but beat the case of Anaxarchus," he appropriates an intimate subjective benefit of publicity's self-abstraction.

Through the conventions that allowed such writing to perform the disincorporation of its authors and its readers, public discourse turned persons into a public. At points in *The Structural Transformation of the Public Sphere,* Jürgen Habermas makes a similar point. One of the great virtues of that book is the care it takes to describe the cultural-technical context in which the public of the bourgeois public sphere was constituted. "In the *Tatler,* the *Spectator,* and the *Guardian* the public held up a mirror to itself. . . . The public that read and debated this sort of thing read and debated about itself."[6] It is worth remembering also that *persons* read and debated this sort of thing, but in reading and debating it *as* a public, they adopted a very special rhetoric about their own personhood. Where earlier writers had typically seen the context of print as a means of personal extension—they understood themselves in print essentially to be speaking in their own persons—people began to see it as an authoritative mediation. That is clearly the case with the Steele passage, and pseudonymous serial essays like the *Spectator* did a great deal toward normalizing a public print discourse.

In the bourgeois public sphere, which was brought into being by publication in this sense, a principle of negativity was axiomatic: the validity of what you say in public bears a negative relation to your person. What you say will carry force not because of who you are but despite who you are. Implicit in this principle is a utopian universality that would allow people to transcend the given realities of their bodies and their status. But the rhetorical strategy of personal abstraction is both the utopian moment of the public sphere and a major source of domination. For the ability to abstract oneself in public discussion has always been an unequally available resource. Individuals have to have specific rhetorics of disincorporation; they are not simply rendered bodiless by exercising reason. And it is only possible to operate a discourse based on the claim to self-abstracting disinterestedness in a culture where such unmarked self-abstraction is a differential resource. The subject who could master this rhetoric in the bourgeois public sphere was implicitly, even explicitly, white, male, literate, and propertied. These traits could go unmarked, even grammatically, while other features of bodies could only be acknowledged in discourse as the humiliating positivity of the particular.

The bourgeois public sphere claimed to have no relation to the body image at all. Public issues were depersonalized so that, in theory, any person would have the ability to offer an opinion about them and submit that opinion to the impersonal test of public debate without personal hazard. Yet the bourgeois public sphere continued to rely on features of certain bodies. Access to the public came in the whiteness and maleness that were then denied as forms of positivity, since the white male qua public person was only abstract rather than white and male. The contradiction is that even while particular bodies and dispositions enabled the liberating abstraction of public discourse, those bodies also summarized the constraints of positivity, the mere case of Anaxarchus, from which self-abstraction can be liberating.

It is very far from being clear that these asymmetries of embodiment were merely contingent encumbrances to the public sphere, residual forms of illiberal "discrimination." The difference between self-abstraction and a body's positivity is more than a difference in what has officially been made available to men and to women, for example. It is a difference in the cultural/symbolic definitions of masculinity and femininity.[7] Self-abstraction from male bodies confirms masculinity. Self-abstraction from female bodies denies femininity. The bourgeois public sphere is a frame of reference in which it is supposed that all particularities have the same status as mere particularity. But the ability to establish that frame of reference is a feature of some particularities. Neither in gender nor in race nor in class nor in sexualities is it possible to treat different particulars as having merely paratactic or serial difference. Differences in such realms already come coded as the difference between the unmarked and the marked, the universalizable and the particular. Their own internal logic is such that the two sides of any of these differences cannot be treated as symmetrical—as they are, for example, in the rhetoric of liberal toleration or "debate"—without simply resecuring an asymmetrical privilege. The bourgeois public sphere has been structured from the outset by a logic of abstraction that provides a privilege for unmarked identities: the male, the white, the middle class, the normal.

That is what Pasolini meant when he wrote, just before his murder, that "tolerance is always and purely nominal":

In fact they tell the "tolerated" person to do what he wishes, that he has every right to follow his own nature, that the fact that he belongs to a minority does not in the least mean inferiority, etc. But his "difference"—or better, his "crime of being different"—remains the same both with regard to those who have decided to tolerate him and those who have decided to condemn him. No majority will ever be able to banish from its consciousness the feeling of the "difference" of minorities. I shall always be eternally, inevitably conscious of this.[8]

Doubtless it is better to be tolerated than to be killed, as Pasolini was. But it would be better still to make reference to one's marked particularities without being specified thereby as less than public. As the bourgeois public sphere paraded the spectacle of its disincorporation, it brought into being this minoritizing logic of domination. Publicness is always able to encode itself through the themes of universality, openness, meritocracy, and access, all of which derhetoricize its self-understanding, guaranteeing at every step that difference will be enunciated as mere positivity, an ineluctable limit imposed by the particularities of the body, a positivity that cannot translate or neutralize itself prosthetically without ceasing to exist. This minoritizing logic, intrinsic to the deployment of negativity in the bourgeois public sphere, presents the subjects of bodily difference with the paradox of a utopian promise that cannot be cashed in for them. The very mechanism designed to end domination is a form of domination.

The appeal of mass subjectivity, I will suggest, arises largely from the contradiction in this dialectic of embodiment and negativity in the public sphere. Public discourse from the beginning offered a utopian self-abstraction, but in ways that left a residue of unrecuperated particularity, both for its privileged subjects and for those it minoritized. Its privileged subjects, abstracted from the very body features that gave them the privilege of that abstraction, found themselves in a relation of bad faith with their own positivity. To acknowledge their positivity would be to surrender their privilege, as for example to acknowledge the objectivity of the male body would be feminizing. Meanwhile, minoritized subjects had few strategies open to them, but one was to carry their unrecuperated positivity into consumption. Even from the early eighteenth century, before the triumph of a liberal metalanguage for consumption, commodities were being used, especially by women, as a kind of access to publicness that would nevertheless link up with the specificity of difference.[9]

Consumption offered a counterutopia precisely in a balance between a collectivity of mass desires and an unminoritized rhetoric of difference in the field of choices among infinite goods. A good deal of noise in modern society comes from the inability to translate these utopian promises into a public sphere where collectivity has no link to the body and its desires, where difference is described not as the paratactic seriality of illimitable choice but as the given constraints of preconscious nature. Where consumer capitalism makes available an endlessly differentiable subject, the subject of the public sphere proper cannot be differentiated. It can represent difference as other, but as an available form of subjectivity it remains unmarked. The constitutional public sphere, therefore, cannot fully recuperate its residues. It can only display them. In this important sense, the "we" in "We the People" is the mass equivalent of the Spectator's prosthetic generality, a flexible instrument of interpellation, but one that exiles its own positivity.

From the eighteenth century we in the modern West have inherited an understanding of printing as publication, but we now understand a vast range of everyday life as having the reference of publicity. The medium of print is now only a small part of our relation to what we understand as the public, and the fictitious abstraction of the Spectator would seem conspicuously out of place in the modern discourse of public icons. So although the bourgeois public sphere continues to secure a minoritizing liberal logic of self-abstraction, its rhetoric is increasingly complicated by other forms of publicity. At present the mass-cultural public sphere continually offers its subject an array of body images. In earlier varieties of the public sphere it was important that images of the body *not* figure importantly in public discourse. The anonymity of the discourse was a way of certifying the citizen's disinterested concern for the public good. But now public body images are everywhere on display, in virtually all media contexts. Where printed public discourse formerly relied on a rhetoric of abstract disembodiment, visual media, including print, now display bodies for a range of purposes: admiration, identification, appropriation, scandal, etc. To be public in the West means to have an iconicity, and this is true equally of Qaddafi and of Karen Carpenter.

The visibility of public figures for the subject of mass culture occurs in a context in which publicity is generally mediated by the discourse of consumption. It is difficult to realize how much we observe public images with the eye of the consumer. Nearly all of our pleasures come to us coded in some degree by the publicity of mass media. We have brand names all over us. Even the most refined or the most perverse among us could point to his or her desires or identifications and see that in most cases they were public desires, even mass-public desires, from the moment that they were that person's desires. This is true not only in the case of salable commodities—our refrigerators, sneakers, lunch—but also in other areas where we make symbolic identifications in a field of choice: the way we bear our bodies, the sports we follow, or our erotic objects. In such areas our desires have become recognizable through their display in the media, and in the moment of wanting them, we imagine a collective consumer witnessing our wants and choices.

The public discourse of the mass media has increasingly come to rely on the intimacy of this collective witnessing in its rhetoric of publicity, iconic and consumerist alike. It is a significant part of the ground of public discourse, the subjective apprehension of what is public. In everyday life, for one thing, we have access to the realm of political systems in the same way that we have access to the circulation of commodities. Not only are we confronted by slogans that continually make this connection for us ("America wears Hanes," "The heartbeat of America"); more important, the contexts of commodities and politics share the same media and, at least in part, the same metalanguage for constructing our notion of what a public or a people is. When the citizen (or noncitizen—for contemporary publicity the difference hardly matters) goes down to the 7–Eleven to buy a Budweiser and a Barbie Magazine and scans from the news headlines to the tabloid stories about the Rob Lowe sex scandal, several kinds of publicity are involved at once. Nevertheless, it is possible to speak of all these sites of publicity as parts of a public sphere, insofar as each is capable of illuminating the others in a common discourse of the subject's relation to the nation and its markets.

In each of these mediating contexts of publicity we become the mass-public subject, but in a new way unanticipated within the classical bourgeois public sphere. Moreover, if mass-public subjectivity has a kind of singularity, an undifferentiated extension to indefinite numbers of individuals, those individuals who make up the "we" of the mass public subject might have very different relations to it. It is at the very moment of recognizing ourselves as the mass subject, for example, that we also recognize ourselves as minority subjects. As participants in the mass subject, we are the "we" that can describe our particular affiliations of class, gender, sexual orientation, race, or subculture only as "they." This self-alienation is common to all of the contexts of publicity, but it can be variously interpreted within each. The political meaning of the public subject's self-alienation is one of the most important sites of struggle in contemporary culture.

2   The Mirror of Popularity

In an essay called "The Image of the Body and Totalitarianism," Claude Lefort speculates that public figures have recently begun to play a new role. He imagines essentially a three-stage history of the body of publicity. Drawing on the work of Kantorowicz, he sketches first a representative public sphere in which the person of the prince stands as the head of the corporate body, summing up in his person the principles of legitimacy, though still drawing that legitimacy from a higher power. Classical bourgeois democracy, by contrast, abstracted the public, corporate body in a way that could be literalized in the decapitation of a ruler. "The democratic revolution, for so long subterranean, burst out when the body of the king was destroyed, when the body politic was decapitated and when, at the same time, the corporeality of the social was dissolved. There then occurred what I would call a 'disincorporation' of individuals."[10]

According to Lefort, the new trend, however, is again toward the display of the public official's person. The state now relies on its double in "the image of the people, which . . . remains indeterminate, but which nevertheless is susceptible of being determined, of being actualized on the level of phantasy as an image of the People-as-One." Public figures increasingly take on the function of concretizing that fantasmatic body image, or in other words, of actualizing the otherwise indeterminate image of the people. They embody what Lefort calls the "Egocrat," whose self-identical representativeness is perverse and unstable in a way that contrasts with the representative person of the feudal public sphere. "The prince condensed in his person the principle of power . . . , but he was *supposed* to obey a superior power. . . . That does not seem to be the position of the Egocrat or of his substitutes, the bureaucratic leaders. The Egocrat coincides with himself, as society is supposed to coincide with itself. An impossible swallowing up of the body in the head begins to take place, as does an impossible swallowing up of the head in the body."[11] Lefort sees the sources of this development in democracy, but he associates the trend with totalitarianism, presumably in the iconographies of Stalin and Mao. But then, Lefort wrote this essay in 1979; since that time it has become increasingly clear that such fantasmatic public embodiments have come to be the norm in the Western democratic bureaucracies.

Jürgen Habermas has an interestingly similar narrative. He too describes a first stage of a representative public sphere in which public persons derived their power in part from being on display. The idealizing language of nobility did not abstract away from the body: "Characteristically, in none of [the aristocracy's] virtues did the physical aspect entirely lose its significance, for virtue must be embodied, it had to be capable of public representation."[12] For Habermas, as for Lefort, this ceased to be the case with the bourgeois public sphere, in which the public was generalized away from physical, theatrical representation. It was relocated instead to the mostly written contexts of rational debate. And Habermas, again like Lefort, speaks of a more recent return to the display of public representatives, a return that he calls "refeudalizing." "The public sphere becomes the court *before* [which] public prestige can be displayed—rather than *in* which public critical debate is carried on."[13]

Why should modern regimes so require a return to the image of the leader in the peculiar form that Lefort calls the Egocrat? We can see both how powerful and how complicated this appeal in mass publicity can be by taking the example of Reagan's popularity. Reagan is probably a better example than others because, more than any other, his figure blurs the boundary between the iconicities of the political public and the commodity public. Bush, Dukakis, and the others have been less adept at translating their persons from the interior of the political system to the surface of the brand-name commodity. The Reagan-style conjunction of these two kinds of appeal is the ideal-typical moment of national publicity against which they are measured. So, regardless of whatever skills they have within the political system, Bush and others like him have not been able to bring to their superbureaucratic persons the full extended reference of publicity. Reagan, by contrast, was the champion spokesmodel for America, just as he had earlier been a spokesmodel for Westinghouse and for Hollywood. It's easy to understand why the left clings to its amnesia about the pleasures of publicity when confronted with a problem like the popularity of a Ronald Reagan. But we do not have a clear understanding of the nature of the public with which Reagan was popular, nor do we have a clear understanding of the attraction of such a public figure.

One recent report in *The Nation* has it that Ronald Reagan was not a popular president at all. Gallup opinion polls, over the duration of his two terms, rated him far less favorably than Roosevelt, Kennedy, or Eisenhower. He was not appreciably more popular than Ford or Carter. For the left-liberal readership of *The Nation,* this surprising statistic spells relief. It encourages us to believe that the public might not be so blind, after all. Indeed, in the story that presents the statistics, Thomas Ferguson claims exactly this sort of populist vindication. For him, the point of the story is simply that journalists who genuflect before Reagan's popularity are mistaken and irresponsible. The people, he implies, know better, and politics would be more reasonable if the media better represented the public. Not without sentimentality, *The Nation* regards the poll as the public's authentic expression, and the media picture as its distortion.[14]

But even if the figures represent an authentic public, it's far from clear how to take reassurance from the fact of such a poll. What could it mean to say that Reagan's popularity was simply illusory? For Congress discovered that it was not. And so did the media, since editors quickly learned that the journalistic sport of catching Reagan in his errors could make their audiences bristle with hostility. Reagan in one sense may have had no real popularity, as polls record it. But in another sense, he had a substantial and positive popularity, which he and others could deploy both within the political system and within the wider sphere of publicity. So if we characterize the poll as the authentic opinion of the public, while viewing the media reports of Reagan's popularity as a distortion, then both the genesis and the force of that distortion become inexplicable. It would be clearly inadequate to say, in what amounts to a revival of old talk about the conspiracy of the bosses, that the media were simply "managed" or "manipulated," despite the Republicans' impressive forensics of spin control.[15]

The Nation, then, gives a much too easy answer to the question of Reagan's attraction when it claims that there simply never was any. If that answer seems mistaken, the poll shows that it would be equally mistaken to see the public as successfully recruited into an uncritical identification with Reagan and an uncritical acclamation of Reaganism. It might otherwise have been comforting to believe, by means of such explanations, that Reagan really *was* popular, that the people were suckered. Then, at least, we could tell ourselves that we knew something about "the people." In fact, we have no way of talking abut the public without theorizing the contexts and strategies in which the public could be represented. If we believe in the continued existence of a rational-critical public, as *The Nation* does, then it is difficult to account for the counter-democratic tendencies of the public sphere as anything other than the cowardice or bad faith of some journalists. On the other hand, if we believe that the public sphere of the mass media has replaced a rational and critical public with one that is consumerist and acclamatory, then we might expect it to show more consumer satisfaction, more acclaim.

"Reagan" as an image owes its peculiar character in large part to the appeal of the other media construction that is jointly offered with it: "the public." In publicity we are given a stake in the imaginary of a mass public in a way that dictates a certain appeal not so much for Ronald Reagan in particular but for the kind of public figure of which he is exemplary. Different figures may articulate that appeal differently, and with important consequences, but there is a logic of appeal to which Reagan and Jesse Jackson equally submit. Publicity puts us in a relation to these figures that is also a relation to an unrealizable public subject, whose omnipotence and subjectivity can then be figured both on and against the images of such men. A public, after all, cannot have a discrete, positive existence; something becomes a public only through its availability for subjective identification. "Reagan" bears in his being the marks of his mediation to a public, and "the public" equally bears in its being the marks of its mediation for identification. Indeed, the most telling thing of all about the story in *The Nation* is Ferguson's remark that the myth of Reagan's popularity is itself "ever-popular." The problem is not Reagan's popularity but the popularity of his popularity. "Reagan," we might even say, is a relay for a kind of metapopularity. The major task of Western leaders has become the task of producing popularity, which is not the same as being popular.

What makes figures of publicity *attractive* to people? I do not mean this to be a condescending question. This question does not ask simply how people are seduced or manipulated. It asks what kinds of identifications are required or allowed in the discourse of publicity. The rhetorical conditions under which the popular can be performed are of consequence not only for policy outcomes but, more important, for who we are.

3 Self-Abstraction and the Mass Subject

Part of the bad faith of the *res publica* of letters was that it required a denial of the bodies that gave access to it. The public sphere is still enough oriented to its liberal logic that its citizens long to abstract themselves into a privileged public disembod-iment. And when that fails, they can turn to another kind of longing, which, as Lauren Berlant shows, is not so much to cancel out their bodies as to trade in for a better model. The mass public sphere tries to minimize the difference between the two, surrounding the citizen with trademarks through which she can trade marks, offering both positivity and self-abstraction. This has meant, furthermore, that the mass public sphere has had to develop genres of collective identification that will articulate both sides of this dialectic.

Insofar as the two sides are contradictory, however, mass identification tends to be characterized by what I earlier called noise, which typically appears as an erotic-aggressive disturb-ance. Here it might be worth thinking about a genre in which the display of bodies is also a kind of disembodiment: the discourse of disasters. At least since the great Chicago fire, mass disaster has had a special relationship to the mass media. Mass injury can always command a headline; it gets classed as immediate-reward news. But whatever kind of reward makes disaster rewarding, it evidently has to do with injury to a *mass* body—an already abstracted body assembled by the simultane-ity of the disaster somewhere other than here. When massive numbers of separate injuries occur, they fail to command the same fascination. This discrepancy in how seriously we take different organizations of injury is a source of never ending frustration for airline executives. They never tire of pointing out that, although the fatality rate for automobiles is astronom-ically higher than for airplanes, there is no public panic of supervision about automobiles. In the airline executives' inter-ested exasperation, that seems merely to prove the irrationality of journalists and congressmen. But I think this fondness of the mass media for a very special kind of injury makes rigorous sense. Disaster is popular because it is a way of making mass subjectivity available, and it tells us something about the desir-ability of that mass subject.

John Waters tells us in *Shock Value* that one of his hobbies in youth was collecting disaster coverage. His all-time favorite photograph, he claims, is a famous shot of the stadium col-lapsing at the Indianapolis 500, a photograph he proudly reproduces. But despite his pride in the aura of perversion that surrounds this disclosure, he is at some pains to point out that his pleasure is a normal feature of the discourse. "It makes the newspapers worth the quarter," he writes, and "perks up the local news shows." What could be the dynamic of this link between injury and the pleasures of mass publicity? Waters stages the intimacy of the link in the following story about his childhood, in what I think of as a brilliant corruption of Freud's *fort/da* game:

Even as a toddler, violence intrigued me. . . . While other kids were out playing cowboys and Indians, I was lost in fantasies of crunching metal and people screaming for help. I would sweet-talk unsuspecting relatives into buying me toy cars—any kind, as long as they were new and shiny. . . . I would take two cars and pretend they were driving on a secluded country road until one would swerve and crash into the other. I would become quite excited and start smashing the car with a hammer, all the while shouting, "Oh, my God, there's been a terrible accident!"[16]

Exactly what kind of pleasure is this? It isn't just the infantile recuperation of power that the *fort/da* game usually represents. The boy Waters, in other words, is not just playing out identification and revenge in the rhythm of treasuring and destroying the cars.

Nor is Waters simply indulging the infantile transitivism of which Lacan writes: "The child who strikes another says that he has been struck; the child who sees another fall, cries."[17] In fact, Waters's pleasure in the scene seems to have little to do with the cars at all. Rather, it comes about largely through his identification with publicity. Not only does Waters have access to auto disaster in the first place through the public discourse of news; he dramatizes that discourse as part of the event. Whose voice does he take up in exclaiming, "Oh, my God, there's been a terrible accident!"? And just as important, to whom is he speaking? He turns himself into a relay of spectators, none of whom are injured so much as horrified by the witnessing of injury. His ventriloquized announcer and his invisible audience allow him to internalize an absent witness. He has been careful to imagine the cars as being on "a secluded country road," so that his imaginary audience can be anywhere *else*. It is, in effect, the mass subject of news.

In this sense, the story shows us how deeply publicity has come to inform our subjectivity. But it also reveals, through Waters's camp humor, that the mass subject's absent witnessing is a barely concealed transitivism. The disaster audience finds its body with a revenge. Its surface is all sympathy: there's been a terrible accident. The sympathetic quality of its identification, however, is only half the story since, as Waters knows, inflicting and witnessing mass injury are two sides of the same dynamic in disaster discourse. Being of necessity anywhere else, the mass subject cannot have a body except the body it witnesses. But in order to become a mass subject it has left that body behind, abstracted away from it, canceled it as mere positivity. It returns in the spectacle of big-time injury. The transitive pleasure of witnessing/injuring makes available our translation into the disembodied publicity of the mass subject. By injuring a mass body—preferably a really massive body, somewhere—we constitute ourselves as a noncorporeal mass witness. (I do not, however, mean to minimize Waters's delirious perverseness in spelling out this link between violence and spectatorship in mass subjectivity. The perverse acknowledgement of his pleasure, in fact, helps him to violate in return the minoritizing disembodiment of the mass subject. It therefore allows Waters a counter-public embodied knowledge in the mode of camp.) The same logic informs an astonishing number of mass publicity's genres, from the prophylaxes of horror, assassination, and terrorism, to the organized prosthesis of sports. (But, as Waters writes, "Violence in sports always seemed so pointless, because everyone was prepared, so what fun could it possibly be?"[18]) The mass media are dominated by genres that construct the mass subject's impossible relation to a body.

In the genres of mass-imaginary transitivism, we might say, a public is thinking about itself and its media. This is true even in the most vulgar of the discourses of mass publicity, the tabloid pasttime of star puncturing. In the figures of Elvis, Liz, Michael, Oprah, Geraldo, Brando, and the like, we witness and transact the bloating, slimming, wounding, and general humiliation of the public body. The bodies of these public figures are prostheses for our own mutant desirability. That is not to say that a mass imaginary identification is deployed with uniform or equal effect in each of these cases. A significant subgenre of tabloid publicity, for instance, is devoted not to perforating the iconic bodies of its male stars but rather to denying them any private power behind their iconic bodies. Johnny Carson, Clint Eastwood, Rob Lowe, and others like them are subjected to humiliating forms of display not for gaining weight or having cosmetic surgery but for failing to exercise full control over their lives. By chronicling their endless romantic/matrimonial disasters, publicity keeps them available for our appropriation of their iconic status by reminding us that they do not possess the phallic power of their images— we do.

In this respect, we would have to say that Ronald Reagan stands in partial contrast to these other male icons of publicity. He does not require a discourse of star puncturing because he seems to make no personal claim on the phallic power of his own image. His body, impossible to embarrass, has no private subject behind it. The gestures stay the same, undisturbed by reflection or management. Reagan never gives a sense of modulation between a public and private self, and he therefore remains immune to humiliation. That is why it was so easy for news reports to pry into his colon without indiscretion. His witless self-continuity is the modern equivalent of virtue. He is the perfect example of what Lefort calls the egocrat: he coincides with himself and therefore concretizes a fantasy-image of the unitary people. He is popularity with a hairdo, an image of popularity's popularity.

The presentation of Reagan's body was an important part of his performance of popularity. J. G. Ballard understood that as early as 1969 in a story entitled "Why I Want to Fuck Ronald Reagan." In that story every subject of publicity is said to share the secret but powerful fantasy of violating Reagan's anus. In sharing that fantasy, Ballard suggests, we demonstrate the same thing that we demonstrate as consumers of the Kennedy assassination: the erotics of a mass imaginary. Like Waters's perverse transitivism, Ballard's generalized sadistic star cult theorizes the public sphere and ironizes it at the same time.

His characters, especially in *Crash,* are obsessed with a violent desire for the icons of publicity. But theirs is not a private pathology. Their longing to dismember and be dismembered with Ronald Reagan or Elizabeth Taylor is understood as a more reflective version of these public icons' normal appeal. In the modern nations of the West, individuals encounter in publicity the erotics of a powerful identification not just with public icons but also with their popularity.

It's important to stress, given the outcome of such a meta-popularity in the realm of policy, that the utopian moments in consumer publicity have an unstable political valence. Responding to an immanent contradiction in the bourgeois public sphere, mass publicity promises a reconciliation between embodiment and self-abstraction. That can be a powerful appeal, especially to those minoritized by the public sphere's rhetoric of normative disembodiment. Mass subjectivity, however, can result just as easily in new forms of tyranny of the majority as it can in the claims of rival collectivities. Perhaps the clearest example now is the discourse on AIDS. As Simon Watney and others have shown, one of the most hateful features of AIDS discourse has been its construction of a "general public."[19] A spokesman for the White House, asked why Ronald Reagan had not even mentioned the word "AIDS" or its problems until late in 1985, explained, "It hadn't spread into the general population yet."[20] In pursuit of a public demanded by good professional journalism, the mass media have pursued the same logic, interpellating their public as unitary and as heterosexual. Moreover, they have deployed the transitivism of mass identification in order to exile the positivity of the body to a zone of infection; the unitary public is uninfected but threatened. In this context, it is heartbreakingly accurate to speak of the prophylaxis held out by mass publicity to those who will identify with its immunized body.

Hateful though it is to those exiled into positivity by such a discourse, in a sense everyone's relation to the public body must have more or less the same logic. No one really inhabits the general public. This is true not only because it is by definition general but also because everyone brings to such a category the particularities from which they have to abstract

themselves in consuming this discourse. Of course, some particularities, such as whiteness and maleness, are already oriented to that procedure of abstraction. (They can scarcely even
be imagined as particularities; think for example of the asymmetry between the semantics of "feminism" and "masculin-
ism.") But the given of the body is nevertheless a site of
countermemory, all the more so since statistically everyone will
be mapped into some minority or other, a form of positivity
minoritized precisely in the abstracting discourse with which
everyone also identifies.

So in this sense, the gap that gay people register within the
discourse of the general public might well be an aggravated
form, though a lethally aggravated form, of the normal relation
to the general public. I'm suggesting, in other words, that a
fundamental feature of the contemporary public sphere is this
double movement of identification and alienation: on one
hand, the prophylaxis of general publicity; on the other hand,
the always inadequate particularity of individual bodies, experienced both as an invisible desire within a visible body and,
in consequence, as a kind of closeted vulnerability. The centrality of this contradiction in the legitimate textuality of the
video-capitalist state, I think, is the reason why the discourse
of the public sphere is so entirely given over to a violently
desirous speculation on bodies. What I have tried to emphasize
is that the effect of disturbance in mass publicity is not a
corruption introduced into the public sphere by its colonization
through mass media. It is the legacy of the bourgeois public
sphere's founding logic, the contradictions of which become
visible whenever the public sphere can no longer turn a blind
eye to its privileged bodies.

For the same reasons, the public sphere is also not simply
corrupted by its articulation with consumption. If anything,
consumption sustains a counterpublicity that cuts against the
self-contradictions of the bourgeois public sphere. One final
example can show how. In recent years, graffiti writing has
taken a new form. Always a kind of counterpublicity, it has
become the medium of an urban and mostly black male subculture. The major cities each devote millions of dollars per
year to obliterate it, and to criminalize it as a medium, while

the art world moves to canonize it out of its counterpublic setting. In a recent article Susan Stewart argues that the core of the graffiti writers' subculture lies in the way it has taken up the utopian promise of consumer publicity, and particularly of the brand name. These graffiti do not say "U.S. out of North America," or "Patriarch go home," or "Power to the queer nation"; they are personal signatures legible only to the intimately initiated. Reproduced as quickly and as widely as possible (unlike their canonized art equivalents), they are trademarks that can be spread across a nearly anonymous landscape. The thrill of brand name dissemination, however, is linked to a very private sphere of knowledge, since the signature has been trademarked into illegibility. Stewart concludes,

Graffiti may be a petty crime but its threat to value is an inventive one, for it forms a critique of the status of all artistic artifacts, indeed a critique of all privatized consumption, and it carries out that threat in full view, in repetition, so that the public has nowhere to look, no place to locate an averted glance. And that critique is paradoxically mounted from a relentless individualism, an individualism which, with its perfected monogram, arose out of the paradox of all commodity relations in their attempt to create a mass individual; an ideal consumer; a necessarily fading star. The independence of the graffiti writer has been shaped by a freedom both promised and denied by those relations—a freedom of choice which is a freedom among delimited and clearly unattainable goods. While that paradise of consumption promised the transference of uniqueness from the artifact to the subject, graffiti underlines again and again an imaginary uniqueness of the subject and a dissolution of artifactual status *per se*.[21]

The graffiti of this subculture, in effect, parodies the mass media; by appearing everywhere, it aspires to the placeless publicity of mass print or televisualization. It thus abstracts away from the given body, which in the logic of graffiti is difficult to criminalize or minoritize because it is impossible to locate. ("Nowhere to look, no place to locate an averted glance" exactly describes the abstraction of televisualized space.) Unlike the self-abstraction of normal publicity, however, graffiti retains its link to a body in an almost parodic devotion to the sentimentality of the signature. As Stewart points out, it claims an imaginary uniqueness promised in commodities but canceled in the public sphere proper. Whenever mass publicity puts its bodies on display, it reactivates this same promise. And although emancipation is not around the corner, its possibility is visible everywhere.

Obviously, the discursive genres of mass publicity vary widely. I group them together to show how they become interconnected as expressing a subjectivity that each genre helps to construct. In such contexts the content and the media of mass publicity mutually determine each other. Mass media thematize certain materials—a jet crash, Michael Jackson's latest surgery, or a football game—to find a way of constructing their audiences as mass audiences. These contents then function culturally as metalanguages, giving meaning to the medium. In consuming the thematic materials of mass-media discourse, persons construct themselves as its mass subject. Thus the same reciprocity that allowed the *Spectator* and its print medium to be mutually clarifying can be seen in the current mass media. But precisely because the meaning of the mass media depends so much on their articulation with a specific metalanguage, we cannot speak simply of one kind of mass subjectivity or one politics of mass publicity. Stewart makes roughly the same observation when she remarks that the intrication of graffiti, as a local practice, with the systemic themes of access—"access to discourse, access to goods, access to the reception of information"—poses a methodological problem, "calling into question the relations between a micro- and a macro-analysis: the insinuating and pervasive forms of the mass culture are here known only through localizations and adaptations."[22]

Nevertheless, some things are clear. In a discourse of publicity structured by deep contradictions between self-abstraction and self-realization, contradictions that have only been forced to the fore in televisual consumer culture, there has been a massive shift toward the politics of identity. The major political movements of the last half century have been oriented toward status categories. Unlike almost all previous social movements—Chartism, Temperance, or the French Revolution—they have been centrally about the personal identity formation of minoritized subjects. These movements all presuppose the bourgeois public sphere as background. Their rallying cries of difference take for granted the official rhetoric of self-abstraction. It would be naive and sentimental to suppose that identities or mere assertions of status will precipitate from this crisis as its solution, since the public discourse makes identity an ongoing problem. An assertion of the full equality of minoritized statuses would require abandoning the structure of self-abstraction in publicity. That outcome seems unlikely in the near future. In the meantime, the contradictions of status and publicity are played out at both ends of the public discourse. We, as the subjects of mass publicity, ever more find a political stake in the difficult-to-recognize politics of our identity, and the egocrats who fill the screens of national fantasy must summon all their skin and hair to keep that politics from getting personal.

For Lauren Berlant

Notes

1. Claude Lefort, "The Image of the Body and Totalitarianism," in his *Political Forms of Modern Society,* ed. John B. Thompson (Cambridge: MIT Press, 1986), p. 306.

2. J. G. Ballard, *Love and Napalm: Export U.S.A.* (New York: Grove Press, 1972), pp. 149–151.

3. The arguments condensed here can be found in full form in *The Letters of the Republic: Publication and the Public Sphere in Eighteenth-Century America* (Cambridge: Harvard Univ. Press, 1990).

4. [Richard Steele], *Spectator,* no. 555, in Angus Ross, ed., *Selections from the Tatler and the Spectator* (New York: Penguin, 1982), p. 213.

5. Lauren Berlant, "National Brands/National Body: *Imitation of Life,*" Hortense Spillers, ed., *Comparative American Identities* (New York: Routledge, 1990), pp. 110–140.

6. Habermas, *The Structural Transformation of the Public Sphere* (Cambridge: MIT Press, 1989), p. 43.

7. The point here about the character of gender difference has been a common one since de Beauvoir's *The Second Sex* (1949); its more recent extension to an analysis of the bourgeois public sphere is in Joan Landes, *Women and the Public Sphere in the Age of the French Revolution* (Ithaca: Cornell Univ. Press, 1988).

8. Pier Paolo Pasolini, *Lutheran Letters,* quoted in Douglas Crimp, "Strategies of Public Address: Which Media, Which Publics?" *Discussions in Contemporary Culture,* vol. 1, ed. Hal Foster (Seattle: Bay Press, 1987), p. 33.

9. Timothy Breen, "Baubles of Britain," *Past and Present* 119 (May 1988): 73–104.

10. Lefort, "Image of the Body," p. 303.

11. Lefort, "Image of the Body," pp. 304–306.

12. Habermas, *Structural Transformation,* p. 8.

13. Habermas, *Structural Transformation,* p. 201. The MIT Press translation reads "whose" where I have corrected the text to "which."

14. "F.D.R., Anyone?" *The Nation* (May 22, 1989), p. 689.

15. For a critique of the still-popular notion of media manipulation, see Hans Magnus Enzensberger, "Constituents of a Theory of the Media," in *Critical Essays* (New York: Continuum, 1982), pp. 46–76.

16. John Waters, *Shock Value* (New York: Dell, 1981), p. 24.

17. "Aggressivity in Psychoanalysis," *Écrits,* trans. Alan Sheridan (New York: Norton, 1977), p. 19.

18. Waters, *Shock Value,* p. 26.

19. Simon Watney, *Policing Desire: Pornography, AIDS, and the Media* (Minneapolis: Univ. of Minnesota Press, 1987), pp. 83–84 and passim.

20. Jan Zita Grover, "AIDS: Keywords," *October* 43 (1987): 23. This issue has since been reprinted as *AIDS: Cultural Analysis, Cultural Activism,* ed. Douglas Crimp (Cambridge, MIT Press, 1988).

21. Susan Stewart, "Ceci Tuera Cela: Graffiti as Crime and Art," in John Fekete, ed., *Life after Postmodernism: Essays on Value and Culture* (New York: St. Martin's, 1987), pp. 175–176.

22. Stewart, "Ceci Tuera Cela," p. 163.

16
Textuality, Mediation, and Public Discourse

Benjamin Lee

The conference on Habermas's work on the public sphere was itself an index of the changing nature of intellectual criticism in the West. The original work, first published in German in 1962, was not translated into French until 1978, and an English translation did not appear until 1989. In both cases, interest in it was catalyzed by earlier translations of such works as *Erkenntnis und Interesse* and *Theorie und Praxis;* in the case of the English translation, Habermas's position as a defender of the Enlightenment project of modernity against postmodern critiques was already well established. The earlier work was a comparative and historical account of the development of the bourgeois public sphere in England, France, and Germany. Its theoretical framework and empirical concerns clearly derived from the Frankfurt School, and its intellectual audience was more locally conceived (it was originally Habermas's *Habilitationsschrift* at the University of Marburg). The later works, especially the two volumes on communicative action and the lectures on modernity, are resolutely metatheoretical and multidisciplinary. The historical account is primarily Weber's rationalization thesis; the theoretical account attempts to create a transhistorical, philosophical grounding for a general theory of communicative action. While expanding upon themes present in the earlier work, the more recent work places them in a framework that is heavily influenced by Anglo-American analytic philosophy, cognitive-developmental psychology, and contemporary and classical social theory. The audience is also

conceived differently; the framework is used not only to analyze social developments but to criticize certain postmodern
trends, particularly the French use of German thinkers such
as Nieztsche and Heidegger. The emphasis on metatheory, the
multidisciplinary scope, and the expanded sense of intellectual
audience all reflect some of the changing parameters of the
current Western public sphere.

The differences between the earlier and later works reflect
an increasing internationalization and interweaving of different critical discourses. The earlier work is an analytic and
historical account of the development of bourgeois forms of
social criticism in England, France, and Germany during the
seventeenth and eighteenth centuries and their effacement in
the nineteenth and twentieth centuries by the forces of mass
culture and industrial capitalism. Although his sympathies are
clearly with the ideals of the bourgeois public sphere, he did
not attempt to develop an immanent critique of capitalism
similar to that of his Frankfurt School mentors and colleagues.
His later work develops an alternative strategy that does an
end run around the entire post-Cartesian philosophical tradition; it seeks to combine a minimal transcendentalism of the
speech act with a conception of communicative action that will
both satisfy the demands of an immanent critique and ground
historical analysis.

Habermas sees much of post-Cartesian philosophy as a philosophy of consciousness caught up in a subject/object epistemology, which inherently distorts the nature of communicative
action. Communicative action is oriented toward understanding; strategic, means-end rationality, insofar as it utilizes communication or communicatively mediated devices, presupposes
communicative action. Subject-centered reason and strategic
rationality are intimately related; strategic rationality presupposes an individual subject who is the source of the controlling
intention, whereas any subject of action must treat his actions
as the object of his intentions. Subject-centered reason, therefore, can never serve as an adequate standpoint of critique of
instrumental action, since it is merely its flip side. Instead,
Habermas argues that a formal pragmatics of communicative
action grounded in the analysis of speech acts reveals that

communicative reason is not reducible to instrumental reason; subject-centered reason and subject/object epistemologies are not presuppositions of communication but its derivatives. The standpoint of critique cannot be that of a transcendental rationality attached to a transcendental subject; instead, it must be located in the very structure of communication itself. The structure of communicative reason is revealed through the reconstruction of the universal presuppositions of communicative action. Such an analysis leads to a typology of "pure types of linguistically mediated action" (Habermas 1984, 329), which can frame both Kant's three critiques of epistemology, morality, and aesthetics and Weber's analyses of the development of science, law, and art. Communicative reason serves as a standpoint of critique, since it can specify what distorted communication is, and it provides an immanent dimension for any analysis, since its presuppositions are the universal presuppositions of communicative action.

With the elucidation of the structure of communicative reason at the end of the first volume of his *Theory of Communicative Action*, Habermas can use it in the second volume to analyze the relations between the lifeworld and system world. From the standpoint of what he calls "the unfinished project of modernity," the development of modern capitalism and a mass-mediated consumer culture appear as encroachments by a system world driven by money and power upon a lifeworld that is the holding environment for the potentially regenerative properties of linguistic and communicative practices. Communicative reason not only provides a backing for the universal relevance of the Enlightenment values of the bourgeois public sphere; it also provides the framework in which he can criticize postmodern theorists, such as Foucault and Derrida, as involved in a kind of intellectual solipsism; their works seem to presuppose the very structures of communicative reason that they criticize (the possibility of free, undistorted communication oriented toward mutual understanding).

On the last day of the conference Nicholas Garnham and Michael Warner were, perhaps appropriately or ironically, the last presenters. Although both papers were heavily influenced by Habermas's early work on the public sphere, they shared an unease with his later formulations, particularly how they deal with the role of the mass media in shaping cultural criticism. At first their overall perspectives seemed to differ considerably, as their comments on postmodern theory indicated. Garnham, coming out of his long association with Raymond Williams and British cultural Marxism and his active interest in rethinking media policy in Great Britain, shares with Habermas a commitment to the Enlightenment project of democracy and the concomitant development of a politically effective public sphere of social criticism. However, he rejects the quasi-transcendental version of speech act rationality that Habermas uses to ground this project, favoring instead a historical grounding. He argues that a viable, modern democratic polity needs some common normative framework to mediate between the dual pressures of an increasingly globalized economy and internal pluralization, and we should make a "Pascalian bet" that universal reason can fulfill these needs. Further support for this wager is "that large numbers of human beings from different cultures have actually believed in it and fought to realize it" and that "only history will show whether the project is in fact realizable." He sees this direction of thinking as incompatible with a "pluralist decentered postmodern politics"; for him, "at some level, cultural relativism and a democratic polity are simply incompatible."

Garnham's distrust of postmodern cultural theory lies in no small part in the transformation in the United States of British cultural studies into a "utopian and romantic pursuit of difference for its own sake," which has been subsumed within an ideology of pluralism and cultural relativism. From the standpoint of a veteran of the battles between Thatcherism and any form of liberal cultural politics, the neutralization of the political thrust of cultural studies in the United States must appear as a debilitating loss of vision and nerve. Warner, on the other hand, speaks from the embattled fields of American identity politics, whose basic premises were formed by the civil-rights movement of the sixties and still shape the debates over the canon, feminism, and multiculturalism. In this context, postmodern theory can be a catalyst for revitalizing a liberal tradition now seen to be under attack by conservative ideologies developed under Reagan and expanded by Bush.

Warner seems to make a postmodern move right at the beginning of his paper by juxtaposing quotes from Claude Lefort's "Image of the Body and Totalitarianism" and J. G. Ballard's "Why I Want to Fuck Ronald Reagan." Although the paper inhabits a terrain common to much of current postmodern discourse, it locates these debates in a wider theoretical framework that overlaps some of Garnham's concerns. Warner places issues such as publicity, identity, status, and their interrelationships within a cultural field of tension; this tension is created by a contradiction between the print-mediated politics of self-abstraction necessary to establish the ideology of the bourgeois public sphere and a "media politics" of self-realization. Warner interprets Habermas's account of the rise of the bourgeois public sphere as showing how its adoption of a rhetoric and ideology of self-abstraction and universal rationality also presupposed a "disembodied public subject," whose moral authority lay in its appeal to universal interests rather than the particular interests of a given class or set of persons. This is an imagined community in which, as Warner puts it, "what you say will carry force not because of who you are but despite who you are."

The principle of self-abstraction that was constitutive of the print-mediated bourgeois public sphere stands in contrast to the embodied sensibilities of self-realization characteristic of a modern, consumerist, mass-mediated public sphere. To create the imagined community of the bourgeois public sphere, differentiating features of persons and collectivities such as gender, class, and ethnicity were neutralized and abstracted from; these same features, augmented by the cultural economy of modern consumerism, have become the diacritics of modern identity movements. Habermas and to a certain extent Garnham see this process as the degradation of the public sphere by the onslaught of a mass-mediated consumer culture. Warner, however, sees these changes as the deepening of an inevitable tension between the founding ideology of the public sphere and its grounding in social life. As this grounded tension became caught up in the expanded cultural economies of modern Western nation states, it became internal to their public spheres. In the early bourgeois public sphere, the disembodied, rational public imaginary gave unity to the nation-state through its ideal of citizenship. In modern capitalist societies the media representation of the body politic now includes those who were previously disenfranchised; the disembodied, rational public imaginary is only one moment in an expanded public sphere. What Habermas had to exclude to give a unity to his account of the bourgeois public sphere has become, with the development of an expanded consumer economy, internal to it.

Although coming out of different political histories, both Garnham and Warner have been influenced by critical traditions that used liberal democracy as their original standpoints of critique and that are trying to respond to conservative successes that are at least in part due to effective use of the mass media. For Garnham, this entails reconsidering the relevance of issues raised by Habermas's work on the public sphere and adapting them "to the conditions of large-scale societies in which both social and communicative relations are inevitably mediated through time and space." For Warner, this involves understanding how the presuppositions of the bourgeois public sphere have a continuing relevancy for current identity politics; they continue to anchor one end of the contradiction between self-abstraction and self-realization, which now structures an enlarged, mass-mediated public sphere. Despite their different emphases, Garnham and Warner share a disquiet with Habermas's later work on communicative reason; their shared unease points to a deeper problem that the mass mediation of public culture presents both to modernist and postmodernist approaches: to what extent do the presuppositions of a historically and culturally grounded liberal social criticism need to be revised in the face of changing conditions of the modern world?

Habermas's answer to this question reflects his philosophical background; by reworking speech-act philosophy, he is able to transform what is essentially a dyadic model of speech communication into an analytic and critical framework for the analysis of social action. The basic model of communication is that of dialogue, with speech as the prototypical medium. A

potential problem is whether the model of speech communication that Habermas develops is adequate for all types of
communication, especially those that characterize a mass-mediated public sphere. Garnham points out that "both the initial
theory and subsequent related ideologies were based upon
face-to-face communication in a single physical space"; basic
human rights such as freedom of assembly guaranteed access
to the channels of communication, while the universal ability
of humans to speak guaranteed equal access to the means of
communication. However, our basic models of democratic politics assume either a face-to-face model of communication or
its indirect mediation, and these are at odds with our theories
and practices of communication. Although his comments are
directed toward romanticized visions of pluralistic democracy,
they also criticize as reductionistic any attempts to analyze
large-scale communicative practices in terms of face-to-face
models.

Warner reinforces this skepticism toward the adequacy of
face-to-face models in his analysis of the mechanism of publicity in modern American society. These mechanisms contrast
sharply with those of the early republican public sphere, which
Warner has written about in his book *The Letters of the Republic*.
The earlier model (which Garnham also comments critically
upon in his chapter) sought "to avoid any rupture of self-
difference between ordinary life and publicity." The ideal republican would "maintain continuity of value, judgment, and
reputation" between his roles as citizen and private person.

The continuity between public and private, mediated by
changing notions of publicity, was created and maintained by
an ideology of print production and consumption. This ideology explicitly represents the roles of authors and readers as
the starting point for constructing a public whose boundaries
are coterminus with the citizenry. The governing metadiscur-
sive principle that organizes this space is that the validity of
what you say bears a negative relation to your self-interest; the
more disinterested a position is, the more likely is it to be
universally valid and rational, and only such positions should
govern social decision making.

Warner argues that "a dialectic of embodiment and negativity in the public sphere" lies behind the appeal of mass subjectivity and is a driving force behind recent identity movements. Thus Warner, like Garnham, would also view as inadequate any attempt to analyze modern communicative practices in terms of a face-to-face communication model. One line of argument might adapt to Habermas's conception of communicative action his critique of subject-centered or instrumental reason as inadequate for the analysis of communication. Can a theory of communicative action based on an essentially dyadic speaker-hearer model of speech acts be adequate for the mixed, large-scale communicative modes characteristic of modern societies?

Habermas argues that developing an adequate theory of communicative action will involve balancing formal and empirical approaches in what he calls "formal pragmactics." This approach begins with three types of idealized speech acts oriented toward mutual understanding (constative, expressive, and regulative), their concomitant speaker attitudes (objectivating, expressive, and norm-conformative), and their corresponding validity claims (truth, truthfulness, and rightness). Formal pragmatics is a reconstruction of "the universal presuppositions of communicative action" (Habermas 1984, 328); it is not just an empirical model of face-to-face communication. Since these presuppositions are universal, they are immanent in naturally occurring speech events, which can be analyzed by "dropping the methodological provisions we began with in introducing standard speech acts" (Habermas 1984, 330); the basic framework is extendable from the initial idealization of isolated speech events to sequences of speech acts, texts, and conversations.

The account presupposes that other forms of discourse, including narrative genres, are analyzable in terms of speech-act functions and can in principle be seen as concatenated sequences of speech events. Larger structures of communicative action, such as science, law, and art, are each organized around a particular validity claim (truth, rightness, and truthfulness, respectively); they are institutionalized differentiations of the validity claims immanent in ordinary, everyday communication.

Perhaps the most trenchant criticism of using a speech-act model of communication as a general framework for the analysis of sign processes is Derrida's critique of Searle. Habermas comments on the Derrida-Searle controversy in his lectures on modernity (1987). Drawing upon Jakobson's analysis of speech functions, he says that because Derrida "overgeneralizes this one linguistic function—namely, the poetic—he can no longer see the complex relationship of the ordinary practice of normal speech to the two extraordinary spheres, differentiated, as it were, in opposite directions" (Habermas 1987, 207). These two spheres are the world-disclosing functions of art and literature and the problem-solving spheres of science, morality, and law. Habermas argues that these two spheres are held together by their grounding in the "functional matrix of ordinary language" and are differentiations worked out "within *one* linguistic function and one dimension of validity at a time." Derrida can use literary critical techniques to "deconstruct" philosophy only because he levels the complex relationships between these spheres and ordinary life.

This argument presupposes that Derrida's deconstructionism can be seen as focusing on the aesthetic functions of language and that there is a continuity between communicative functions at the level of individual speech events and larger-scale institutional organizations of discourse. However, Derrida's critique of Searle can be interpreted in a different way that lends support to Garnham's and Warner's doubts over the extendibility of face-to-face models of communication to larger-scale communicative practices.

In "Signature Event Context" (1988) Derrida raises several doubts about the univocality of the meaning of the term "communication," especially as it is used by philosophers. His target is the sender-receiver model of communication in which a speaker transmits his thoughts or impressions to an addressee or audience. Within such a general model of communication, writing is seen as overcoming the spatial and temporal limitations of face-to-face communication by extending communication through a more powerful means; writing allows the speaker's message to be extended to those not present. The absence of the addressee is "determined . . . as a continuous modification and progressive extenuation of presence" (Derrida 1988, 5). Derrida argues that an essential quality of writing is its "iterability," which is its property of remaining intelligible despite the absence of any particular addressee or receiver, or even sender or author. At the same time, this iterability also allows the written message to break with its context of production. These two properties are built into the structure of the written sign through its spacing vis-à-vis other elements in a given stretch of writing. Derrida then argues that these properties are constitutive not only of the written sign but also of linguistic signs in general. The functioning of any particular sign is a determination or regimentation of these semiotic processes; face-to-face communication in a given context and its attendant communicative functions are local determinations of these more general semiotic processes, and there is no direct or transparent relation between these two levels of functioning.

Replacing the sender-receiver models that Derrida criticizes with Habermas's formal pragmatics of the speech situation would not change the terms of Derrida's critique. First, it is arguable whether even an enlarged conception of speech-act communication can ground the different senses of communication as one switches between spoken and written communications. Second, questions still arise over whether semiotic processes must be grounded first in acts of communication. Are there properties of semiolinguistic functioning not reducible to speech-act communicative functions?

One line of argument comes from Peirce's semiology. Peirce first establishes a general sign theory in which the value of any given sign is its place in a general semiotic process. Communication presupposes the existence of semiosis. As Peirce put it, to interpret his general sign theory as a theory of communication between senders and receivers was "a sop to Cerberus" that obscured his contention that a general theory of signs constructed the very parameters of communication, including the participant. The connection between Peirce's model and deconstructionism was seen by de Man in an article entitled "Semiology and Rhetoric" (1979), who used it to develop what could be called a rhetoric of semiosis. This approach contrasts sharply with Habermas's and Apel's use of Peirce to create an ideal speech community that could ground a discourse-based ethics. De Man sees Peirce as linking rhetoric not to the aesthetic function but to the general process of sign generation; pure rhetoric is the process by means of which "one sign gives birth to another" (de Man 1979, 9). The property that Derrida identifies as the iterability of a semiolinguistic sign would correspond at a linguistic level to the role of pure rhetoric in Peirce's account of semiosis; it would be a general property of all such signs and would not be restricted to the poetic function.

Instead of working out the critical implications of the poetic/ aesthetic function of language, as Habermas maintains, Derrida's notion of iterability can be interpreted as pointing to a set of language-specific functions that have been overlooked by speech-act theorists and even such linguistic functionalists as Buhler and Jakobson, whom Habermas draws upon. Even Peirce, in his development of a general semiotics, did not analyze the language-specific devices that constitute its ability to form texts. More recent functional approaches to language, such as Halliday's, recognize the textual/cohesive properties of language as constituting a unique and irreducible function. As Halliday describes it, the textual function "comprises the resources that language has for creating text . . . , for being operationally relevant, and cohering within itself and with the context of situation" (Halliday and Hasan 1976, 27). It consists of devices for ellipsis, coreference, and texture maintenance and is a precondition for the intelligibility of discourse. For example, the locutionary or propositional cores of speech acts isolated by Austin and Searle are products of how language-specific cohesive mechanisms, such as coreference, coordinate indexical and semantic levels of reference.

The irreducibility of the textual function of language to speech-act functions has several implications that call into question some of the assumptions of Habermas's formal pragmatics. First, any account of speech act functions that leaves out the textual function cannot be adequate to an analysis of communication that produces understanding, since it is the textual function that makes possible the intelligibility of any linguistic communication.

Second, since larger-scale linguistic interactions, such as different types of dialogues or narrative genres, are at least in part constituted by their specific textual properties, their communicative functioning and that of the social practices they mediate may not be analyzable in terms of speech-act functions. For example, as Bakhtin and others have tried to show, genres are sociohistorical products whose internal structures are built up through complicated metalinguistic mechanisms of voicing, "centrifugal" and "centripetal tendencies," and "dialogicality," which are the sources of our ability to represent speech. If different genres such as the realistic novel, the scientific article, formal modes of calculation, or historical narratives are constitutive moments in particular social practices, then an analysis of even the communicative properties of such practices in terms of speech-act functions may be inadequate.

Finally, recent work on speech acts (Silverstein 1979) and narrativity (Fleischman 1990) indicates that not only are textual functions not reducible to speech-act functions, but also the segmentation of communication into discrete speech events is an objectification of language-specific metalinguistic structures, especially those involved in text cohesion. This is particularly noticeable in the various devices we have for reporting speech, such as quotation and indirect discourse, all of which involve highly language-specific devices. Speech acts are the unmarked, residual products of the objectification of these devices when certain textual mechanisms such as coreference are held constant. The ability to posit a segmented speech act as the starting point for an analysis of communicative functions is thus a product of a textual functioning whose constitutive role is effaced by the analysis.

The last line of argument could lead to a relativism of linguistic structure and functioning that would undercut Habermas's claim to have identified universal pragmatic functions of communication from the examination of a restricted subset of languages. Even if all languages had cohesive devices that allowed segmenting communication into discrete speech events (for example, all languages seem to have such devices as quotation for reporting speech), this would not entail that the functions of speech or speech-event types that Habermas has identified in what Whorf would have called "standard average" European languages are universal; such a claim would require a comparative functional examination of these devices in other languages to see if they correspond to the three macrofunctions that Habermas claims are universal. The additional claim that all languages contain speech acts that fit our typologies would also not entail the universality of such acts but would rather point to the robustness of our schemes of translation.

Although several other points that Derrida raises against Searle's analysis would also seem to overlap with the implications of textual functions for speech-act analysis, perhaps the most important claim is that the semiotic functioning of writing cannot be reduced or subsumed under a sender-receiver model of communication. There may be no general model of communication under which specific modes may be subsumed or which can serve as a standpoint of a critique. However, since the various textual/cohesive devices and functions analyzed by Halliday and others are specific to language, questions could also be raised about the applicability of a general theory of writing or textuality to mixed modes of semiosis, such as television and movies, which combine visual and oral modalities and whose production includes print-mediated processes as diverse as script writing and audience surveying.

Of course, ideologies of textuality can make a unity out of divergent communicative processes. Warner's 1990 work on the early republican public sphere in the United States shows how an ideology of print exploited certain functional possibilities of print textuality, interwove them with models of direct communication and political representation, and thereby created the republican political and literary ideologies. In his later work Habermas sees the breakdown of the bourgeois public sphere as the invasion of the lifeworld by the system world; the lost historical unity is replaced by a unity of vision in his standpoint of critique. Garnham and Warner, despite their acknowledged debts to Habermas and their theoretical differences with one another, seem to suggest that the analysis of the historical reality of the intertextual, multimedia, and multimediated modern public sphere requires a similar diversity of models of communication. Garnham hopes that this diversity will ultimately lead to the empirical and historical validation of his claim that only a nonrelativistic conception of reason can mediate the centrifugal tendencies of the communicative practices characteristic of modern society. For Warner, such a claim can also only be located historically, albeit as one moment in a continually unfolding dialectic between abstraction and embodiment.

All three reactions to the themes of Habermas's earlier work on the public sphere point to different ways of dealing with the problem of how communicative forms mediate social action. Habermas's own reaction in his later works is to create a critically grounded vantage point from which to analyze specific communicative practices and their institutional organizations. Because of the transhistorical nature of its analytic categories, the vantage point is itself neutral with respect to the different forms of communication that mediate the public sphere. This leads to a tension between the analytic framework and its usefulness for cultural-historical research, as evidenced by the inevitable complaints by anthropologists of ethnocentrism. On the other hand, the relative indifference to communicative difference allows Habermas clearly to state a communicative presupposition of critical discourse in modern civil societies: that of communication uninhibited by inequalities of status and power. Perhaps the price of a certain opacity to comparative cultural history is a transparency to the ideals that structure ongoing critical discourse, which would thereby allow a clearer articulation of a cultural/political stance than other contemporary positions.

From another perspective, such clarity seems to be the issue. Foucault, whom Habermas accuses of a performative paradox in that his criticisms of the ideals of reason presuppose those norms, can be interpreted as enacting in his writing the very dialectic of abstraction and embodiment that Warner points to as constitutive of the modern public sphere. Derrida's critique of Searle implies that no single model of communication can serve as a critical vantage point to assess the possibilities and deficiencies of different communicative media. Instead of being a one-sided emphasis on the poetic function of language, deconstruction can be seen as exploring the generative implications of an expanded notion of textuality, of which face-to-face communication is only one possibility.

An expanded notion of textuality would have interesting implications for any analysis of communication. First, the textuality of language raises questions about the relations between oral and written communication. The interplay between textual and metatextual devices such as coreference, citation, quotation, and indirect discourse allows language to represent itself, making possible what Bakhtin called "speech about speech." The feeling that speech acts are primary seems to arise because any form of discourse, spoken or written, seems to be embeddable as a quotation, i.e., he *said* ". . ." or the author *said* ". . . ." Thus, written communication can be seen as derivative of speech; any written communication is a kind of speech act. However, from the standpoint of narrative theory, Banfield (1982) and others have emphasized that in certain standard historical and novelistic discourses there are no linguistic signs of the speaker and hearer. Instead, within these genres there develops "a sentence type which falls outside any framework structured by the communicative relation between *I* and *you*" (Banfield 1982, 141). Some of Derrida's criticisms of face-to-face communication may be a recognition of the nonreducible properties of narrative discourse. An expanded notion of textuality reveals a potential tension between speech and narration that is mediated by the unique ability of language to represent itself.

This tension can be a site of contestation between different genres and ideologies of communication. Such genres as stream of consciousness, historical narration, and "skaz" are particular functional configurations of textual and metatextual devices. At the same time, differences between genres are the source for certain ideologies of communication. For example, the early republican model maintained a consistency between the expressive potentials of speech and print while using the expanded distributional potential of print to create a print-based, imaginary public that embedded any particular oral community or face-to-face communication. This model also governed the interpretive norms for both the politics and literature of that era (Warner 1990).

An expanded notion of textuality would also raise questions about the relations between language and other media whose "textuality" seems organized along other principles. Television and movies are mixed media in which speech is directly represented; they are also indirectly related to print culture through script writing, which is usually done by elites. In many contemporary societies the political public is coextensive with the mass-media audience, which may be mostly illiterate. The "public spheres" of such societies seems to be organized around the tensions between different modes of communication, each of which possesses a particular cultural organization of "textuality." Instead of the degradation of a preexisting bourgeois public sphere by the forces of consumer capitalism, what we see is the coeval emergence of different publics, public spheres, and public spaces, each with their own forms of communicative organization. The study of such communicative difference might found a comparative and critical multicultural studies. In such an expanded context, Habermas's early work on the public sphere can be seen as developing the foundation for a communication-based and empirically driven critical cultural studies, which is now being updated to fit the changing conditions of the modern world. For Habermas, the possibility of a coherent critical stance for such a project has entailed redefining its cultural and historical dimensions. For Garnham and Warner, on the other hand, to return to culture and history is to redefine the possibilities of critique.

References

Banfield, Ann. 1982. *Unspeakable Sentences.* London: Routledge and Kegan Paul.

De Man, Paul. 1979. *Allegories of Reading.* New Haven: Yale University Press.

Derrida, Jacques. 1988. *Limited Inc.* Evanston, Ill.: Northwestern University Press.

Fleischman, Suzanne. 1990. *Tense and Narrativity.* Austin: University of Texas Press.

Habermas, Jürgen. 1984. *The Theory of Communicative Action.* Vol. 1, *Reason and the Rationalization of Society.* Boston: Beacon Press.

Benjamin Lee

Habermas, Jürgen. 1987. *The Philosophical Discourse of Modernity.* Cambridge: MIT Press.

Halliday, M. A. K., and Ruqaiya Hasan. 1976. *Cohesion in English.* London: Longman.

Silverstein, Michael. 1979. "Language Structure and Linguistic Ideology." In *The Elements: A Parasession on Linguistic Units and Levels, April 20–21, 1979,* ed. P. Clyne et al., pp. 193–247. Chicago: Chicago Linguistic Society.

Warner, Michael. 1990. *The Letters of the Republic: Publication and the Public Sphere in Eighteenth-Century America.* Cambridge: Harvard University Press.

IV

Conclusion and Response

17

Further Reflections on the Public Sphere

Jürgen Habermas

Translated by Thomas Burger

Rereading this book after almost thirty years, I was initially tempted to make changes, eliminate passages, and make emendations. Yet I became increasingly impressed with the impracticability of such a course of action: the first modification would have required me to explain why I did not refashion the entire book. This, however, would be asking too much of an author who in the meantime has turned to other matters and has recalled that the original study emerged from the synthesis of contributions based in several disciplines, whose number even at that time almost exceeded what one author could hope to master.

There are two reasons that may justify the decision in favor of an unrevised new printing of the eighteenth edition, which had gone out of print.[1] For one, there is the continuing demand for a publication that in a variety of programs of study has become established as a sort of textbook. For another, there is the contemporary relevance bestowed on the structural change of the public sphere by the long-delayed revolution occurring before our eyes in central and eastern Europe.[2] The current relevance of this topic—and of its multifaceted treatment—is confirmed by the reception of the book in the United States, where an English translation[3] finally appeared last year.[4]

I want to use this occasion for a few comments intended less to downplay the temporal distance created by the span of a generation than to throw it into clear relief. It is trivial to state that research and theoretical problems are different now from what they were in the late 1950s and early 1960s, when this study originated. Since the Adenauer regime, the contemporary scene has changed, i.e., the extrascientific context that shapes the horizon of experience from which social-scientific research derives its perspective. My own theory, finally, has also changed, albeit less in its fundamentals than in its degree of complexity. On the basis of a first and certainly only superficial acquaintance with current thinking on some relevant topics, I want to remind the reader of those changes, at least by way of illustration and in the hope of stimulating further studies. I shall proceed by following the structure of the book in that I shall first deal with the historical genesis and the concept of the bourgeois public sphere (chapters 1 to 3), then with the structural change of the public sphere with regard to the transformation toward the social welfare state and the change of the structures of communication through the mass media (chapters 5 and 6). After that, I shall discuss the study's theoretical perspective and its normative implications (chapters 4 and 7), where my focus will be on the possible contribution of the study to the newly relevant questions of the theory of democracy. This is the aspect in relation to which the book has received most attention, not so much at the time of its first publication but in connection with the student rebellion and the neoconservative reaction it triggered. In the process it has occasionally been the object of polemical treatment coming equally from the right and from the left.[5]

1   The Genesis and Concept of the Bourgeois Public Sphere

(1)

As was stated in the preface to the first edition, my first aim had been to derive the ideal type of the bourgeois public sphere from the historical context of British, French, and German developments in the eighteenth and early nineteenth centuries. The formation of a concept specific to an epoch requires that a social reality of great complexity be stylized to give prominence to its peculiar characteristics. As is the case with any sociological generalization, selection, statistical relevance, and weighting of historical trends and examples pose a problem involving great risks, especially for someone who, unlike the historian, does not go back to the sources but instead relies on the secondary literature. Historians have rightly complained of empirical shortfalls. Yet I have been put somewhat at ease by Geoff Eley's friendly assessment in his extensive and comprehensively documented contribution to the conference: "On rereading the book . . . , it is striking to see how securely and even imaginatively the argument is historically grounded, given the thinness of the literature available at the time."[6]

The basic lines of my analysis have been corroborated by H. U. Wehler's summarizing presentation of a wide body of literature. By the end of the eighteenth century there had emerged, in Germany, "a public sphere, although a small one, where critical-rational discussion was carried on."[7] With the growth of a general reading public that transcended the republic of scholars and the urban bourgeoisie and who no longer limited themselves to a careful reading and rereading of a few standard works but oriented their reading habits to an ongoing stream of new publications, there sprang from the midst of the private sphere a relatively dense network of public communication. The growing number of readers, increasing by leaps and bounds, was complemented by a considerable expansion in the production of books, journals, and papers, an increasing number of authors, publishers, and book sellers, the establishment of lending libraries, reading rooms, and especially reading societies as the social nodes of a literary culture revolving around novels. The relevance of the associational life that began to take off late in the German Enlightenment has by now been acknowledged, although its significance for future developments lay more with its organizational forms than with its manifest functions.[8] The societies for enlightenment, cultural associations, secret freemasonry lodges, and orders of *illuminati* were associations constituted by the free, that is, private, decisions of their founding members, based on voluntary membership, and characterized internally by egalitarian practices of sociability, free discussion, decision by majority, etc. While these societies certainly remained an exclusively bourgeois affair, they did provide the training ground for what were to become a future society's norms of political equality.[9]

The French Revolution eventually triggered a movement toward the politicization of a public sphere that at first revolved around literature and art criticism. This is true not only of France, but holds for Germany as well.[10] A "politicization of associational life," the rise of a partisan press, the fight against censorship and for freedom of opinion characterize the change in function of the expanding network of public communication up to the middle of the nineteenth century.[11] The policies of censorship, with which the states of the German Federation fought against the institutionalization of a political public sphere and managed to delay its advent until 1848, only made it more inevitable that literature and criticism would be sucked into the whirlpool of politicizations. Peter U. Hohendahl has used my concept of the public sphere to trace this process in detail, although for him it is the collapse of the revolution of 1848 that marks the turning point for the beginning structural transformation of the early liberal public sphere.[12]

Eley has directed attention to several recent studies in English social history that fit well into the proposed theoretical framework for the analysis of the public sphere. With reference to the popular liberalism of nineteenth-century Great Britain,[13] these studies investigate the processes of class formation, urbanization, cultural mobilization, and the emergence of new structures of communication along the lines of those voluntary associations that became constituted in the eighteenth century.[14] Raymond Williams's studies in the sociology of communications are particularly illuminating on the transformation of a public sphere characterized initially by an educated bourgeoisie interested in literature and the critical discussion of cultural issues into a sphere dominated by mass media and mass culture.[15]

At the same time, Eley repeats and substantiates the objection that my overly stylized depiction of the bourgeois public sphere leads to an unjustified idealization involving more than an overdrawn emphasis on the rational aspects of a public communication whose basis is reading and whose main vehicle is conversation. It is wrong to speak of one single public even if we assume that a certain homogeneity of the bourgeois public enabled the conflicting parties to consider their class interest, which underneath all differentiation was nevertheless ultimately the same, as the basis for a consensus attainable at least in principle. Apart from introducing a greater internal differentiation of the bourgeois public, which by means of a more detail-oriented focus could also be accommodated within my model, a different picture emerges if *from the very beginning* one admits the coexistence of competing public spheres and takes account of the dynamics of those processes of communication that are excluded from the dominant public sphere.

(2)

We may use "excluded" in Foucault's sense when we are dealing with groups that play a *constitutive* role in the formation of a particular public sphere. "Exclusion" assumes a different and less radical meaning when the same structures of communication simultaneously give rise to the formation of several arenas where, beside the hegemonic bourgeois public sphere, additional subcultural or class-specific public spheres are constituted on the basis of their own and initially not easily reconcilable premises. The first case I did not consider at all at the time; the second I mentioned in the preface but left it at that.

With regard to the Jacobin phase of the French Revolution and the Chartist movement, I spoke of the beginnings of a "plebeian" public sphere, and considering it merely a variant of the bourgeois public sphere that remained supressed in the historical process, I believed neglecting it to be justifiable. However, in the wake of E. P. Thompson's pathbreaking *The Making of the English Working Class* there appeared a multitude of investigations concerning the French and English Jacobins, Robert Owen and the activities of the early socialists, the Chartists, and also the left-leaning populism in early-nineteenth-century France.[16] These studies have provided a different perspective on the political mobilization of the rural lower classes and the urban workers. Günter Lottes, in direct confrontation with my concept of the public sphere, studied the theory and practice of English radicals in the late eighteenth century, as exemplified by the London Jacobins. He shows how under the influence of radical intellectuals and under the conditions of modern communication, the traditional culture of the common people brought forth a new political culture with organizational forms and practices of its own. "The emergence of the plebeian public sphere thus marks a specific phase in the historical development of the life relations of the petite bourgeoisie and the strata below it. It is, on the one hand, a variant of the bourgeois public sphere, for it takes it as a model. On the other hand it is more than a mere variant, since it develops the bourgeois public sphere's emancipatory potential in a new social context. The plebeian public sphere is, in a manner of speaking, a bourgeois public sphere whose social preconditions have been rendered null."[17] The exclusion of the culturally and politically mobilized lower strata entails a pluralization of the public sphere in the very process of its emergence. Next to, and interlocked with, the hegemonic public sphere, a plebeian one assumes shape.

Within the traditional forms of representative publicness, the exclusion of the people operated in a different manner. Here the people functioned as the backdrop before which the ruling estates, nobility, church dignitaries, kings, etc. displayed themselves and their status. By its very exclusion from the domination so represented, the people are part of the constitutive conditions of this representative publicness.

I continue to believe that this type of publicness (only sketchily described in section 2 of *Structural Transformation*) constitutes the historical background to modern forms of public communication. Had he kept this contrast in mind, Richard Sennett might have been able to avoid orienting his diagnosis of the collapse of the bourgeois public sphere toward a wrong model. For Sennett makes certain features of representative publicness an integral part of the classical bourgeois public sphere; he does not grasp the specifically bourgeois dialectic of inwardness and publicness that in the eighteenth century, through the ascendancy of the audience-oriented privateness of the bourgeois intimate sphere, begins to capture the literary world as well. Since he does not sufficiently distinguish between the two types of publicness, he believes that he can document the correctness of his diagnosis of the end of "public culture" by reference to the decline in the forms of an impersonal, cere-monialized role-playing esthetic of self-presentation. However, staging the presentation of oneself behind a mask that removes private emotions and everything subjective from sight should properly be considered part of the highly stylized framework of a representative publicness whose conventions had already crumbled in the eighteenth century, when bourgeois private people formed themselves into a public and therewith became the carriers of a new type of public sphere.[18]

I must confess, however, that only after reading Mikhail Bakhtin's great book *Rabelais and His World* have my eyes be-come really opened to the *inner* dynamics of a plebeian culture. This culture of the common people apparently was by no means only a backdrop, that is, a passive echo of the dominant culture; it was also the periodically recurring violent revolt of a counterproject to the hierarchical world of domination, with its official celebrations and everyday disciplines.[19] Only a stereoscopic view of this sort reveals how a mechanism of ex-clusion that locks out and represses at the same time calls forth countereffects that cannot be neutralized. If we apply the same perspective to the bourgeois public sphere, the exclusion of women from this world dominated by men now looks different than it appeared to me at the time.

(3)

No doubt existed about the patriarchal character of the con-jugal family that constituted both the core of bourgeois society's private sphere and the source of the novel psychological ex-periences of a subjectivity concerned with itself. By now, however, the growing feminist literature has sensitized our awareness to the patriarchal character of the public sphere itself, a public sphere that soon transcended the confines of the reading public (of which women were a constituting part) and assumed political functions.[20] The question is whether women were excluded from the bourgeois public sphere *in the same fashion* as workers, peasants, and the "people," i.e., men lacking "independence."

Both women and the other groups were denied equal active participation in the formation of political opinion and will. Under the conditions of a class society, bourgeois democracy thus from its very inception contradicted essential premises of its self-understanding. This dialectic could still be grasped within the categories of the Marxist critique of domination and ideology. Within this perspective I investigated how the relationship between public and private spheres changed in the course of the expansion of the democratic right of participation and the social-welfare state's compensation for class-specific disadvantages. Nevertheless, *this* structural transformation of the political public sphere proceeded without affecting the patriarchal character of society as a whole. Equality of civil rights, finally attained in the twentieth century, has no doubt created for hitherto underprivileged women the opportunity to improve their social status. Yet women who, through equal political rights, also managed to come to enjoy increased social-welfare benefits did not therewith accomplish the modification of the underprivileged status tied to gender.

The progress toward emancipation, for which feminism has struggled for two centuries, has by now been set into motion on a broad front. Like the social emancipation of wage workers, it is a phenomenon of the universalization of civil rights. However, unlike the institutionalization of class conflict, the transformation of the relationship between the sexes affects not only the economic system but has an impact on the private core area of the conjugal family. This shows that the exclusion of women has been constitutive for the political public sphere not merely in that the latter has been dominated by men as a matter of contingency but also in that its structure and relation to the private sphere has been determined in a gender-specific fashion. Unlike the exclusion of underprivileged men, the exclusion of women had structuring significance.

This is the thesis advocated by Carol Pateman in an influential essay first published in 1983. She deconstructs the contract-theoretical justifications of the democratic constitutional state to demonstrate that rationalist legal criticism of the *paternalistic* exercise of domination merely functions to *modernize patriarchy* in the form of a rule of brothers: "Patriarchalism has two dimensions: the paternal (father versus son) and the masculine (husband versus wife). Political theorists can represent the outcome of the theoretical battle as a victory for contract theory because they are silent about the sexual or conjugal aspect of patriarchy, which appears as nonpolitical or natural."[21] Pateman remains skeptical concerning women's integration on equal terms into a political public sphere whose structures continue to be wedded to the patriarchal features of a private sphere removed from the agenda of public discussion: "Now that the feminist struggle has reached the point where women are almost formal civic equals, the opposition is highlighted between equality made after a male image and the real social position of women as women" (p. 122).

Of course, this convincing consideration does not dismiss rights to unrestricted inclusion and equality, which are an integral part of the liberal public sphere's self-interpretation, but rather appeals to them. Foucault considers the formative rules of a hegemonic discourse as mechanisms of exclusion constituting their respective "other." In these cases there is no communication between those within and those without. Those who participate in the discourse do not share a common language with the protesting others. This is how one may conceive of the relationship between the representative publicness of traditional domination and the devalued counterculture of the common people: people were forced to move and express themselves in a universe that was different and *other*. In this system, therefore, culture and counterculture were so interlinked that one went down with the other. Bourgeois publicness, in contrast, is articulated in discourses that provided areas of common ground not only for the labor movement but also for the excluded other, that is, the feminist movement. Contact with these movements in turn transformed these discourses and the structures of the public sphere itself from within. From the very beginning, the universalistic discourses of the bourgeois public sphere were based on self-referential premises; they did not remain unaffected by a criticism from within because they differ from Foucaultian discourses by virtue of their potential for self-transformation.

(4)

The two shortcomings remonstrated by Eley have implications for an ideal-typical model of the bourgeois public sphere. The modern public sphere comprises several arenas in which, through printed materials dealing with matters of culture, information, and entertainment, a conflict of opinions is fought out more or less discursively. This conflict does not merely involve a competition among various parties of loosely associated private people; from the beginning a dominant bourgeois public collides with a plebeian one. From this it follows, especially if one seriously tries to make room for the feminist dynamic of the excluded other, that the model of the contradictory institutionalization of the public sphere in the bourgeois constitutional state (developed in section 11 of *Structural Transformation*) is conceived too rigidly. The tensions that come to the fore in the liberal public sphere must be depicted more clearly as potentials for a self-transformation. As a result, the contrast between an early political public sphere (lasting up to the middle of the nineteenth century) and the public sphere of the mass-democratic social-welfare states, which has been subverted by power, no longer has the ring of a contrast between an idealistically glorified past and a present distorted by the mirror of cultural criticism. This implicit normative gradient bothered many reviewers. As I shall discuss, it was a consequence not only of the ideology-critical approach as such but also of the blocking out of aspects that I mentioned, to be sure, but whose significance I underestimated. Still, a mistake in the assessment of the significance of certain aspects does not falsify the larger outline of the process of transformation that I presented.

2 The Structural Transformation of the Public Sphere: Three Revisions

The structural transformation of the public sphere is embedded in the transformation of state and economy. At the time, I conceived of the latter within a theoretical framework that had been outlined in Hegel's philosophy of right, had been elaborated by the young Marx, and had received its specific shape in the German constitutional-law tradition since Lorenz von Stein.

The constitutional construction of the relationship between a public authority that guarantees liberties and a socioeconomic realm organized on the basis of private law has two sources: on the one hand, the liberal theory of constitutional rights developed during the period of German history known as *Vormärz* (pre-March), insisting (with obvious political intention) on a strict separation of public and private law; on the other hand, the consequences of the failure of the "dual German revolution of 1848/9" (Wehler), that is, the development of a state based on the rule of law but without democracy. E. W. Böckenförde highlights this specifically German retardation in the gradual enactment of political equality for all citizens as follows:

Once "state" and "society" have begun to confront each other, the problem of society's *share* in the state's decision-making power and its exercise arises. . . . The state put individuals and society into a condition of civil liberty, and it maintained them in this condition through the creation and enforcement of the new general legal order. Yet individuals and society did not attain *political* freedom, that is, no share in the political decision-making power concentrated in the state, and no institutionalized possibility to exert an active influence upon it. The state as an organization of domination rested as it were within itself, that is to say, sociologically speaking, it was supported by the monarchy, the civil service and the army, and partially also by the nobility, and thus was "separated" both organizationally and institutionally from the society represented by the bourgeoisie.[22]

This historical background also supplies the context for the specific interest in a public sphere. The latter is capable of assuming a political function only to the extent to which it enables the participants in the economy, via their status as citizens, to mutually accommodate or generalize their interests and to assert them so effectively that state power is transformed into a fluid medium of society's self-organization. This is what the young Marx had in mind when he spoke of the reabsorption of the state into a society that has become political in itself. The idea of such a self-organization, channeled through the public communication of freely associated members of society, demands (in a first sense) that the "separation" of state and society, as sketched by Böckenförde, be overcome.

Connected with the conception of this separation on the level of constitutional law is another, more general one: the emergence, through differentiation, of an economy controlled through market mechanisms from the premodern orders of political domination. Since the early-modern period, this differentiation had accompanied the gradual ascendency of the capitalist mode of production and the emergence of modern state bureaucracies. In the retrospective view of liberalism, these developments are interpreted as having their point of convergence in the autonomy of a "bourgeois society" in Hegel's and Marx's sense, that is, in the economic self-regulation of an economic society organized through activities under private law upheld by a constitutional state. This model of a progressive separation of state and society, no longer specially geared toward the specific development in the German states of the nineteenth century but informed more by the prototypical development in Great Britain, supplied the foil for my analysis of the *reversal of this trend* that began in the latter part of the nineteenth century. For this interlinking of state and economy removes the ground from under the model of society assumed by bourgeois private law and the liberal view of the constitution.[23] The de facto negation of the tendency toward a separation of state and society I conceptualized, by reference to its juridical reflections, as a neocorporatist "societalization of the state," on the one hand, and as a "state-ification of society," on the other, both occurring as a result of the interventionist policies of a now actively interfering state.

All this has by now been investigated with much greater precision. I merely want to bring back to mind the theoretical perspective that emerges when the normative meaning of the self-regulation of a society characterized by a radical democratic elimination of the separation between state and economic sphere is compared with the functional interlinkage of the two systems as it actually became reality. My guiding point of view was that of the potential for societal self-regulation inhering in the political public sphere, and I was interested in the repercussions of those complex developments toward the social-welfare state and organized capitalism in the Western type societies. In particular, I was concerned with the repercussions on the private sphere and the social bases of private autonomy (subsection 1 below), the structure of the public sphere as well as the composition and behavior of the public (subsection 2), and finally, the legitimation process of mass democracy itself (subsection 3).

With regard to these three aspects, my presentation in chapters 5 to 7 of *Structural Transformation* exhibits a number of weaknesses.

(1)

In the modern natural-law conceptions, but also in the social theories of the Scottish moral philosophers, civil society (*bürgerliche Gesellschaft*) was always contrasted with public authority or government as a sphere that is private *in its entirety*.[24] According to the self-conception of early modern bourgeois society, stratified by occupational groupings, the sphere of commodity exchange and social labor as well as the household and the family relieved from productive functions without distinctions were deemed to belong to the private sphere of "civil society." Both were structured in a like sense; the position and decision-making latitude of private owners involved in production constituted the basis for a private autonomy whose psychological flip side, so to speak, lay in the conjugal family's intimate sphere. For the economically dependent classes, a tight structural connection of this sort never existed. But only with the onset of the social emancipation of the lower strata and with the politicization of class conflicts on a massive scale in the nineteenth century did awareness also arise in the life-world of the bourgeois social strata that the two realms, the family's intimate sphere and the occupational system, were structured at *cross-purposes*. What a later literature conceptualized as the tendency toward an "organizational society," as the progressing autonomy of the level of the organization vis-à-vis the network of basic interactions, I described in section 17 as the "polarization of the social sphere and the intimate sphere."

Jürgen Habermas

The realm of private life, defined by family, neighborly contacts, social occasions, and all sorts of informal relations, does not merely become a distinct entity through differentiation; it is simultaneously transformed differently for each social stratum in the course of long-term tendencies such as urbanization, bureaucratization, the concentration of enterprises, and finally the shift to mass consumption accompanied by ever more leisure time. Yet I am interested here not in the empirical aspects (which need to be supplemented) of this structural transformation of the circumstances of life experience but in the theoretical point of view from which I described at the time the changing status of the private sphere.

After the universalization of equal civil rights, the private autonomy of the masses could no longer have its social basis in the control over private property, in contrast to those private people who in the associations of the bourgeois public sphere had come together to form the public of citizens. To be sure, the actualization of the potential for societal self-regulation presumptively contained in an expanding public sphere would have required that the culturally and politically mobilized masses make effective use of their rights to communication and participation. But even under ideally favorable conditions of communication, one could have expected from economically dependent masses a contribution to the spontaneous formation of opinion and will only to the extent to which they had attained the equivalent of the social independence of private property owners. Obviously, the propertiless masses could no longer gain control of the social preconditions of their private existence through participation in a system of commodity and capital markets organized under private law. Their private autonomy had to be secured through reliance on the status guarantees of a social-welfare state. This derivative private autonomy, however, could function as an equivalent of the original private autonomy based on control over private property only to the degree to which the citizens, as clients of the social-welfare state, came to enjoy status guarantees that they *themselves* bestowed on themselves in their capacities as citizens of a democratic state. This in turn appeared to become possible in proportion to the expansion of democratic control to the economic process in its entirety.

This consideration had its place in the context of a drawn-out controversy among scholars of constitutional law in the 1950s. Ernst Forsthoff and Wolfgang Abendroth were protagonists in this dispute over an issue of legal systematics, i.e., the compatibility of the social-welfare principle with the handed-down architectonics of the constitutional state.[25] The Carl Schmitt school argued that the preservation of the structure of the constitutional state required the unconditional priority of the protection of the classical legal freedoms over the demands of social welfare provisions.[26] Abendroth, in contrast, interpreted the social-welfare principle simultaneously as the preeminent hermeneutic governing the interpretation of the constitution and as a policy-shaping maxim for the political legislator. The idea of the social-welfare state was to provide the leverage for a radical democratic reformism that preserved at least the possibility for a transition toward democratic socialism. Abendroth maintained that the constitution of the Federal Republic of Germany aimed at "*extending* the idea of a substantively democratic constitutional state (which means especially the principle of equality and its combination with the notion of participation in the idea of self-determination) to the entire economic and social order" (*Structural Transformation*, pp. 226–227, my emphasis). Within this perspective, of course, the political public sphere is reduced to function as a sort of adjunct for a legislator whose judgment is theoretically and constitutionally predetermined and who knows a priori in what fashion the democratic state has to pursue "the substantive shaping of the social order" that is incumbent on it, namely through "the state's interference with that ownership . . . that makes possible private control over large means of production and therewith control over economic and social positions of power that cannot be democratically legitimated."[27]

As much as the insistence on the dogmas of the liberal constitutional state has failed to do justice to the changed social conditions, one cannot but be struck by the weaknesses of a Hegelian-Marxist style of thought, all wrapped up in notions of totality, as is evidently the case with Abendroth's fascinating program. Even though in the meantime I have distanced my-self more from such an approach, this circumstance does nothing to diminish my intellectual and personal debt to Wolfgang Abendroth, which I acknowledged in my dedication. I must state my conviction, however, that a functionally differentiated society cannot be adequately grasped by holistic concepts of society. The bankruptcy of state socialism now witnessed has once again confirmed that a modern, market-regulated economic system cannot be switched as one pleases, from a monetary mechanism to one involving administrative power and democratic decision making, without threatening its performance capacity. Additionally, our experiences with a social-welfare state being pushed to its limits have sensitized us to the phenomena of bureaucratization and intrusive legalism (*Verrechtlichung*).[28] These pathological effects are consequences of the state's interventions in spheres of activity structured in a manner that renders the legal-administrative mode of regulating them inappropriate.

(2)

The central topic of the second half of the book is the structural transformation, embedded in the integration of state and society, of the public sphere itself. The infrastructure of the public sphere has changed along with the forms of organization, marketing, and consumption of a professionalized book production that operates on a larger scale and is oriented to new strata of readers, and of a newspaper and periodical press whose contents have also not remained the same. It changed with the rise of the electronic mass media, the new relevance of advertising, the increasing fusion of entertainment and information, the greater centralization in all areas, the collapse of the liberal associational life, the collapse of surveyable public spheres on the community level, etc. It seems that these tendencies were assessed correctly, even if in the meantime more detailed investigations have been presented.[29] In conjunction with an ever more commercialized and increasingly dense network of communication, with the growing capital requirements and organizational scale of publishing enterprises, the channels of communication became more regulated, and the opportunities for access to public communication became subjected to ever greater selective pressure. Therewith emerged a new sort of influence, i.e., media power, which, used for purposes of manipulation, once and for all took care of the innocence of the principle of publicity. The public sphere, simultaneously prestructured and dominated by the mass media, developed into an arena infiltrated by power in which, by means of topic selection and topical contributions, a battle is fought not only over influence but over the control of communication flows that affect behavior while their strategic intentions are kept hidden as much as possible.

A realistic description and analysis of the power-infiltrated public sphere certainly prohibits the uncontrolled infusion of valuing points of view. Yet by the same token, it is too high a price to pay if, in exchange for such a prohibition, empirically important differences are paved over. Therefore, I introduced a distinction between, on the one hand, the critical functions of self-regulated, horizontally interlinked, inclusive, and more or less discourse-resembling communicative processes supported by weak institutions and, on the other hand, those functions that aim to influence the decisions of consumers, voters, and clients and are promoted by organizations intervening in a public sphere under the sway of mass media to mobilize purchasing power, loyalty, or conformist behavior. These *extractive* intrusions into a public sphere no longer perceived as anything else than an environment of one's own system of reference encounter a public communication whose spontaneous source of regeneration is to be found in the life-world.[30] This was the meaning of the thesis that "publicity operating under the conditions of a social-welfare state must conceive of itself as a self-generating process. Gradually it has to establish itself in competition with that other tendency which, within an immensely expanded public sphere, turns the principle of publicity against itself and thereby reduces its critical efficacy" (*Structural Transformation*, p. 233).

While on the whole I would stick to my descriptions of the changed infrastructure of a public sphere infiltrated by power, its analysis needs to be revised, especially my assessment of the changes in the public's behavior. In retrospect, I discern a number of reasons for the insufficiency of my interpretation: the sociology of voter behavior was only in its beginnings, in Germany at least. What I came to grips with at the time were my own first-hand experiences with the first election campaigns run along the lines of marketing strategies on the basis of opinion polls. I presume that the population of the German Democratic Republic has been similarly shocked by the campaigns of the West German parties currently invading its territory. Also, at the time television had barely made its start in the Federal Republic. I became acquainted with such sociology only years later in the United States; thus I was not able to check the literature with experiences of my own. Furthermore, the strong influence of Adorno's theory of mass culture is not difficult to discern. Additionally, the depressing results of the just-finished empirical investigation for *Student und Politik* may have contributed to an underestimation of the positive influence of formal schooling, especially of its expanding secondary level, on cultural mobilization and the promotion of critical attitudes.[31] It should be remembered, however, that the process later called the "educational revolution" by Parsons, had not yet started up in the Federal Republic. Finally there is the glaring absence of anything belonging to the dimension that by now has come to attract great attention under the label of "political culture." As late as 1963 Gabriel Almond and Sidney Verba had still attempted to capture the "civic culture" by means of a few attitudinal variables.[32] Even the more broadly conceived research on value change, initiated by Ronald Inglehart's *Silent Revolution* (Princeton 1977), did not yet extend to the entire spectrum of political mentalities that are firmly engrained in a culture and in which a mass public's repertory of responses is historically rooted.[33]

In fine, my diagnosis of a unilinear development from a politically active public to one withdrawn into a bad privacy, from a "culture-debating to a culture-consuming public," is too simplistic. At the time, I was too pessimistic about the resisting power and above all the critical potential of a pluralistic, internally much differentiated mass public whose cultural usages have begun to shake off the constraints of class. In conjunction

with the ambivalent relaxation of the distinction between high
and low culture, and the no less ambiguous "new intimacy
between culture and politics," which is more complex than a
mere assimilation of information to entertainment, the standards of evaluation themselves have also changed.

I cannot even begin to comment on the diversified literature
in the sociology of political behavior, since I have paid only
sporadic attention to it.[34] Just as relevant to the topic of the
structural transformation of the public sphere is the research
on the media,[35] especially the investigations in the sociology of
communication concerned with the social effects of television.[36]
At the time, I had to rely on the results of the research tradition
established by Lazarsfeld, which in the 1970s was heavily criticized for its individualist-behaviorist approach constrained by
the limitations of small-group psychology.[37] At the opposite
pole, the ideology-critical approach has been continued in a
more empirical vein.[38] It has directed the attention of communication researchers to the institutional context of the media, on the one hand,[39] and, on the other, to the cultural
context of their reception.[40] Stuart Hall's distinction between
three different interpretive strategies on the part of spectators
(who either submit to the structure of what is being offered,
take an oppositional stance, or synthesize it with their own
interpretations) illustrates well how the perspective has
changed from the older explanatory models still assuming linear causal processes.

(3)

In the last chapter of the book I had attempted to bring the
two strands together: the empirical diagnosis of the breakdown
of the liberal public sphere and the normative aspect of a
radical democratic vision that takes into account and turns to
its own purpose the functional intertwining of state and society
that objectively goes on above the heads, as it were, of the
participants. These two aspects are reflected in two diverging
conceptualizations of "public opinion." As a fictitious construct
of constitutional law, public opinion continues, in the normative theory of democracy, to be endowed with the unitariness

of a conterfactual entity. In the empirical investigations of media research and the sociology of communication this entity has long since been disassembled. However, both aspects must be kept in mind if one wants to grasp the mode in which the creation of legitimacy has actually come to operate in mass democracies constituted as social-welfare states, yet does not want to gloss over the distinction between genuine processes of public communication and those that have been subverted by power.

This intention provides the rationale for the provisional model, sketched at the end of the book, of a mass-media-dominated arena in which opposing tendencies clash. The degree of its infusion with power was supposed to be measured by the extent to which the informal, nonpublic opinions (i.e., those attitudes and assessments that are taken for granted within a culture and that make up the lifeworld constituting the context and ground of public communication) are not fed into the circuits of formal, quasi public opinion making by the mass media (which state and economy, considering them system environments, try to influence) or by the degree to which both realms are brought into conflict by means of a critical publicity. At the time, I could not imagine any other vehicle of critical publicity than internally democratized interest associations and parties. Intraparty and intra-associational public spheres appeared to me as the potential centers of a public communication still capable of being regenerated. This conclusion was derived from the trend toward an organization society in which it is no longer associated individuals but rather members of organized collectivities who, in a polycentric public sphere, compete for the assent of passive masses in order to achieve a balance of power and interests against each other and especially against the massive complex of state bureaucracies. As recently as the 1980s, Norberto Bobbio, for example, has proposed a theory of democracy based on the same premises.[41]

However, this model again ran up against that pluralism of irreconcilable interests that already moved the liberal theoreticians to object to the "tyranny of the majority." Tocqueville and John Stuart Mill were perhaps not so mistaken in their belief that the early liberal notion of a discursively accomplished formation of opinion and will was nothing but a veiled version of majority power. From the point of view of normative considerations, they were at most prepared to admit public opinion as a constraint on power, but in no way as a medium for the potential rationalization of power altogether. If "a structurally ineradicable antagonism of interests would set narrow boundaries for a public sphere reorganized . . . to fulfill its critical function" (*Structural Transformation,* p. 234), it would certainly be sufficient simply to charge liberal theory with an ambivalent conception of the public sphere, as I did in section 15 of *Structural Transformation.*

3 A Modified Theoretical Framework

In spite of the objections raised, I continue to stay with the intention that guided the study as a whole. The mass democracies constituted as social-welfare states, as far as their normative self-interpretation is concerned, can claim to continue the principles of the liberal constitutional state only as long as they seriously try to live up to the mandate of a public sphere that fulfills political functions. Accordingly, it is necessary to demonstrate how it may be possible, in our type of society, for "the public . . . to set in motion a *critical* process of public communication through the very organizations that mediatize it" (*Structural Transformation,* p. 232). This question drew me back, at the close of the book, to the problem on which I had touched but failed to address properly. The contribution of *Structural Transformation* to a contemporary theory of democracy had to come under a cloud if "the unresolved plurality of competing interests . . . makes it doubtful whether there can ever emerge a general interest of the kind to which a public opinion could refer as a criterion" (*Structural Transformation,* p. 234). On the basis of the theoretical means available to me at the time, I could not resolve this problem. Further advances were necessary to produce a theoretical framework within which I can now reformulate the questions and provide at least the outline of an answer. I want to recall, by way of a few brief remarks, the major way stations of this development.

(1)

Only to a superficial glance would it have appeared possible to write *Structural Transformation* along the lines of a developmental history of society in the style of Marx and Max Weber. The dialectic of the bourgeois public sphere, which determines the book's structure, wears the ideology-critical approach on its sleeve. The ideals of bourgeois humanism that have left their characteristic mark on the self-interpretation of the intimate sphere and the pubic and that are articulated in the key concepts of subjectivity and self-actualization, rational formation of opinion and will, and personal and political self-determination have infused the institutions of the constitutional state to such an extent that, functioning as a utopian potential, they point beyond a constitutional reality that negates them. The dynamic of historical development too was to be fueled by this tension between idea and reality.

Unfortunately, this thought makes it tempting to idealize the bourgeois public sphere in a manner going way beyond any methodologically legitimate idealization of the sort involved in ideal-typical conceptualization. But it is also propped up, at least implicitly, by background assumptions belonging to a philosophy of history that have been refuted by the civilized barbarisms of the twentieth century. When these bourgeois ideals are cashed in, when the consciousness turns cynical, the commitment to those norms and value orientations that the critique of ideology must presuppose for its appeal to find a hearing becomes defunct.[42] I suggested, therefore, that the normative foundations of the critical theory of society be laid at a deeper level.[43] The theory of communicative action intends to bring into the open the rational potential intrinsic in everyday communicative practices. Therewith it also prepares the way for a social science that proceeds reconstructively, identifies *the entire spectrum* of cultural and societal rationalization processes, and also traces them back beyond the threshold of modern societies. Such a tack no longer restricts the search for normative potentials to a formation of the public sphere that was specific to a single epoch.[44] It removes the necessity for stylizing particular prototypical manifestations of an institutionally embodied communicative rationality in favor of an empirical approach in which the tension of the abstract opposition between norm and reality is dissolved. Furthermore, unlike the classical assumptions of historical materialism, it brings to the fore the relative structural autonomy and internal history of cultural systems of interpretation.[45]

(2)

The perspective from which I inquired into the structural transformation of the public sphere was linked to a theory of democracy indebted to Abendroth's concept of a socialist democracy evolving out of the democratic, constitutional welfare state. In general, it remained captive of a notion that became questionable in the meantime, i.e., that society and its self-organization are to be considered a totality. The society that administers itself, that by means of a legal enactment of plans writes the program controlling all spheres of its life, including its economic reproduction, was to be integrated through the political will of the sovereign people. But the presumption that society as a whole can be conceived as an association writ large, directing itself via the media of law and political power, has become entirely implausible in view of the high level of complexity of functionally differentiated societies. The holistic notion of a societal totality in which the associated individuals participate like the members of an encompassing organization is particularly ill suited to provide access to the realities of an economic system regulated through markets and of an administrative system regulated through power. While in *Technik und Wissenschaft als "Ideologie"* (1968) I had still tried to differentiate between the action systems of state and economy on the level of a theory of action, proposing the predominance of purposive and rational (or success-oriented) action versus that of communicative action as a distinguishing criterion, this all-too-handy parallelization of action systems and action types produced some nonsensical results.[46] This caused me, in *Legitimation Crisis* (1973), to link the concept of lifeworld, introduced in *On the Logic of the Social Sciences* (1967), to that of the boundary maintaining system. From this emerged, in *The Theory of*

Communicative Action (1981), the two-tiered concept of society as lifeworld and as system.[47] The implications for my concept of democracy were considerable.

From that time on I have considered state apparatus and economy to be systemically integrated action fields that can no longer be transformed democratically from within, that is, be switched over to a political mode of integration, without damage to their proper systemic logic and therewith their ability to function. The abysmal collapse of state socialism has only confirmed this. Instead, radical democratization now aims for a shifting of forces within a "separation of powers" that itself is to be maintained in principle. The new equilibrium to be attained is not one between state powers but between different resources for societal integration. The goal is no longer to supersede an economic system having a capitalist life of its own and a system of domination having a bureaucratic life of its own but to erect a democratic dam against the colonializing *encroachment* of system imperatives on areas of the lifeworld. Therewith we have bid a farewell to the notion of alienation and appropriation of objectified essentialist powers, whose place is in a philosophy of praxis. A radical-democratic change in the process of legitimation aims at a new balance between the forces of societal integration so that the social-integrative power of solidarity—the "communicative force of production"[48]—can prevail over the powers of the other two control resources, i.e., money and administrative power, and therewith successfully assert the practically oriented demands of the lifeworld.

(3)

The social integrative power of communicative action is first of all located in those particularized forms of life and lifeworlds that are intertwined with concrete traditions and interest constellations in the "ethical" sphere ("*Sittlichkeit*"), to use Hegel's terms. But the solidarity-generating energies of these fabrics of life do not directly carry over into democratic procedures for the settling of competing interests and power claims on the political level. This is especially so in posttraditional societies in which a homogeneity of background convictions cannot be assumed and in which a presumptively shared class interest has given way to a confused pluralism of competing and equally legitimate forms of life. To be sure, the intersubjectivist formulation of a concept of solidarity that links the establishment of understandings (*Verständigung*) to validity claims that can be criticized, and therewith to the ability on the part of individuated subjects fully in a position to make up their own minds (*zurechnungsfähig*) to announce their disagreement (*Neinsagenkönnen*), already does away with the usual connotations of unity and wholeness. However, even in this abstract formulation the word "solidarity" must not suggest the false model of a formation of will à la Rousseau that was intended to establish the conditions under which the empirical wills of separate burghers could be transformed, *without any intermediary*, into the wills, open to reason and oriented toward the common good, of moral citizens of a state.

Rousseau based this expectation of virtuousness (illusory from the beginning) on a separation of the roles of "*bourgeois*" and "*citoyen*," which made economic independence and equality of opportunity a precondition of the status of autonomous citizen. The social-welfare state negates this role separation: "In the modern Western democracies this relationship has been severed. The democratic formation of the will has become instrumental to the promotion of social equality in the sense of maximizing the even distribution of the national product among the individuals."[49] Preuss justifiably underscores that nowadays the public role of the citizen and the private role of the client of the social-welfare state's bureaucracies are interlinked in the political process. "The mass democracy established as a social-welfare state [has] produced the paradoxical category of the 'societalized private person,' whom we commonly call 'client' and who becomes one with the role of citizen to the extent to which he becomes societally universal" (ibid., p. 48). Democratic universalism flips over into "generalized particularism."

In section 12 of *Structural Transformation* I criticized Rousseau's "democracy of nonpublic opinion" because he conceives of the general will as a "consensus of hearts rather than of arguments." The morality with which Rousseau demands the citizens to be imbued and that he places in the individuals' motives and virtues must instead be anchored in the process of public communication itself. The essential aspect here is pinpointed by B. Manin:

It is necessary to alter radically the perspective common to both liberal theories and democratic thought: the source of legitimacy is not the predetermined will of individuals, but rather the process of its formation, that is, deliberation itself. . . . A legitimate decision does not represent the will of all, but is one that results from the deliberation of all. It is the process by which everyone's will is formed that confers its legitimacy on the outcome, rather than the sum of already formed wills. The deliberative principle is both individualist and democratic. . . . We must affirm, at the risk of contradicting a long tradition, that legitimate law is the result of general deliberation, and not the expression of general will.[50]

Therewith the burden of proof shifts from the morality of citizens to the conduciveness of specific processes of the democratic formation of opinion and will, presumed to have the potential for generating rational outcomes, of actually leading to such results.

(4)

This is why "political public sphere" is appropriate as the quintessential concept denoting all those conditions of communication under which there can come into being a discursive formation of opinion and will on the part of a public composed of the citizens of a state. This is why it is suitable as the fundamental concept of a theory of democracy whose intent is normative. In this sense Jean Cohen defines the concept of deliberative democracy as follows: "The notion of a deliberative democracy is rooted in the intuitive ideal of a democrative association in which the justification of the terms and conditions of association proceeds through public argument and reasoning among equal citizens. Citizens in such an order share a commitment to the resolution of problems of collective choice through public reasoning, and regard their basic institutions as legitimate insofar as they establish a framework for free public deliberation."[51] This discourse-centered concept of democracy places its faith in the political mobilization and utilization of the communicative force of production. Yet, consequently, it has to be shown that social issues liable to generate conflicts are open to rational regulation, that is, regulation in the common interest of all parties involved. Additionally, it must be explained why engaging in public arguments and negotiations is the appropriate medium for this rational formation of will. Otherwise, the premise of the liberal model would be justified, that the only way in which irreconcilably conflicting interests can be "brought to terms" is through a strategically conducted struggle.

In the last two decades John Rawls, Ronald Dworkin, Bruce Ackermann, Paul Lorenzen, and K.-O. Apel have contributed arguments intended to clarify how practical-political questions, insofar as they are of a moral nature, can be decided rationally. These authors have made explicit the "moral point of view" that permits an impartial assessment of what, in a particular case, is in the general interest. Regardless of how they have formulated and justified their universalizing principles and moral axioms, this much seems to have become clear in this wide-ranging discussion: there are solid reasons available that can provide a foundation for a universalization of interests and for an appropriate application of norms embodying such general interests.[52] Beyond that, with K.-O. Apel,[53] I developed a discourse-centered approach to ethics that views the exchange of arguments and counter-arguments as the most suitable procedure for resolving moral-practical questions.[54] Therewith the second of the two above-mentioned questions receives an answer. The discourse-centered approach to ethics does not limit itself to the claim that it can derive a general principle of morality from the normative content of the indispensable pragmatic preconditions of all rational debate. Rather, this principle itself refers to the discursive redemption of normative validity claims, for it anchors the validity of norms in the possibility of a rationally founded agreement on the part of all those who might be affected, insofar as they take on *the role of participants in a rational debate*. In this view, then, the settling of political questions, as far as their moral core is concerned, depends on the institutionalization of practices of rational public debate.

Of course, although issues of political principle almost always also have a moral dimension, by no means all questions institutionally defined as part of the bailiwick of political decision makers are of a moral nature. Political controversies frequently concern empirical questions, the interpretation of states of affairs, explanations, prognoses, etc. Also, certain problems of great significance, so-called existential issues, often concern not questions of justice but, as questions concerning the good life, have to do with ethical-political self-image, be it of a whole society, be it of some subcultures. After all, the majority of conflicts have their sources in the collision of group interests and concern distributive problems that can be resolved only by means of compromises. Yet this differentiation within the field of issues that require political decisions negates neither the prime importance of moral considerations nor the practicability of rational debate as the very form of political communication. Empirical and evaluative questions are frequently inseparable and evidently cannot be dealt with without reliance on arguments.[55] The ethical-political process of coming to an understanding about how, as members of a particular collectivity, we want to live must at least not be at odds with moral norms. Negotiations must rely on the exchange of arguments, and whether they lead to compromises that are *fair* depends essentially on procedural conditions subject to moral judgment.

The discourse-centered theoretical approach has the advantage of being able to specify the preconditions for communication that have to be fulfilled in the various forms of rational debate and in negotiations if the results of such discourses are to be presumed to be rational. Therewith this approach opens up the possibility of linking normative considerations to empirical sociological ones.

(5)

Since the discourse-centered concept of democracy first of all has to be clarified and made plausible within the framework of a normative theory, the question remains of how, under the conditions of mass democracies constituted as social-welfare states, a discursive formation of opinion and will can be institutionalized in such a fashion that it becomes possible to bridge the gap between enlightened self-interest and orientation to the common good, between the roles of client and citizen. Indeed, an element intrinsic to the preconditions of communication of all practices of rational debate is the presumption of impartiality and the expectation that the participants question and transcend whatever their initial preferences may have been. Meeting these two preconditions must even become a matter of routine. Modern natural law's way of coming to terms with this problem was the introduction of legitimate legal coercion. And the subsequent problem entailed by this solution, how the political power required for the coercive imposition of law could itself be morally controlled, was met by Kant's idea of a state subject to the rule of law. Within a discourse-centered theoretical approach, this idea is carried further to give rise to the notions that additionally the law is applied to itself: it must also guarantee the discursive mode by means of which generation and application of legislative programs are to proceed within the parameters of rational debate. This implies the institutionalization of legal procedures that guarantee an approximate fulfillment of the demanding preconditions of communication required for fair negotiations and free debates. These idealizing preconditions demand the complete inclusion of all parties that might be affected, their equality, free and easy interaction, no restrictions of topics and topical contributions, the possibility of revising the outcomes, etc. In this context the legal procedures serve to uphold within an empirically existing community of communication the spatial, temporal, and substantive constraints on choices that are operative within a presumed ideal one.[56]

For instance, the rule to abide by majority decisions can be interpreted as an arrangement squaring a formation of opinion that seeks truth and is as discursive as circumstances permit with the temporal constraints to which the formation of will is subject. Within a discourse-centered theoretical approach, decision by majority must remain internally related to a practice of rational debate, which entails further institutional arrangements (such as the requirement to state one's reasons, rules allotting the burden of proof, repeated readings of legislative proposals, etc.). A majority decision must be arrived at in such a fashion, and only in such a fashion, that its content can be claimed to be the rationally motivated but fallible result of a discussion concerning the judicious resolution of a problem, a discussion that has come temporarily to a close because coming to a decision could no longer be postponed. Other institutions too may be interpreted from this same perspective of a legal institutionalization of the general conditions of communication for a discursive formation of will, as, for example, the regulations concerning the composition and mode of operation of parliamentary bodies, the responsibilities and immunities of elected representatives, the political pluralism of a multiparty system, the necessity for broad-based parties to package their programs so that they appeal to various interest constellations, etc.

The deciphering of the normative meaning of existing institutions within a discourse-centered theoretical approach additionally supplies a perspective on the introduction and testing of *novel* institutional arrangements that might counteract the trend toward the transmutation of citizens into clients. These must reinforce the gradation between the two roles by interrupting the short circuit that abandons the field to the play of immediate personal preferences and the generalized particularism of interests organized in special-interest associations. The novel idea of connecting the vote to a "multiple preference ordering" is a case in point.[57] Such suggestions must be based on an analysis of the inhibiting factors at work in the existing arrangements that condition citizens to an unpolitical follower mentality and prevent them from reflecting and being concerned with anything but their own short-term personal interests. In other words, the unlocking of the democratic meaning of the constitutional state's institutions within a discourse-centered theoretical approach must be supplemented with the critical investigation of the mechanisms that in democracies constituted as social-welfare states function to alienate citizens from the political process.[58]

(6)

To be sure, the normative content of a concept of democracy that refers to processes of norm and value formation taking the form of discursive public communications is not restricted to appropriate institutional arrangements at the level of the democratic constitutional state. Rather, it pushes beyond formally instituted processes of communication and decision making. Corporatively organized opinion formation resulting in responsible decision making can serve the goal of a cooperative search for truth only to the extent to which it remains *permeable* to the free-floating values, topics, topical contributions, and arguments of the *surrounding* political communication. Such opinion formation must be facilitated by the constitution, but it cannot be formally organized in its entirety. Instead, the expectation deriving from a discourse-centered theoretical approach, that rational results will obtain, is based on the interplay between a constitutionally instituted formation of the political will and the spontaneous flow of communication unsubverted by power, within a public sphere that is not geared toward decision making but toward discovery and problem resolution and that in this sense is *nonorganized*. If there still is to be a realistic application of the idea of the sovereignty of the people to highly complex societies, it must be uncoupled from the concrete understanding of its embodiment in physically present, participating, and jointly deciding members of a collectivity.

There may actually be circumstances under which a direct widening of the formal opportunities for participation and involvement in decision making only intensifies "generalized particularism," that is, the privileged assertion of local and group-specific special interests that, from Burke to Weber, Schumpeter, and today's neoconservatives, has provided the arguments of a democratic elitism. This can be prevented by procedurally viewing the sovereignty of the people as comprising the essential conditions that enable processes of public communication to take the form of discourse. The one remaining "embodiment" of the altogether dispersed sovereignty of the people is in those rather demanding forms of subjectless

communication that regulate the flow of the formation of political opinion and will so as to endow their fallible results with
the presumption of practical rationality.[59] This sovereignty
turned into a flow of communication comes to the fore in the
power of public discourses that uncover topics of relevance to
all of society, interpret values, contribute to the resolution of
problems, generate good reasons, and debunk bad ones. Of
course, these opinions must be given shape in the form of
decisions by democratically constituted decision-making bodies.
The responsibility for practically consequential decisions must
be based in an institution. Discourses do not govern. They
generate a communicative power that cannot take the place of
administration but can only influence it. This influence is limited to the procurement and withdrawal of legitimation. Communicative power cannot supply a substitute for the systematic
inner logic of public bureaucracies. Rather, it achieves an impact on this logic "in a siegelike manner." If the sovereignty of
the people is in this fashion dissolved into procedures and
attempts, the symbolic place of power—a vacuum since 1789,
that is, since the revolutionary abolishment of paternalistic
forms of domination—also remains empty and is not filled with
new identity-conveying symbolizations, like people or nations,
as Rödel, following Claude Lefort, would have it.[60]

4 Civil Society or Political Public Sphere

Having thus changed my premises and upgraded their precision, I can finally return to the task of describing a political
public sphere characterized by at least two crosscutting processes: the communicative generation of legitimate power on
the one hand and the manipulative deployment of media
power to procure mass loyalty, consumer demand, and "compliance" with systemic imperatives on the other. The question
that had been left pending concerning the basis and sources
of an informal formation of opinion in autonomous public
spheres now can no longer be answered with reference to the
status guarantees of the social-welfare state and with the holistic
demand for the political self-organization of society. Rather,
this is the place where the circle closes between the structural

transformation of the public sphere and those long-term trends that the theory of communicative action conceives as a *rationalization of the lifeworld*. A public sphere that functions politically requires more than the institutional guarantees of the constitutional state; it also needs the supportive spirit of cultural traditions and patterns of socialization, of the political culture, of a populace accustomed to freedom.

The central question in *Structural Transformation* is nowadays discussed under the rubric of the "rediscovery of civil society." The global reference to a "supportive" spirit of differentially organized lifeworlds and their potential for critical reflection is not sufficient. It must be made more concrete, and not only with regard to patterns of socialization and to cultural traditions. A liberal political culture rooted in motives and value orientations certainly provides a favorable soil for spontaneous public communications. But the forms of interchange and organization, the institutionalizations of support of a political public sphere unsubverted by power, are even more important. Here is the point of departure for Claus Offe's most recent analyses. Offe uses the concept of "relations of association," intending "to confront the global categories of lifeworld and form of life that are to provide the discourse ethic with an anchorage in the social realm, with rather more sociological categories."[61] The vague concept "relations of association" is not by accident reminiscent of the "associational life" that at one time constituted the social stratum of the bourgeois public sphere. It also recalls the now current meaning of the term "civil society," which no longer includes a sphere of an economy regulated via labor, capital, and commodity markets and thus differs from the modern translation, common since Hegel and Marx, of "*societas civilis*" as "bourgeois society" ("*bürgerliche Gesellschaft*"). Unfortunately, a search for clear definitions in the relevant publications is in vain. However, this much is apparent: the institutional core of "civil society" is constituted by voluntary unions outside the realm of the state and the economy and ranging (to give some examples in no particular order) from churches, cultural associations, and academies to independent media, sport and leisure clubs, debating societies, groups of concerned citizens, and grass-roots petitioning drives all the way to occupational associations, political parties, labor unions, and "alternative institutions."

John Keane attributes to these associations the following task or function: "to maintain and to redefine the boundaries between civil society and state through two interdependent and simultaneous processes: the expansion of social equality and liberty, and the restructuring and democratization of the state."[62] In other words, he refers to opinion-forming associations. Unlike the political parties, which to a large extent have become fused with the state, they are not part of the administrative system but manage to have a political impact via the public media because they either participate directly in public communications or, as in the case of projects advocating alternatives to conventional wisdom, because the programmatic character of their activities sets examples through which they implicitly contribute to public discussion.

Similarly, Offe endows the relations of associations with the function of establishing contexts conducive to a political communication that, through sufficiently convincing arguments, readies citizens to engage in "responsible behavior": "To behave responsibly means for the actor to adopt toward his own actions, in the *futurum exactum*, the evaluative perspectives of the expert, the generalized other, and his own self all at once, thus subjecting the criteria governing the behavior to functional, social, and temporal validation."[63]

The concept of civil society owes its rise in favor to the criticism leveled, especially by dissidents from state-socialist societies, against the totalitarian annihilation of the political public sphere.[64] Here Hannah Arendt's concept of totalitarianism, with its focus on communication, plays an important role. It provides the foil that makes it understandable why the opinion-shaping associations, around which autonomous public spheres can be built up, occupy such a prominent place in the civil society. It is precisely this communicative praxis on the part of citizens that, in totalitarian regimes, is subjected to the control of the secret police. The revolutionary changes in eastern and central Europe have confirmed these analyses. Not coincidentally, they were triggered by reform policies initiated under the banner of *glasnost*. As if a large-scale experiment in social science had been set up, the apparatus of domination was overthrown by the increasing pressure of peacefully proceeding citizen movements; the German Democratic Republic is the primary case in point. In a first step, out of these citizen movements grew the infrastructure of a new order, whose outline had already become visible in the ruins of state socialism. The pacesetters of this revolution were voluntary associations in the churches, the human rights groups, the oppositional circles pursuing ecological and feminist goals, against whose latent influence the totalitarian public sphere could from the beginning be stabilized only through reliance on force.

The situation is different in Western-type societies. Here voluntary associations are established within the institutional framework of the democratic constitutional state. And here a different question arises, one that cannot be answered without considerable empirical research. This is the question of whether, and to what extent, a public sphere dominated by mass media provides a realistic chance for the members of civil society, in their competition with the political and economic invaders' media power, to bring about changes in the spectrum of values, topics, and reasons channeled by external influences, to open it up in an innovative way, and to screen it critically. It seems to me that the concept of a public sphere operative in the political realm, as I developed it in *Structural Transformation,* still provides the appropriate analytical perspective for the treatment of this problem. This is why Andrew Arato and Jean Cohen, in their attempt to make the concept of civil society fruitful for an up-to-date theory of democracy, adopt the architecture of "system and lifeworld" as it was proposed in *The Theory of Communicative Action.*[65]

I conclude with the reference to an inventive study dealing with the impact of electronic media on the restructuring of basic interactions. Its title, *No Sense of Place,* stands for the claim of the dissolution of those structures within which individuals living in society have hitherto perceived their social positions and have placed themselves. Now even those social boundaries that defined the lifeworld's coordinates of space and historical time have begun to move:

Many of the features of our "information age" make us resemble the most primitive of social and political forms: the hunting and gathering society. As nomadic peoples, hunters and gatherers have no loyal relationship to territory. They, too, have little "sense of place"; specific activities are not totally fixed to specific physical settings. The lack of boundaries both in hunting and gathering and in electronic societies leads to many striking parallels. Of all known societal types before our own, hunting and gathering societies have tended to be the most egalitarian in terms of the roles of males and females, children and adults, and leaders and followers. The difficulty of maintaining many separate places or distinct social spheres tends to involve everyone in everyone else's business.[66]

An unforeseen confirmation of this somewhat overblown thesis is again provided by the revolutionary events of 1989. The transformation occurring in the German Democratic Republic, in Czechoslovakia, and in Romania formed a chain of events properly considered not merely as a historical process that happened to be shown on television but one whose very *mode of occurrence* was televisional. The mass media's worldwide diffusion had not only a decisive infectious effect. In contrast to the nineteenth and early twentieth centuries, the physical presence of the masses demonstrating in the squares and streets was able to generate revolutionary power only to the degree to which television made its presence ubiquitous.

With regard to the normal conditions of Western societies, Joshua Meyrowitz's thesis that the mass media induced the dismantling of socially defined boundaries is too linear. There are obvious objections. The dedifferentiation and destructuring affecting our lifeworld as a result of the electronically produced omnipresence of events and of the synchronization of heterochronologies certainly have a considerable impact on social self-perception. This removal of barriers, however, goes hand in hand with a multiplication of roles becoming specified in the process, with a pluralization of forms of life, and with an individualization of life plans. Deracination is accompanied by the construction of personal communal allegiances and roots, the leveling of differences by impotence in the face of an impenetrable systemic complexity. These are complementary and interlocking developments. Thus the mass media have contradictory effects in other dimensions as well. There is considerable evidence attesting to the ambivalent nature of the democratic potential of a public sphere whose infrastructure is marked by the growing selective constraints imposed by electronic mass communication.

Thus if today I made another attempt to analyze the structural transformation of the public sphere, I am not sure what its outcome would be for a theory of democracy—maybe one that could give cause for a less pessimistic assessment and for an outlook going beyond the formulation of merely defiant postulates.

Notes

1. The question of a new printing has arisen for rather extrinsic reasons. The sale of the Luchterhand-Verlag, to which I am much obliged for the promotion of my early books, necessitated a change of publishers. At the same time, this edition by the Reclam-Verlag in Leipzig represents the first publication of any of my books in the German Democratic Republic.

2. J. Habermas, *Die nachholende Revolution* (Frankfurt, 1990).

3. *The Structural Transformation of the Public Sphere* (Cambridge: MIT Press, 1989).

4. This provided the occasion for a conference at the University of North Carolina at Chapel Hill in September 1989. In addition to sociologists, political scientists, and philosophers, there were participants from the disciplines of history, literature, communication, and anthropology. I found the meeting extraordinarily instructive, and I am grateful to the participants for suggestions.

5. W. Jäger, *Öffentlichkeit und Parlamentarismus: Eine Kritik an Jürgen Habermas* (Stuttgart, 1973). For a listing of reviews, see R. Görtzen, *J. Habermas: Eine Bibliographie seiner Schriften und der Sekundärliteratur, 1952–1981* (Frankfurt, 1981).

6. G. Eley, "Nations, Publics, and Political Cultures: Placing Habermas in the Nineteenth Century" (manuscript, 1989).

7. H. U. Wehler, *Deutsche Gesellschaftsgeschichte*, vol. 1 (Munich, 1987), pp. 303–331.

8. R. v. Dülmen, *Die Gesellschaft der Aufklärer* (Frankfurt, 1986).

9. K. Eder, *Geschichte als Lernprozeß* (Frankfurt, 1985), pp. 123 ff.

10. For France, see the contributions by Etienne François, Jack Censer, and Pierre Rétat in R. Koselleck and R. Reichardt, *Die französiche Revolution als Bruch des gesellschaftlichen Bewußtseins* (Munich, 1988), pp. 117 ff.

11. H. U. Wehler, *Deutsche Gesellschaftsgeschichte*, vol. 2, pp. 520–546.

12. P. U. Hohendahl, *Building a National Literature: The Case of Germany, 1530–1870* (Ithaca: Cornell University Press, 1989), especially chapters 2 and 3.

13. Patricia Hollis, ed., *Pressure from Without* (London, 1974).

14. J. H. Plumb, "The Public, Literature, and the Arts in the Eighteenth Century," in M. R. Marrus, ed., *The Emergence of Leisure* (New York, 1974).

15. R. Williams, *The Long Revolution* (London, 1961); R. Williams, *Communications* (London, 1962).

16. E. Thompson, *The Making of the English Working Class* (London, 1963).

17. G. Lottes, *Politische Aufklärung und plebejisches Publikum* (Munich, 1979), p. 110. See also O. Negt and A. Kluge, *Erfahrung und Öffentlichkeit. Zur Organisationsanalyse bürgerlicher und proletarischer Öffentlichkeit* (Frankfurt, 1972).

18. R. Sennett, *The Fall of Public Man* (New York, 1977).

19. N. Z. Davis, *Humanismus, Narrenherrschaft und Riten der Gewalt* (Frankfurt, 1987), especially chapter 4. On traditions of countercultural festivals going way back before the Renaissance, see J. Heers, *Vom Mummenschanz zum Machttheater* (Frankfurt, 1986).

20. C. Hall, "Private Persons versus Public Someones: Class, Gender, and Politics in England, 1780–1850," in C. Steedman, C. Urwin, V. Walkerdine, eds., *Language, Gender, and Childhood* (London, 1985), pp. 10 ff.; J. B. Landes, *Women and the Public Sphere in the Age of the French Revolution* (Ithaca, 1988).

21. C. Pateman, "The Fraternal Social Contract," in J. Keane, ed., *Civil Society and the State* (London, 1988), p. 105. The same point is made by A. W. Gouldner, *The Dialectic of Ideology and Technology* (New York, 1976), p. 103: "The integration of the patriarchical family system with a system of private property was the fundamental grounding of the private; a sphere that did not routinely have to give an accounting of itself, by providing either information about its conduct or judification for it. Private property and patriarchy were thus indirectly the grounding for the public."

22. E. W. Böckenförde, "Die Bedeutung der Unterscheidung von Staat und Gesellschaft im demokratischen Sozialstaat der Gegenwart," trans. in E. W. Böckenförde, *State, Society and Liberty: Studies in Political Theory and Constitutional Law* (New York: St. Martin's Press, 1991).

23. D. Grimm, *Recht un Staat der bürgerlichen Gesellschaft* (Frankfurt, 1987).

24. J. Habermas, "Die klassische Lehre von der Politik in ihrem Verhältnis zur Sozialphilosophie," also "Naturrecht und Revolution," both trans. in J. Habermas, *Theory and Practice*, trans. John Viertel (Boston: Beacon Press, 1973). In addition, see J. Keane, "Despotism and Democracy: The Origins and Development of the Distinction between Civil Society and the State, 1750–1850," in Keane, *Civil Society and the State*, pp. 35 ff.

25. E. Forsthoff, ed., *Rechtsstaatlichkeit und Sozialstaatlichkeit* (Darmstadt, 1968).

26. E. Forsthoff, "Begriff und Wesen des sozialen Rechtsstaates"; E. R. Huber, "Rechtsstaat und Sozialstaat in der modernen Industriegesellschaft"; both contained in Forsthoff, *Rechtsstaatlichkeit und Sozialstaatlichkeit*, pp. 165 ff. and 589 ff.

27. W. Abendroth, "Zum Begriff des demokratischen und sozialen Rechtsstaates," in Forsthoff *Rechtsstaatlichkeit und Sozialstaatlichkeit*, pp. 123 ff.

28. F. Kübler, ed., *Verrechtlichung von Wirtschaft, Arbeit und sozialer Solidarität* (Baden-Baden, 1984); J. Habermas, "Law and Morality," in *The Tanner Lectures on Human Values*, vol. 8 (Salt Lake City and Cambridge, 1988), pp. 217–280.

29. R. Williams, *Television: Technology and Cultural Form* (London, 1974); R. Williams, *Keywords: A Vocabulary of Culture and Society* (London, 1983); D. Prokop, ed., *Medienforschung*, vol. 1, *Konzerne, Macher, Kontrolleure* (Frankfurt, 1985).

30. See W. R. Langenbucher, ed., *Zur Theorie der politischen Kommunikation* (Munich, 1974).

31. J. Habermas, L. v. Friedeburg, C. Öler, and F. Weltz, *Student und Politik* (Neuwied, 1961).

32. *The Civic Culture: Political Attitudes and Democracy in Five Nations* (Princeton, 1963). Also see G. Almond, S. Veba, eds., *The Civic Culture Revisited* (Boston, 1980).

33. See, however, R. N. Bellah et al., *Habits of the Heart* (Berkeley, 1985).

34. See, for example, S. H. Barnes, Max Kaase, eds., *Political Action: Mass Participation in Five Western Democracies* (Beverly Hills, 1979).

35. See the anniversary issue "Ferment in the Field," *Journal of Communication* 33 (1983). For this reference my thanks go to Rolf Megersohn, who himself has been active for decades in the fields of the sociology of mass media and of mass culture.

36. A summary of results is provided by J. T. Klapper, *The Effects of Mass Communication* (Glencoe, 1960).

37. T. Gitlin, "Media Sociology: The Dominant Paradigm," *Theory and Society* 6 (1978): 205–253. For a response, see the rebuttal by E. Katz, "Communication Research since Lazarsfeld," *Public Opinion Quarterly*, Winter 1987, 25–45.

38. C. Lodziak, *The Power of Television* (London, 1986).

39. T. Gitlin, *The Whole World is Watching* (Berkeley, 1983); H. Gans, *Deciding What's News* (New York, 1979). A survey is provided by G. Tuckmann, "Mass Media Institutions," in N. Smelser, ed., *Handbook of Sociology* (New York, 1988), pp. 601–625. Instructive from the point of view of society as a whole is C. Calhoun, "Populist Politics, Communications Media, and Large Scale Societal Integration," *Social Theory* 6 (1988): 219–241.

40. S. Hall, "Encoding and Decoding in the TV-Discourse," in S. Hall, ed., *Culture, Media, Language* (London, 1980), pp. 128–138; D. Morley, *Family Television* (London, 1988).

41. N. Bobbio, *The Future of Democracy* (Oxford, 1987).

42. For a critique of Marx's concept of ideology, see J. Keane, *Democracy and Civil Society: On the Predicaments of European Socialism* (London, 1988), pp. 213 ff.

43. S. Benhabib, *Critique, Norm, and Utopia* (New York, 1987).

44. J. Habermas, *Theory of Communicative Action*, vol. 2, *Lifeworld and System: A Critique of Functionalist Reason*, trans. T. McCarthy (Boston: Beacon Press, 1989).

45. J. Habermas, "Historischer Materialismus und die Entwicklung normativer Strukturen," in J. Habermas, *Zur Rekonstruktion des Historischen Materialismus* (Frankfurt, 1976), pp. 9–48.

46. A. Honneth, *Kritik der Macht* (Frankfurt, 1985), pp. 265 ff.

47. See my Reply to objections in A. Honneth and H. Joas, eds., *Kommunikatives Handeln* (Frankfurt, 1986), 377 ff.

48. See my interview with H. P. Krüger in J. Habermas, *Die nacholende Revolution*, pp. 82 ff.

49. U. Preusss, "Was heißt radikale Demokratie heute?" in Forum für Philosophie, ed., *Die Ideen von 1789* (Frankfurt, 1989), pp. 47–67.

50. B. Manin, "On Legitimacy and Political Deliberation," *Political Theory* 15 (1987): 351 ff. Manin's explicit reference is not to *Structural Transformation* but to "Legitimationsprobleme" (see note 36, p. 367).

51. J. Cohen, "Deliberation and Democratic Legitimacy," in A Hamlin, P. Pettit, eds., *The Good Polity* (Oxford, 1989), pp. 12–24. Cohen too refers not to *Structural Transformation* but to three of my later publications (in English) (see note 13, p. 33).

52. K. Günther, *Der Sinn für Angemessenheit* (Frankfurt, 1987).

53. See K.-O. Apel, *Diskurs und Verantwortung* (Frankfurt, 1988).

54. J. Habermas, *Legitimation Crisis*, trans. T. McCarthy (Boston: Beacon Press, 1975); J. Habermas, *Moral Consciousness and Communicative Action* (Cambridge: MIT Press, 1990).

55. J. Habermas, "Towards a Communication Concept of Rational Collective Will-Formation," *Ratio Juris* 2 (1989): 144–154.

56. See my "Law and Morality," pp. 246 ff.

57. The paraphrase is based on R. E. Goodin, "Laundering Preferences," in J. Elster and A. Hylland, eds., *Foundations of Social Science Theory* (Cambridge, 1986), pp. 75–101. C. Offe develops this consideration in his ingenious essay "Bindung, Fessel, Bremse: Die Unübersichtlichkeit von Selbstbeschräkungsformeln," in A. Honneth, T. McCarthy, C. Offe, A. Wellmer, *Zwischenbetrachtungen* (Frankfurt, 1989), pp. 739–775.

58. C. Offe and U. K. Preuss, "Can Democratic Institutions Make Efficient Use of Moral Resources?" manuscript.

59. J. Habermas, "Volkssouveränität als Verfahren: Ein normativer Begriff der Öffentlichkeit?" in *Die Ideen von 1789* (1989), pp. 7–36.

60. U. Rödel, G. Frankenberg, and H. Dubiel, *Die demokratische Frage* (Frankfurt, 1989), chapter 4.

61. Offe, in Honneth et al., *Zwischenbetrachtungen*, p. 755.

62. Keane, *Democracy and Civil Society* (1988), p. 14.

63. C. Offe, in Honneth et al. *Zwischenbetrachtungen,* p. 758.

64. See the contributions by J. Rupnik, M. Vajda, and Z. A. Pelczynski in Keane, ed., *Civil Society and the State* (1988), part 3.

65. A. Arato and J. Cohen, "Civil Society and Social Theory," *Thesis Eleven,* no. 21 (1988), pp. 40–67; Arato and Cohen, "Politics and the Reconstruction of the Concept of Civil Society," in Honneth et al., *Zwischenbetrachtungen,* pp. 482–503.

66. J. Meyrowitz, *No Sense of Place* (Oxford, 1985).

18

Concluding Remarks

Jürgen Habermas: I'm pleased, of course, by the strange fact that a book that I started to write more than thirty years ago is still able to stimulate serious academic discussion. I was the last to expect that. I particularly appreciate the gentle style and face-to-face kindness, including Fredric Jameson's jokes, that provided the context for several boring but necessary premises. I also am impressed with the talent of Craig Calhoun in bringing together more than a dozen colleagues from many different fields who are, nonetheless, able to speak at least similar languages, so that convergent lines of discussion emerge from a thoughtful diversity of approaches. I admire, moreover, the quality of the presentations, including those of some commentators who clearly exposed the topics of the speakers and transformed their thoughts into something of their own.

Rather than give an overall comment, I would like to confine myself to the limited role of a highly selective listener and mention some of the problems and several aspects that will provide me with starting points for a renewal of interest in research that I set aside for several decades.

The book was criticized when it appeared in Germany for confusing descriptive and normative aspects. The concept of the public sphere, *Öffentlichkeit,* is meant as an analytical tool for ordering certain phenomena and placing them in a particular context as part of a categorical frame. This concept also

Condensed and edited by Craig Calhoun, Leah Florence, and Rekha Mirchandani.

has inevitable normative implications, of course, and is related (and this is the confusing part) to certain positions in normative political theory. These are connotations that link the historical analysis with our value-laden and future-oriented enterprise of making some sort of diagnosis of our present situation, particularly for those who are still committed to the project of radical democracy.

This uneasy tension was one of the implications of Michael Schudson's careful analysis of certain trends in the American case. In response, Moishe Postone correctly restated the original intention of the book, which I now see more clearly than at the time. *Structural Transformation* moved totally within the circle of a classical Marxian critique of ideology, at least as it was understood in the Frankfurt environment. What I meant to do was to take the liberal limitations of public opinion, publicity, the public sphere, and so on, at their worst, and then try to confront these ideas of publicness with their selective embodiments and even the change of their very meaning during the process of transformation from liberal to organized capitalism, as I described it at that time. But even within this model, I can rightly be accused of having idealized what were presented as features of an existing liberal public sphere; I was at least not careful enough in distinguishing between an ideal type and the very context from which it was constructed. And I think it was due to this slight idealization that the collapsing of norm and description came into this book.

But the real problem is, I think, something else. Let me put it in the form of a question: Is the form or frame of ideology critique in need of revision? I have convinced myself that at least some presuppositions are no longer viable, at least insofar as ideology critique was linked to background assumptions that were still somehow relying on some kind of a materialist philosophy of history. I have been criticized for trying to separate several levels of analysis and of being a bit naive at each of these levels—naive insofar as I tried to keep up with established discourses as I found them. So on one level, through speech-act theory, I just wanted to get hold, independently of some sort of philosophy of history, of a notion of rationality that does have certain normative implications. But once you fix any normative implication in terms of implications of a notion of rationality, it is not *just* a value choice. Nor is it just a reference to norms that can be found in the self-understanding of some people, norms that you can then leaf back through and say, "Oh, it's they who maintain them."

Now on the second level, moral and legal theory are still clearly normative enterprises. Only the next step, institutional analysis of a more conventional sociological type (in a reformulated way), proceeds on an empirical level. And then the next step, historical analysis, comes in, particularly historical analysis of informal settings. The schedule of this conference even shows that these levels are now inhabited by totally different people—I mean people moving in different academic universes. And yet we can still talk to each other. The real problem is that even if we leave this frame of ideology critique and try somehow to split it up into more inconspicuous bunches of analyses, there may linger in the background the danger of an overintegrative approach. So that is a challenge to social theory, especially social theory in the Marxian tradition, which I've quite fiercely decided to defend as a still-meaningful enterprise.

The book has also been criticized for its Marxist or economic approach. I'm referring to the discussions by David Zaret and Lloyd Kramer. I learned a lot from these and other presentations as far as the necessity of taking into consideration cultural factors like science, like the interaction of elitist and popular cultures (popular culture even as early as seventeenth-century English Protestantism) is concerned. But I think that I have in the meantime also changed my own framework so that the permanent autonomy of cultural developments is taken more accurately into account. Simply, I have incorporated a bit more of Max Weber and of changes in religious thought, moral belief systems, the impact of the authority of science in secularized, everyday practices, even as pacesetters of social change. So I'm more open today to integrating some of the evidence of more recent anthropological approaches in history.

Let me mention one reservation. I think that a public sphere, in the sense in which I've tried to define it, only arose with the transformation of the split between high culture and popular culture that has been characteristic of premodern societies. A convenient or, in that sense, popular public sphere emerged only in competition with the literary public sphere of the late eighteenth century; it can already by observed in late-eighteenth-century France during the revolution. I have some doubts about how far we can push back the very notion of the public sphere into the sixteenth and seventeenth centuries without somehow changing the very concept of the public sphere to such a degree that it becomes something else.

The problem raised by the well-taken objections of historians is whether the format or size of the theoretical frame of historical analysis is not too extensive. With reference to Keith Baker's fascinating presentation, I think the question is whether constructing public opinion as a rhetorical device (this is, of course, how many of you now look at history) is not at least accompanied by the danger of an overculturalized view of history, where the hard facts of institutions or economic imperatives and of social and political struggles are then too easily assimilated into fights over symbolic meanings. Although I'm one of the first proponents of that view (I'm sorry to keep referring to myself; it's a narcissistic situation into which you have led me), I was one of the first to stand against the then dominating empiricist approaches. I argued that for all sociologists, and historians as well, the objective domain is constituted by a symbolically prestructured objectification. Today there is a different jargon, but I don't see that it has any different meaning from what we said in the more hermeneutically laden language of the early sixties. Nevertheless, that doesn't mean that everything is just the product of some sort of interpretational achievement of those who are somehow embedded in linguistic or other symbolic structures.

I found highly stimulating Michael Warner's talk on dialectics of identification and self-alienation in terms of the bodily aspects of self-representation in the public sphere. One can learn from this really refreshing new view, but one has to see, as Tom McCarthy suggested, that these are false questions. There is no longer any attempt to link such an analysis with any remnants of a normative political theory. This is okay, but one has to distinguish what one is doing. This type of analysis, as far as I understand it (I know you are going to hit me), is part of a social psychological approach to some sort of analysis of an expressivist, somehow aesthetic, need for self-representation in public space. I don't think this can lead back to a theory of democracy, and to be fair, it is not intended in this way. This sort of self-representation in the public space relates in a funny way to a strain in the tradition of normative political theory, namely that of a republican political theory of honor, glory, and giving oneself eternal identity by donating funds and having a university hall named after one. I know that from deconstruction to this, there is no real path [laughter from audience], but if you looked from a background of political history and the history of political theory, you could easily make that connection.

The third aspect is how we relate the historical analysis of actions and events not only to structures of language, forms of life, and symbolic forms in general but also to those systemic aspects of the social world that have been analyzed since the rise of political economy and other systems, approaches, in terms of latent functions and processes that work behind or beyond the intuitive knowledge of agents.

Now two related problems: one on the empirical level and one on the more normative level. Empirically, I've learned most from the criticisms that point to the exclusionary mechanisms of the public sphere, liberal or postliberal. Geoff Eley's marvelous paper and Mary Ryan's beautiful presentation were very convincing to me. These illuminating studies benefit, of course, from Foucault and similar recent methodological approaches. I'm the last not to recognize or acknowledge them. But one problem comes to mind. How far should we go along with Foucault, if I may label it this way, on his road to a self-referential critique of the supposedly totalitarian features of the Enlightenment tradition and its social embodiments?

An analysis of the exclusionary aspects of established public spheres is particularly revealing in this respect, the critique of that which has been excluded from the public sphere and from my analysis of it too: gender, ethnicity, class, popular culture. This critique can be carried out only in the light of the declared standards and the manifest self-understanding of the proponents and participants of these very same public spheres, at least if you refer to the most articulate forms of these limitations. The peculiar feature of this discourse formation is that the rules that constitute the participants' self-understanding at the same time provide the resources for a critique of its own selectivity, of the blind spots and the incompleteness of its own transitional embodiments. This non-Foucaultian feature of such discourse is brought into focus by the fact that the only other exclusion on which a public sphere can legitimately rely, by its own standards, is violence. Once you invent these universalistic Enlightenment concepts, forms of communication, like court cases, that are meant to settle practical conflicts in terms of mutual understanding and intended agreement manifestly rely on the force of more or less good reasons as the only alternative to overt or covert violence.

So, the question is, How could you critically assess the inconspicuous repression of ethnic, cultural, national, gender, and indentity differences if not in the light of this one basic standard, however interpreted, of procedures that all parties presume will provide the most rational solution at hand, at a given time, in a given context? If you look at it from this point of view, then the question is not that these people are just interested in keeping order, in the sense of keeping a blind order; the question is how we can best institutionalize procedures that presumably have those characteristics, at least until somebody convinces us, in the light of these same procedures, that the very implantations are highly selective and repressive. So, keeping order is not the issue here; rather, it is solving problems of action coordination with as little violence as possible. There seems to be in the minds of many of my interlocutors over the past years an alternative that I've never quite understood: that when there are differences, we also have the choice of escaping these repressive procedures and just going off in peace. That's not a meaningful alternative choice. There are problems that are inescapable and can be solved only in concert. Who, then, makes up the concert?

I think an empirically meaningful approach to our selective and even colonized forms of public communication is to see how they work within certain procedural dimensions of formal inclusion, of the degree of political participation, of the quality of discussion, of the range of issues, and, finally and most important, of how the presuppositions of those public debates are really institutionalized. Of course, I too look at American television. When I see debates between presidential candidates, I get sick. But we at least have to explain *why* we get sick, not just leave it at that and only explain the bodily gestures, although that is also an interesting business.

And now, the last point: speech-act theory. Of course, speech-act theory is not designed to do everything. But the very presuppositions of forms of communication that are true, presumably, and the self-understanding of their participants display the very curious property of proceeding according to rules that are recognized by the participants as the most neutral procedures available at a given time. These presuppositions can best be analyzed if you focus on the ideal, on isolated and abstract types of simple speech-act changes. The second problem is related: Is it possible to defend a more or less radical form of proceduralism? This means, Is it possible to institutionalize procedures that can be interpreted differently by all parties and yet are recognized as the same procedures fulfilling, as best they can, the intention of the movement? That's just up for discussion; I won't talk another hour on that. [Laughter from audience.]

[Some questions and answers are deleted here.]

Nancy Fraser: I want to ask a political question, which I think many people have been shying away from, about the political program for an emancipatory transformation of contemporary society that follows from this analysis of the public sphere and its structural transformation. At the end of *Structural Transformation* you picture a democratic transformation as internally democratizing a number of institutions whose activities impinge on the formal political process of decision making. More recently, you've argued that markets and state bureaucracies are a necessary feature of life in complex societies, that only relatively uninstitutionalized social movements can exercise the function of a critical, rational opinion formation that in a way is a watchdog. What are the social and economic conditions for effective participation in a nonexclusionary and genuinely democratic public sphere? Isn't economic equality—the end of class structure and the end of gender inequality—the condition for the possibility of a public sphere, if we are really talking about what makes it possible for people to participate? Is capitalism compatible with this? I mean, I don't know where you're going. . . .

Jürgen Habermas: I'll have to get over the shock to answer such a question. . . . As I understand you, you are saying, Let's try to be early socialists, political socialists, and utopian socialists and then say what we think the design should be. . . . I do think that I have been a reformist all my life, and maybe I have become a bit more so in recent years. Nevertheless, I mostly feel that I am the last Marxist. I think, in fact, that there is a definite need to counter those imperatives that are still reproduced according to the capitalist mode of accumulation and come from a highly bureaucratized capitalist nation, to cope with and to reverse them, at least to modify these imperatives. This should grow from what I would like to call autonomous publics of an *Öffentlichkeit* type, so that we can have a lifeworld-system interaction that redirects the imperatives in such a way that we can contain, from the system's perspective, those side effects that not only make us suffer but almost destroy core areas of class and racially specific subcultures. Now let me lay out how it should work (why I think that it could work is even less believable). I don't think that there can be any type of revolution in societies that have such a degree of complexity; we can't go back anyway, in spite of all the romanticist antimovements. For academics, revolution is a notion of the nineteenth century.

Audience member: Except for Communist governments.

Jürgen Habermas: Okay, if you call it revolution. We are in the first period, and we don't know what will happen. So an easy way back to capitalism? I still can't believe it! [Laughter from audience.] I do believe that there is only one way to push back the boundaries (if I may speak so metaphorically) between lifeworld and systems without those forces that are the most probable historically—that means without weapons, without bribery and money, without legal repression, and so on. The only way is to radicalize those institutions that we have already established in Western countries, to direct them toward a form of radical democracy that makes it possible, just in terms of delegitimization, to change or at least to affect administration. Administration is still the entry to economies, at least insofar as syndicalistic forms are not easily at hand. Maybe there is a positive outlook toward change in the Eastern Hemisphere, toward the reinvention of some sort of social democratic capitalism, tamed capitalism. Maybe there will be a development of syndicalist forms. Then we would have a somewhat different economy, open for political intervention from within, or at least from the border, and not only via political intervention that comes in a legal language.

In talking this way, you talk me into a kind of response that, I must say, I hate, because this seems to be loose thought. We must be much more specific; we could talk, for example, just of what is going on in West Germany. This question is immediately political: What can we do, what would a liberal-Red coalition in Berlin and Frankfurt mean in the setting of German political culture and the German political system? In any case, we must try to give a reasonable economic analysis. It is startling that in the last ten years there has not been any economic analysis with a lasting political impact. It was, after all, the privilege of the left to provide these analyses. I don't think that we have just to give in to Friedman or to popular slogans. But popular slogans are replacing economic analysis.

Stephen Leonard: Your last comment raises interesting questions about the nature of your project here as a whole. On the one hand, you suggest that we need more historically specific, contextually specific analyses of possibilities; at the same time, the notion of the discourse here about the public sphere has been carried on at a high level of abstraction. I'm having difficulty moving from the ideal or from the empirical to the normative or from the reality to the ideal. It seems to me that a project of this sort ought to be judged in terms of the intentions of the theory itself, which is basically to help change practice.

Would you address this translation of the empirical or this relationship between the empirical and the normative? How are we going to bridge this gap, if it is bridgeable? And if it is bridgeable, doesn't that presuppose the need to have a more contextually and historically specific analysis of social movements and the arguments they make? It seems to me those things can't be prejudged in terms of some ideal. Rather they have to be judged in terms of arguments that are advanced by those movements or by their representatives or spokesmen.

Jürgen Habermas: I'm not quite sure whether the spokesmen of a more or less successful social movement are the best ones to interpret the opportunities that the movement is facing. I don't think that we can ever again, or even that we should ever again, bridge the institutional differentiation between the science system and political agitation and political organization and political action. That is what Lenin tried to do. And I think that it's a part of the past that we don't want to retrieve. So there are just bridges between us as participants in some sort of political action and as members of the science community. I know that Horkheimer began his career with a famous article denying just this. . . .

On the other hand, you are completely right to ask me why I am engaging in these abstract things, speech-act theory, moral theory, and whatever without entertaining a historically focused, straightforward analysis. And this I can take to heart. This is why I have a sentimental relation to this first work, which we have been discussing here for the past three days.

Stephen Leonard: My intention was not to suggest that there's a problem with the work, the position, as much as that there may be a problem with the metatheoretical implications of this project. In other words, if it is supposed to be practically effective, shouldn't that guide our metatheoretical self-understanding of how this project should be carried out, what its standards are?

Jürgen Habermas: I can only give an example from my own work in legal theory and research. It makes a difference whether you approach simple court decisions, in proceedings in the supreme court in Germany or here, from a critical legal-

studies perspective, where you have only an interest in identifying the rhetorical devices that are working against what they
are taken to be working for. This is a debunking interest, which
is similar to formal approaches in ideology critique. I appreciate what Duncan Kennedy is doing in this sphere. But if one
engages in legal theory with a certain political motivation, I
find it more reasonable to start with something that sounds
more idealistic and abstract, namely with the attempt to rationally reconstruct the very presuppositions under which a particular court procedure is going on. Only if you pin down the
established practice with its own implicit presuppositions as
something presumably rational do you have all the means not
only to debunk but also to politically criticize them. This means
that when you have given a description, the very description is
a critique in the light of established legal norms, only radical-
ized to such an extent that everybody is rolling their eyes and
saying, "Oh, maybe we didn't mean it that way."

On the other hand, I do think that historical analysis—I
mean empirical analysis not only of social movements but also
of new crystallizations—is very impressive. That's your field,
the analysis of new crystallizations of what I think to be the
nucleus of autonomous publics. First, you go into this analysis
with a seemingly abstract frame, mainly an organizational
model. This is designed so that you can identify, say, the stage
of a certain process of organizational self-stabilization. The
function and declared purpose of the organization is now moving away from participants' orientations, even those orientations on which the participants can, to a certain degree, gain
consent. Second, there is an evaluation of the wheeling and
dealing, the interactions, particularly the will formations within
this group. I find it telling to look into these mixed up, lively,
bodily expressive, elliptic, noisy discussions where some issue
is at stake, with a certain analytical tool to see which issues are
at stake, which argument is finally brought up, and where it
changes and can be abstracted. And how they evaluate it in
ethical, moral, practical, and legal terms. This abstraction, I
think, is adequate for what we are interested in, for what I
would be interested in if I were to study processes of opinion
formation. In fact, opinions are going into a communicative

process, from which the agents are in a way disowned. From this context, finally, arise topics and designs, which mean programs and arguments, which mean reasons, that are then translated into communication processes in which this very collective cannot, in bodily presence, participate at all.

Seeing this is the condition for coping with Nicholas Garnham's point that our face-to-face communications are all mediated through time and space. So this abstraction is done. It's a realistic abstraction but an unobtainable one, and not a real abstraction in Marx's sense. It alienates us, but these media tied up with a natural language are open to retrieval by any agents for reassessment, retranslation, rereception; they are open for and even rely on face-to-face communication and interactions. This is what totally distinguishes this type of communication from money and administrative power. These are also languages, but these languages are by definition alienated from agents, from natural languages. If you look closely, you will see that they don't have the features of a natural language.

James Peacock: I understood you to say that for rational discourse or communication there is only one condition necessary, and that is that one can imagine it could be otherwise, in other words, that reflexivity is the essential condition for rational communication. If there must be reflexivity, then I'm curious to hear your comment on the theoretical status of psychiatry in rational communication, since psychiatry attempts to produce a reflexivity that is more rational.

Jürgen Habermas: In a tense situation, where we are under pressure and don't know what to do, we come to feel the necessity, and have the capability, the opportunity, to push these questions to a certain level. We try to come to terms with the questions "Who am I?" and "Who do I want to be?" And these two questions can only be answered simultaneously. So we are trying to come to terms with what we have done (from which we want to disassociate ourselves) and with certain future projects that we would like to identify with. I think there is an everyday-life type of hermeneutic, an ethical reasoning of ourselves as those who are embedded in a particular life history, in particular historical conditions, and who want somehow to reappropriate relevant parts of their own life history to find out what is good for them now. On the other side, there are psychiatrists who, in an artificial communicational setting, try to bring themselves to engage in this sort of discourse.

But this means to become reflective within a certain given context, from which you cannot escape. Your whole identity is linked up with your life history. The only thing you can do is to convert totally, but even then you make the connection to your past and give reasons to yourself. Augustine, for instance, does this in an exemplary fashion. This is a level of reflexivity that is still context-bound and only gives a way to an illumination of inescapable traditions from within—to which, however, you can say either yes or no.

If it really comes to moral questions proper—and this happens in politics too—then I do think that reflexivity means that we must take even another step back from our own heritage. Only with this step back—what George Herbert Mead meant by ideal role taking, putting yourself in the shoes of another person—can we perceive the differences of different identities. This, of course, is what happens in everyday life and more so in a multicultural society like Europe, where other identities remain impenetrable to us but are somehow mutually acknowledged. That is reflexivity. Reflexivity is a criterion for an attempt at least to identify thresholds between what we call premodern and modern. I know that's an uneasy topic, but nobody helps us; we find ourselves in the modern condition. I *do* think you can identify cultures that did invent second-order concepts and those that didn't. There is no discrimination involved in saying that.

Michael Warner: If the step back to acknowledge and to obtain the mutual acknowledgment of otherness is the sine qua non here, doesn't that presuppose the elimination of certain significant asymmetries and of how those differences are originally defined? Since they aren't symmetrical differences, they do not have that structure of mutuality built into their logic. Doesn't it presuppose that the very nature of the difference has already been redefined, so that it can be recognized in that symmetrical acknowledgment? Isn't it problematic, then, to say that this step of drawing back, by recognition of mutual otherness, is the procedure by which you surmount asymmetrical inequalities?

Jürgen Habermas: No, it is a precondition for perceiving asymmetries that cannot be overcome just by will but require institutional and social change. This is not a question only of language. The very precondition for realizing that there is more involved, not just money or even just education, is the step to which I am referring. In a discussion, debate, or conversation—we can imagine a thousand different settings. When we realize that we are running into a wall in the attempt to really understand the other's situation, there is no way out but to recognize this as a sphere of integrity that can't be violated in constituting an identity. This is the first step for a neutrality in recognition, which does not imply any real change in the real world. But I have the feeling that this whole indifference turns things upside down. We are caught in these forces that are homogenizing and interpreting differences in such a way that a preexisting asymmetry is conferred. . . . If you shift from an observer's role to a participant's role and carry over your insight into it, at least you would be in a favorable situation, which I take to be the position that is desirable as a model position. I mean not a position that we in fact take but a position that everybody should take and is supposed to take in a public discourse that would live up to its own standard.

Lloyd Kramer: Doesn't the functioning of the public sphere— that is, coming together, rational discourse, a decision that is finally made—carry with it the necessity of implicit violence against those who don't accept the consensus? At the very least, if the behavior is ruled legal or illegal, there is the claim of violence against those who don't go along with it—they can be put in jail, punished, even executed. So, despite your clear desire to exclude violence from the public sphere, isn't it always, in some sense, dependent on an implicit or explicit threat or use of violence?

Jürgen Habermas: I would question only the word "always." Every public sphere I know still depends on violence. Nevertheless, what is the outcome of this criticism? If it has any impact, it is to redefine the conditions of access and the level of discussion to do away with the identified exclusionary mechanism. Now, you ask, must it not always be that? This is only the case if the measures of institutions of procedural rationality are in principle a contradictory enterprise. Must the attempt to find rules that, under ideal conditions, could be recognized for all parts of the world necessarily reflect one's own interests, desires, identities, and so on? I can't see how one can make such an a priori argument. Historically, there is also evidence for the self-corrective process of overcoming the selections by which all public spheres as complete embodiments of that one idea [of procedural rationality] have been marred. So we are back to the question, Is procedural rationality an idea on which all publics can agree? If so, there is a regulatory embodiment that can be interpreted differently from different parts but that is seen by all parts as the best embodiment of that idea of procedural impartiality at a given time, in a given context, for the time being. That means until the next argument is able to show how in fact everything is biased. I think that is the issue: procedural rationality.

Gerald Postema: I want to raise a question about your account of rational discourse at the most general or abstract level. It really has to do with the role of consensus. In some of your remarks you mentioned that two of the conditions, identified very abstractly, would be the desire for mutual understanding and intended agreement. How, at this rather abstract level, is that notion of intended agreement worked out? It's known that there are certain conditions for any kind of rational interaction, discussion, discourse. Many have thought that what is needed is agreement on the rules of logic, others agreement on more substantive rules. In any case, many think that what is needed is agreement on general principles. Then rational discourse really is a matter of applying those principles and having different views about them and working things out, but with all the foundations already agreed upon. The thrust of your approach is that rationality and rational discourse about the ground rules of the discourse are also possible. We don't start with consensus, but consensus plays what Seyla Benhabib called a kind of regulative role. I find that attractive, but I don't know exactly what it means.

Jürgen Habermas: I think that this sense can only be identified against the background of the intended agreement. There are conceptual necessities, but beyond these conceptual necessities there are pragmatic presuppositions. What would it mean to have a discussion if we did not presuppose the possibility that we can agree, and of course disagree, on certain issues and propositions? It wouldn't be meaningful.

In fact, I think that the ground rules for public debate are only attempts to give a context-bound and historically specific articulation of an idea that is more widely shared, actually intuitively shared, by everybody who uses a natural language in one way, namely to come to a certain understanding with somebody else about something in the world. What does that mean if not to use the same terms with the same meaning? We know that this ideal is not perfectly reachable. Nevertheless, if we don't presuppose that we assign the same meaning to the same terms, we wouldn't even start to speak. The whole enterprise would be meaningless. There are other presuppositions of that type; for instance, I wouldn't talk in the same way if I couldn't look into your eyes, and you into mine, to find a specific indication of performative attitude. You realize that I am talking to you and not about you. In a psychiatric situation you immediately see the very moment that the doctor reasons about you. You see it in the eyes. Then he shifts from the performative attitude to an observer's position. While taking this performative attitude, I cannot but presuppose that you are able to give some sort of reason for what you say. I'm attributing accountability.

We know there are not only normative presuppositions but also idealizing presuppositions that everyone can in principle give for what he did or is going to do, or whatever. Try to interact with somebody without that presupposition. He will immediately ask you, What are you thinking about? What are you doing now? You are not communicating to me. So it is this range of intuitive knowledge that we presuppose, and I do think that under some conditions and in some cultures, some contexts, we draw from these intuitions to explain, for instance, what we mean by a neutral or impartial procedure. It's not the notion that makes the difficulties; it's the implementation of it. But implementation can be criticized in light of its own notion, and that is the non-Foucaultian feature of discourse. That is why I think that a radical Foucaultian analysis is a blind alley.

Goram Kindem: I'm trying to understand the difference in the way in which you use the term "discourse" and the way in which I understand Foucault to use the term. Foucault suggests that there is no such thing as a neutral discourse, that all discourses have built into them some kind of heirarchy, some power relations. Yet you seem to suggest that reasoned discourse is neutral, or that somehow the process of coming to a consensus will work out the disparities between competing alternative discourses.

Jürgen Habermas: I do think that the Foucaultian notion is useful for the empirical analysis of, for instance, our present discussion. We would then find, not very surprisingly, certain hierarchies, asymmetries, overpowerings, and so on. It's clear that a first-term student who enters a discussion about Foucault's theory is underprivileged. I think it's also useful for revealing hidden asymmetries and power structures (and this is, of course, the purpose for which Foucault introduced the concept). It's a good guess to suppose that most discourses are of that kind, that they do imply power structures that are not only hidden but systematically latent, that is, structurally concealed from their participants.

In spite of this I think that there are several types of discourses that are self-corrective in terms of being sensitive to a critique of systematic exclusionary mechanisms built into them. It may well be that no participant is able, say, to look into the back of the mirror. But once an observer's information enters that same and so far unchanged discourse, it is implied that participants cannot go on, in light of their self-understanding, without identifying the rules of the games they have been playing as being selective and revising them. What we call argumentation or rational discourse is of that type. Then there are institutionalizations of what we call argumentations of a special sort. For instance, in institutions like this, we have selective and incomplete institutionalizations of arguments that are specialized in certain scientific fields. These institutionalized discourses are supposedly selective only for these sorts of selectivities. So once ethnomethodology entered the scene—you remember it? [laughter]—a parallel criticism was deconstructionism, not introduced into sociology but into literature departments. What happened was that the institutions themselves became more sensitive to what they were doing, not only in terms of methodologies but also in actual implementations of certain types of discourses.

So this sort of self-correctiveness is what makes me hesitant when, as Professor Kramer maintains, one says discourses are always some type of power-discourse formations. At some point all these attempts to institutionalize a public sphere from the liberal model or on a different model have been efficiently identified as exclusionary. But even if we changed from the role of observer to a performative attitude, what would be the alternative for the political problem of settling controversies? At least the public sphere is an attempt to exclude violence, if only to reproduce some sort of violence internally again but in a criticizable fashion. This may be the best we can achieve in the domain of politics. The core of it is certainly politics: fighting all modes of settlements that are somehow unjust.

Contributors

Keith Michael Baker, Professor of History at Stanford University, is principally interested in French political culture in the Old Regime and revolutionary periods and in the intellectual history of early modern Europe. His most recent book is *Inventing the French Revolution* (Cambridge University Press, 1990).

Seyla Benhabib is Professor of Politics and Philosophy at the New School for Social Research. She is the author of *Critique, Norm, and Utopia: A Study of the Foundations of Critical Theory* (New York, 1986) and *Situating the Self: Gender, Community, and Postmodernism in Contemporary Ethics* (forthcoming from Routledge and Kegal Paul and Polity Press) and is coeditor, with Drucilla Cornell, of *Feminism as Critique* (Minnesota, 1987).

Harry C. Boyte is Senior Fellow and Director of Project Public Life at the Hubert H. Humphrey Institute of Public Affairs, University of Minnesota. His most recent book is *Commonwealth: A Return to Citizen Politics* (New York, 1990).

Craig Calhoun is Professor of Sociology and History at the University of North Carolina at Chapel Hill. He is also Chair of the Curriculum in International Studies and Director of the Program in Social Theory and Cross-Cultural Studies. Calhoun's books include *The Question of Class Struggle: Popular Protest in Industrializing England* (Chicago, 1982) and *Beijing*

Spring: Students and the Struggle for Democracy in China, 1989
(forthcoming, University of California Press).

Geoff Eley teaches history at the University of Michigan in
Ann Arbor. He is the author of *Reshaping the German Right:
Radical Nationalism and Political Change after Bismarck* (London
and New Haven, 1980), *From Unification to Nazism: Reinterpret-
ing the German Past* (London, 1986), and *Wilhelminismus, Nationalismus, Faschismus: Zur historischen Kontinuität in Deutschland*
(Münster, 1991). He is coauthor with David Blackbourn of *The
Peculiarities of German History: Bourgeois Society and Politics in
Nineteenth-Century Germany* (Oxford, 1984). He is finishing a
book on the European left between 1848 and the present and
has a long-term interest in the relationship between democracy
and nationalism.

Nancy Fraser is Associate Professor of Philosophy and Research Faculty, Center for Urban Affairs and Policy Research,
at Northwestern University. She is the author of *Unruly Practices: Power, Discourse, and Gender in Contemporary Social Theory*
(University of Minnesota Press and Polity Press, 1989) and the
coeditor with Sandra Bartky of *Revaluing French Feminism: Critical Essays on Difference, Agency, and Culture* (University of Indiana Press, 1991). She is currently working on *Keywords of the
Welfare State*, coauthored with Linda Gordon.

Nicholas Garnham is Professor of Communications and Director of the Center for Communication and Information
Studies at the Polytechnic of Central London. He has written
many studies on the media, both empirical and theoretic, and
was previously a producer with the BBC. He has recently published *Capitalism and Communication: Global Culture and the Economics of Information* (Sage, 1991).

Jürgen Habermas is Professor and Head of the Faculty of
Philosophy in the Johann Wolfgang Goethe University of
Frankfurt. He is the author of numerous books on political,
social, and moral theory, on the history of philosophy, on sociology, and on political analysis. He is among the most influ-

ential philosophers and social theorists of the contemporary era.

Peter Uwe Hohendahl is Jacob Gould Schurman Professor of German and Comparative Literature at Cornell University. He is the author of several works on literary criticism and the public sphere. Some of these are collected in his *Institution of Criticism* (Cornell, 1982).

Lloyd Kramer is Associate Professor of History and a member of the Steering Committee for the Program in Social Theory and Cross-Cultural Studies at the University of North Carolina at Chapel Hill. He is the author of *Threshold of a New World: Intellectuals and the Exile Experience in Paris, 1830–1848* (1988).

Benjamin Lee is Director of the Center for Psychosocial Studies in Chicago. An anthropological linguist by training, he has published on a wide range of topics in semiotics, philosophy of language, and cultural studies.

Thomas McCarthy is Professor of Philosophy at Northwestern University. He is the author of *The Critical Theory of Jürgen Habermas* and *Ideals and Illusions: On Reconstruction and Deconstruction in Contemporary Critical Theory*. He is General Editor of Studies in Contemporary German Social Thought, a series published by The MIT Press, and he has translated a number of Habermas's works into English.

Moishe Postone is Associate Professor of Sociology, Social Theory, and European History at the University of Chicago. He has recently completed a work on Marx and critical theory.

Mary P. Ryan is Professor of History and Women's Studies at the University of California, Berkeley, and the author of several books, including *Cradle of the Middle Class* (Cambridge, 1981) and *Women in Public* (Johns Hopkins, 1990). She is currently completing a study of the people's and the public's discovery of each other in nineteenth-century American cities.

Michael Schudson is Professor in the Department of Communication and the Department of Sociology at the University of California, San Diego. He is the author of *Discovering the News: A Social History of American Newspapers* (Basic, 1978) and *Advertising, the Uneasy Persuasion* (Basic, 1984) and is coeditor, with Chandra Mukerji, of *Rethinking Popular Culture* (California, 1991). He is presently writing on collective memory and the place of Watergate in American politics and culture and on a historical overview of American citizens' political knowledge and participation from 1690 to 1990.

Michael Warner is Associate Professor in the English Department at Rutgers University. He is author of *The Letters of the Republic: Publication and the Public Sphere in Eighteenth-Century America* (Harvard, 1990) and is coeditor, with Gerald Graff, of *The Origins of Literary Studies in America: A Documentary Anthology* (Routledge, 1988). His most recent articles, on American literature and on gay theory, are forthcoming in *Raritan*, in *Social Text*, and in *American Literature*.

David Zaret is Associate Professor of Sociology at Indiana University, Bloomington. His areas of interest are historical sociology, the sociology of knowledge, and social theory. He is the author of *The Heavenly Contract: Ideology and Organization in Prerevolutionary Puritanism* (Chicago, 1985). His contribution to this book derives from ongoing work that investigates the origins of democratic ideology in Anglo-American societies.

Index

Studies in Contemporary German Social Thought
Thomas McCarthy, General Editor

Reinhart Koselleck, *Critique and Crisis: Enlightenment and the Pathogenesis of Modern Society*

Reinhart Koselleck, *Futures Past: On the Semantics of Historical Time*

Harry Liebersohn, *Fate and Utopia in German Sociology, 1887–1923*

Herbert Marcuse, *Hegel's Ontology and the Theory of Historicity*

Guy Oakes, *Weber and Rickert: Concept Formation in the Cultural Sciences*

Claus Offe, *Contradictions of the Welfare State*

Claus Offe, *Disorganized Capitalism: Contemporary Transformations of Work and Politics*

Helmut Peukert, *Science, Action, and Fundamental Theology: Toward a Theology of Communicative Action*

Joachim Ritter, *Hegel and the French Revolution: Essays on the* Philosophy of Right

Alfred Schmidt, *History and Structure: An Essay on Hegelian-Marxist and Structuralist Theories of History*

Dennis Schmidt, *The Ubiquity of the Finite: Hegel, Heidegger, and the Entitlements of Philosophy*

Carl Schmitt, *The Crisis of Parliamentary Democracy*

Carl Schmitt, *Political Romanticism*

Carl Schmitt, *Political Theology: Four Chapters on the Concept of Sovereignty*

Gary Smith, editor, *On Walter Benjamin: Critical Essays and Recollections*

Michael Theunissen, *The Other: Studies in the Social Ontology of Husserl, Heidegger, Sartre, and Buber*

Ernst Tugendhat, *Self-Consciousness and Self-Determination*

Mark Warren, *Nietzsche and Political Thought*

Albrecht Wellmer, *The Persistence of Modernity: Essays on Aesthetics, Ethics and Postmodernism*

Thomas E. Wren, editor, *The Moral Domain: Essays in the Ongoing Discussion between Philosophy and the Social Sciences*

Lambert Zuidervaart, *Adorno's Aesthetic Theory: The Redemption of Illusion*